Norfolk Record Society
Volume LXXIX for 2015

Alice Stubbe, wife of Sir Hamon Le Strange, 1585–1656,
portrait by John Hoskins, 1617

Her Price is Above Pearls

Family and Farming Records of Alice Le Strange, 1617–1656

Edited by
Elizabeth Griffiths

Norfolk Record Society
Volume LXXIX
2015

In memory of Paul Rutledge 1936–2015

A dear friend and a wise counsellor

First published in 2015
by the Norfolk Record Society

ISBN 978-0-9556357-8-6

Typeset by Carnegie Book Production, Lancaster
Printed and bound by Short Run Press, Exeter

Contents

Illustrations

Tables

Preface

My association with Alice Le Strange dates back to 1981 when I was selecting archives for a PhD thesis on medium-sized Norfolk estates in the seventeenth century. The sheer size of the Le Strange archive made it an unwieldy subject for a comparative study, but I promised Alice I would return. This happened quite by chance twenty years later when Jane Whittle asked me to join her in a research project on the household accounts of Alice Le Strange. Despite being in full-time employment, I accepted with alacrity; the proposal was successful and I started work on the project, funded by the Economic and Social Research Council, in 2003. The result, *Consumption and Gender in the Early Seventeenth Century Household: The World of Alice Le Strange* was published in 2012, delayed by the arrival of Jane's two daughters.

The book on the household fulfilled a specific purpose but it did not do justice to Alice's achievement as a farmer, estate manager and guardian of the family finances. This is the task of the present volume. For allowing me to pursue that theme, my thanks, first and foremost, go to the Norfolk Record Society; the publication of a sample of Alice's records helps to demonstrate the ability and range of this extraordinary woman, a real native of Norfolk.

Anything to do with Alice Le Strange turns into a Herculean task, so thanks are also due to several people: in the early stages to Elizabeth Rutledge for her guidance on the layout of accounts, later to Jean Agnew for her technical expertise, good ideas and endless patience, and more generally to Carole Rawcliffe and Alan Metters. I would also like to thank Rachel Clarke at Carnegie Publishing for her generous advice, English Heritage Publishing for permission to use their colour version of the portrait of Dame Alice Le Strange, and last but not least, the ever helpful staff of the Norfolk Record Office.

Elizabeth Griffiths

Introduction

The huge archive left by Alice, the wife of Sir Hamon Le Strange of Hunstanton, forms part of one of the most important collections held at the Norfolk Record Office. In their scale and quality these records are exceptional; they include six bound volumes of general disbursements and household books, dating from 1610 to 1654, Alice's sheep accounts from 1617, records for her own estate at Sedgeford from 1620, and accounts and field books for the entire Hunstanton estate from 1632.

The general disbursements and the household books have recently been the subject of a major research project on the organisation of an early seventeenth-century household.[1] This volume examines Alice's life as a farmer, estate manager and guardian of the family finances. In many ways, her performance in this field was even more remarkable than her management of her household, traditionally the province of gentlewomen. Women, of course, were no strangers to accounts or managing estates, but usually they assumed the role as widows or as single women or in the absence of a male alternative. It was most unusual for a wife to undertake such a task alongside her husband. Over the years, the Le Stranges created a family management team with Sir Hamon providing strategic direction and masterminding the rebuilding programme, Alice acting as accountant and co-ordinator, and their eldest son, Sir Nicholas, working on various projects including the drainage of the coastal marshes.[2] By their joint efforts, they

---

1. J.C. Whittle and E.M. Griffiths, *Consumption & Gender in the Early Seventeenth Century Household: The World of Alice Le Strange* (Oxford, 2012).

2. Sir Hamon left memoranda books full of details on his projects: LEST/Q36, Q37, Q38. For a perspective on Sir Hamon's activities see E.M. Griffiths, 'A Country Life: Sir Hamon Le Strange of Hunstanton, Norfolk, 1583–1654', in R.W. Hoyle, ed., *Custom, Improvement and the Landscape in Early Modern Britain* (Farnham, 2011). Sir Hamon was knighted in 1603; his son Sir Nicholas was granted a baronetcy in 1629. Sir Nicholas created at least eight farming notebooks, four of which survive: LEST/KA6, KA9, KA10, KA24, *see* E.M. Griffiths, 'Draining the coastal marshes in north west Norfolk: the Le Stranges at Hunstanton, 1604–1724', *Agricultural History Review* (forthcoming).

rebuilt their estate 'out of the ground', as Alice noted in her summary of the family finances.[3] Sir Hamon had no doubts as to her ability and the value of her contribution to the management of his affairs. On the front of the fifth household book, concealed under a flap, he left a message, 'who shall finde a virtuous woman for her price is above pearls, the very heart of her husband trusteth in her … she overseeth the ways of her household and eateth not the brede of idleness'.[4] In his will he praised her 'incessant industry in straynes of knowledge above her sex to the just, faithfull and laudable advantage and advancement of my estate'.[5]

Alice's modernization of the estate records and accounting system in the early seventeenth century is of the utmost significance. In this period of steeply rising prices, it was essential for landowners to update their management structures and put their estates on a sound commercial footing. Norfolk was littered with examples of old gentry families, like the Cleres of Ormesby and Blickling, and the Heydons of Baconsthorpe, who failed to do so; from the outset the Le Stranges were determined not to join their ranks. Soon after their marriage in 1604, Sir Hamon started compiling details of their titles and rights in his memoranda books, commissioning surveys of the estate, clarifying the content of rentals and firmals, and keeping his own accounts.[6] Alice first became involved in estate management in 1613, receiving rents from the bailiffs and recording the receipts at the end of her household books.[7] In 1617, she set up individual accounts for the sheep which she and her father, Richard Stubbe of Sedgeford, gave to her children. On his death in 1620, Alice inherited the Sedgeford estate and assumed responsibility for its management. She took the job very seriously, gradually building up her knowledge, taking advice, creating new accounts, rationalizing the complex field systems and organising new field books and rentals. From 1632, she used this experience to radically improve the records for the rest of the estate at Hunstanton, Ringstead, Holme and Heacham. Set out clearly and precisely, these records served as a reference work for succeeding generations. The estate, commended by Arthur Young as a model of improvement, owed much to Alice.[8] It would be no exaggeration to claim that her meticulous record keeping secured the survival of the

---

3. LEST/P10, see below, pp. 67–85.

4. LEST/P8, based on the Book of Proverbs 31, v. 10, 27.

5. PROB 11/238/248, see below, pp. 353–7; *see also* LEST/AE8 for a later transcription.

6. For Sir Hamon's early rentals, firmals and accounts see LEST/BK1, BK2, BK3, BK4, BK5, BK6/1, BK6/2 and LEST/P6. Rentals listed manorial rents; firmals listed farm rents.

7. LEST/R9.

8. A. Young, *The Farmer's Tour through England, vol. 2* (1770), pp. 23–9. In 1760, on the

estate in the early seventeenth century and laid the foundation for its success in the eighteenth century and beyond.

Alice produced no single estate book, like that of William Windham of Felbrigg, so a selection for transcription had to be made from the scores of paper books which survive for every part of the estate.[9] We decided that Alice's particular contribution was best understood from her work with sheep and on her own estate at Sedgeford. These records demonstrate her wide knowledge and deep understanding of farming systems in this part of Norfolk and explain why she came to play such an influential role in the wider management of the Hunstanton estate. With the expertise she learned from her father she was able to reorganise and keep the accounts for the flocks that the family farmed in hand from 1625 to 1654.[10] By the 1630s the sale of sheep, lambs and wool, and the associated production of corn, formed a significant part of their revenues. But it was not all plain sailing. From the sheep accounts we learn of the loss of Sir Hamon's flocks, corn and horses to the parliamentary forces in 1643.[11] Bravely, Alice started again, recording the painfully slow restocking process, with sheep supplied by sons, cousins, tenants and friends. This was not the only reversal they suffered at this time. Sir Hamon's later years were blighted by fines, sequestration and legal disputes, which may explain why Alice made a summary of their family finances.[12] These notes provide a useful overview of their family and financial affairs, and are the first to be transcribed. Both their wills have been included as they cast further light on their relationship, family life and values.[13]

Alice's farming records for Sedgeford are of particular value to the historian. They provide a unique picture of the working of an infield and outfield system in the early seventeenth century and the methods used to improve it. The system, a way of farming the light upland soils of west and north-west Norfolk, lies at the heart of our understanding of Norfolk agriculture and how it developed in the eighteenth century.[14] In 1631, on the

---

death of Sir Henry Le Strange, 6th bt, the Hunstanton estate passed to Nicholas Styleman of Snettisham through his marriage to Sir Henry's sister, Armine.

9. *William Windham's Green Book, 1673–88*, ed. E.M. Griffiths (Norfolk Record Society, XLVI, 2002).

10. LEST/P10. Alice's sheep accounts, see below, pp. 87–193.

11. R.W. Ketton-Cremer, 'Sir Hamon Le Strange and His Sons', *A Norfolk Gallery* (1948), pp. 56–94; Ketton-Cremer, *Norfolk and the Civil War* (1969), pp. 206–17.

12. LEST/P10, see below, pp. 67–85.

13. PROB 11/238/248; PROB 11/262, see below, pp. 353–62.

14. H.C. Darby & J. Saltmarsh, 'The Infield-Outfield System of a Norfolk Manor', *Economic History Review*, III (1935), pp. 30–44; S. Wade Martins and T. Williamson, 'Roots

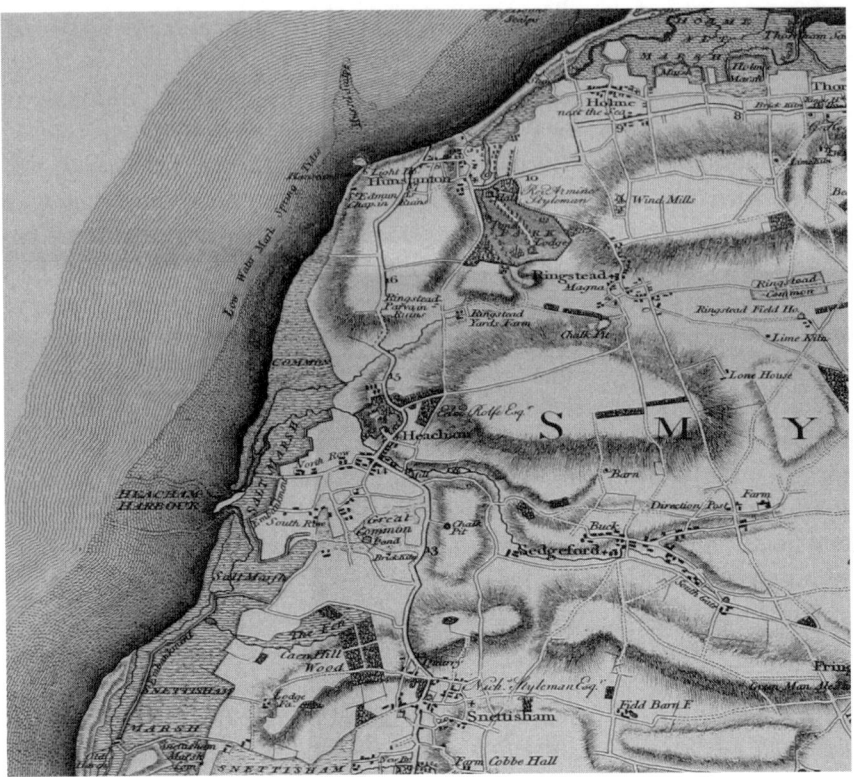

Figure 1. Faden's Map of Norfolk, 1797 – around Hunstanton.[15]

death of her cousin Francis Guybon, the principal tenant at Sedgeford, Alice commissioned a survey of the estate.[16] This consists of three interlocking maps representing the three flocks and foldcourses of Sedgeford and a written survey explaining the organisation and use of the 'Sedgeford Brecks and Infield Lands'.[17] The book lists the rotations, the lands to be exchanged, while the maps provide a visual base for identifying the holdings

---

of Change: Farming and the Landscape in East Anglia, c. 1700–1870', *Agricultural History Review, Supplement Series 2* (1999), pp. 9–12.

15. J.C. Barringer, *Faden's Map of Norfolk* (1989); although the map dates from 1797, much of the detail of commons, brecks, marsh and fens was the same in the sixteenth and seventeenth centuries, *see* A. Macnair & T. Williamson, *William Faden and Norfolk's Eighteenth Century Landscape* (2010). Ringstead Parva, south of Hunstanton Park, was more commonly known as Barrett Ringstead.

16. Francis Guybon's mother, Anne, was the sister of Richard Stubbe, Alice's father.

17. LEST/OC1, LEST/IC58, see below, pp. 40–1, 309–48.

at a glance. Later records show how Alice built on this method and how her successors developed the system.[18] Gradually, the distinction between brecks and infields was broken down. By 1702, new farms had been created, fallows eliminated with turnips and clover grown in rotation with wheat, barley, peas and vetches.[19] From this evidence, we can see that the process of improving the brecks and bringing them into regular cultivation, the cornerstone of the agricultural revolution, was underway on this estate from the early seventeenth century.

The documents selected do scant justice to the range of Alice's involvement in farming and estate management, but to include more would require several volumes exhausting the energies of both readers and editors, so in this introduction we will briefly consider her wider activities and assess her place in Norfolk history.[20] Just how unusual was she? To answer this question, we need to know more about Alice Stubbe, the girl from Sedgeford, who became Lady Le Strange.

Born in 1585, Alice was the younger daughter of Richard Stubbe and his second wife Anne Goding, the widow of John Le Strange of Sedgeford.[21] Stubbe was not a native of west Norfolk. From a relatively modest background, his family came from Scottow and migrated to Bungay in

18. LEST/IC55, IC64, IC65, IB85, IB89, IB90, IB93.

19. LEST/IB91.

20. Until the publication of Whittle & Griffiths, *Consumption & Gender*, little had been written about Alice, yet academics have long been aware of her archive. Ketton-Cremer briefly drew attention to her in *Norfolk Gallery*, pp. 64–5, and *Norfolk and the Civil War*, pp. 41, 190, 217–18. She appears in C. Hussey, Hunstanton Hall I – Norfolk (*Country Life*, 10 April 1926) protesting against Sir Hamon's viol playing and insisting he build a garden house to practice in. References often attest to the bawdy quality of her jokes recorded by her son, Nicholas Le Strange, in his jest book, *Merry Passages and Jests*, ed. H.F. Lippincott (Salzburg, 1974). Her husband and sons all have entries in *Oxford Dictionary of National Biography*, but Alice did not until the omission was corrected, 'L'Estrange, Alice, Lady L'Estrange (1585–1656)', *Oxford Dictionary of National Biography* (Oxford, 2005). The editors changed the spelling to that used for the men folk devised by their youngest son, Sir Roger L'Estrange, but modern authors tend to use Le Strange, *see also* A. Moore & C. Crawley, *Family and Friends: A Regional Survey of British Portraiture* (Norfolk Museums Service, 1992), pp. 84–6.

21. John (d. 1582) was the third son of Sir Nicholas Le Strange (1511–1580) and uncle of Sir Hamon. In 1562, John was assigned, by his father, the lease of the two Sedgeford manors held by the dean and chapter of Norwich. By 1601, Richard Stubbe was the lessee, NRO, DCN (Dean and Chapter of Norwich) 59/30/10. F. Blomefield & C. Parkin, *An essay towards a topographical history of the county of Norfolk*, X (2nd edn, 1805–10), p. 314 for the definitive family tree of the Le Stranges of Hunstanton, *see also*, Whittle & Griffiths, pp. 18–23; W. Rye, *Norfolk Families* (Norwich, 1913).

1534.[22] In 1561 he married Elizabeth, daughter of a local landowner, Anthony Gurney of Ellingham, and they had a daughter, Dionisia. Over the years, he built up an estate across the county, which included lands at Harpley and Rougham, following the marriage of Dionisia to William Yelverton of Rougham, and in Sedgeford, Hunstanton, and Holme, after he married Anne Le Strange in about 1583.[23] Trained in the law, Stubbe was active in county circles, resolving disputes and advising gentry families. He became closely involved in the affairs of the Le Strange family after the death of Sir Nicholas Le Strange in 1592. As the family lawyer, he worked alongside the trustees, Sir John Peyton, Sir Henry Hobart and Sir Henry Spelman, guiding and securing the future of Sir Nicholas's orphan son, the eight year old Sir Hamon.[24] In 1602 the trustees arranged the marriage of Sir Hamon to Stubbe's daughter, Alice. For her settlement, he assigned his lands in Sedgeford and the leases and lands of John Le Strange which had passed to his widow, Alice's mother.[25]

The marriage was quite a coup. Sir Hamon was the scion of an ancient

22. Rye, *Norfolk Families*, p. 859, *see also* W. & M. Vaughan Lewis, *See You in Court: The Potts Family of Mannington, 1584–1737* (2009), pp. 572–4, for a background of the Stubbe family. Alice may have been named after Richard Stubbe's mother, Alice, daughter and co-heiress of John Richers of Bungay.

References to Stubbe's land purchases include: Edgefield, Blomefield & Parkin, *Norfolk*, IX, p. 303; Harpley, Blomefield & Parkin, *Norfolk*, VIII, p. 455; Holme Parsonage, Blomefield & Parkin, *Norfolk*, X, p. 333. Stubbe was involved in a dispute over the warren and chase at Castle Rising, Blomefield & Parkin, *Norfolk*, IX, p. 56.

23. Sir William Yelverton of Rougham, 1558–1631, baronet in 1620 and sheriff of Norfolk in 1622, married Dionisia, daughter and co-heir of Richard Stubbe of Sedgeford. They had two sons: Sir William, 2nd bt, 1590–1648, married Ursula, daughter of Sir Thomas Richardson; their son Sir William, 3rd bt, 1621–1649, was a royalist, fined heavily, died unmarried, and the title became extinct; the other son Sir Henry, kt, married but d.s.p. Blomefield & Parkin, *Norfolk*, X, pp. 31–2.

24. The trustees were all related to Sir Hamon. Sir John Peyton (1544–1630), the Elizabethan soldier and administrator, had married Sir Hamon's grandmother, Dorothy, daughter and heiress of Edward Beaupre of Outwell and widow of Sir Robert Bell; she was the mother of Mary Bell who married Sir Nicholas Le Strange (1562–92) and died in 1585. Sir Henry Hobart of Intwood, who rose to be lord chief justice of the Court of Common Pleas, married Mary's sister Dorothy Bell. Sir Henry Spelman of Congham, antiquarian and bibliophile, married Eleanor, daughter of John Le Strange and Anne Goding. Thus the Spelmans were first cousins to both Sir Hamon and Alice Stubbe, who were also first cousins. All the trustees merit entries in the *Oxford Dictionary of National Biography*; *see also* E.M. Griffiths, 'Sir Henry Hobart: A New Hero of Norfolk Agriculture?', *Agricultural History Review*, 46 (1998), pp. 15–34.

25. LEST/AA66–73: documents concerning the marriage settlement of Sir Hamon Le Strange and Alice Stubbe, 1602.

Norfolk family which had lived at Hunstanton since the twelfth century. Illustrious forebears included the first Sir Hamon, a hero of the battle of Crecy, who built the original medieval gatehouse, and Sir Thomas Le Strange, who served Henry VIII at the Field of the Cloth of Gold; he later greatly benefitted from the dissolution of the monasteries and secured the most prestigious offices in the county.[26] However, in the second half of the sixteenth century, the Le Strange fortunes were in decline, the family having failed to grasp the need for reform. By the time Sir Hamon inherited the estate in 1604, the rental and his income was a fraction of that enjoyed by his great-great-grandfather. He at once settled down to the task of reviving their fortunes, ably assisted by his guardians, principally Richard Stubbe and Sir Henry Spelman.[27]

When Hamon and Alice married they were still in their teens. The union lasted for over fifty years, a long time even by modern standards. During that period their relationship and the management of the family, household and estate went through several phases. Their first three children – Nicholas, Hamon and Dorothy – were born in 1604, 1605 and 1608, and not surprisingly Alice left no records from this time. Her involvement in Sir Hamon's affairs began in 1610 when he handed over responsibility for household expenditure.[28] Dorothy had died in 1609 and this may have been a tactful diversion for Alice, but more likely Hamon needed her assistance so that he could concentrate more fully on estate management.[29] With Alice in charge the general disbursements immediately became more organised and rigorous. She itemized every payment, whereas Hamon had relied on the honesty of servants and tradesmen. For example, while he paid his groom Thomas Hogan, 'his halfe yeares wages and 13s which he disbursed for me', Alice paid him for 'his diet 2s 6d and for 2 horses each of them 2 days in Norwich 4s 6d, so in all 7s'.[30] It is true that Sir Hamon often referred to bills kept in files, but his method left him open to fraud, as Alice soon found out, dismissing Hogan within weeks. Realistically, Hamon had little option but to trust his servants; his good fortune lay in having a wife able and willing to take on such a tedious task.

Alice soon started categorizing entries in the accounts: wages to servants,

26. C. Oestmann, *Lordship and Community: the Lestrange Family and the Village of Hunstanton, Norfolk in the First Half of the Sixteenth Century* (Woodbridge, 1994).

27. Griffiths, 'A Country Life', pp. 203–20.

28. LEST/P6.

29. Sir Hamon had purchased the large manor at Heacham from the earl of Arundel in 1609 which added significantly to his portfolio, LEST/Q38.

30. LEST/P6.

expenditure on the children, repairs to buildings, and food for the household. In time, food and buildings were siphoned off into separate accounts giving her greater control over detail and providing a framework for expansion into new enterprises. At the end of her first book of disbursements, 1610–13, Alice jotted down an estimate of their estate income and expenditure. Of the £905 per annum income from rents, she had to set aside nearly a third to pay annuities, another third for the household, leaving the family just under a third for everything else; so there was not much room for manoeuvre.[31] She clearly understood the idea of a budget.

The household books, sometimes described as 'kitchen books', provided a weekly record of food for the household.[32] In the first few weeks Alice experimented with the layout and arrived at a formula which remained unchanged. Every half year she started with a stock take, followed by the weekly accounts recording items in store, purchased and delivered as gifts from tenants and suppliers. Then, for a standard list of staple foods, she noted the amounts received, bought, made, spent, sold and remaining. The limited range – beef, bread and corn – soon increased to include butter, cheese, and different types of saltfish, beer, bread and prepared food. This routine provided effective controls over stock, was easily checked and could be used to predict consumption and expenditure from year to year. Payments for labour, mainly working on the home farm and in the gardens, concluded the weekly account; the half year ended with a further stock take including details of the piggery and dairy. The dairy first appears in the household books in 1620 although we know from the document, 'A Reckoning of the proffit of my Deyrey' that it was a profitable venture from 1617.[33] The herd, milked by a succession of dairy maids, ranged in size from twenty-three to twenty-six cows by 1634; it produced huge amounts of butter and cheese for the household, often leaving enough for sale. Alice had no qualms about squeezing a profit from the household budget. The receipts from the estate, including farm rents, sales of timber, corn, livestock, wool, butter, milk and cheese were entered at the back of each household book.

The building accounts stemmed from Hamon's plans to rebuild the hall and the buildings on the estate which gathered momentum in 1620 with Alice's inheritance of the Sedgeford estate. These accounts consist of two

---

31. LEST/P6.

32. Whittle & Griffiths, *passim;* nine household books survive: LEST/P6 from 1613–1621 (1st, 3rd, 4th) with a gap from 1614–1616; LEST/P8 from 1621–1633 (5th, 6th, 8th) with a gap from 1627–1629; LEST/P9 from 1633–1642 (9th, 10th) with a long gap from 1642–1650, followed by a book for 1650–1653 in LEST/P11.

33. LEST/P8.

to four pages inserted in the general disbursements at the end of every half year; they can be cross-referenced to Hamon's memoranda books where he kept notes of projects, contracts with suppliers, and jotted down his own ideas and designs. In this way, Alice paid the bills and itemized expenditure, while Hamon concentrated on managing the building process. His growing confidence in her meant that he could reliably predict his income stream and plan ahead with a degree of certainty. He knew at a glance his day-to-day expenses, his income, and the spare cash he could allocate to various projects; this enabled him and Nicholas to carry out a rolling programme of building and repairs which continued without a break despite the financial setbacks of the 1640s.

Alice's involvement in farming and estate management increased greatly with the addition of Sedgeford. Prior to that date, she kept the estate receipts and the children's sheep accounts with her household accounts. From 1620, she initiated a quite separate range of estate accounts and records for Sedgeford. In 1625, once she controlled all the flocks on the estate, she devised a more organised sheep account, which gradually absorbed the children's accounts. In the early years at Sedgeford, Alice had relied on her cousin, Francis Guybon, but, as we have seen, on his death she commissioned the survey by John Fisher which facilitated her programme of improvements. At the same time, the marriage of Nicholas opened up new possibilities. He and his wife, Anne, and their growing family, lived with Hamon and Alice at Hunstanton Hall, giving them every opportunity and incentive to develop the management of the family estates.[34] As Nicholas embarked on his drainage schemes, Alice took on the accounts for the remainder of the estate at Hunstanton, Ringstead, Holme and Heacham.

The estate was managed through four different types of record: field books provided a description of the landholding structure in each parish; rentals listed the manorial tenants owing freehold and copyhold rents; firmals listed those tenants leasing demesne land from the Le Stranges and paying farm rents; finally, bailiffs' accounts recorded the allowances granted and the payments made to the receiver. Before 1630 these records were kept separately, making it difficult to trace what each individual tenant owed for his lands, which might be scattered through several parishes, and the type of rent he paid. Hamon made some attempt to synthesize this detail, but it was left to Alice to modernize the system. She vastly improved the

34. Anne, daughter of Sir Edward Lewkenor of Denham, Suffolk, 1587–1618, see below, p. 12.

layout and legibility of the field books and drew together the rentals, firmals and bailiffs' accounts into a single volume; this is best illustrated in the Hunstanton estate account, 1623–1653.[35] It starts with a combined rental and firmal, listing each tenant with his farm lands and manorial rents. Against each item Alice noted the rents paid, distinguishing between types of farm land according to the rent paid per acre. Subsequently, the rental and firmal were included at four-yearly intervals, noting any change of occupancy. Every year she entered a summary of the bailiff's accounts, recording the rent charge: customary and farm rents, profits of court, payments from rights and liberties; the amount allowed to the bailiff for repairs, expenses and outrents, and finally, the sum received 'at several times by mee Alice Le Strange'. From 1638, she attached with a pin, 'a note how this account was received and written in my [Household] Booke'; later these receipts were entered more securely in the account, and can be cross-referenced to the entries in household book. In this way, Alice created a fully integrated system, linking estate and household accounts.

From her estate accounts, we can see a management strategy unfolding with attention focused on foldcourses, marshes, and those areas of demesne where the Le Stranges exercised total control. Elsewhere, they accepted the fragmented land-holding structure and worked with these large village communities, sustained by fishing and farming, to effect the improvements on the estate. At the same time, the Le Stranges resolved to collect every rent due to them and to protect their own interests. This was Alice's achievement. By methodical accounting and record keeping, she reduced the task to a simple routine, allowing Hamon and Nicholas to concentrate on improvement. The design of her account books as a work of reference also proved to be invaluable to future generations, notably Sir Nicholas, the fourth baronet, from the 1680s. By creating a modern accounting system, Alice not only placed the business of the estate on a sound commercial footing, but facilitated the improvements of the 1630s and 1640s, and the substantial reforms of the late seventeenth and early eighteenth centuries.

From this brief description, Alice's activities can be compared with those of her relatives and other gentlewomen who kept household and estate accounts. To what extent was she typical? Alice herself consulted accounts kept by Le Strange women in the sixteenth century and adopted a similar format for her kitchen books before adding her own modifications. Catherine Calthorpe, the sister of her daughter-in-law, Anne, married to Sir James Calthorpe, kept an account from 1652–1662 which remains in

---

35. LEST/BK15.

the Le Strange archive.[36] Slight variations in handwriting from the 1630s suggest that Anne may have assisted Alice with entries from time to time. Further afield, her cousin by marriage, Lady Frances Hobart of Blickling, was influential in reforming the accounts and finances of her husband, bringing clarity and control to existing methods and recruiting the right men to perform the various tasks involved.[37] Later, in the 1690s, Katherine Windham of Felbrigg kept the estate accounts for a while following her husband's early death, and supervised the family finances for the next forty years.[38] Clearly, these women were familiar with accounts. What is so unusual, possibly unique, about Alice is the scale of her activity, her enthusiasm for the task and her understanding of what was required for an effective accounting system. She never ceased perfecting her methods, showing a very firm grasp of accounting techniques. Her knowledge of farming and estate business was also exceptional. It allowed her to develop her role almost indefinitely, taking on the most intricate tasks. Most significantly, the benefits of her work outlived her, providing as they did a model for succeeding generations of improvers in this corner of Norfolk. She may not have been typical, but Alice shows what a woman could achieve in the first half of the seventeenth century with encouragement, training and support. The next section, explaining the documents, and the transcriptions that follow, will start to demonstrate the scale of her achievement.

---

36. The Calthorpes were a vast Norfolk family and closely related to the Le Stranges. Sir James Calthorpe of East Barsham, 1604–1652, married in 1641 as his second wife, Catherine Lewkenor, daughter of Sir Edward Lewkenor, and sister of Anne Le Strange, wife of Sir Nicholas, *see* Moore & Crawley, *Family & Friends*, pp. 77–88, for several references to the Calthorpes, Le Stranges and Lewkenors, and *see also*, LEST/BE6, LEST/P20. Catherine's son, Sir Christopher Calthorpe, kt, 1661, acted as trustee for Sir Nicholas Le Strange, 4th bt, between 1669–1682; he married Dorothy, daughter of Sir William Spring and his wife, Elizabeth Le Strange. Their daughter Anne married Sir Thomas Le Strange, *see* Blomefield, *Norfolk*, VII, p. 57.

37. Frances, d. 1664, daughter of John Egerton, 1st earl of Bridgewater, second wife of Sir John Hobart, 2nd bt, 1593–1647; Sir Hamon's first cousin through their mothers, Dorothy and Mary Bell, see above, fn. 24, p. 6.

38. Katherine 1652–1729, daughter of Sir Joseph Ashe, wife of William Windham, 1647–1689.

Figure 2. Le Strange Family Tree, 1600–1762[39]

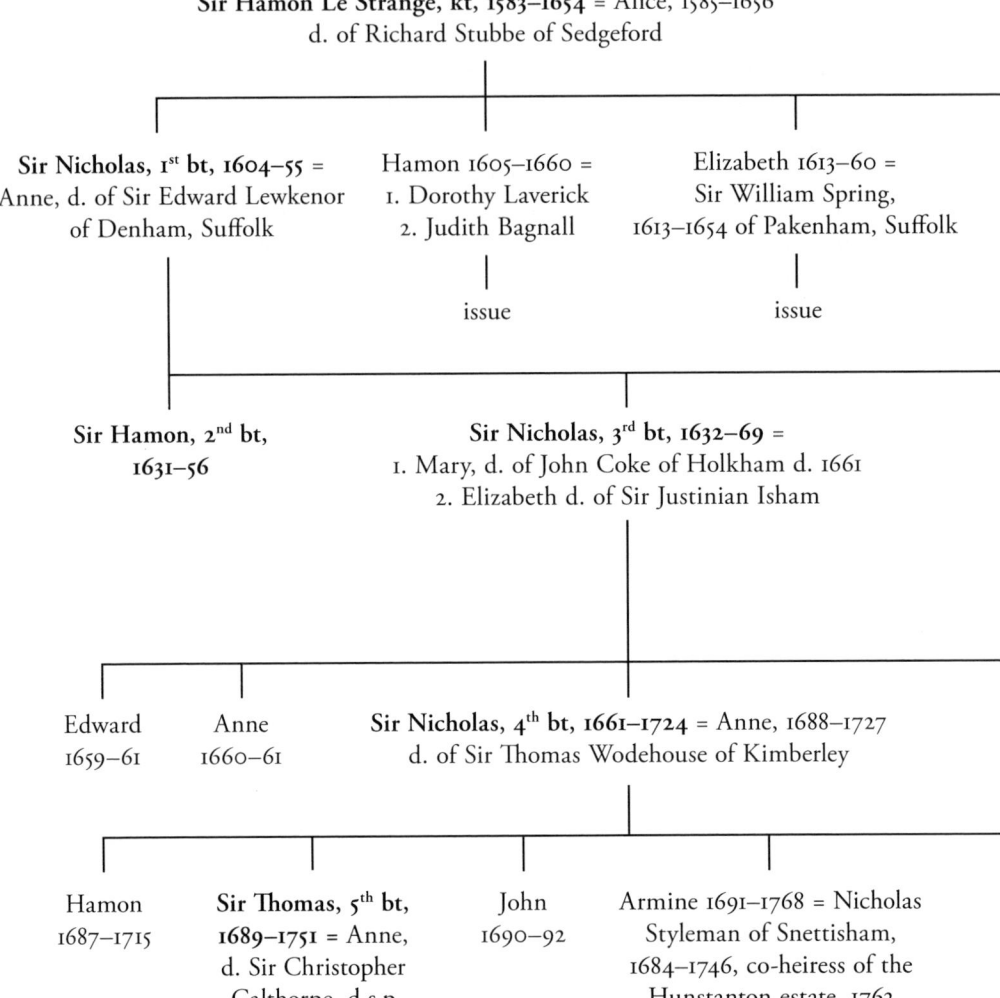

Sir Hamon Le Strange, kt, 1583–1654 = Alice, 1585–1656
d. of Richard Stubbe of Sedgeford

Sir Nicholas, 1st bt, 1604–55 =
Anne, d. of Sir Edward Lewkenor
of Denham, Suffolk

Hamon 1605–1660 =
1. Dorothy Laverick
2. Judith Bagnall

issue

Elizabeth 1613–60 =
Sir William Spring,
1613–1654 of Pakenham, Suffolk

issue

**Sir Hamon, 2nd bt,
1631–56**

Sir Nicholas, 3rd bt, 1632–69 =
1. Mary, d. of John Coke of Holkham d. 1661
2. Elizabeth d. of Sir Justinian Isham

Edward
1659–61

Anne
1660–61

Sir Nicholas, 4th bt, 1661–1724 = Anne, 1688–1727
d. of Sir Thomas Wodehouse of Kimberley

Hamon
1687–1715

**Sir Thomas, 5th bt,
1689–1751** = Anne,
d. Sir Christopher
Calthorpe, d.s.p

John
1690–92

Armine 1691–1768 = Nicholas
Styleman of Snettisham,
1684–1746, co-heiress of the
Hunstanton estate, 1762

---

39. Based on Blomefield & Parkin, *History of Norfolk*, vol. X, p. 314. In 1760 the baronetcy passed to a distant cousin, Sir Roger L'Estrange of Hoe who died without issue in 1762 rendering the title extinct. The Le Strange estate was then divided between the two surviving daughters of Sir Nicholas, 4th bt: the Hunstanton estate passed to Armine, married to Nicholas Styleman of Snettisham; the Gressenhall estate to Lucy, the wife of Sir Jacob

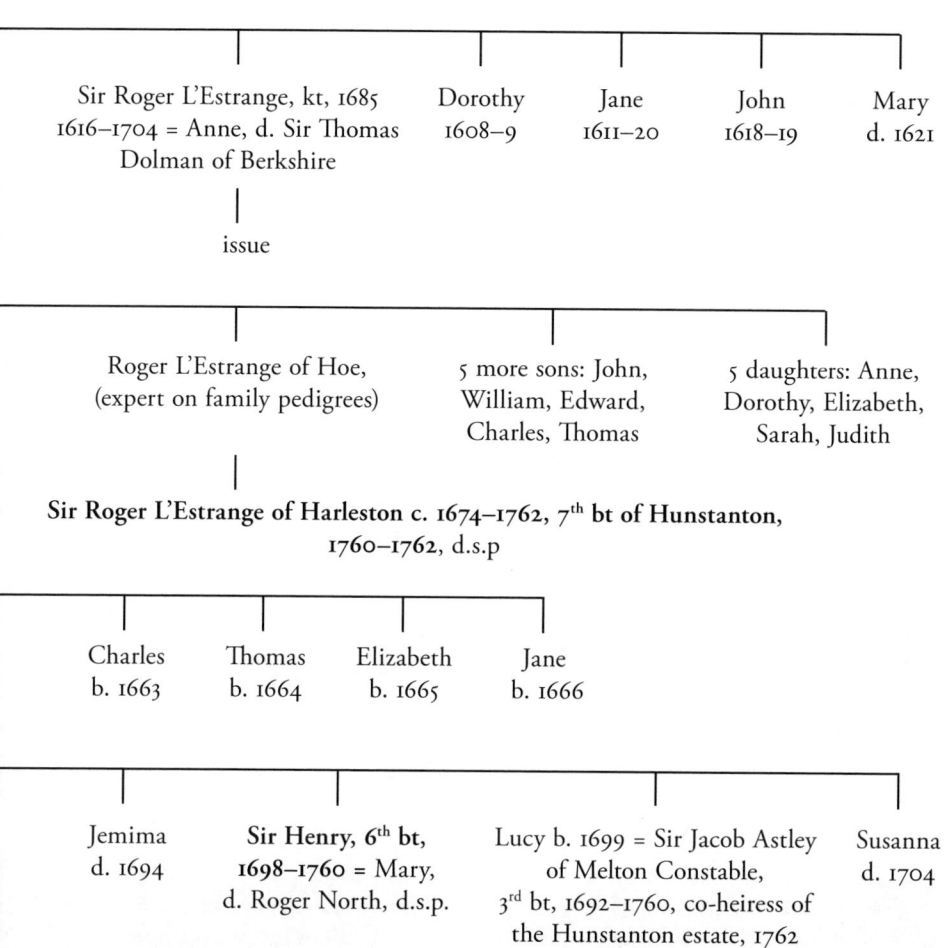

Sir Roger L'Estrange, kt, 1685, 1616–1704 = Anne, d. Sir Thomas Dolman of Berkshire

Dorothy 1608–9

Jane 1611–20

John 1618–19

Mary d. 1621

issue

Roger L'Estrange of Hoe, (expert on family pedigrees)

5 more sons: John, William, Edward, Charles, Thomas

5 daughters: Anne, Dorothy, Elizabeth, Sarah, Judith

Sir Roger L'Estrange of Harleston c. 1674–1762, 7ᵗʰ bt of Hunstanton, 1760–1762, d.s.p

Charles b. 1663

Thomas b. 1664

Elizabeth b. 1665

Jane b. 1666

Jemima d. 1694

Sir Henry, 6ᵗʰ bt, 1698–1760 = Mary, d. Roger North, d.s.p.

Lucy b. 1699 = Sir Jacob Astley of Melton Constable, 3ʳᵈ bt, 1692–1760, co-heiress of the Hunstanton estate, 1762

Susanna d. 1704

Astley of Melton Constable, see NRO, LEST/R23 for the valuation carried out by N. Kent and J. Claridge in 1784. In 1834, the Stylemans added Le Strange to the family name; in 1874, following the sale of the Snettisham estate, Hamon Styleman Le Strange, dropped the name Styleman by deed poll, NRO, LEST/12/6/1976. This line of the Le Stranges remains in possession of the Hunstanton estate.

Explaining the Documents

This section offers readers, daunted by the rows and columns of figures, some explanation of the accounts in the hope that it will encourage them to delve more deeply. Reflecting the order of the documents, the chapter has been divided into three parts: Family and Finance, the Sheep Accounts and the Improvements at Sedgeford. The transcriptions are mainly drawn from four paper books: LEST/P10, LEST/BK7, LEST/IC58 and LEST/IB90, but also include the wills of Sir Hamon Le Strange, PROB 11/238/248, and Dame Alice Le Strange PROB 11/262, and other relevant documents which provide a fuller context.

Family and Finance

The first document, which includes details of the Le Strange family finances, can be found with the final book of general disbursements, 1645–1654.[40] We do not know when or why Alice Le Strange wrote these notes but it was most likely after the difficulties the family encountered in the early 1640s, as a way of explaining their indebtedness to their successors. What is noticeable is her aggrieved tone, first directed against her half-sister Dionisia Yelverton and her father, and then against anyone else who tried to do them down: principally those who challenged their rights and titles to their estate, and her husband's enemies during the Civil War. The first extract begins with Alice comparing the settlement made by her father for his two daughters. On marriage, both sisters were given cash sums and continuing assistance from Stubbe until his death in 1619, but Alice's total of £4,669 13s 4d was substantially less than the £6,392 allowed to

---

40. LEST/P10 consists of two books bound together by Hamon L' Estrange Styleman in 1853. The first includes Alice Le Strange's final book of disbursements, followed by her notes on the family finances; the second, principally her sheep accounts, also contains Nicholas and Hamon's expenses at Eton, Roger's expenses at Cambridge, a ship account, and inventories of furniture and linen taken in 1620 and 1632.

the Yelvertons.[41] Even allowing for the £513 16s given to her family in gifts and legacies, this still amounted to a substantial difference: 'my sister had more in money more than myself £1,209 15s 8d'. She also emphasized that much of the Yelvertons' money was used to pay off debts, while £1,000 was deducted from her own account to pay Sir John Peyton's expenses.[42] The management of the trustees was another bone of contention.[43] However, despite these grievances, Alice's early household accounts show a close relationship between father and daughter, with the old man taking a keen interest in her growing family, lending them money, giving them sheep and offering advice: her sister was also a frequent visitor and came to live at Hunstanton during her widowhood. Nevertheless, Alice's notes on the settlement, carefully documented for posterity, provide a striking picture of an assertive woman strong in defence of herself, her husband and her family.

These notes on the family finances are not continuous but separated by blank pages, indicating that Alice wanted to leave space for adding to them if necessary. After the sisters' settlement, she left twelve blank pages, before listing the 'Sale of Lands and Purchases' from 1630. The date is significant as it coincides with the marriage of their eldest son, the newly created Sir Nicholas Le Strange, to Anne, daughter of Sir Edward Lewkenor of Denham, Suffolk.[44] By this time Hamon and Alice had raised and educated four children: the three boys, Nicholas, Hamon and Roger, went to Eton, Cambridge and the Inns of Court, while Elizabeth was groomed for marriage by her mother. They had also made progress improving the estate, rebuilding Hunstanton Hall, increasing their income and reducing their debts. As their children achieved maturity and needed to be settled, their family finances became much more complex with huge sums passing through the accounts. The impression is that Alice wanted to explain how this process was skilfully managed. Anne Lewkenor's dowry of £3,000 was used, not to repay debts as was so often the case, but to purchase the Benacre estate in Suffolk. The estate was sold two years later to finance the marriage of their second son, Hamon, to Dorothy Laverick in 1634 – there is no evidence of a dowry. In all, young Hamon's settlement amounted to nearly £2,600, with £1,800 paid to Sir William Yelverton for an estate

---

41. For the Yelverton family, see above, fn. 23, p. 6.

42. The assumption being that this charge, Sir Hamon's release of wardship, should not have been set against her estate. For Sir John Peyton, see above, fn. 24, p. 6.

43. See below, p. 83 under 'Losses in my Husbands Estate'.

44. Sir Edward Lewkenor of Denham, Suffolk, 1587–1618, www.historyofparliament online.org.uk.

at West Winch and a further £800 in cash. By 1635 this transaction was completed with Alice noting 'Debts Remayne 1635 – none'.

This happy state of affairs was about to change with Elizabeth's marriage in 1636 to William Spring of Pakenham, Suffolk, and the need to raise a dowry of £3,500.[45] The sum was raised principally by loans from relatives, such as the Lewkenors and Springs, friends, tenants, employees, including the Guybons and the Banyards, and more formal money lenders, like Mr Simons who loaned £800 from 1637 to 1648.[46] These borrowings might appear profligate but were sustainable against a background of rising estate revenues; the family continued to spend money on buying land, building, adventuring on Boston Fen and their own drainage schemes. From 1636 to 1654, Alice recorded the 'Debts Owing' and how they were financed from year to year with loans repaid and new borrowings arranged. There is no mention of interest rates until 1654, when Alice paid the London money lenders 6%; however, her books of disbursements record interest payments of 6% and 8%, with the higher rate often paid to relatives and tenants.[47] By 1642 the level of debt had been reduced from £3,400 to £2,100. But the downward trend did not last: it was brutally interrupted by the costs and losses incurred during the Civil War with Sir Hamon's dramatic intervention in the royalist uprising of Kings Lynn.[48]

The crisis started on 13 August 1643 when the royalist faction of west Norfolk and Kings Lynn, led by Sir Hamon, declared their support for the King. The earl of Manchester, newly appointed commander of the Eastern Association, responded by imposing a siege on the town, awaiting the arrival of relief forces and supplies.[49] Inside the town, John Percival and Thomas Toll, the puritan members for the borough, busily conspired against the royalists. Within a month resistance collapsed and terms were agreed which

---

45. Sir William Spring of Pakenham, 1613–1654, www.historyofparliamentonline.org.uk. Roger, the youngest surviving child, did not marry until the 1670s, but caused plenty of trouble and expense to his parents in the 1640s and 1650s, *see* H. Love, 'L'Estrange, Sir Roger (1616–1704)', *Oxford Dictionary of National Biography* (Oxford, 2004).

46. Reference to these kinds of loans can be found in *The Papers of Nathaniel Bacon of Stiffkey, vol. III, 1586–1595*' (Norfolk Record Society, LIII, 1987 and 1988), pp. 222–3.

47. LEST/P7 for 1631 to 1645; LEST/P10 for 1645–1654. For a similar variation of interest rates, *see* Griffiths, *William Windham's Green Book*, pp. 254–7. My thanks to John Broad for this point, and to Jean Agnew who suggested that the different rates might reflect the absence of a broker's fee.

48. Ketton-Cremer, *Norfolk in the Civil War*, pp. 206–17.

49. The first of these troops was led by Captain William Poe who figures prominently in Alice's sheep accounts as the architect of the raid on the Le Strange flocks. LEST/P10, see below, p. 152.

included the payment of a levy to the besieging soldiers in lieu of plunder, and later, by parliamentary ordinance, compensation for any damage inflicted on 'well affected persons' of the borough. So, in addition to the loss of their flocks and corn during the siege, the Le Stranges were liable for the payment of their share of the levy to the soldiers, damages to Toll, Percival and others, and suffered the vigorous enforcement of the sequestration of their estates. Sums relating to these issues can be found scattered through the document from 1643: they amounted to over £3,000 excluding the value of the sheep and corn.

Despite these reverses, the family continued as before buying parcels of land and paying off debt; by the early 1650s it had fallen to £1,300. In 1654, on Sir Hamon's death, the family borrowed £2,000 to cover undisclosed sums leaving a total debt of £3,300. Given what they had suffered over the previous ten years, and the continuing high levels of taxation, this sum was not excessive.[50] Nevertheless, at the end of the list of debts, Alice clearly felt the need to summarize and explain their position and perhaps to justify her management of their affairs.

The summary starts, after a gap of ten pages, with the final agreement of a long running legal case with the Cremer family showing that it had been fully resolved. The suits against the Cremers and Styleman, over parcels of land in Heacham, had been an ongoing problem throughout the 1630s and 1640s. The principal issue was settled out of court in 1648, but it seems that Robert Styleman had exacted a payment from Sir Hamon in 1646, as Alice noted them 'being over powered by the times'.[51] She then listed the lands sold and purchased from the earliest years of their marriage. These included the sale in 1609 of the manor of Fring for £2,140 to pay for the purchase of the manor of Heacham Lewis from the earl of Arundel for £4,400.[52] She explains how the shortfall was met with the sale of Grint Mill and Holme Parsonage, Chappell Mill, South Linne, and the reversion of the Irish lands. As if to underline her financial rectitude, she noted that the expectation of improvement at Heacham would 'make the land bought as much as the land sold'; in other words, that improvement would cover the initial outlay. Alice then poignantly itemized the 'Losses in my Husbands Estate'. As a preamble, she emphasized the debts left by the executors and their neglect of the household and buildings during Sir Hamon's minority, which required

---

50. For an account of reckless borrowing, *see* Sir John Hobart's experience at Blickling, in E.M. Griffiths, 'The management of two East Norfolk estates in the seventeenth century: Blickling and Felbrigg' vol. 1, 1596–1654' (PhD Thesis, UEA, 1987), pp. 248–53.

51. See below, p. 84, and Griffiths, 'A Country Life', p. 230.

52. LEST/Q38, fol. 26; LEST/Q37, fol. 18; LEST/P6.

them to rebuild 'most of them out of the ground'. This difficult inheritance was compounded by the 'many chargeable sutes' and 'unkinde losses'; these included the 'adventuring' in the East Indies and Boston Fens, and the draining of marshes at Heacham. The section ends with an emotional reference to the 'Tirannical Oppression' of Mr Toll and his faction in Lynn which cost them £1,088, 'beside our greate Losse where we were plundered of all our Sheep and Corn'. Alice closed her summary on a calmer note listing 'Lands and other guifts of Father', restating his contribution to their children; this is followed by an inventory of household stuff left to her by her father. The final item, a list of church repairs at Sedgeford and Ringstead in 1653, has not been transcribed: they amount to less than £25 but they do indicate what Alice thought useful to include in this context.

Alice died in 1656, two years after Sir Hamon. Their wills tell us so much about the richness of their relationship: there was no lack of affection in this marriage.[53] As we can see, he fulsomely acknowledged Alice's intelligence and her role in the education of their children and the advancement of his estate; she simply desired to be 'decently interred ... neere the Body of ... my late Deare husband'. Neither will is concerned with property, which had already been dealt with, but each provides a list of various bequests to family, friends, servants and the poor; these indicate the value attached to particular goods and people. By this time Alice had retired to Sedgeford and bequeathed all her brewing and dairy equipment to her favourite grandson, Sir Nicholas. At the same time, she ensured that her daughter-in-law, Anne, had enough bedding, curtains, furniture, kitchen stuff and tableware for her own widowhood at Sedgeford. Beyond small legacies and bequests to her own daughter, Elizabeth, and particular grandchildren, Alice singled out female relations, including her cousin Elizabeth Guybon, friends and servants. Francis Guybon, son of Alice's cousin and principal tenant, and John Fisher, the surveyor, appear as witnesses.[54] Both wills indicate a couple striving to ensure the future of their family and estate, and living at ease with their servants, tenants and wider rural communities.

---

53. PROB 11/238/248; PROB 11/262, see below, pp. 353–62.

54. There were in fact two John Fishers who both appear in both wills: John Fisher the surveyor of Heacham and John Fisher of Honing, gt. The latter is differentiated by his gentility; we may assume that when John Fisher stands on its own it was the surveyor. See further fn. 49 below, p. 77.

The Sheep Accounts, 1617–1655

Alice Le Strange's sheep accounts are the first evidence of her working with farming records. Her initial purpose was to keep a record of her own sheep and those of her five children: Nicholas, Hamon, Jane, Elizabeth and Roger. She was continuing a family tradition, established by her father, whereby children were trained in the arts of sheep farming by allocating them ewes and allowing them the profit of lambs and wool. Richard Stubbe died in 1619 leaving each grandchild forty sheep.[55] Evidence of his enduring influence can be found in her description of the flocks on the estate where she refers to folios in 'my father's booke'.[56]

The sheep accounts are contained in a separate book bound with the disbursements and family finances.[57] The cover lists various accounts: the flocks and foldcourses by Alice 'for divers years'; the profits of a ship in which they had a share; her sons' expenses at Eton and Cambridge, and inventories of furniture and bedding. The last two items are not transcribed, but the ship account has been included as it has direct relevance to their business concerns – Alice used some of the profits to buy sheep – and it has not been considered elsewhere.[58] So, all appears straightforward, but in fact, the sheep accounts proved to be a minefield. The entries, at the front of the book, date from 1625 to 1653; however, at the end of the book, there are some scruffy, faded and untitled accounts, which turned out to be the sheep accounts for the children and Alice, dating from 1617 to 1627; to add to the confusion, other related accounts had been inserted by Alice on spare pages. For the sake of the reader, we decided to put the sheep accounts in chronological order and to group related accounts at the end; the footnotes explain where these accounts appear in the original document.[59] An entirely separate sheep account appears in Alice's first farming book for Sedgeford. This brief account will be considered first as it illustrates Alice's development as a sheep farmer and her progression to managing all the sheep accounts for the estate in 1625.

---

55. Richard Stubbe's will PROB 11/135.
56. LEST/P10, see below, p. 192.
57. LEST/P10, see above, fn. 40.
58. For a discussion of these topics, see Whittle & Griffiths, pp. 120–40, 174–83.
59. See also, Notes to the Reader, below pp. 59–60.

The Sedgeford sheep account, 1620–22[60]

Alice's inheritance of the Sedgeford estate was not straightforward. In his will, Richard Stubbe had allowed Sir William Yelverton, his son-in-law, to enjoy the profits for a year. In 1620 we find Alice buying Yelverton's holding in the Sedgeford flocks, paying £355 14s 8d for 1,333 sheep.[61] The short account provides much explanatory detail and a useful introduction to her system and sheep accounting methods. The first page records that 1,239 sheep were delivered to three shepherds: 557 ewes to Woods at East Ground, 250 ewes to Rose at South Ground and 432 wethers to Corner at North Ground leaving a shortfall of ninety-four sheep. In addition, tenants were allowed to put 'Joyce Sheep' into the flocks, amounting to 496 sheep.[62] Francis and William Guybon placed 313 in the East Flock, nineteen in the South Flock and thirty-nine in the North Flock; George Frammingham put thirty-six in the South Flock and twelve in the North Flock, while seven other tenants put seventy-seven into the South Flock. Francis Guybon placed a further 120 in the South Flock from Alice 'in lieu of the 1C [120] I have of wethers going in his part of Ringsted Flock'. The shortfall of ninety-four sheep highlights some of the difficulties with Alice's accounting system. For example, there is no consistency in her use of Roman and Arabic numerals, and some confusion in her use of the long hundred, 1C or 120 instead of 100 or vxx [i.e. five score], traditionally used for counting sheep. She refers to the 1C wethers she has exchanged with Guybon and later refers to them as a hundred wethers. When these figures are converted into Arabic numerals further problems emerge. Frequently, her totals at the end of each account do not coincide with the actual totals: this can be seen in the discrepancy in the total for the South Flock in 1620 showing an excess of almost sixty sheep over the actual total of 502. This type of difference of twenty, forty or sixty sheep is a regular feature of the sheep accounts; a payment to Rose, the shepherd of the South Flock, in 1620 explains why. He was allowed two half-yearly payments of fifteen shillings 'for 60 sheep which we are to lay at 6d the sheepe which are not layd this year'. The inclusion of this allowance brings the total figure for the three flocks up to 1,299, reducing the initial shortfall to thirty-four;

60. LEST/BK7, fols. 3–15; see below, pp. 199–206.

61. LEST/P10, Richard Stubbe left the Yelvertons a year's profit from the estate at Sedgeford which Alice recorded in the Sedgeford estate accounts 1621–1635, LEST/BK7, see below, p. 209.

62. For joyce or cullett sheep, see Sheep Glossary, pp. 63–4, and D. Yaxley, *A Researcher's Glossary of words found in historical documents in East Anglia* (Fakenham, 2003) for all technical and local terms.

this reflects fourteen morts [i.e. deaths] and possibly a hidden allowance of twenty for Woods or Corner. With this understanding of what was happening on the ground, Alice's accounts begin to add up, but they are not foolproof.

From the Sedgeford account, it is possible to follow the cycle of sheep management. With the delivery of the sheep to the shepherds at Midsummer 1620, they were 'charged' with a certain number of sheep, which they had to account for at the 'clipping' the following year. Alice then itemized expenditure for the intervening months. The largest outlay was for the remuneration of shepherds with wages at 16s 8d a quarter, livery (clothes and food) at 6s 8d per annum, and the value of placing sheep in the flock at 6d a sheep.[63] In this way, Rose enjoyed £5 3s 4d per annum, amongst the highest wages on the estate. Payments were also made to nameless contractors for washing, dragging, clipping, greasing, branding, winding wool, and other necessities such as pitch, tar and hurdles.[64] These expenses were set against receipts from tathe,[65] skins, the sale of lambs, crones, wethers and wool, payments for joyce sheep, and rents for foldcourses when they were let. Following the clipping in 1621, Alice calculated a profit of £21 6s 2d made on the sale of sheep, with a further £57 12s on the sale of wool. The tithe paid on wool and lambs had been deducted at source from the shepherd. Crucially, the account provided information on the movement of sheep from flock to flock: for example, in 1621 Sedgeford wethers were shifted into Crisp's South Flock at Ringstead, as well as into Corner's North Flock. Crisp also received wethers from Barrett Ringstead, including those of the children.[66] The short account ceases at this point as Alice began to rationalize her management of the sheep on the estate.

Alice's general sheep accounts do not, as a rule, contain the same level of information. From 1625, they become in effect a centralized stock account, incorporating individual shepherd's accounts, designed to keep a tally of numbers and the movement of sheep; they contain some references to prices received for lambs, wethers, crones and wool, but there is no attempt

---

63. This package compares to 15s a quarter and 5s for livery, with a more generous allowance for sheep, albeit in a larger flock, at Sedgeford in the 1500s, *see* M. Bailey 'The Sheep Accounts of Norwich Cathedral Priory 1484 to 1534', p. 9, in *Poverty and Wealth: Sheep, Taxation and Charity in Late Medieval Norfolk*, eds. M. Bailey, M. Jurowski & C. Rawcliffe (Norfolk Record Society, LXXI, 2007).

64. Dragging usually means literally dragging unwilling sheep to the clipping.

65. i.e. manure, see Sheep Glossary.

66. The Crisps were an old Sedgeford family; Richard was making payments for tathing in the 1490s, *see* Bailey, above, pp. 37, 42–3.

to strike a balance of profit and loss. Alice entered money received in her receipt book at the end of each household book, while she noted expenses in her books of general disbursements. This is a more personal arrangement, tailored to fit in with her domestic accounts, than the traditional system found on large estates. For example, at Raynham, shepherds submitted their own accounts to the sheep reeve, who kept a centralized stock account of the seven flocks under his control with a separate account summarizing receipts, expenditure, profits and loss.[67] Between 1603 and 1617 these were presented to Jane, Lady Berkeley, grandmother of Sir Roger Townshend, who administered the estate during his long minority.[68] The structure at Raynham, noted for its long history of keeping large flocks, conforms to the practice of the Norwich Cathedral Priory; these include the accounts of their flocks at Sedgeford, Gnatingdon and nearby Fring.[69] Alice's system was more idiosyncratic, reflecting her personal control of the flocks and their management; the accounts were not designed for an estate bureaucracy, but to provide her with the information she needed which varied from time to time.

The early accounts for the children and herself are haphazard with Alice's objectives unclear. The format is clarified in 1625 when she started her new book. This initiative followed the acquisition of the three Sedgeford flocks in 1620 and their absorption into the Le Stranges' general management of

---

67. The Townshend papers are held by the family at Raynham Hall, but *see* E.M. Griffiths and M. Overton, *Farming to Halves: The Hidden History of Sharefarming in England from Medieval to Modern Times* (Basingstoke, 2009), pp. 56–132.

68. Jane, Lady Berkeley (c. 1547–1617), daughter of Sir Michael Stanhope of Shelford (c. 1508–1552), married Sir Roger Townshend (1544–1590) and in 1597, Henry, 7th baron Berkeley (1534–1613). On the death of her profligate son, Sir John Townshend, in 1603, she managed the Raynham estate until her death in 1617, *see* L. Campbell, 'Sir Roger Townshend and his Family: A Study of Gentry Life in Early Seventeenth Century Norfolk' (PhD thesis, UEA, 1990).

69. Bailey, 'The Sheep Accounts of Norwich Cathedral Priory' in *Poverty and Wealth*, pp. 1–96, see fn. 63. In 1498, Sedgeford was their largest flock accounting for more than a quarter of the total of 6,212 sheep. In 1509, Fring dropped out of the account, but a new flock, with similar numbers, appears at Gnatingdon south west of Sedgeford village; the following year, another flock appears in Sedgeford, 'Westmannor', known as the 'farmers flock'. From 1514 the Sedgeford flock is described as the Northflock indicating further segregation between ewes, wethers and lambs. From this point, numbers averaged 2,500 sheep, about a third of the total as the Priory had raised their numbers by placing cullett sheep into flocks at Bintree, Sparham, Wood Norton, Ryburgh, and increasing the size of their flocks around Norwich. Blomefield lists Gnatingdon separately, but it lies within Sedgeford parish and is also known as Eaton, *see* Blomefield & Parkin, *Norfolk*, X, pp. 390–1.

their six flocks and foldcourses.[70] From 1625 the family kept three flocks in hand at Sedgeford East Ground, Barrett Ringstead and the South Ground at Great Ringstead. They let the North Flock at Ringstead to a syndicate of tenants,[71] while at Sedgeford, Alice let the South Foldcourse to her cousin William Guybon in 1621 and the North Foldcourse to John Cremer in 1625. The system prospered until 1643 when the flocks were plundered by the parliamentary forces, leaving the Le Stranges to stock the foldcourses mainly with cullett sheep from relatives, friends and tenants.[72] Recovery was slow, but this did not prevent Alice from continuing the policy of providing her male grandchildren with sheep from 1634. The sheep accounts, in many ways, mirror the family fortunes, the turning point being Alice's inheritance of the Sedgeford estate from her father and her purchase of the flocks from her brother-in-law, Sir William Yelverton, in 1620.

The sheep accounts for Alice and her children, 1617–1627

In the original document, Alice's own account comes after the children's, as it does in the transcriptions, but it will be considered first as it sets the context. The start of the account is obscured as the top half of the page is missing, so we don't really know how and when Alice began her venture into sheep farming. The first entry dates from Midsummer 1617, when Page and Goodman, the shepherds at Barrett Ringstead, took delivery of 204 wethers, lambs and hoggs, of which 194 were safely brought to the clipping at Midsummer 1618. This appears to be the sum total of Alice's holding, suggesting a new enterprise. In 1619, she repaid a loan to her father of £73 8s 2d, which would have covered the cost of buying these sheep, indicating that he was underwriting the project; she still owed him £30 when he died. The children's accounts start in 1618. In effect, Alice managed the children's sheep as an offshoot of her own, shifting animals around, selling crones and fatstock, replacing them with young ewes and wether lambs, organising the tasks that needed to be done during the year, and keeping a record of numbers and movements. In her first account, she bought Nicholas twenty ewes which we find in his account for 1618, delivered to Page, who took responsibility for the children's sheep.

In these early accounts, Alice recorded expenses and receipts in some

---

70. Alice's sheep accounts exclude the two flocks at Heacham leased to tenants, LEST/DH16, but she included payments for the Heacham tithe after 1643.

71. LEST/EK5. In 1632, the North Foldcourse at Ringstead was let to J. Constable, R. Constable, T. Thurlow and N. Powle for £16 a year.

72. In these accounts Alice referred to cullett rather than joyce sheep, see Sheep Glossary.

detail. As at Sedgeford, the largest outlay was the payment of shepherds, but apparently at lower rates. In 1619, she paid the 'sheppheardes wages for a yeare ... £1 13s 4d' and in 1620, £1 18s 4d. In the same year, she noted 'to the shepheardes for their quarter wages 14s 2d'. In a later note, Alice set out the regulations governing the different flocks which included details of the shepherds' covenants, livery and wages, showing that they were all paid comparable rates at £3 6s 8d a year, or 16s 8d a quarter.[73] However, we know from the books of disbursements that Alice was not averse to adjusting wage rates downwards.[74] As before, payments were made to contractors to carry out seasonal tasks: washing, dragging, clipping and greasing, branding and winding wool. Necessities included oil as well as the pitch and tar, used to mark the sheep and protect them from diseases to which they were notoriously susceptible.[75] On the first page of Alice's account, she 'Lost 25 sheep, bought of Mr Waters, which were stricken'; we note she quickly sold them off at a reduced rate, taking a loss of 12d per sheep. Large quantities of hurdles were also bought to fold the sheep on the arable. A further cost was the payment of the tithe on wool and lamb to the vicar, which was deducted directly from the shepherd. These expenses were set against receipts from the sale of crones, pooks (undersized lambs), fat lambs and wethers, and from wool. Income was also drawn from payments for cullett sheep and rents for foldcourses when they were let.

As at Sedgeford, the annual life cycle turned around Midsummer when shepherds were charged with a certain number of sheep which they had to account for at the clipping the following year.[76] At the 'reckoning', the shepherd brought the skins of dead sheep 'morts', to make up the numbers; if these did not tally, he had to 'make good' the difference. At the same time, crones and pooks were 'taken off' and sold with fatstock, while other sheep, mainly wether lambs, were moved to different flocks. From the small numbers involved in the early accounts it is easy to follow the natural cycle of the flock and to explain the terms used to describe the sheep at various ages. Lambs, born in the spring, were fattened and sold before the winter, or kept as hoggs until they were shorn the following year in May or June. Once clipped, they appear as shearlings or shorlins in Alice's accounts. The ewe shorlins were put to the ram, with the older ewes, in late autumn and

---

73. LEST/P10, see below, pp. 192–3.

74. LEST/P7 and P10 see also, Whittle & Griffiths, pp. 210–38.

75. Pitch was used for marking sheep, applied with a branding iron; black tar was used to protect sheep against parasites and tick-borne diseases, *see* J.A.S. Watson & J.A. More, *Agriculture: The Science and Practice of Farming* (11th edn, 1962), pp. 576–90.

76. See Sheep Glossary: Life cycle of a sheep, p. 63.

lambed the following spring; the gestation period for a ewe is about five months.[77] When they arrived at the clipping with their lambs, they were counted as ewes or mother ewes. As they grew old and barren, they were croned or weeded out of the flock with the small lambs. The male lambs were kept as ram lambs, or castrated as wether lambs, becoming wether hoggs, wether shorlins and wethers of two, three, four and even five sheare. This seems a great age, but wethers were kept for their wool and tathing as well as meat; their fleeces were heavier and more valuable than those of ewes. Wether lambs were taken from the breeding flocks at Sedgeford East Ground and Barrett Ringstead, and kept in wether flocks, principally Crisp's South Flock at Ringstead. Later on, we find Alice selling more fat lambs in the summer and autumn, restricting the size of the flocks and the numbers over wintered. The children were allocated ewes with the idea of building up little breeding flocks; once established their wether lambs were sent to Crisp's flock, or to Corner at Sedgeford North Ground before it was let in 1625.

The children's flocks varied in size suggesting there might have been an element of favouritism. Nicholas steadily built up his numbers, buying twenty more ewes, selling wethers and establishing a breeding flock of fifty-five animals by 1619. Hamon, a year younger, made a slow start in 1619 with just seven ewes and two lambs, and never caught up. Roger, on the other hand, received financial help from his grandfather in 1618, aged just two years, with twenty ewes and twenty-three lambs delivered to Page in that year. Jane started in 1619 with five young females, while Elizabeth received three in 1620; the forty ewes from Stubbe in 1620 were a significant boost to their numbers. When Jane died in 1621, Roger and Bess divided her forty-four ewes, while Dorothy Guybon received her twenty lambs. In 1622 Alice started diverting wether lambs and shorlins to the wether flocks. By 1623 the children held a total of 790 sheep in three different flocks. In 1627 they sold their entire holding of 924 sheep to their father for a total of £292 4s 8d, as shown in Table 1, possibly as a way of simplifying an increasingly complex system.

These little individual accounts are painfully repetitive, leaving us to wonder why Alice bothered. We can only surmise that their purpose was to educate the children and give them a sense of ownership over their ewes and lambs. But did the effort pay dividends? Certainly, Nicholas became an enthusiastic improver and worked closely with his mother at Sedgeford while Hamon farmed at Ringstead. From 1644, he helped in the recovery

---

77. 147–51 days, *see* Watson & More, *Agriculture,* pp. 576–90.

Table 1: Sale of the children's sheep to their father, Sir Hamon Le Strange, 1627[a]

	Nicholas	Hamon	Roger	Elizabeth	Total	Prices	£	s	d
Mother ewes	120	72	121	50	363	7s	127	1	0
Ewe shorlins	25	16	15	12	68	6s	20	8	0
Rams	3	5	6	4	18	5s	4	10	0
Lambs	57	35	56	32	180	3s 8d	34	10	0
Wethers	60	55	84	96	295	6s 8d > 8s	105	15	8
Total	265	183	282	194	924		292	4	8

a Tables 1–3 are based on LEST/P10.

after the plunder of 1643, placing 120 cullett sheep in the flock at Barrett Ringstead with a further 200 sheep in Ringstead North Flock from 1648.[78]

Despite growing commitments elsewhere on the estate, Alice also kept sheep accounts for her grandchildren.[79] These start in 1634 with her providing twenty ewes for 'little Nicholas LeStrange' and '1 Lambe for little Ham'. In 1640 'little Jack' received two store sheep and four store lambs and 'little Wills' one store lamb in 1642. In 1643 Captain Poe 'tooke of the little Boyes' forty-five sheep, including '1 store lambe of little Neds'. In 1644, Goodman's charge 'after the plundering' included 'one [lambe] for little Roger', and in 1648, 'ewe lambes twinnes' for Charles Le Strange. By this time, the sheep allocated to the five younger boys were listed separately; in 1651, the youngest son, Thomas, joined them with '11 Ewes and 5 Lambes', see also Figure 3. No provision was made for Sir Nicholas's five daughters, or for Hamon's children. Alice did not repeat the individual accounts, but simply accounted for them in Goodman's account for Barrett Ringstead.

---

78. Hamon Le Strange, 1605–1660 married 1. Dorothy Laverick, and 2. Judith Bagnall, and raised numerous children at Ringstead.

79. Sir Nicholas and Anne Lewkenor had thirteen children. Ham (Sir Hamon, 2nd bt 1631–56) held fewer sheep than his younger brother, Nick (3rd bt 1632–1669); the elder son, who died prematurely in his early twenties, might have been mentally impaired as he hardly figures in the documents. In 1652 Alice drew up a detailed sheep account for Nick but not for Ham. The younger boys were John, b. 1636, William, b. 1639, Edward, b. 1641, Roger, b. 1644, Charles, b. 1647, and Thomas, b. 1651.

She did, however, draw up 'A Reckoning of the Sheepe of Nicholas le Strange my Grandchilde' in 1655.[80] This account started in 1652 when she bought a hundred ewes for him from his uncle Hamon for £48. She also calculated the profit he made of the sheep he held as a small child between 1634 and 1642 before selling them to his grandfather; alongside she listed the losses at Barrett Ringstead. Alice clearly believed that such methods developed the business sense of her children and grandchildren, and helped to instil the idea of profit and loss.

The sheep accounts for the Le Strange estate, 1625–1655[81]

Alice's venture into large scale sheep farming began in earnest when she inherited the Sedgeford estate and bought the flocks from her brother-in-law, Sir William Yelverton. We saw how she purchased 1,333 sheep divided into three flocks located on the East, North and South Grounds. From 1622, with the South Ground let to Francis Guybon, Alice incorporated the two remaining Sedgeford flocks, the East Ground and North Ground, into her main sheep account. By 1623, with the sheep at Barrett Ringstead, she had a total of 2,517 sheep under management. By 1624, all the shepherds, apart from Crisp of South Flock, Ringstead, had been replaced, with Allen at Sedgeford East Ground, Lennnard at Sedgeford North Ground and Pyper at Barrett Ringstead; these are the shepherds in Alice's new account which begins with the shepherds' charge at Midsummer 1625, as shown in Table 2.

Damage obscures the start of the new account, but we know from the children's accounts, which continued until 1627, that the first account is Pyper's charge for Barrett Ringstead. Fading also affects Allen's and Lennard's charges at Sedgeford, but Crisp's account of the Ringstead South Flock appears intact. In 1626 Lennard made his final appearance at the clipping as Sedgeford North Ground was let to John Cremer reducing the total numbers to below 2,000. Between 1626 and 1643 the figure averaged 1,825. There is some evidence that Alice reduced the size of flocks. The notes on the regulation and stocking of the flocks, based on 'my father's booke', set the size of flocks at significantly higher levels than what prevailed after 1626.[82] This may reflect a change of policy with Alice selling off more fat lambs: her receipts show a growing proportion of income from the sale of sheep rather than wool, and in the Sedgeford account of 1621, she expressed her concern about the over-grazing by sheep and the impact on profits.[83]

---

80. LEST/P10, see below, p. 179.
81. LEST/P10, see below, pp. 121–93.
82. LEST/P10, see below, pp. 192–3.
83. LEST/BK7, see below, p. 209.

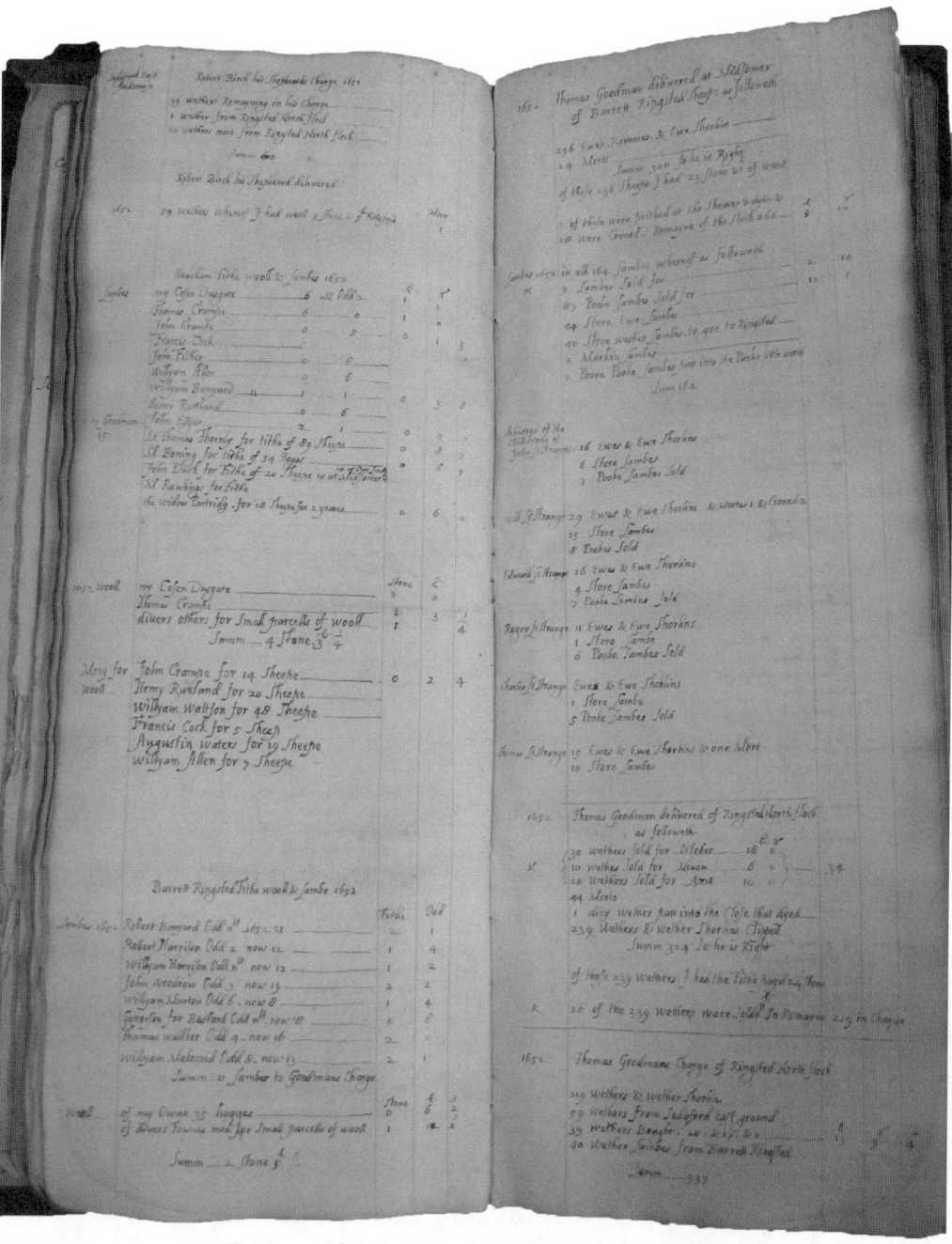

Figure 3: Alice Le Strange's Sheep Account 1651–52
(LEST/P10)

Table 2: Flocks in hand 1626–1643
showing flock size and shepherds' allowances

Charge	Sedgeford East Flock	Barrett Ringstead Flock	Ringstead South Flock	Total
Father's booke	Lord 940 Shepherd 120	Lord 700 Shepherd 100	Lord 400 Shepherd 100	
Charge				
1626	Allen: 912ᵃ [952]	Pyper: 674 + 40ᵇ [694]	Crisp: 409 [429]	[2115]c
1627	Allen: 917 [957]	Pyper: 550 + 40 [650]	Crisp: 409 [489]	[2096]
1628	Allen: 812	Pyper: 586 + 40 [606]	Crisp: 404 [424]	[1882]
1629	Thistle: 879 [890]	Pyper: 599 + 40 [619]	Crisp: 419 [434]	[1983]
1630	Thistle: 906 [926]	Pyper: 600 + 40 [621]	Crisp: 418 [463]	[2050]
1631	Thistle: 908 [928]	Pyper: 548 [568]	Crisp: 408 [448]	[1944]
1632	Greenwood: 797 [837]	Cooper: 526 [566]	Crisp: 413 [433]	[1836]
1633	Greenwood: 713 [763]	Cooper: 418 + 10 [438]	Crisp: 367 [387]	[1598]
1634	Greenwood: 871 [891]	Cooper: 520 + 36 [540]	Goodman: 411 + 70 in North flock	[1948]
1635	Osborn: 771 [791]	Goodman: 457 + 56	F. Crisp: 346 [366] + 46 in N. flock	[1716]
1636	Osborn: 802 [822]	Goodman: 475 [515] + grandsons 64	Crisp: 324 [344] + 99 in North flock	[1780]
1637	Osborn: 807 + 21	Goodman: 536 [556]ᵈ	Crisp: 393 + 101 [121] in North flock	[1898]

Charge	Sedgeford East Flock	Barrett Ringstead Flock	Ringstead South Flock	Total
1638	Osborn: 807	Goodman: 472 [492] + grandsons 84	Crisp: 562 [582] with North flock	[1965]
1639	Osborn: 819 [839]	Goodman: 487 [507] + grandsons 101	Crisp: 462 [482]	[1929]
1640	Osborn: 817 [837]	Goodman: 586 [606]	Willis: 440 [460]	[1903]
1641	Osborn: 815 [835]	Goodman: 572 [592] + cullet 74	Willis: 482 [502]	[2003]
1642	Osborn: 726 [780]	Goodman: 590 [630] + 131 [151]	Willis: 410	[1971]
1643	Osborn: 774 [794]	Goodman: 553 [573] + 105 cullet/grandsons	Willis: 419 [439]	[1911]
Plunder	Osborn: 753	Goodman: 530	Willis: 410 + 22	1715

a Alice's total, followed by the actual total which includes a shepherd's allowance.
b Cullet or joyce sheep.
c Total for three flocks including shepherds' allowances and cullett sheep.
d Total includes grandsons, as in 1640 and 1641.

However, the fall in numbers may also hide cullet sheep and shepherds' allowances. A continuing difficulty is that the actual totals, shown in square brackets, rarely coincide with Alice's totals. As mentioned, the discrepancy is usually in round figures of twenty to eighty sheep indicating shepherds' allowances, but there might be other sheep lost to the accounts.

Further insights into Alice's management policy can be obtained by working out the lambing rates. Do they improve over the course of time? How do they compare with those found at Sedgeford in the fifteenth and sixteenth centuries? Mark Bailey used the figure of 0.6 and 0.8 lambs and this is the range found amongst the children's ewes at Barrett Ringstead in the early 1620s. There are instances of it rising to 0.9%, but never reaching one lamb per ewe.[84] At Sedgeford East Ground, the rate was slightly lower. In 1624, Alice noted 'of these 680 ewes I had 394 lambes', a rate of 0.57 per ewe; in 1623, with tithe lambs included, it was 0.53. From 1626, the rate at Sedgeford averaged 0.7, while at Barrett Ringstead it ranged between 0.75 and 0.9 per ewe. The explanation might be the reduced flock size, but also the improved ratio of rams to ewes. In 1623, at Sedgeford, nine rams were expected to serve 842 ewes, while in 1626, twenty-four rams served 674 or one ram to twenty-eight ewes. At Barrett Ringstead the ratio averaged one ram to twenty ewes. Even by today's standards this is generous.[85] From 1630, in the accounts, the ewes are counted at the clipping with ewe shorlins (yet to lamb), and rams, so the lambing rate is more difficult to calculate. However, it appears that Alice quickly achieved a measure of improvement. In 1641 she could look back on twenty years of steady progress: then disaster struck – of the 1,911 sheep charged to shepherds in 1643, 1,715 were taken by the parliamentary forces.[86]

The plunder left Alice with less than a hundred sheep, as shown in Table 3. She quickly assembled a scratch flock for Barrett Ringstead buying 143 ewes and 141 wethers to run with sixty-five sheep gathered from the park, close, and the other shepherds. For the South Flock, the tenants laid on 311 sheep, '11 more than they ought for which they are to pay 2d a sheep', while the shepherd, allowed a hundred sheep, appears to have placed only sixty in the flock.[87] In 1644, for stocking the North Flock, she sent wethers from Barrett Ringstead, while relatives, friends and tenants placed cullett

---

84. Bailey, 'Sheep Accounts', pp. 12–18, see fns 63, 69, pp. 22–3.

85. About 40 ewes to a ram, Watson & More, *Agriculture*, pp. 576, 590.

86. Alice's figure is 1,653, forty short of the actual total; she missed out twenty-two stolen from the park.

87. 'A note of such sheepe as the Tenants layd on the South flock of Ringsted in 1643', see below, pp. 191–2.

Table 3: After the plunder: re-stocking the flocks 1643–1654

Charge	Sedgeford East Flock	Barrett Ringstead Flock	Ringstead South & North Flocks
1643	Let to Robert Birch	Goodman: 309 [*349*]	**Ringstead South Flock** Let to tenants: 311 [*371*]
1644		Goodman: 203 [*223*] cullett : 462 [*502*]	**Ringstead North Flock** Gates: 151; cullett: 280 [*298*]
1645		Goodman: 125 [*145*] grandsons: 6 cullett: 510 [*560*]	Willis: 201 cullett: 243
1646		Goodman: 214 [*234*] grandsons: 9 cullett: 440 [*470*]	Strett: 236 [*256*] cullett: 465 [*505*]
1647		Goodman: 257 [*276*] grandsons: 15 cullett: 416 [*456*]	Strett: 249 [*259*] cullett: 410 [*450*]
1648		Goodman: 309 [*350*] grandsons: 25 cullett: 330 [*370*]	Strett: 208 [*227*] cullett: 500 [*534*]
1649	Layd for Birch 40 wethers	Goodman: 272 [*292*] grandsons: 39 cullett: 320 [*380*]	Goodman: 311 [*351*] cullett: 440 [*480*]
1650	40 wethers from Ringstead	Goodman: 295 + grandsons: 66 [*361*] cullett: 302 [*342*]	Goodman: 345 [*385*] cullett: 400 [*420*]
1651	Shepherd: 60	Goodman: 300 [*334*] grandsons: 98 cullett: 205 [*225*]	Goodman: 324 [*364*] cullett: 400 [*440*]
1652	Shepherd: 60	Goodman: 303 [*320*] grandsons: 134 [*154*]; cullett: 130 [*150*]	Goodman: 337 [*357*] cullett: 100 [*350*]
1653	Shepherd: 61	Goodman: 420 grandsons: 173 [*193*] cullett: 47	Goodman: 341 [*361*] cullett: 359 [*390*]
1654		Goodman: 419 grandsons: 206 [*249*] cullett: 49	Goodman: 370 [*390*] cullett: 359 [*390*]

sheep in these two flocks raising numbers to almost pre-1643 levels. From 1646 the 'fearmours of South flock' placed 260 sheep in the North Flock for which they paid full cullet rates of between 8d and 10d; the rates for Barrett Ringstead ranged between 12d and 14d. In 1653, Alice clarified the stocking rates for the North and South Flock.[88] In the new agreement of 1650, Sir Hamon and Sir Nicholas undertook to stock the North Flock, leaving scope for the tenants to place their 300 sheep in the South Flock.[89] At Sedgeford, the East Flock was let to Robert Birch for £25.[90] Notice in Table 3 how the grandsons rebuilt their holdings in the flock. During this period, Alice also paid more attention to the collection of tithes on lambs and wool, recording the smallest amounts; for the first time, she summarized the sales of wool from 1643 to 1654, identifying quantities, prices and markets. The income from sheep and wool halved over the next few years, but by 1650, by working closely with their tenants and village communities, and by acting decisively, Alice and her husband were able to stage a relatively quick recovery. Alice's wider task was to build up the income from sheep and wool on the estate, which through the management of the brecks and foldcourses had a direct impact on the income from corn. Before 1621, their income from sheep had been minimal, partly because Alice reinvested profits in breeding stock. With the acquisition of the Sedgeford flocks in 1622, income rose sharply and averaged between £200 and £250 a year until 1641. The income from sheep partially recovered from the plunder of 1643, but not to the levels achieved in the 1620s and 1630s. Receipt books do not survive for the 1640s, so we rely on the sheep accounts to explain what happened in those difficult years. The income from corn proved even more impressive and resilient, rising from an average of £315 between 1621 and 1626, to £550 between 1630 and 1641, principally due to the improvements at Sedgeford. By the 1650s, the family also benefitted from the drainage of the coastal marshes which produced quantities of marsh barley, notably from Heacham, but at a significant cost: in 1638 Alice noted a loss of £600 on Heacham Marsh.[91] At Sedgeford income rose from £464 in 1621, with £287 paid in corn, to £690 in 1636 with £418 paid in corn. Sedgeford was a particular success story to which we will now turn.

---

88. 'A note for laying of sheep in Ringsted before the Agreement with the Townsmen of Ringsted for laying the North flock Intire', see below, p. 182.

89. LEST/Q38.

90. LEST/IB89.

91. See below, p. 84.

The Improvements at Sedgeford, 1621–1656

Alongside the sheep accounts, Alice managed the estate at Sedgeford which she inherited from her father, Richard Stubbe, in 1619. Her purchase of Sir William Yelverton's sheep in 1620 was followed by her first set of estate accounts which date from 1621 and end in 1633 following the death of her cousin, Francis Guybon.[92] When he died in 1631, she commissioned the survey of the estate comprising three maps, covering the extent of each of the three foldcourses, with an accompanying book explaining the use and organisation of the 'Sedgeford Brecks and Infield Lands'.[93] The surveyor, John Fisher of Heacham, frequently referred to an earlier survey, 'Mr Shepheards Booke' drawn up in 1582, a copy of which he included in his own book, indicating that Sedgeford had always been difficult to manage. By repeating the policy of engaging a professional, Alice showed her appreciation of the challenge and her determination to succeed. As with the sheep accounts, she clearly understood that her successors needed instruction and information on the estate if her improvements were to be sustained.

The documents, selected for Sedgeford, focus on this early period from 1621 to 1635; they include the Sedgeford sheep account of 1620–1622, the Sedgeford estate account of 1621–1633 and an estate rental of 1634,[94] followed by Fisher's written survey of 1631.[95] Tracings of the three maps have been reproduced and fit into a pocket at the end of the book, but a simplified version, outlining the principal features of a classic infield-outfield system, has also been included in the text, as shown in Figure 4. Taken together, these documents laid the foundation for a new system of record keeping which continued into the eighteenth century. The most complete example of Alice's later work is the 'Sedgford Firmall & Breck Book 1647/8/9 and 1650'.[96] The original intention was to include the document in its entirety, but it proved impractical given the complexity and amount of the material,

---

92. Francis Guybon's will: NRO, NCC will register, Purgall 201, MF 91; and inventory DN/INV37/176.

93. LEST/OC1, LEST/IC58. The maps are not signed or dated by Fisher, but his references in his 'Breck Book' indicate they were drafted alongside this work. Minor changes in the ownership of holdings in 1634 and further reorganisation of the brecks in 1641 suggest that the survey took several years to complete and in fact omissions can be found: some furlongs have no numbers, some strips no tenants.

94. LEST/BK7, see below, pp. 199–307.

95. LEST/IC58, see below, pp. 309–47.

96. LEST/IB90, see below, pp. 349–52.

and the dense layout which made editing problematic. There is also much repetition as Alice included Fisher's survey, adding her own amendments and further details which she considered relevant. We decided to include just the table of contents and the 'Generall Directory for using all the Brecks', which shows how Alice's ideas developed in the late 1640s and early 1650s. Reference is also made to the other documents and most particularly to the Sedgeford firmal of 1707 which refers back and uses Alice's 'old book' of 1647 as a starting point.[97] A few tables have been included to better explain the working of these intricate documents. However, the first task is to provide some background on the geography, landholding structure and farming systems of this large Norfolk parish.

The parish of Sedgeford extends to 4,214 acres which is close to the seventeenth-century estimates found in the documents.[98] The lands were divided between the two manors of the dean and chapter of Norwich, Easthall and Westhall, and a much smaller manor known as Sedgefords which came into the possession of John Le Strange, the second son of Sir Nicholas (1511–1580) in the second half of the sixteenth century.[99] In 1539, the dean and chapter had granted Sir Thomas Le Strange (c. 1490–1545) a ninety-nine year lease of their estate for a rent fixed at £61 7s 6d per annum, a fraction of what it was worth upon improvement.[100] This lease was confirmed to Sir Nicholas in 1562 who assigned it to John to make up his estate in Sedgeford.[101] On John's death in 1582 the lease passed to his widow Anne and subsequently came into the hands of her second husband, Richard Stubbe.[102] In 1602, Stubbe assigned the lease, with the manor of Sedgefords and other lands he had purchased in Sedgeford, to their daughter Alice as part of her marriage settlement to Sir Hamon Le

---

97. LEST/IC64, IC65, LEST/IB85, IB89, IB91.

98. 2001 Census. In 1619, the townsmen estimated Richard's Stubbe's holding at 2,300 acres and their own at 1,800 acres with 100 acres of common making a total of 4,200 acres. In 1670 the balance was adjusted to 2,400 acres and 1,700 acres reflecting the purchases made by the Le Stranges in the intervening period LEST/IC64; Fisher's survey offers more precise calculations, see below, p. 37.

99. Blomefield & Parkin, *Norfolk*, X, pp. 385–90.

100. LEST/AA67; NRO, DCN 51/91. The parliamentary survey of 1649 of the dean and chapter lands estimated the improved value at £304 10s, but in fact the income from Sedgeford by this time was more than double that figure. The dean and chapter was abolished in 1649, and by act of parliament the cathedral estates were sold. At the restoration, these sales were declared void.

101. LEST/AA67.

102. LEST/AA70–73.

Strange, to take effect two years after his death.[103] In 1637, the dean and chapter renewed the lease to Sir Hamon Le Strange at the same rent for a further ninety-nine years. However, it was not renewed to the family in 1736 being let on a twenty-one year lease to a William Smith.[104] In 1733 Sir Thomas Le Strange had paid £75 a year for an estate valued at £696: no wonder the dean and chapter sought a more profitable solution.[105]

In the documents, the demesne lands in Sedgeford leased from the dean and chapter can be identified as belonging to 'The Lord' or 'Dms'; the demesne of the manor of 'Sedgefords' owned by the Le Stranges and the land purchased by Richard Stubbe are ascribed to 'Sir Hamon Le Strange'.[106] The lands of the dean and chapter formed by far the largest portion estimated at 1,734 acres out of a total of the 2,232½ acres of demesne land in Fisher's survey; Sedgefords amounted to 138 acres leaving 360½ acres purchased by Stubbe. Of these 2,232½ acres, Fisher classified 631¾ acres as infield and 1,600¾ acres as brecks, sheep's pasture and furze ground.[107] The manorial tenants, freeholders and copyholders, dominated the infields holding 1,720½ acres with 213½ acres scattered through the brecks making a total of 4,166½ acres, excluding the commons.[108] These tenants, paying nominal fixed rents for nearly half the farmland in the parish, were a force to be reckoned with.

The infield-outfield system, devised to farm and utilize the sandy soils and heathland of west Norfolk, was made possible by the existence of river valleys which provided a core of fertile lands, the infields, where manorial tenants were able to grow their crops, keep their stock and sell their labour to the lords cultivating the brecks, the outfields.[109] Sedgeford was particularly favoured in this respect. Its lands rise from the broad and fertile valley of the river Heacham to the light thin soils of the uplands, which become progressively less fertile to the east of the parish around the commons and the sheep pasture known as 'The Whins', named after the gorse and furze

---

103. LEST/AA67.

104. DCN 49/49.

105. DCN 59/30/1.

106. LEST/OC1, LEST/BK7, LEST/IC58.

107. LEST/OC1, LEST/IC58, see below, pp. 335, 347.

108. Fisher's map for East Field suggests that part of the commons had been encroached and no longer amounted to 100 acres; this would bring his total figure closer to the modern estimate of 4,214 acres. The parliamentary survey of 1649 says the common was 'about 100 acres', see below, p. 38.

109. Wade Martins & Williamson, 'Roots of Change', pp. 10–11; Darby & Saltmarsh, 'The Infield-Outfield System of a Norfolk Manor', pp. 30–44.

which flourished there.[110] The extensive infields enabled Sedgeford to sustain a large population located in the river valley mainly along the highway from Heacham to Docking. The lords, principally the lessees of the dean and chapter, concentrated their energies on improving the brecks, sub-letting their demesne lands to large farmers who drew on the labour of the village to plough the arable and harvest the corn. These farm tenants, principally the Guybon family, paid their rent in money and corn, with barley rents often exceeding money rents. By 1625 two of the Sedgeford flocks were leased to large tenants, while the large East Flock with its ground, which required the most attention, remained in hand until 1643.[111]

The system was ingenious, but required careful regulation and management, particularly as it was combined with the organisation of three flocks and foldcourses: this explains the purpose of the three maps. Each map shows the extent and location of the eight brecks allocated to each foldcourse, as shown in Figure 4. Each breck was cultivated on an eight year rotation: first year, summerley and breaking up the land; three years with grain crops – rye, barley, barley and oats – followed by four years of grass.[112] When the brecks were out of cultivation, manorial tenants had to be compensated with arable elsewhere. The purpose of John Fisher's book was to set out the rotations and specify these exchanges. This was done by matching brecks, so that Breck 1 was matched with Breck 5, Breck 2 with 6, Breck 3 with 7, and Breck 4 with 8.[113] 'The Parliamentary Survey of the Leasehold Estate of the Dean and Chapter of Norwich in Sedgeford in 1649' explained how these arrangements worked:

> There is a fouldcourse for 1200 sheep belonging to the Lord of the sd mannors [Westhall and Easthall] which are to be kept in this manner: viz partly upon the Common whereof there is about 100 acres and partly upon the shack of all the arable ground (whether they be customary, freehold or demesne lands of the sd mannors) and none else are to keep sheep there or the sd common butt the lords, and partly upon the lay or unplowed ground of the sd brecks whereof 5 parts (the whole being divided into 8 parts) are every year to be lay for the pastures of the sd sheep, and where it fall out in course that any of the copyhold or freehold

---

110. Whins is a word for gorse or furze, used for fuel, making dead hedges etc. Yaxley, *Glossary*, p. 235.

111. See above, Tables 2 and 3.

112. LEST/IC58, see from p. 311. Summerley or summerland refers to land uncropped, but not necessarily unploughed, in the summer, Yaxley, *Glossary*, p. 207.

113. LEST/IC58, see below, p. 309.

lands are to ly for the purpose aforesaid, the Lord allows to the tenants in exchange & recompense for the same alike quantity of his demesne arable lands.[114]

The potential for disputes was ever present. Not only was the grazing restricted to the lord, but the issue of exchange of lands and compensation was constantly open to challenge. In a long running dispute with Richard Stubbe, the tenants claimed grazing rights for their 'great cattle' over the brecks. Stubbe conceded the right, but the terms of the agreement of 1619 show that the tenants were confined to The Whins and not allowed to graze their cattle on his severals.[115] This long drawn out dispute may well have persuaded Alice of the need for a full survey once Francis Guybon had departed the scene. Such a complex farming system depended on the collaboration and the acquiescence of the entire farming community if it was to succeed. Having been brought up in Sedgeford, Alice was fortunate in the close ties and kinship she enjoyed with the community, but she still needed to be on her guard and act with firmness and clarity.

The maps show the extent of the brecks and the grazing regime of the three flocks and foldcourses in the 1630s, but they also show what existed before and what confronted Alice in 1621. The maps overleaf show that: the north plot, south plot and east plot fit together like a jigsaw and indicate an earlier structure based on 'precincts' and 'quarentena'. The north plot includes the lands of the first, second, third and sixth precincts, the south plot, seventh and eighth precincts, and the east plot fourth and fifth precincts. The purpose of the precincts is not clear, but seems to relate to the ecclesiastical origins of the principal manor of Sedgeford and the need to divide up such a large parish; it may even represent an earlier attempt at rationalization. The term 'quarentena' corresponds to the more common furlong. In the 1621–1633 account, Alice uses these terms interchangeably but with greater emphasis on the furlong after 1630 which may reflect Fisher's usage of the term in his survey. In the rental of 1634 Alice reverted to the ancient forms to identify the strips and parcels of land, abbreviated

114. DCN 51/90, Parliamentary Survey of 1649. Note the compensation paid to tenants, *see also* Wade Martins & Williamson, 'Roots of Change', pp. 10–11.

115. LEST/IC64 includes notes on the final agreement of this dispute. This farming book, started by Alice's favourite grandson, Sir Nicholas (1632–1669) has much information on Richard Stubbe's estate in Sedgeford, see below, Table 4, p. 43. References are also made to Fisher's survey of 1630, with a sketch of the commons, and Bradford's survey of 1653, indicating the continuing reliance on Alice's management techniques. 'Severals' means privately owned land as opposed to common, *see* Yaxley, *Glossary*, p. 185.

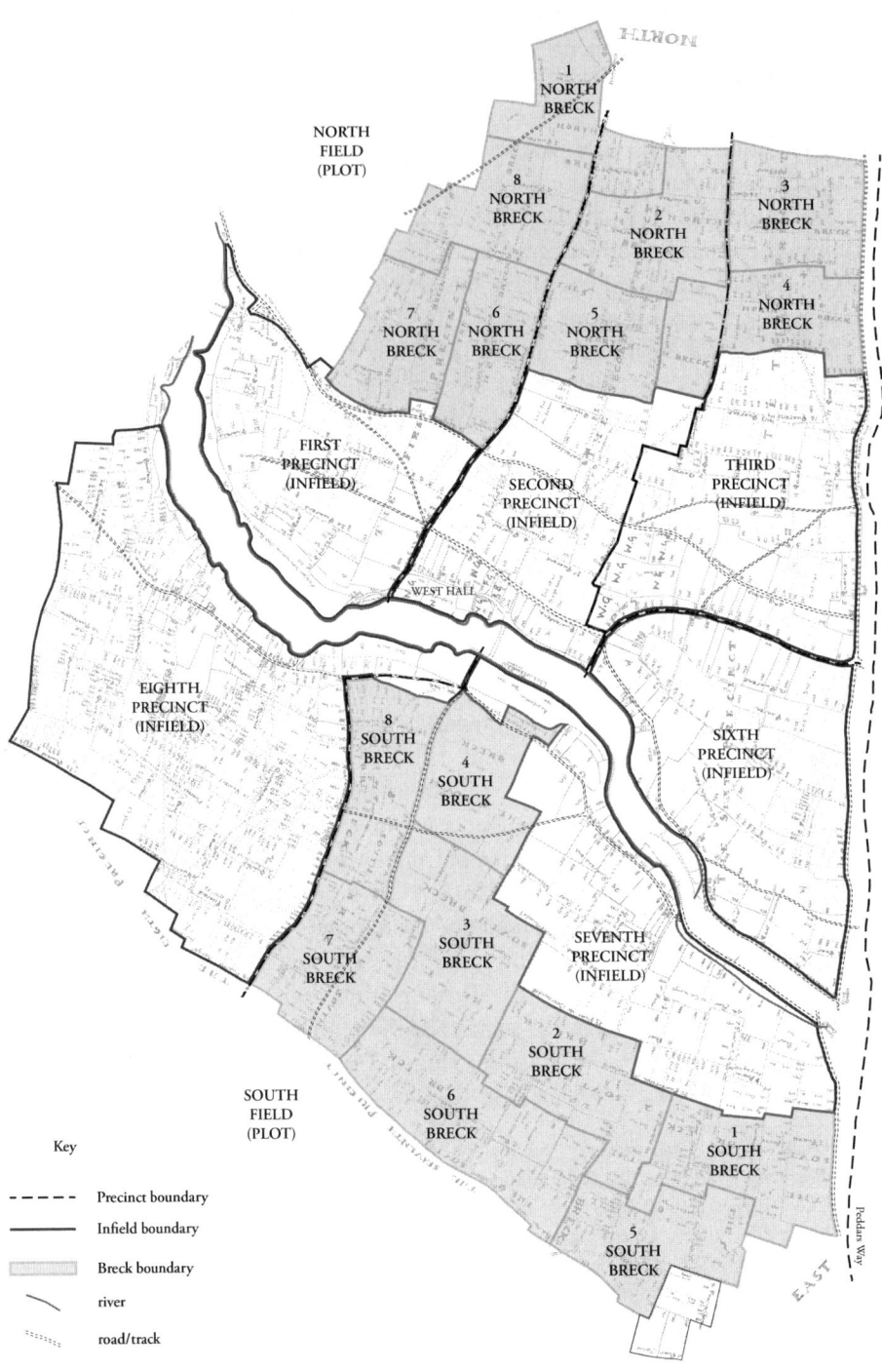

NORTH

1
NORTH
BRECK

NORTH
FIELD
(PLOT)

8
NORTH
BRECK

2
NORTH
BRECK

3
NORTH
BRECK

4
NORTH
BRECK

7
NORTH
BRECK

6
NORTH
BRECK

5
NORTH
BRECK

FIRST
PRECINCT
(INFIELD)

SECOND
PRECINCT
(INFIELD)

THIRD
PRECINCT
(INFIELD)

WEST HALL

EIGHTH
PRECINCT
(INFIELD)

8
SOUTH
BRECK

4
SOUTH
BRECK

SIXTH
PRECINCT
(INFIELD)

7
SOUTH
BRECK

3
SOUTH
BRECK

SEVENTH
PRECINCT
(INFIELD)

2
SOUTH
BRECK

SOUTH
FIELD
(PLOT)

6
SOUTH
BRECK

1
SOUTH
BRECK

5
SOUTH
BRECK

EAST

Peddars Way

Key

– – – – Precinct boundary

———— Infield boundary

▨ Breck boundary

╱ river

⋯⋯ road/track

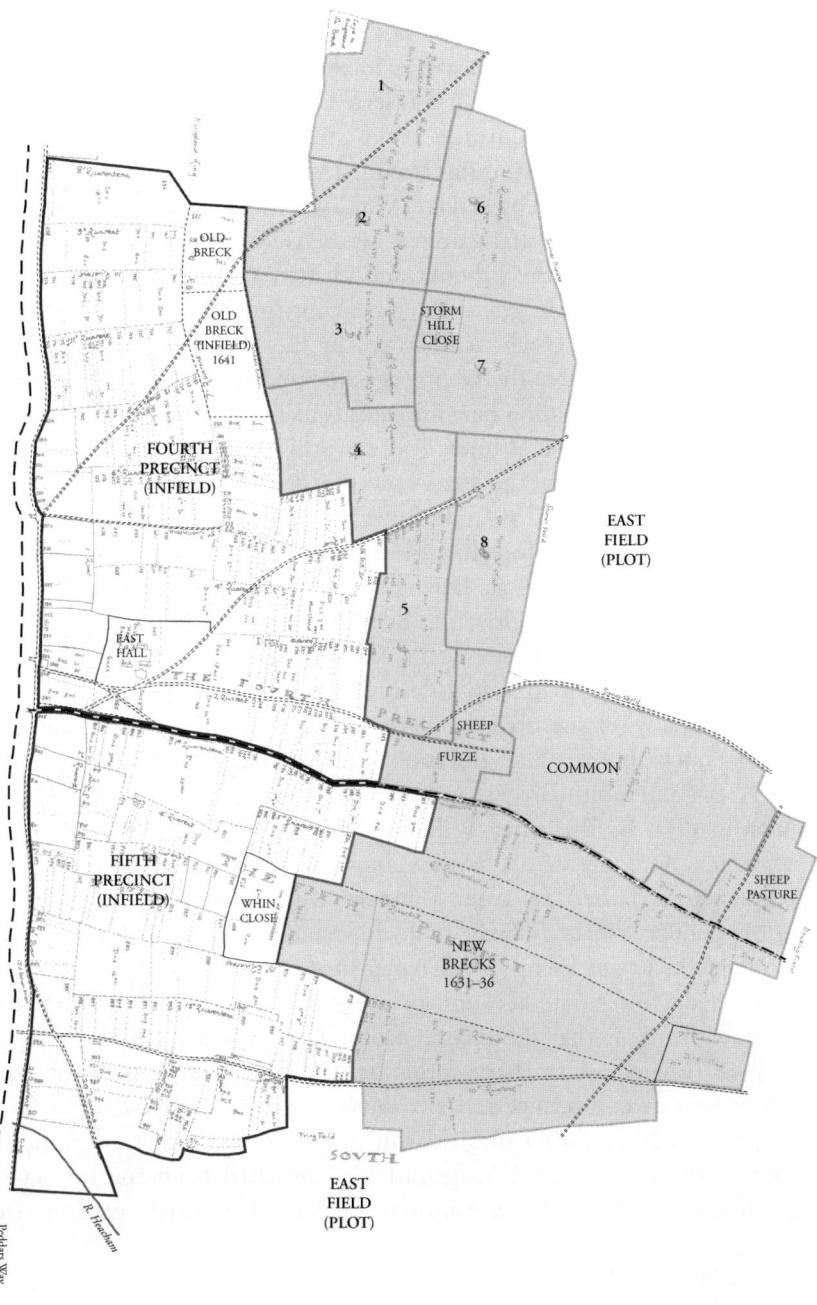

Figure 4 John Fisher's maps of Sedgeford, c. 1631 (diagram)
(LEST/OC1)

to 'pre' and 'q' followed by 'num' in the margin.[116] However, from the 1640s she adopted Fisher's format, but occasionally the abbreviation 'q' or 'qr' slips into the text. 'Num' refers to the new numbering system that Fisher introduced for the maps and inserted into his written survey; more erratically Alice inserted them into her estate rental of 1634. Each strip or close was given a number running from 1–1759.

Fisher's maps are divided by Peddars Way and the river Heacham. On each map he superimposed the area covered by the eight brecks, making it easy to cross reference to the breck books and identify the strips and parcels in cultivation or laid down to grass. The most congested area was in the north plot, dominated by the Guybons, followed by the south and finally the less fertile east. This was where the Le Stranges focused their efforts, re-ordering the East Brecks and building new farmsteads at Easthall and the Magazine which, with Stormhill and Whin Close, can still be seen on the OS map.[117] A table exists comparing the extent of the demesne lands in the eight precincts between 1604 and 1660; it shows how 738 acres of the East Brecks, Stormhill, and the East Whins had been absorbed into the fourth and fifth precincts during that period, as shown in Table 4. In this way we can see the gradual process of regular cultivation being extended to the brecks. What is significant is how much had been achieved at Sedgeford by 1660.

The estate account of 1621–1633 describes the situation facing Alice and how she gradually restructured the management of her new inheritance. The first entries, which are a later insertion, include evidence of reorganisation of the North and South Brecks, and of land being exchanged with William Guybon in 1634. By this time, William had succeeded his father as Alice's principal tenant alongside his brother, another Francis. The first account of 1621 shows their father 'my cosen [Francis] Guybon' paying farm rent for almost her entire acreage in Sedgeford; this remained the situation until the North Foldcourse was let to John Cremer in 1627.

In the Sedgeford estate account for 1621–1633, as shown in Table 5, the first point to note is that the income from farm rents was far exceeded by the sale of tithe and farm barley; this derived from the payment of tithe and corn rent at one bushel and two bushels per acre. Payments in kind may seem an odd medieval survival, but in fact it meant that a significant portion of the income from Sedgeford was insulated from the impact of inflation and benefitted from rising corn prices. This partly explains the

---

116. LEST/BK7, see below, pp. 259–307.

117. LEST/KA6 ff. 185–213 for the building of the Magazine, 1639–40; it was used as a depot for military supplies, see www.wikipedia.com which has a useful reference under 'Gunpowder Magazine', OS Map: Explorer 250.

Table 4: Lands in Sedgeford in 1604 and in 1660

1604				1660				
Precinct	a	r	p	Precinct	a	r	p	
1	234	0	0	1	290	2	10	
2	199	3	30	2	200	2	15	
3	122	1	0	3	124	1	35	
4	185	1	0	4	752	2	20	East Brecks
5	129	2	0	5	393	2	8	Whins
6	24	1	0	6	28	1	0	
7	559	1	30	7	578	1	30	
8	119	3	30	8	184	1	20	
Sub-total	1574	2	10	Total	2552	3	18	
East Brecks & Stormhill	405	0	0	[*Tenants' lands*]	1700	0	0	
In the East Whinns	333	0	6					
Sub-total	2312	2	10					
Purchased	140	1	8					
Total[a]	2452	3	18					
[*Tenants' lands*][b]	1800	0	0					

a Totals include 100 acres of common.
b LEST/IC64. See fn. 115, p. 39.

fluctuation in total income, but farm rents also varied from year to year as brecks of different sizes dropped out of cultivation. Apart from the leasing of the South and North Foldcourse, and the creation of a new breck in 1633, farm rents remained more or less static. In 1632 the collection of the manorial rents, which were fixed, was simplified to twice rather than three times a year. The table also shows that certain income and expenditure was removed from the account. From 1622, Alice entered sheep and wool sales in the receipt book, while most of the expenditure on building repairs and construction was recorded in the new building accounts inserted in the books of disbursements.[118] By 1630 expenditure was confined to outrents,

118. LEST/P7 and P10.

Table 5: Sedgeford Estate Account, 1621–1633[a]

Income	1621 £	1622 £	1623 £	1624 £	1625 £	1626 £	1627 £	1628 £	1629 £	1630 £	1631 £	1632 £	1633 £
Manorial rents	25.7	25.7	26.1	25.6	25.45	25.45	25.35	25.35	25.35	25.35	25.84	26.38	26.6
Court profits	2.7	0.5	3.95	4.6	10.5	8.5	14.7	5.55	6.78	10.54	1.83		
Farm rents:													
Francis Guybon											new breck		16.5
Westhall	64.93	64.93	64.93	66.17	67.12	67.12	67.12	67.12	67.12	67.12	66.84	66.84	68.94
E. & S. Brecks	67.5	59.5	58.45	55.5	58.87	69	71.25	74.12	70.63	60	54.68	51.94	57.37
South Foldcourse	18	18	18	18	18	18	18	18	18	18	18	18	18
Easthall Farm	6.97	6.97	6.97	6.97	6.97	6.97	6.97	6.97	6.97	6.97	6.97	6.97	6.97
North Foldcourse	in hand					J. Cremer	25	25	25	25	25	25	20
Widow Mason	5.5	5.5	5.5	5.55	5.55	5.75	5.75	5.75	5.75		5.75	5.75	5.75
F. Costen	0.8	0.8	0.8	0.8	1.8	1.6	1.6	1.6	1.6	1.6	0.8	0.8	0.8
J. Sallter	1.5	1.5	1.5	1.6	1.6	1.6	1.6	1.6	1.6	1.1			
Hempland	0.65	0.65	0.65	sold						J. Cremer	0.34	0.34	0.34
Tithe – Mills	0.58	0.58	0.58	0.58	0.91	0.91	0.91	0.91	0.91	1.16	0.91	0.91	0.91
Tithe barley	126.45												

	1621	1622	1623	1624	1625	1626	1627	1628	1629	1630	1631	1632	1633
Farm barley	87.35	295.95	238.2	222.45	258.1	226.44	207.45	200.2	248.91	365.62	256.87	288.55	298.1
Tithe peas		11.55	1.55	4.1	0.42	0.35		2.48	2.5		1.2		
Sheep, wool etc	73.3			1.23	1.9					2.35			
Total	463.93	492.13	427.18	413.15	457.19	431.69	445.7	434.65	481.12	584.81	465.03	491.48	520.28
Expenses													
Outrents	52.5	72.85	72.85	72.85	75.54	75.54	75.54	75.54	75.54	75.54	75.54	75.54	75.54
Bailiff's fee	2	2	2	2									
Tax	0.95			4.05									
Poor	3.7	4	7.05	8.87	17.65	6.45	7.7	5.8	6.6				
Building	5.55	19.55	50.35	57.7	122.5	123.2	38.2	3.5	25.2				
Total	64.7	98.4	132.25	145.47	215.69	205.19	121.44	84.84	107.34				

a LEST/BK7. For compactness, the table has been decimalized.

mainly to the dean and chapter of Norwich. So, there is not a complete picture of the income from Sedgeford.

In the layout of the account we can see Alice developing her understanding and refining her methods; this particularly concerned the rotations employed by Francis Guybon on 'the great farme', based at the principal manor of Westhall. In the 1621 account, she entered the details of his holding in two parts distinguishing between 260 acres of infield land and inclosed ground and 279 acres of brecks. He paid 5s per acre for both infield and outfield, but as the brecks were often out of cultivation it had the effect of reducing the rent. So, in 1622, when the amount in cultivation declined from 279 acres to 238 acres, the rent fell from £67 10s to £59 10s. In 1621 Alice granted her cousin an abatement of 45s for Hall Bottom Close (nine acres in precinct 2, q. 10, n. 243) 'because the year was so hard, as the sheep had it for so longe he could reape no proffit from it', indicating her understanding of the need for improvement. In 1622, she started to clarify the rotation of the brecks, placing entries on different lines; by 1625 she had figures in the margin, by 1627, titles distinguishing between East Brecks and South Field, and by 1631 she had adopted the rotation used by Fisher in his breck book identifying the first, second, last crop and summerley.[119] At the same time, she started listing the holdings of tenants, noting the rents paid in money and barley; those not paying money are paying barley rent, as can be seen in Sallters lands 1630 (folio 50), and more clearly in folios 58–60. In 1632 (folio 55), she set this out describing 'the great farme' of 'my cosen Guybon' and other farms letten for money in Sedgeford. In 1633, the final account shows that Guybon's holding had been divided between his two sons, Francis and William; the latter had also taken on the lease of the North Foldcourse from John Cremer.

The account ends in 1633 with a summary of the reorganisation after Francis Guybon's death. The summary starts in 1634 with lands let for money, followed by infield and brecks let for barley (folios 63–72), and repeats the detail in a slightly abridged version in 1635; it shows William Guybon occupying Westhall and his brother Francis at Easthall enlarged with the addition of 'the new farme' and the East Brecks making a holding worth £50 9s; rents averaged 3s 6d per acre for the 'first farme' and the brecks, and 5s for the new farm.[120] William Guybon enjoyed a much larger holding with a greater proportion of infield, renting meadow, yards and closes around Westhall at 7s and 9s per acre, lands and closes in first, second and third

---

119. LEST/IC58, see below from p. 311.
120. LEST/BK7, see below, p. 240.

precinct at 6s 4d, and outfield closes on the brecks at 5s 4d and 5s 2d. Linked to these brecks, he leased the North and South Foldcourses for £20 each, and the brecks in South Field for 5s per acre. In addition he leased two areas of 'new broken ground' in the East Foldcourse for £31 or 10s per acre.[121] Altogether, he paid £164 13s for 389 acres, with seven acres for the manor site for which he paid no rent. Only two other tenants, Thomas Longstreth and Francis Costen, paid money rent amounting to just £7 7s 9d. In total, the money rent for Sedgford in 1634 amounted to just over £222 with the Guybons accounting for £215; this compares to £188 in 1633. The difference was the rent for the East Brecks, showing the impact of improvement.

These four tenants, with another fourteen tenants, paid barley rent on 276½ acres of infield land in Sedgeford, estimated to produce 138 combs, one bushel and one peck of barley, and barley rent on the North and South Brecks, while Francis Guybon paid the rent for the East Brecks. The North Pasture as it was called extended to 143½ acres, producing 71 combs 3 bushels 1 peck of barley; the South Field of 69½ acres, 34 combs 3 bushels, and the East Brecks, 61½ acres, 30 combs 3 bushels. In other words, they paid two bushels of barley to the acre. In this section on the brecks, Alice detailed the area of each of the crops in cultivation rented by each tenant in the North and South Brecks, showing once again the domination of William Guybon with 98 acres in the north and 51 acres in the south.

At the other end of the book Alice entered a rental of the Sedgeford manorial tenants for 1634.[122] This was a further part of the reorganisation following the death of Francis Guybon; it was probably devised to overcome the growing deficiencies of the account book and accommodate the new information arising from Fisher's survey.[123] Using the rental and the estate account for the year 1634, it has been possible to construct a table showing the farming profile of the Sedgeford tenants with their manorial and farm lands as shown in Table 6. The total figure for manorial land and the number of tenants is slightly less than recorded in Fisher's survey indicating ongoing rationalization. For the location of manorial tenants and a breakdown of those paying free and bond rents, see Table 7. The estate account does not give the total acreage of demesne lands, as cultivation, particularly for the brecks, varied with the rotation from year to year. Notice the continuing dominance of the Guybon brothers.

---

121. This figure seems excessive, but note it says, 'the first crop' *i.e.* after being laid to grass for 4 years.

122. LEST/BK7, see below, pp. 259–307.

123. The most significant of these changes was the appearance of the new numbering system, listing the strips and closes from 1–1759, see above, p. 42.

Table 6: Farming profile of the Sedgeford manorial tenants and farmers, 1634

Manorial Lands		Demense (Farm) Lands											
Manorial tenants paying	manorial rents ½d to 4d per ac (fol. 15–59)			let for money rent (fol. 63–67) at 3s to 9s per acre						let for barley rent (fol. 66–73) at 2 bushels per acre			
				Infield			Outfield			Infield			Brecks
	a	r	p	a	r	p	a	r	p	a	r	p	a	r	p
Robert Rose	242	1	10												
Rob. Banyard	211	0	0												
W. Guybon	169	3	15	144	0	0	252	0	0	36	2	0	149	1	20
Mr Gurling, clerk	162	3	35							1	2	10			
J. Lawes	155	0	20												
H. Cremer	104	0	0												
J. Ellgar	101	1	21												
R. Attwood	100	2	20												
R. Bird	81	3	0							0	1	30			
H. Minns	73	3	10												
W. Banyard	72	2	0												
H. Lawes heirs	64	2	30												
Rich. Banyard	63	2	30							17	2	10	4	2	0
G. Framingham	57	1	15										1	3	0
A. Collen	44	1	0							1	3	0	10	2	20
Ellgars heirs	20	2	0												
F. Guybon	17	3	20	123	3	0	127	0	0	23	0	0	61	2	0
J. Lingey	13	3	30										2	0	0
R. Bankes, sen.	13	2	0										2	0	0
R. Dey	11	0	0												
Mr Waters, clerk	9	0	0												
E. Creamer	8	3	20												
E. Jenners	8	1	0												
R. Lawes	6	3	20												

	Manorial Lands			*Demense (Farm) Lands*											
Manorial tenants paying	*manorial rents ½d to 4d per ac*			*let for money rent (fol. 63–67) at 3s to 9s per acre*						*let for barley rent (fol. 66–73) at 2 bushels per acre*					
	(fol. 15–59)			*Infield*			*Outfield*			*Infield*			*Brecks*		
	a	r	p	a	r	p	a	r	p	a	r	p	a	r	p
J. Adams	4	0	0							8	1	20	6	0	0
J. Crisp	1	1	16								2	0	2	3	0
T. Spalding	1	0	0										2	0	0
9 tenants: 1–5 acs — H. Lawes, R. Hancell, W. Minnes, J. Roll, Mrs D. Redmans, C. Powley, W. Adams, W. Billament, T. Awdly	27	1	36												
6 tenants: 0–1 acs + barley rent — R. Bankes, junior, T. Bassam, G. Hargate, R. Gould, W. Byrd, T. Outlawe	1	1	0										1	0	0
	1850	0	0ª												
T. Longstreth,				27	0	0				20	1	0	1	2	0
F. Costen				3	3	10				40	0	0			
M. Smith										69	1	0	2	0	0
Mr Loades, clerk,										26	2	0	7	2	0
Widow Acres										14	1	20			
Widow Vickers, B. Crisp, W. Hill, W. Segon, G. Estick, J. Sallter, L. Vile, T. Banyard, R. Crisp, P. Eade, Osburn										16	2	0	16	2	0
Infield not let										9	2	20			
Total acreage	1850	0	0	295	2	10	379	0	0	276	2	20	274	2	0

a The total for manorial tenants is slightly lower than Fisher's figures, but conforms to totals in Table 4. The figures for the brecks are for 1634 with half the brecks out of cultivation.

Table 7: Location and legal status of tenants' holdings, 1634

Location of tenants		Tenants in order of size of holding	Free rent @ ½d to 3d per acre			Bond rent @ 2d to 4d per acre		
Maps	Precincts		a	r	p	a	r	p
E, N, S	5, 6, 7	Robert Rose	7	3	0	234	2	10
E, N, S	3, 4, 5, 6, 7	Rob. Banyard	41	3	0	169	1	0
N	1, 2, 3, 6	W. Guybon	50	1	15	119	2	0
N, E	3, 4, 5, 6	Mr Gurling, clerk	1	2	0	160	1	35
N	1, 2, 3	J. Lawes	38	3	20	116	1	1
E, N, S	5, 6, 7, 8	H. Cremer	60	2	0	43	2	0
E, N, S	4, 5, 6, 7	J. Ellgar				101	1	21
N, E	1, 2, 3, 5, 6	R. Attwood	18	0	20	82	2	0
N, E	1, 2, 3, 5, 6	R. Bird	11	0	20	70	3	0
N, E, S	1, 2, 3, 4, 7	H. Minns				73	3	10
E, N, S	5, 6, 7	W. Banyard				72	2	0
N, E	3, 4, 5	H. Lawes heirs				64	2	30
N, E	1, 2, 3, 5, 6	Rich. Banyard	16	3	0	46	3	30
E, N, S	5, 6, 7	G. Framingham				57	1	15
E, N, S	5, 6, 7	A. Collen				44	1	0
N	1, 2	Ellgars heirs	1	1	0	19	1	0
N, E	1, 2, 3, 4	F. Guybon				17	3	20
N, E	3, 4, 5, 6	J. Lingey				13	3	30
N, E	3, 4, 6	R. Bankes, sen.				13	2	0
N, E, S	3, 4, 5, 7	R. Dey	3	1	0	7	3	0
N	1, 2	Mr Waters, clerk				9	0	0
N	1, 2	R. Lawes				6	3	20
	Heacham	E. Creamer				8	3	20
	Heacham	E. Jenners				8	1	0
N, E	3, 4, 5	H. Lawes	4	2	0			
N, E	3, 5	R. Hancell				4	1	0
N, E	2, 4, 5	W. Minnes				4	0	16
N	6	J. Adams				4	0	0
N	2	J. Roll				3	2	20

Location of tenants		Tenants in order of size of holding	Free rent @ ½d to 3d per acre			Bond rent @ 2d to 4d per acre		
Maps	Precincts		a	r	p	a	r	p
	Heacham	Mrs D. Redmans				3	2	0
N	2	C. Powley, clerk				2	3	0
N, S	6, 8	W. Adams				2	3	0
N	2	J. Crisp				1	1	16
N, E	3, 4	T. Spalding				1	0	0
N	3	W. Billament				1	0	0
N	2	R. Bankes, jun.				0	2	0
S	8	G. Hargate				0	1	30
N	6	T. Bassam				0	1	10
N	6	R. Gould				0	1	0
E	5	W. Byrd				0	0	20
N	6	T. Outlawe				0	0	20
		Total 1850 acres	255	3	35	1594	1	0

Underpinning all these developments was John Fisher's written survey of 1631.[124] As we have seen, it was designed to clarify the landholding structure as it existed on the death of Francis Guybon, and to provide the information necessary for further reorganisation and improvement of the infield-outfield system. The survey begins by explaining the principle of exchange whereby lands in cultivation in one breck are matched with lands laid down to grass in another breck: Breck 1 was matched with 5, Breck 2 with 6, Breck 3 with 7 and Breck 4 with 8. The three fields, with their eight brecks each, are then dealt with in turn: 'Southfield', 'North Pasture' and finally 'Eastfield'. Starting in 'Southfield', for each breck the description of each entry includes the precinct, furlong and number of strip, details of ownership, acreage and how the land was farmed.[125] With this information, the reader can cross reference to the maps and find the location of each tenant's holding, see also Table 7. At the end of the entry for each breck, the demesne lands are totalled, followed by that of the tenants, those lands to be exchanged, and

---

124. LEST/IC58, see below, pp. 309–47.

125. Note the references made to Mr Shepheard's book, the survey dating from 1582, and the amendments made to his assessments of acreage which have been recalculated 'by measure'.

the allowance for the shepherds. In the bottom left hand corner, Fisher sets
out the rotation to be followed; for how this worked across the eight brecks
of 'Southfield' between 1631 and 1643.

For the organisation and management of the brecks in the three fields,
see Table 8. The columns, reading from left to right, show the number of
the breck, the extent of the lord's lands and those of the manorial tenants,
with the lands exchanged in matching brecks in columns three and five.
The 'exchanged lands' show the lands out of cultivation in each breck;
as you read from Breck 1 to 5, 2 to 6, 3 to 7, and 4 to 8. The remaining
columns show the allowance made to shepherds and the land let by the lord
for money and barley, less the land out of cultivation. The table confirms
that collaboration with manorial tenants was well established in South and
North Brecks, while the East Brecks were almost entirely dominated by the
lord. Notice how the tenants in North Field paid only barley rent, and how
W. Guybon was consolidating his holding.

The information in Fisher's written survey and on the maps illustrates
the dramatic improvements undertaken in 'Eastfield'. The east map shows
Easthall occupied by young Francis Guybon in 1634, extended with the
addition of 'the new farm' and his responsibility for farming the East
Brecks. Using the estate account for the years 1634 and 1635, we can trace
the composition of this new holding carved out of the least fertile part
of Sedgeford. The section on 'Eastfield' in the breck book begins with a
reference to the maps of Sedgeford made in 1631; also to the fact that the
furlongs and pieces have been carefully re-measured and noted on the
east map. See Figure 5 showing a page of Fisher's survey. In 1641 further
amendments were made in the second, third, fifth, seventh and eighth
brecks with breckland being laid into the infield. At the end of the section
on the brecks, Fisher summarized the lord's holding in all three fields. He
then provided a description of the new brecks in 'Eastfield', broken up
in 1631, which can be identified on the east map as lying to the south of
the Sedgeford to Docking road and Sedgeford Common; these were the
newly broken grounds in East Foldcourse farmed by William Guybon in
1634 and 1635. Fisher concluded by setting out the re-division of the East
Brecks into eight blocks of forty acres each and how they were farmed in
1641. The section on the brecks is followed by a listing of the lord's infield
lands in 1631, set out in a similar way with references to Mr Shepheard's
book. Fisher concluded by summarizing the demesne lands let for money
and barley, with half the brecks in cultivation.

Fisher's book of the brecks and infield lands became the model for
management at Sedgeford, repeatedly referred to and updated over the

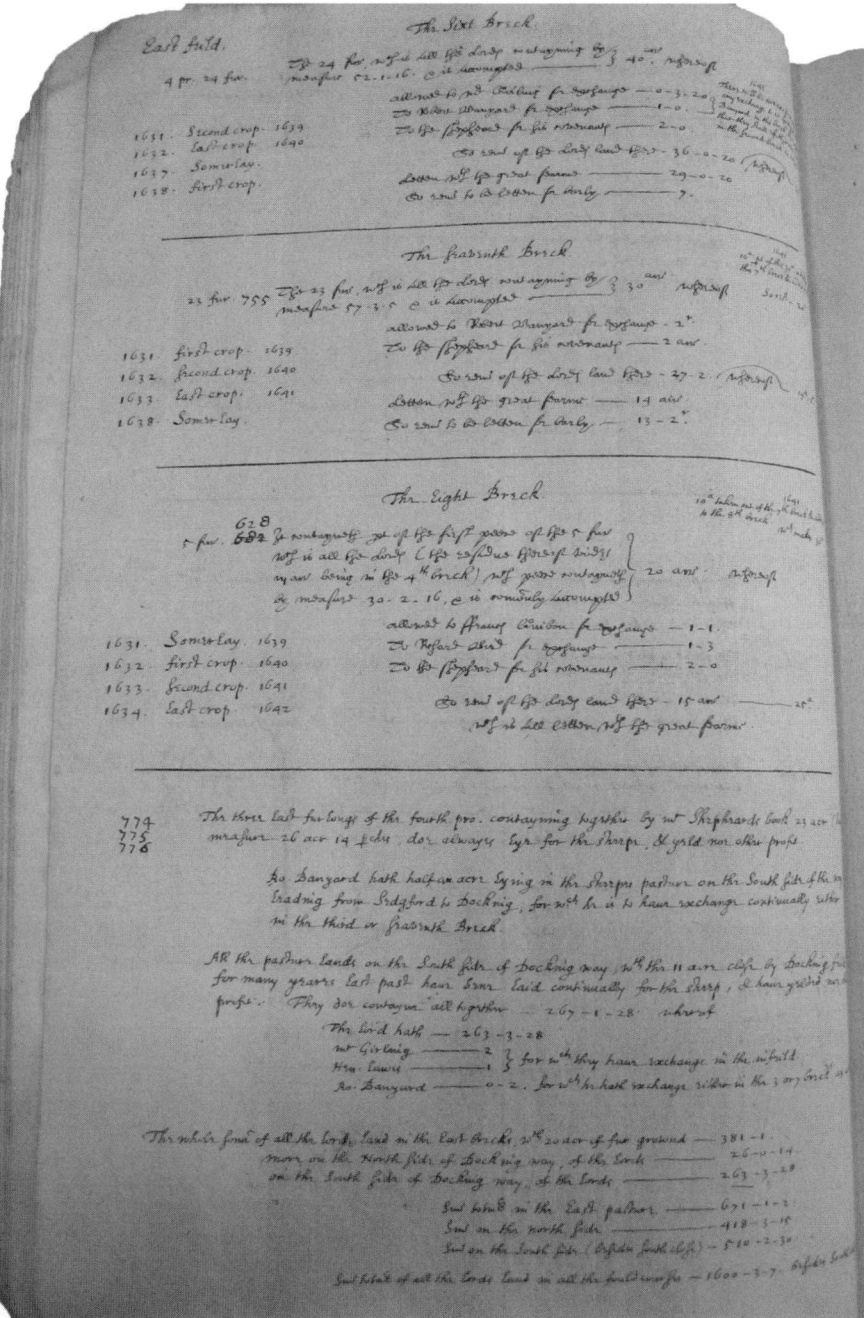

Figure 5 John Fisher's survey of Sedgeford showing East Field Brecks 6–8
(LEST/IC58)

Table 8: Organisation of the brecks at Sedgeford, 1631

South Brecks	acres	acres	acres	acres	acres	acres	
---	---	---	---	---	---	---	
Breck no:[130]	Lord's lands	Tenant lands	Shepherd covenant	Lord's land exch	Lord let to farm	Lord let to barley	Lord let Total
1	64.00	9.50	2.00	27.75	27.25	3.00	30.25
2	70.75	12.50	2.00	38.00	15.50		15.50
3	67.00	5.00	2.00	12.75	32.00	4.00	36.00
4	65.00		2.00		53.00	10.00	63.00
5	45.00	27.75	2.00	9.50	24.50	19.75	44.25
6	47.25	38.00	2.00	11.00	32.00	13.25	45.25
7	64.25	12.75	2.00	5.00	37.75	34.25	72.00
8	65.50		2.00		49.25	14.25	63.50
Furze	18.50						
Total	510.75	105.00	16.00	104.00	271.25	98.50	369.75

North Brecks	acres	acres	acres	acres	acres	acres	acres	acres
Breck no:	Lord's lands	tenants lands	Shepherd covenant	Lord's land exch	Lord let to barley	Total Lord let	Exch to Guybon	Sold to Guybon
1	48.25	1.00	2.00	4.25	38.25	38.25	3.00	0.50
2	58.50	7.50	2.00	27.25	12.00	12.00	3.25	14.00
3	82.75	29.25	2.00	9.75	68.00	68.00		3.00
4	38.00	7.75	2.00	14.00	5.75	5.75		16.25
5	33.50	4.25	2.00	1.00	30.75	30.75	0.50	3.00
6	60.25	27.25	2.00	7.50	33.75	33.75	14.00	3.25
7	38.00	9.75	2.00	29.25	3.75	3.75	3.00	
8	53.75	14.00	2.00	7.75	27.75	27.75	16.25	
Total	418.75	100.75	16.00	100.75	220.00	220.00	40.00	40.00

years. As we shall see, in 1647, Alice started a new book reflecting the changes that had taken place in the intervening years.[126] Other farming books provide useful information as to what was happening in that period. For example, the 'Corn Tithe and Farm Accounts' from 1643 to 1653 detail the corn received from different tenants for tithe and barley rent,

---

126. LEST/IB90.

East Brecks	acres	acres	acres	acres	acres	acres	acres	acres
Breck no:	Lord's lands	tenants lands	Shepherd covenant	Lord's land exch	Lord let to farm	Lord let to barley	Lord let Total	Exch to Guybon
1	50.00		2.00	2.00	26.00	20.00	46.00	
2	62.00	1.75	2.00		44.00	16.00	60.00	
3	70.00	0.50	2.00		42.00	25.50	67.50	
4	47.25	3.00	2.00		36.00	3.50	39.50	3.00
5	42.75	2.00	2.00		34.25	6.50	40.75	
6	40.00		2.00	1.75	29.00	7.00	36.00	
7	43.00		2.00	0.50	14.00	13.50	27.50	
8	20.00		2.00	3.00	15.00		15.00	
Furze	20.00							
Total	382.00	7.25	16.00	7.25	240.25	92.00	332.25	
Sheep	26.00							
New	263.25							
	671.25							

the sale of the corn with prices and names of buyers, and the shipping of it to Newcastle, Norway and Dunkirk.[127] These accounts supplement the receipts paid directly into Alice's receipt book. There is no estate account for Sedgeford after 1633; expenditure and outpayments for Sedgeford appear in Alice's books of disbursements, which also contain the building accounts.

A memoranda book dating principally from the 1660s includes biographical notes on farm tenants dating back to the sixteenth century: these thumbnail sketches cast light on the families, their origins and how they rose to wealth, providing a picture of a buoyant peasant economy and land market.[128] The families, who proved more resilient than the Guybons, include the Banyards, Lawes, Elgars, Roses, Hargates, Birds, Bankes, Longstreths, and Robert Birch who succeeded Francis Guybon at Easthall in 1641.[129] Several,

---

127. LEST/IC65, see below Alice's ship account with the sheep accounts, pp. 195–8.
128. LEST/IB85. The Banyards appear in the Hunstanton accounts from 1525, see Oestmann, Lordship and Community, pp. 70–2. The Roses appear in the Sedgeford sheep accounts in 1498 and the Elgars in 1514–15, Bailey, 'Sheep Accounts', pp. 71, 81.
129. For Birch's lease for Easthall 1641, see LEST/P10. Birch's lease includes a reference to the 'Breck Book', indicating its purpose to guide and control the activities of tenants and farmers.

like William Banyard, Thomas Hargate, Randolph Bird, Lionel Bankes and Thomas Longstreth were 'strangers out of the North country', who came to work and live in Sedgeford and married local heiresses.[130] Another group migrated from within Norfolk: Ralph and Henry Lawes from Fring, William Gurling from Sandringham, John Albert from Thornham, Robert Attwood from Sustead, John Roll from Scarning and William Minns from Little Fransham. Robert Birch from Swanton Morley 'was but a youth and lived with Thomas Hargate ... then he married and had 3 wifes wch were all very rich to him, then he purchased the house of Willyam Guybon...'[131] and took over the tenancy of Francis Guybon.

The main link between Fisher's survey and Alice Le Strange's book of 1647–1649 is another book containing various rentals and firmals from 1640 to 1645.[132] These relate to three significant developments: the renewal of the lease from the dean and chapter in 1637, the termination of Francis Guybon's lease in 1641, and William Guybon's departure in 1644. For the first time, the rental of 1640 distinguishes between the dean and chapter, Sedgefords and the lands of Sir Hamon Le Strange, adding to its complexity. A new firmal – i.e. a list of farm tenancies – was made in 1642 when Robert Birch entered Easthall, and much crossing out and insertions occur when William Guybon's lands were let in 1644. While Easthall, with the East Foldcourse, was re-let almost in its entirety, Westhall, the larger farm, was broken up with several 'fearmours' leasing the North and South Foldcourses. This suggests the difficulty of finding tenants with sufficient capital to take on these large holdings; the first tenant for Westhall was soon replaced by Mr Henry Farror who appears in Alice's new book.[133]

Alice's 'Sedgford Firmall and Breck Book 1647/8/9 & 1650' forms a comprehensive reference work which she drew up towards the end of her life.[134] As explained, only the first three pages, which list the contents and the directions for using the brecks, have been transcribed, but a brief description of the whole document is included here. The most striking aspect of the book are the names and dates inserted by Alice's successors showing how they systematically used the document until the 1700s.[135] Creating a manual for posterity was clearly Alice's intention. The directions for using

---

130. Banyard came to work for Mr Stone of Sedgeford, while Hargate worked at Hunstanton Hall.
131. LEST/IB85, Birch is wrongly spelt Bircham.
132. LEST/IB89.
133. LEST/IB90.
134. LEST/IB90.
135. Sir Nicholas le Strange, 4th bt; LEST/IB91.

the Sedgeford Brecks show her trying to fit the relevant information on to a single page for ease of reference with tables summarizing the start of each rotation for the next twenty five years. Unfortunately the acreage for each breck squeezed into the left hand margin has been worn away. For Southfield brecks the figures have been inserted later above the acreage sold for barley. In the same hand, Alice's years for summerley stretching to 1670 have been extended to 1703. Likewise, in folio two, where she provided a full rotation for North Pasture, we can see her successors using the table, systematically crossing out and inserting years down to 1702.

Alice's new breck book runs from folios three to thirty-nine and largely follows the format devised by Fisher. However, changes have been made to reflect the growing complexity of the holdings after the breakup of 'the great farme' leased to old Francis Guybon, the purchase of more land by the Le Stranges and the renewal of the lease from the dean and chapter in 1637. In contrast to Fisher's survey the East Brecks, farmed entirely by the Le Stranges, occupy only a single page, folio seventeen, while the North Brecks, with a host of manorial tenants to accommodate, follow the old format and occupy ten pages. The table of contents highlights further points of interest. For example, folios thirteen and fourteen include a table of the South Brecks which specifies the acreage paid in money and corn for each cultivated breck from 1650 with dates inserted up to 1705.

The firmals, which run from folios forty to sixty, illustrate life in Sedgeford after the departure of the Guybons with demesne lands and foldcourses leased to a variety of tenants: Westhall to Mr Henry Farror, Easthall to Robert Birch with the East Foldcourse, while the north 'fearmours' leased the North Foldcourse, the south 'fearmours' the South Foldcourse, and a further eight tenants leased holdings worth a total of £55 6s.[136] The total money rents for these lands amounted to £288 10s 2d compared to £222 in 1635. The increase can be explained by analysing Birch's rent for Easthall; it included £44 15s for infield, £30 16s for brecks and £9 1s 4d for the Whin Close. The rent for 150 acres of infield consisted of 22 acres at 6s 8d per acre, 5 acres at 6s 4d, 6 acres with the houses, 117 acres at 5s, with a further 32 acres at 3s 6d, recently enclosed from the brecks. This confirms the trend identified in 1641 with parcels of breckland being gradually drawn into the

---

136. The 1650 firmal includes a lease for the North and South Foldcourses listing the north farmers: Edward Lawes, John Roll, Bartholomew Crisp, Henry Minns; the south farmers: Nicholas Hallman, John Ellgar senior, William Banyard, Robert Banyard junior; and the further eight tenants: Edmond Ellgar, John Albert, Allen Collen, Thomas Royston, Francis Costen, Edmond Smith, Thomas Burnham, John Jenner.

infields and regular cultivation.[137] Gradually, we see outfields being whittled away and rents being raised. Similarly, the area yielding corn rent was reduced. Folios fifty-two to fifty-eight list the tenants paying 'fearme barley' in 1653 for a total of 467 acres compared to 551 acres in 1635.[138] The last firmal shows that Robert Birch was replaced by 'My cosen Bagge' paying the same rent for Easthall and the East Foldcourse, but overall, with a few vacant holdings, the rent had declined to £273 12s 2d.

The book ends abruptly at this point; Alice's involvement in farming more or less ceased in 1654 with the death of her husband.

The inserted names of early eighteenth-century tenants, notably Edward Potter, Ambrose Allen and William Hooke, which run through the firmals, indicate quite clearly that Alice's book was still being used by her successors in the 1700s. In fact, it formed the basis of Sir Nicholas Le Strange's Sedgeford firmal of 1702 which was 'entered fayre and more perfect into a new book 1707'.[139] This book in its format and frequent references to Alice's book of 1647 to 1654, attests to Alice's enduring legacy as a farmer and estate manager. The Sedgeford documents are not an isolated example. The pattern of innovation and meticulous recording keeping, with successors quoting her work, was repeated across the Hunstanton estate, notably at Ringstead which shared many features with neighbouring Sedgeford. Alice's contribution to the family and the estate was not only the skilful day to day management of their affairs, but the creation of exceptional records which, handed down from generation to generation, helped to secure the survival and future of the Le Strange family at Hunstanton. Her price was truly above pearls.

---

137. LEST/IC58, see below, pp. 331–8.
138. See Table 6, p. 49.
139. LEST/IB91.

Notes to the Reader

In editing this sample of the family and farming records of Alice Le Strange every effort has been made to retain the spirit and experimental nature of the original documents. As far as possible editing has been confined to modernizing the use of capitals and punctuation, but inevitably some compromises have had to be made with the layout; this is particularly true of the sheep accounts. These accounts do not appear chronologically in the large bound volume LEST/P10. In the transcriptions they have been placed in order and given titles where they are obscured by faded or torn pages. The list below shows the original order of the sheep accounts accompanied by the page numbers of the transcriptions in square brackets. In this way, the reader can follow the changes made and cross reference back to the original if they wish. This order, and the number of blank pages that occur in the document, are also indicated in the footnotes.

The original order of the Sheep Accounts in LEST/P10
'Accounts of Flocks & Foldcourses by the Lady Alice L' Estrange'
[*pp. 46–103*]:[140]

Sheep accounts 1625–43 [*pp. 46–74*]

Plundering of the flocks by parliamentary forces 1643 [*p. 74*]

Cullett sheep, tithe wool & lamb accounts, grandchildren's sheep
[*pp. 74–95*]

'A reckoning of the sheep of Nicholas Le Strange, my grandchilde'
[*pp. 95–7*]

'A reckoning of the profit of my grandchilde Nicholas Le Stranges sheepe'
[*p. 98*]

---

140. Page numbers of transcriptions.

'A note of what sheep were layd upon Barrett Ringsted ground' [*p. 98*]

'A note for laying of sheepe at Ringstead' [*p. 100*]

'A reckoning for sheepe beginning from Midsomer 1653' [*pp. 100–2*]

'A reckoning of the Kitching Sheepe 1654' [*pp. 102–3*]

'Accounts of the charges and profitts of a shippe in divers voyages'
[*pp. 110–12*]

Children's accounts, 1618–1627 [*pp. 15–35*]

A note of the tenants' sheep on the South Flock of Ringstead in 1643, and
a note of flocks, foldcourses and shepherds' covenants [*pp. 108–10*]

Alice Le Strange's own sheep account, 1617–1625 [*pp. 35–46*]

Wool accounts 1642–1654 [*pp. 103–8*]

The system of numbering sheep has also been standardized. At first
Alice used both Roman and Arabic numerals, but we have used Arabic
throughout. For various reasons – uncertainty over the use of the long
hundred, the inclusion of a shepherd's allowance or simply poor arithmetic
– the totals are sometimes inaccurate. In the text the actual number of sheep
is placed in [*italics*]. For those not familiar with the long hundred used to
count sheep it amounts to 120; in the original document it is shown with a
C[*entum*] as in iiiC = 360; XX is a score, as in iiiXX = 60.

To capture the experimental nature of the Sedgeford documents, all
insertions have been *marked* in their original positions. In this way the
reader begins to understand the process of change as well as the content.
Similarly, in John Fisher's written survey of Sedgeford, commissioned by
Alice in 1631, the original diagrammatic format has been retained with
minor adjustments. In these documents where acres, rods and perches
dominate, acres is abbreviated to 'ac' when it stands alone with a single
figure, and reduced to 'a' with rods and perches, as in 'a', 'r', 'p'. At the start
of each document, more specific detail on the editing can be found in the
footnotes.

More generally, the usual conventions apply:

   **   ** words inserted within an insertion;

   < > indicates words that have been deleted; << >> words deleted within a deletion;

   /*italics*/ indicates marginal entry or annotation; *italics* indicates editorial remarks outside the text, e.g. *undated, signed, endorsed*; [*italics*] indicates editorial remarks within the text.

Variations in spelling the Le Strange family name appear in all the documents. The most common form Le Strange appears 209 times compared to L' Estrange or L'estrange, 14 times mostly in wills and titles, and Lestrange, 29 times. Cord Oestmann used Lestrange in his study of the family during the sixteenth century; the version L'Estrange started to appear in the 1630s, as can be seen in the title of the first document.[141] This form was made famous by Roger Le Strange in the second half of the seventeenth century. 'Le Strange' is used throughout the book on the household and that is the form adopted in this volume, as it is in the Norfolk Record Office catalogue.[142]

---

141. Oestmann, *Lordship and Community, passim.*
142. Whittle & Griffiths, *passim.*

Sheep Glossary[143]

Life-cycle of a sheep

Lamb: male or female sheep, wether and ewe lambs, up to about six months old.

Pooks: undersized or small lambs.

Hoggs: sheep before first clipping, i.e. ewe hoggs and wether hoggs.

Shearling or shorlins: sheep after first clipping, i.e. ewe shorlins and wether shorlins.

Ewe: female sheep after lambing and second shearing, i.e. ewe lambs, ewe hoggs, ewe shorlins, ewes or mother ewes.

Wether: castrated male sheep after second shearing, i.e. wether lambs, wether hoggs, wether shorlins and wethers of 2, 3, 4, 5 shear.

Ram: uncastrated male sheep, ram lambs, ram hoggs, ram shorlins and rams.

Rixsey: adult male sheep, half castrated or born with one testicle.

Crone: an old sheep, usually female.

Morts: dead sheep

Sheep-farming terms

Agistment: the provision of grazing for animals, usually on someone else's land involving a financial charge.

Bell wether: refers to the practice of placing a bell around the neck of a wether leading his flock of sheep. The movements of the flock could be noted by hearing the bell before the flock was in sight.

---

143. Watson & More, *Agriculture*; R. Trow Smith, *A History of British Livestock Husbandry to 1700* (1957); Yaxley, *Glossary*.

Cullett or joyce: sheep belonging to other people grazing with the flock of another person, usually the manorial lord to whom they make a payment.

Dizy sheep: mentioned sixty times in the sheep accounts, probably refers to a range of viral disorders found in lambs making them tremble uncontrollably, known as hair-shaker disease, fuzzy lamb syndrome or border disease. Also dotty sheep, said of sheep that have hydatids, a cyst containing the larva of tapeworm on the brain causing erratic motion and behaviour.

Dragging: term used to describe dragging sheep to the clipping.

Foldcourse: the lord's exclusive right to erect a sheep fold and to graze his sheep over the open field strips of his manorial tenants and other specified areas.

Hurdles: light and portable wattle fencing used to pen sheep, also known as clattes.

Livery: food and clothes given to a shepherd.

Long hundred: 120 sheep, rather than 100 sheep.

Marking lambs: lambs gifted to shepherds at the time of marking with red dye.

Murrain: generic term for the diseases afflicting sheep.

Oil: for greasing sheep.

Pitch: for marking sheep, applied with a branding iron.

Raddle: red dye transferred from the ram to the ewes he has serviced.

Shack: feed for livestock on the stubble of the open fields after the harvest.

Skins: skins of dead sheep brought to the clipping to prove they are dead.

Store lambs: lambs kept for fattening, often sold on to others for fattening.

Tally: the process of reckoning, counting or scoring sheep (or other livestock or commodities which implies the use of a stick or counting).

Tar: used to protect sheep against parasites and ticks.

Tathe: sheep or cattle dung spread as fertilizer by the producer, i.e. corn tathed by sheep, dunging, trampling the fields over which they have been folded.

Tithe: payments to the clergy, or the lay impropriators, of an agreed share of the produce, mainly corn, wool and lambs.

Transcriptions of the Documents

Notes on the Family Finances

Accounts of the Lady L'Estrange from 1645 to 1654

The severall purchases & sales made by Sir Hamon L'Estrange
are at the latter end of this book[1]

	£	s	d
[*My*] fathers estate & how he [*settled it upon*] my sister Yellverton & myselfe[2]			
Lands settled upon my sister Yellverton & other lands after given to her chilldren			
Edgefield & Harpley mannours by the yeare	180	0	0
Rent charges out of Rougham & Scullthorp given at his death by yeare	90	0	0
Lands given to Anne Cademan[3] at Litcham by yeare	30	0	0
Westwinch settled upon Sir Willyam Yellverton by the yeare[4]	118	0	0
part of Linne lande given to Sir Henry Yellverton at my fathers death	80	0	0
Sum[5] <488> in land yearely	498	0	0

---

1. The title on the cover of LEST/P10.

2. These pages on the family finances follow Alice's general disbursements for 1645–1654. After twelve blank pages, Alice set out the above settlement with her sister. After fourteen blank pages, she listed information on sales and purchases, and debts owing to 1654. After ten further blank pages she included the final agreement of a long running legal case, and a summary of lands sold, purchased and lost, with gifts from her father. Finally, she added details of church repairs and an inventory of household stuff given to her by her father. Apart from the book of disbursements, which runs to 167 folios, LEST/P10 is not numbered, indicating that these notes were entered as Alice thought necessary. Note the reference to L'Estrange rather than Le Strange, see p. 61.

3. The Cademans were substantial manorial tenants in Great Ringstead. Anne may have been related to Thomas Cademan of Rougham, gent., or his son Robert, clerk to Sir William Yelverton in 1620, NRO, NRS 7907. For details of the Yelverton family see above fn. 23, p. 6.

4. For Stubbe's involvement at West Winch *see* Blomefield & Parkin, *Norfolk*, IX, p. 156.

5. Alternative spellings of summe, summ, and sum have been standardized throughout the text as 'sum'.

Monyes at my fathers death & debts payd for my brother Yellverton
& his sonnes and monyes payd at my sisters maryage

payd to Mr Yellverton upon my sisters marryage	500	0	0
given to my brother Yellverton as by my fathers accompt booke doth appeare fol 17 upon a reckoning between my brother & him	358	0	0
payd for debts for my nephew Willyam Yellverton	100	0	0
payd for debts for Sir Henry Yellverton as by the accompt booke doth apeare fol. 32	204	9	0
my fathers inventory at his death beside desperate debts	3500	0	0
my husbands debt to my father which was not in the inventory *& payd*	400	0	0
my brother Yellverton did owe my father at his death	600	0	0
to Sir Willyam Yellverton, junior, by 100 marks the yeare for 6 years during my fathers life	400	0	0
my brother Yellverton received for a yeares profitt of Sedgford, after my fathers death	330	0	0
Sum	6392	9	0

/Abate out of the £6392 9s/[6] For beding & plate & a diamond ring

& a horse to my husband, the residue given to myselfe & my chilldren in my fathers will[7]	120	16	0
for legasyes given to myselfe and my chilldren out of Westwinch	350	0	0
for 160 sheepe give to my chilldren by my fathers will	43	0	0
Sum	513	16	0

[p] The £513 being deducted out of £6392 9s remayne of my sister Yellvertons part in mony	5879	9	0

Lands settled upon me at my marriage

Sedgford mannours cleare from rent to the Deane & Chappiter whereof lease £220	330	0	0
Linne land	120	0	0
given to my sonne Hamon at my fathers death his lands at Holme late Bigges	23	0	0
Sum	3473	0	0

Monyes given at my marriage by my father & other monyes to
my selfe & chilldren

payd to Sr John Peiton upon his accompt at my marryage	1000	0	0
allowed me by my father by 100 markes by the yeare during my fathers life for 16 yeare	1066	13	4

---

6. The LH margin has been removed and these incidental notes have been brought into the main text.

7. See the inventory below, pp. 84–5.

	£	s	d
he gave me for the manour of Runton	40	0	0
given me & my chilldren by his will in houshold stuffe & plate & a diamond ring & a horse to my husband	116	16	0
given to my chilldren 160 sheepe	43	0	0
given to my sonne Nicholas the lands late Simons which cost him	320	0	0
given to my sonne Hamon Holme Parsonage which cost him of my husband	800	0	0
given in legasyes to my selfe & my chilldren out of Westwinch	350	0	0
my father remitted to me in debt that I ought him a little before his death *£30 for sheepe & £20 I borrowed of Mr Strange*	50	0	0
at his death part of the Linn land sold for	880	0	0
Sum	4669	13	4
so my sister had in land more than my self by the yeare	26	0	0
my sister had in mony more than my selfe beside Sherringham Parsonage[8]	1209	15	8
[p] */1623/ Bought of Cleare Francis 134ac in Ringsted[9]*	325	15	0

Sale of Lands & Purchases

/1630 Benacre bought wth £2550 of my daughter Stranges portion/

	£	s	d
to Mr Yarmouth for Benacre[10]	2520	0	0
layd out in buylding at Benacre	145	0	0
layd out for lands bought of Mr Utting & Smith	240	0	0
layd out for a postfine	7	10	0
layd out for surveighing of Benacre	12	10	0
Sum	2925	0	0

	£	s	d
/1633 Westwinch purchased/ payd to Sir Willyam Yellverton	950	0	0
due from Sir Willyam to Doctour Edmund Stubbe[11]	172	19	9
due from him to Sir Henry Yellverton	166	16	3
due from him to my sister Yellverton	83	8	1
due from him to Elizabeth Le Strange	172	19	9

8. Fourteen blank pages follow this entry.

9. Cleare Francis was a substantial manorial tenant of Great Ringstead who sold his lands in 1623.

10. Several men linked with the purchase of the Benacre estate came from the Lowestoft area: William March held lands at Aldeby; the Yarmouths were lords at Blundeston; John Utting was vicar of Corton; the Gooch and North families had long associations with Benacre, see A. Suckling, *The History and Antiquities of the County of Suffolk*, vol. 1 (1846). The £ s d are placed where Alice put them.

11. Edmund, cousin of Richard Stubbe who left him lands in his will, PROB 11/135.

due from him to Roger Le Strange	166	16	3
due from him to my selfe	83	8	1
Sum beside assurance[12]	1792	0	0

/*1632 Chappell Mill sold*/ Received of Mr Beacon for Chappell Mill which payd part of the purchase of Westwinch	600	0	0
/*1636 Linne land sold*/ Sold to Mr Willyam Paston[13] the land at South Linne which my father gave me at his death for which Mr Paston payd in 1636	500	0	0
/*1637*/ Mr Paston payd more	300	0	0
/*1638*/ Mr Paston payd more £20 and £60	80	0	0
Sum	880	0	0

/*1637 Linne house sold*/ Received of Richard Hayward for an house in the Checker at Linne late Sr Nicholas Le Stranges	360	0	0

Sum of both £1240 this did pay part of my daughter Springs[14] portion and /*£221 10s 0d* / the sute for the Irish lands 1637 £10 & 1638 £100 & £50 & £61 10s in all £221 10s[15]
/*£106 13s 4d* /& for diking of Boston Fenne 1636 £80, and 1637 £26 13s 4d in all for the fenne, beside £400 the purchase 1631 – £106 13s 4d

/*1644*/ payd to Will Guybon for land bought[16]	158	15	0
/*1645*/ payd to John Hancell for an house with an orchyarde in Ringstead late Whittles[17]	50	0	0
/*1648*/ payd to Willyam Guybon for land[18]	256	10	0
/*1648*/ payd to Mr Samuel Gurling for 2a 2r of land[19]	24	12	0
/*1649*/ payd to Thomas Banyard for a pasture close called London Yardes	68	0	0
Sum	557	17	0

---

12. Actual total of £1796 8s 2d may include the assurance, possibly a fee. The 'sums' are not always accurate as they sometimes do not reflect payments inserted in the LH margin, see fn. 20 below.

13. William son of Sir Edward Paston of Appleton, Kings Lynn, *see* Blomefield & Parkin, *Norfolk*, VIII, pp. 329–30.

14. Elizabeth married William Spring of Pakenham, Suffolk in 1636.

15. Sir Hamon inherited land in Ireland, in the province of Connacht, with dubious titles; he sold a portion in 1609 for £500, but failed to establish further titles in 1638, which accounts for the payments recorded by Alice, LEST/NL 21–24 and 27. There is no further mention of the land after 1650.

16. A landholder and principal tenant in Sedgeford, William Guybon was a cousin of Alice Le Strange, see also pp. 75, 83, for this transaction.

17. Small landholders in Great Ringstead.

18. See below, pp. 78, 82–3, for more detail of this transaction with William Guybon.

19. Gurling was a landholder and rector of Sedgeford; Thomas Banyard was from Sedgeford, *see* Whittle *&* Griffiths, pp. 218, 235.

[p]

Debts owing 1632

/Debts payd £150/[20] to my sonne Hamon Le Strange	800	0	0
/£40/ to Mr Willyam March[21]	40	0	0
/£100/ to Sir John Hare[22]	100	0	0
to Mr Phillip Calthorp[23]	200	0	0
/£40 to Mr Gooch[24]	40	0	0
Sum	1180	0	0

This yeare I payd Sir John Hobert[25] for John Cremer[26]	300	0	0
more payd to my sonne Hamon Le Strange for him	100	0	0

Debts owing 1633 at our Lady

/payd £610/ to my [son] Hamon Le Strange	650	0	0
/£200/ to Mr Phillip Calthorp	200	0	0
Borrowed more of my sonne Hamon Le Strange £60 & £100	160	0	0
/£231/ to Mr James Calthorp[27]	231	0	0
/£50/ to Mr Willyam Reade[28]	150	0	0
/£350/ to Mr Clement Spelman[29]	350	0	0
Sum	1741	0	0

This yeare I received of Mr North in part of £2880 for Benacre[30]	2000	0	0
and putt into Mr Barrets hand with £20 added[31]	900	0	0

---

20. These sums of money, from the LH margin, show the gradual repayment of debt which sometimes affects the 'Sum' total'.

21. See above, fn. 10, p. 69, for William March.

22. Sir John Hare of Stow Bardolph, 1603–1637, www.historyofparliamentonline.org.uk.

23. Phillip Calthorpe was the second son of Sir James Calthorpe of Cockthorp, 1558–1615, and tenant of the Le Stranges' estate at Gressenhall, *see* Whittle & Griffiths, pp. 63, 193; Blomefield & Parkin, *Norfolk*, IX, p. 217.

24. See above, fn. 10, p. 69.

25. See above, fn. 50, p. 18.

26. John Cremer, 1582–1652, of Ingoldisthorpe, *see* Blomefield & Parkin, *Norfolk*, X, p. 336; he and this brothers Henry, Edmund and Thomas, leased and held manorial lands from the Le Stranges in Heacham and Sedgeford, *see* Whittle & Griffiths, pp. 83, 218, and below, p. 83.

27. Later knighted as Sir James Calthorpe of East Barsham, 1604–1652, he married Catherine Lewkenor as his second wife in 1641, see fn. 36, p. 11.

28. The Read family were large landholders in Great Ringstead until the early 1620s when they sold most of their lands to Cleare Francis, LEST/EH4.

29. Clement Spelman, 1598–1679, was fourth son of Sir Henry Spelman, *see* Blomefield & Parkin, *Norfolk*, VIII, p. 384.

30. See above, fn. 10, p. 69.

31. Possibly, Edmund Barrett of Dersingham, 1637, NRO, ANW 22/4/96.

/1633/ payd to Sir Willyam Yellverton for Westwinch besides £423 4s 1d that was due to me and my chilldren	1373	4	1

Debts owing 1634

/£200/ to my sonne Hamon Le Strange	200	0	0
/£100/ to Mr Willyam Reade	100	0	0
Sum	300	0	0

Debts remayne 1635 – none

/1636/ payd for diking of Boston Fennes £80 & 1637 £26 13s 4d	160	13	4
/1646/ [recte 1636] my daughter Elizabeth was married & wee were to pay for her portion	3500	0	0
whereof payd the £900 put out to Mr Barrett & £100 more in all	1000	0	0
& payd more	1000	0	0

Debts owing 1636

Borrowed of my Lady Grey[32] £100 & £100	200	0	0
/£100/ Borrowed of Mr Henry Beck[33]	300	0	0
Borrowed of Thomas Banyard £100 & of Dorothe Banyard £40	240	0	0
to Sir Willyam Spring the remaynder of the portion	1500	0	0
Sum	2240	0	0

Debts owing 1637

to the Lady Grey	200	0	0
/£200/ to Mr Henry Beck	200	0	0
/£1200/ to Sir Willyam Spring *900 & 300*	1500	0	0
/£140/ to Thomas Banyard & Dorothe *[£]100 Thomas*	240	0	0
/£10/ Borrowed of Dorothe Banyard	10	0	0
Borrowed of Mrs Dorothe Gurney[34] *£100 & £50*	150	0	0
Borrowed of Mr Simons *20 October*	800	0	0
/£200/ Borrowed of Sir John Hare	200	0	0
Borrowed of Robert Banyard of Sedgford	60	0	0
/£40/ Borrowed of Will Guybon	40	0	0
Sum	3400	0	0

---

32. Lady Grey, widow of Sir William de Grey of Merton, who died in 1632; she was the daughter of Sir James Calthorpe of Cockthorpe, 1558–1615, and sister of Phillip Calthorpe of Gressenhall, see Blomefield & Parkin, *Norfolk*, II, p. 306.

33. Henry Beck appears as a signatory in several documents associated with Sir Edward Coke's purchase of lands at Anmer, Flitcham and Appleton between 1604 and 1617, NRO, FLT 1/440, 456.

34. 'Dol Gurney' appears in Sir Nicholas Le Strange's book, *Merry Passages and Jests,* ed. H.F. Lippincott (Salzburg, 1974), see Whittle & Griffiths, p. 194. She may have been related to Alice and Dionisia through Richard Stubbe's first wife, Elizabeth Gurney of Ellingham.

[*p*]

Debts owing 1638

to my Lady Grey	200	0	0
to my sister Spring[35]	300	0	0
to Mr Simons[36]	800	0	0
to Mrs Dorothe Gurney	150	0	0
/£100/ to Thomas Banyard	100	0	0
/£60/ to Robert Banyard of Sedgford	60	0	0
Borrowed of my sister Spring	100	0	0
Borrowed of my cosen Katherin Lewkenour[37]	50	0	0
Borrowed of Mrs Dorothe Gurney	50	0	0
Borrowed of Thomas Patterick	100	0	0
Borrowed of Mr Nash	100	0	0
Sum	2010	0	0

/1638/ Layd out for imbanking of Heacham Marsh	307	7	11

Debts owing 1639

to my Lady Grey	200	0	0
to my sister Spring	400	0	0
to Mr Simons	800	0	0
to Mrs Dorothe Gurney	200	0	0
to my cosen Katherin Lewkenour	50	0	0
/£100/ to Thomas Patterick	100	0	0
to Mr Nash	100	0	0
Borrowed of my cosen Katherin Lewkenour	50	0	0
Borowed of my cosen Mary Lewkenour[38] *£50 & £50*	100	0	0
Borowed of Mr Nash £60 & £50	110	0	0
Borowed of Lawrence Michaell[39]	30	0	0
Borowed of Mr Willyam Reade	100	0	0
Sum	2240	0	0

---

35. Elizabeth, widow of Sir William Spring, was the mother of Alice's son-in-law.

36. Mr Simons, Thomas Patterick, Mr Nash and Mr Thomson can not be indentified with any certainty.

37. Catherine Lewkenor, the sister of Anne Le Strange, who was to marry Sir James Calthorpe of East Barsham in 1641, see fn. 27, p. 71.

38. Mary, widow of Sir Edward Lewkenor and mother of Catherine Calthorpe and Anne Le Strange, www.historyofparliamentonline.org.uk.

39. Sir Hamon's London tailor, who also lent the family money, *see* Whittle & Griffiths, pp. 67–8, 130, 162.

[*p*]

Debts owing 1640

to my Lady Grey	200	0	0
to my sister Spring	400	0	0
to Mr Simons	800	0	0
to Mrs Dorothe Gurney	200	0	0
to my cosen Katherin Lewkenour	100	0	0
to my cosen Mary Lewkenour	100	0	0
/*£60*/ to Mr Nash	210	0	0
/*£30*/ to Lawrens Michaell	30	0	0
to Mr Willyam Read	100	0	0
Borrowed of Mr Nash	100	0	0
Sum	2240	0	0

/*1640*/ Layd out more for imbanking of Heacham Marsh	472	12	1

Debts owing 1641

to my Lady Grey	200	0	0
/*£100*/ [*payd*] to my sister Spring	400	0	0
to Mr Simons	800	0	0
to Mrs Dorothe Gurney	200	0	0
/*£100*/ to my cosen Katherin Lewkenour	100	0	0
to my cosen Mary Lewkenour	100	0	0
to Mr Nash	250	0	0
to Mr Willyam Reade	100	0	0
Sum	2150	0	0

/*1641*/ Payd to my sonne Nicholas Le Strange to pay his debts	400	0	0

Debts owing 1642

to my Lady Grey	200	0	0
to my sister Spring	400	0	0
to Mr Simons	800	0	0
to Mrs Dorothe Gurney	200	0	0
to my cosen Mary Lewkenour	100	0	0
to Mr Nash	250	0	0
/*£100*/ to Mr Willyam Reade	100	0	0
Borowed of Mr Nash £50 & £50 & £50	150	0	0
Sum	2100	0	0

Debts owing 1643

to my Lady Grey	200	0	0
/*£200*/ to my sister Spring	300	0	0

to Mr Simons	800	0	0
/£50/ to Mrs Dorothe Gurney	200	0	0
/£100/ to my cosen Mary Lewkenour	100	0	0
/£250/ to Mr Nash	400	0	0
Borowed of little John Le Strange[40] £50 & £50	100	0	0
Borowed of my cosen Mary Lewkenour *2 May*	200	0	0
Borowed of Nurse Guybon	40	0	0
Borowed of Mr Thomson of Cambridg	300	0	0
Borowed of Mr Nash *22 Dec*	50	0	0
Borowed of Mr Francis Boyton[41] *3 Febru[ary]*	200	0	0
Sum	2890	0	0

[p]

/1643/ wee payd to the rebells for our 5th & 20th part	300	0	0
/1643/ wee were plundered by the rebells of 1660 sheep all our corne & divers horses			

Debts owing 1644

to my Lady Grey	200	0	0
/£100/ to my sister Spring	100	0	0
to Mr Simons	800	0	0
/£100 & £50/ to Mrs Dorothe Gurney	150	0	0
/£50/ to Mr Nash	200	0	0
to little Jo[hn] Le Strange	100	0	0
to my cosen Lewkenour	200	0	0
/£40/ to Nurse Guybon	40	0	0
/£300/ to Mr Thomson	300	0	0
to Mr Francis Boyton *18 June*	200	0	0
Borowed of Mr Nash *17 May*	50	0	0
Borowed of Edmond Barrett *24 June*	100	0	0
Borowed of Mr Henry Boyton *18 June*	100	0	0
/12 Oct £300/ [payd] Borowed of my cosen Lewkenour: £50*of Mrs Gurneys* & £300	350	0	0
Sum<3140>	2940	0	0

/1644/ payd to Willyam Guybon for land	158	15	0
/1644/ wee payd to the advance of the Skottish rebels	200	0	0

---

40. John was the third son of Sir Nicholas born in 1636, see above, p. 27.

41. The Boytons of Flitcham, linked by marriage to the Cremers, were visitors to Hunstanton Hall, see Whittle & Griffiths, p. 193.

Debts owing 1645

to my Lady Grey	200	o	o
to my sister Spring[42]	ooo	o	o
to Mr Simons	800	o	o
/£50/ to Mr Nash[43]	[150]	o	o
to little Jack[44]	[100]	o	o
to my cosen Lewkenour	550	o	o
to Mr Francis Boyton	200	o	o
/£100/ to Edmond Barrett	100	o	o
to Mr Henry Boyton	100	o	o
Borowed of Mrs Miller	200	o	o
Borowed of my cosen Lewkenour	100	o	o
Sum	2600	o	o

/1645/ payd to John Hancell for an house at Ringsted	50	o	o
/1645/ payd to May, Wormwell etc for their pretended losses[45]	225	11	2

Debts owing 1646

to my Lady Grey	200	o	o
to my sister Spring	ooo	o	o
to Mr Simons	800	o	o
to Mr Nash	o	o	o
to little Jack	100	o	o
to my cosen Lewkenour	650	o	o
to Mr Francis Boyton	200	o	o
to Mr Henry Boyton	100	o	o
to Mrs Miller	200	o	o
Borowed of my cosen Lewkenour	50	o	o
Borowed of Thomas Patterick	200	o	o
Borowed of Mr Willyam Calvert	100	o	o
Sum	2750	o	o

[p]
/1646/ payd to Stileman upon a sute pretending the falce imprisonment
of his father when he refused to pay the mony apoynted for him to pay

---

42. Sister Spring's debt was repaid in 1644; the figure has been amended and can be read as £100, which would account for the sum of £2600; see also footnotes below.

43. The figure for Mr Nash is illegible and based on the figure for 1644 less £50.

44. The figure for little Jack is also illegible and based on the figure for 1644.

45. After the siege of Kings Lynn, the Le Stranges were forced to pay compensation for alleged losses, see above, pp. 17–18.

by my Lord Martiall in the Court of Honour[46]   385 0 0
/1647/ to Mr Percivall for pr[et]ended imprisoning[47] [£]86
to Mr Toll for the like in part [£]40
payd for the almes house [£1]88 4s 10d[48]   324 4 10
to Robert /clerke/ for a heystack fired by the rebels

Debts owing 1647

to my Lady Grey   200 0 0
to Mr Simons   800 0 0
/£150/ to Mr Nash   150 0 0
to little Jack   100 0 0
to my cosen Lewkenour   700 0 0
/£200/ to Mr Francis Boyton   200 0 0
/£100/ to Mr Henry Boyton   100 0 0
/£200/ to Mrs Miller   200 0 0
/£200/ to Thomas Patterick   200 0 0
to Mr Willyam Calvert   100 0 0
Borowed of Mrs C[althorpe] Sum £2850   200 0 0
Borrowed of John Fisher[49]   130 0 0
Borrowed of Robert Banyard   100 0 0
                                            Sum 1230 0 0

1648/ to Mr Toll upon his pretended imprisonment   50 0 0
to Willyam Johnson upon a second order   12 11 8

---

46. Robert Styleman of Snettisham who encouraged his nephew, Robert Cremer of Little Massingham, to challenge the Le Stranges over the status of his copyhold land in Heacham, see below, pp. 81–2 for the final agreement with Robert Cremer in 1654; see also Whittle & Griffiths, p. 236; Griffiths, 'A Country Life', p. 230. For a full transcript of the case see www.court-of-chivalry.bham, case 372, 1638–1640. The Earl Marshall was at this time the 21st earl of Arundel. 1646.

47. Percival and Toll, see above, p. 17, and below, p. 83.

48. Figure not entirely clear; actual total is £314 4s 10d.

49. There were two John Fishers. The surveyor, who drew the Sedgeford maps and produced the written survey was John Fisher of Heacham; he had a son also John who is mentioned in Sir Nicholas's drainage note books, LEST/KA24. In their wills, Sir Hamon and Alice both also refer to John Fisher of Honing gt, who was closely connected to the Hobarts of Blickling. To add to the confusion, Sir Hamon referred to his wife as Mary, while Alice referred to her as Margaret, my cousin. In the will of John Fisher of Honing, gt. who died in 1652, PROB 11/224, he referred to his wife as Helen, and his son John, but with no named wife. It may be that the wills of Sir Hamon and Alice were referring to this son, see pp. 353–62. The likelihood is that the loans to Sir Hamon were made by John Fisher of Honing, while the more local references refer to John Fisher, father and son, of Heacham. The NCC will register shows three generations of John Fishers at Heacham, with wills from 1608, 1668 and 1684.

to John Johnson for composition	30	0	0
[Sum][50]	92	11	8

Debts remayning owing 1648

to my Lady Grey	200	0	0
/£800/ to Mr Simons	800	0	0
to Mr Nash	000	0	0
to little Jack	100	0	0
to my cosen Lewkenour	700	0	0
to Mr Willyam Calvert	100	0	0
to Mrs Calthorp	200	0	0
to John Fisher	130	0	0
to Robert Banyard	100	0	0
Borowed of Mrs Elizabeth Calthorp	300	0	0
Borowed of John Fisher	20	0	0
Sum	2650	0	0

/1648/ payd to Willyam Guybon for land *21a 1r 20p*	256	10	0
/1648/ payd to Mr Gurling for 3a 2r of land	24	12	0

Debts owing 1649 at our Lady

to my Lady Grey	200	0	0
to little Jack	100	0	0
to my cosen Lewkenour	700	0	0
/£100/ to Willyam Calvert	100	0	0
to Mrs Anne Calthorp	200	0	0
to Mrs Elizabeth Calthorp	300	0	0
to John Fisher	150	0	0
to Robert Banyard	100	0	0
/£100/ Borrowed of Willyam Holly[51]	100	0	0
Borrowed of Mr Nash	100	0	0
Sum	2050	0	0

[p]

/1649/ payd to Thomas Banyard a pasture close called London Yardes	68	0	0
/1650/ payd as appeareth by reckonings for the composi[ti]on for			
Sedgford lease beside £165 16s 10d that was received for double monyes	683	6	1
/1649/ to Mr Toll for Mr Jegons part unjustly	136	8	0

---

50. See above, p. 77 and under 'Losses in my Husbands Estate', pp. 83–4.

51. William Holly was a substantial manorial tenant in Great Ringstead and Holme.

Debts owing 1650 at our Lady

to my Lady Grey	200	0	0
to little Jack	100	0	0
to my cosen Lewkenour	700	0	0
to Mrs Anne Calthorp[52]	200	0	0
to Mrs Elizabeth Calthorp	300	0	0
/payd/ to John Fisher	150	0	0
/pd £50 & £50/ to Robert Banyard *pd £50, 1651*	100	0	0
/pd 1651/ to Mr Nash	100	0	0
Borrowed of Mrs Jane Grey 9 Aprill 1650	400	0	0
/£2300 payd/ Borrowed of Thomas Patterick 10 July 1650	50	0	0

Debts payd for my sonne Strange [sic] 1650

to my cosen Lewkenour	20	0	0
to Robert Birch	30	0	0
to John Bride	44	0	0
to Robert Banyard	20	0	0

Debts owing at our Lady 1651 & 1652

/1652/ to the Lady Grey	200	0	0
to little Jack	100	0	0
/pd £200 1652/ to my cosen Lewkenour	700	0	0
to Mrs Anne Calthorp	200	0	0
/pd/ to Mrs Elizabeth Calthorp	300	0	0
/payd 1653/ to Mrs Jane Grey	400	0	0
/pd £1950/ to Robert Banyard *pd 1651*	50	0	0
Borrowed of my sonne Spring 17 March 1652	100	0	0

Debts owing at our Lady 1653

/pd/ to my sonne Spring 17 March	100	0	0
to John Le Strange 25 March	100	0	0
Borrowed of Mrs Elizabeth Calthorp jun[io]r Aprill 1	100	0	0
to Mrs Anne Calthorpe Aprill 7	200	0	0
to my cosen Mary Lewkenour April 12	500	0	0
/£1300/ to Mrs Elizabeth Calthorp senior April 19	300	0	0

Debts owing in Aprill 1654

to little Jack at our Lady 1653	100	0	0
to Mr Phillip Calthorp the first of Aprill	200	0	0
to Mrs Anne Calthorp the 6 of Aprill	200	0	0

---

52. Anne and Elizabeth Calthorpe were probably wives of two of the six brothers of Sir James Calthorpe of East Barsham.

to Mrs Elizabeth Calthorpe the 12 of Aprill	200	0	0
to my cosen Lewkenour the 12 of April	500	0	0
to Mr Pepis to pay at Midsomer 1654[53]	50	0	0
to Denham Hunlock[54] to pay at Christmas	50	0	0
Sum	1300	0	0

[*p*]

Debts owing the 20th May 1654

to little Jack at St Michaell	100	0	0
to Mr Phillip Callthorp the first of October	200	0	0
to Mrs Anne Calthorp the 6th of October	200	0	0
to Mrs Elizabeth Calthorp the 12th of October	200	0	0
to my cosen Lewkenour the 12th of October	500	0	0
to Mr Pepis at Midsomer 1654	50	0	0
to Denham Hunlock a weeke after Christmas	50	0	0
to Mr Rant & Mr Francis Rowland first of Decemb[55]	1500	0	0
to Edward Hale the 15 of May[56]	500	0	0
Sum	3300	0	0

A note of the place of payment of these debts above mentioned with the severall uses for them
/place/ Mr John Rant & Mr Francis Rowland to be payd at the Common Dining Room in the Middle Temple

/uses/ first of December for the use of £1500 in 1654	45	0	0
2 of June in 1655	45	0	0
First of December 1655	45	0	0
3 of June 1656 *qv or 2*	45	0	0
2 December in 1656	45	0	0
3 of June in 1657	1545	0	0

/place/ Mr Edward Hales to Mr Willyam Sanders draper upon Ludgate Hill at the Signe of the Falcon

/use/ 15 of November to Mr Hales *1654*	15	0	0
15 May 1655	15	0	0

---

53. There are several references to 'Pepis', 'Pepys'; this may be John Pepys of Ashstead, Surrey, a man with substantial Norfolk connections, NRO, BL/WA1/8/1–2.

54. Merchant of St Clement Danes, London.

55. Creditors based in London, *see* LEST/BN9 and BN10 for the mortgage on Barrett Ringstead, also, Whittle & Griffiths, p. 163. John Rant had significant Norfolk connections, *see* www.nrocat.org.uk.

56. Sir Edward Hales of Tunstall, Kent, 2nd bt, 1626–1684, succeeded to the baronetcy in 1654, lent money to Sir Nicholas Le Strange for the use of his friend Roger L'Estrange, *see* NRO, MR 311, 242X5.

Debts owing after Midsomer 1654

	£	s	d
/25 March/ to little Jack at St Michaell	100	o	o
/1 Aprill/ 1 October to Mr Phillip Calthorp, 1 October	200	o	o
/6 Aprill/ to Mrs Anne Calthorp, 6 October	200	o	o
/12 Aprill/ to Mrs Elizabeth Calthorp, 12 October	200	o	o
/12 Aprill/ to my cosen Mary Lewkenour, 12 October	500	o	o
[15 May] to Mr Hales, 15 November	500	o	o
/2 June/ to Mr John Rant & Mr Francis Rowland, 1 December	1500	o	o
to Denham Hunlock a weeke after Christmas	50	o	o
to Mr Pepis to be payd at Midsomer	50	o	o
Sum by bond[57]	3300	o	o

[p]

Robert Cremers agreement with Sir Hamon Le Strange the 24ᵗʰ May
1654[58]

Sir Hamon Le Strange doth remitt to Robert Cremer for all his
arrearage of rent and fowles for his land forfeited, but for 2 years last
past at St Micheall 1653 he is to pay, and to take up by coppy 5r &
2r holden of the manour of Heacham & 2r holden of the manour of
Sedgford & to pay the rents past for them for 2 yeares due at St Michaell
1653 & to pay the fines for them, & to take a lease for 1000 years of all
his foreited lands (except 5r at Cattgore wich Sr H Le Strange is to have
the residue of his forfeited lands being 17ac 3r is /for 1000 yeares/ leased
to Robert Cremer upon such conditions as are expressed in an indenture
dated May 24 1654 for which he is to pay Sir Hamon Le Strange £34

	£	s	d
/Due from Robert Cremer/ for 2 yeares rent for his forfeited lands at Mich last past 1653 at 7s 8¾d		15	5½
for 2 yeares rent for 5r late Constables 1653		1	o
for 2 yeares rent for of 2r at Stamerden 1653			4
for 2 yeares rent of 2r of Sedgford 1653			4
for 6 rent hennes to Heacham for 2 yeares 1653		4	o
for a rent capon due to Hunston 1653		1	o
For his forfeited lands being 17ac 3r beside 5r at Cattgore reserved to Sir Hamon Le Strange	34	o	o
Sum	35	2	1½

beside the fine of 5r late Constables 2s 9d & the fine of 2r of
Stamerden 6d & for the fine of 2r bond of Sedgford 5d in all 3s 8d
which was payd to the severall baylifes

	£	s	d
/Due to Robert Cremer/ to Robert Cremer for 2ac or 20p of land q169 n.1 which he selleth for 9r at £10 10s 6d the acre	23	13	9

---

57. This entry is followed by ten blank pages.
58. See above, p. 18, and below, p. 84 under 'Losses in my Husbands Estate'.

to him for 5ac 2r of land in 4 pieces q168 n.3 & 4 & 5 & 6 which he
selleth for 6ac at £8 12s the acre: the rent of these lands were 12½d   51 12 0
                                                        Sum   75   5 9
of this sett off with Robert Cremer due for his 2 yeares rents & fines   1   5 9
more sett off for his forfeit lands   34   0 0
more sett off with him for 3ac of land late Robert Overmans q112
n.11 at £10 the acre   30   0 0
payd to Robert Cremer in satisfaction of this agreement the
24 May 1654   10   0 0
                                                        Sum   75   5 9

A note how Willyam Guybon was payd his £256 10s for 21ac of land
& how written[59]
/1648/ 14 of March payd to him & sett off with him in reckonings
then due to him   76 10 0
/1648/ 14 of March payd to Robert Waters of Docking for Willyam
Guybon   40   0 0
/1649/ 22 of Aprill payd to Mr Phillip Browne for Willyam Guybon
beside his use   90   0 0
/1649/ 26 of January payd to my sonne Hamon Le Strange for
Willyam Guybon beside use   50   0 0
                                                        Sum   256 10 0

                    Lands sold by my Husband
sold to Edmond Riches the manour of Fring worth yearly[60]   130   0 0
sold Grint Mill worth yearly   30   0 0
sold Chappell Mill worth yearely   30   0 0
sold Holme Parsonage worth yearely   70   0 0
sold South Linne worth yearely   120   0 0
                                        Sum [by] the yeare 380   0 0

more sold by my husband
sold his revertion of his Irish lands   600   0 0
sold to my father the rents of Runton manor   40   0 0
sold to Willyam Paston the land in South Linne that my father gave
me at his death   880   0 0
            Sum £1520 beside Linne House that was sold for £360

---

59. See above, p. 70.
60. Blomefield & Parkin, *Norfolk*, X, p. 305.

Lands purchased by my Husband
The manour of Heacham as it is letten 1648 for rents & fearmes,

beside £10 which wee did pay for rents of asize to Heacham	252	0	0
the parsonage of Heacham worth yearly	100	0	0
Sum [*by year*] <& £80 the parsonage>	352	0	0

Heacham may be improved £30 a yeare which will make the land
bought as much as the land that was sold *with profitts of court*

Bought of Edmond Cremer Brownes house & close	80	0	0
/1623/ Bought of Mr Reads land in the pasture	325	15	0
/1644/ Bought land of Willyam Guybon	158	15	0
/1645/ Bought of John Hancell an house in Ringsted	50	0	0
/1648/ Bought of Willyam Guybon land cost[61]	256	10	0
/1648/ Bought of Mr Samuel Girling 2a 2r	24	12	0
/1649/ Bought of Thomas Banyard 5 acres a close called London Yardes	68	0	0
Sum	957	17	0

/1633/ more he purchased Westwinch which was settled upon my sonne Hamon Le Strange which cost him beside the assurance	1796	8	2
my husband was left in debt by his fathers executors with mony due to his uncle Roger Le Strange	1500	0	0

he was left neyther household stuffe nor stock & his cheife house
halfe built, and all his fearme houses in such decay so as he hath
built most of them out of the ground
he hath had many chargable sutes and unkinde losses

Losses in my Husbands Estate

lost by adventuring in the East Indies[62]	500	0	0
/1633/ lost by John Creamer the bankrupt[63]	400	0	0
/1638/ lost by Heacham Marsh about[64]	600	0	0
/1639/ lost by in sute for our Irish lands[65]	221	10	0
lost by adventuring in Boston Fennes[66]	500	0	0
payd and spent in sute by the unjust and tirannicall oppression of Mr Toll & other of his faction in Linne concerning the seige[67]	1088	0	0

---

61. See above, pp. 70, 82.

62. With the assistance of Sir Henry Spelman, Sir Hamon secured admittance to the East India Company in 1617, investing in stock worth £600. LEST/Q38, folio 9.

63. See fn. 26, p. 71 for John Cremer.

64. See above, pp. 73, 74.

65. See above, p. 70.

66. See above, p. 70.

67. For several references, see above, pp. 75–91.

recovered by Stileman in an unjust sute being over powered by the
times[68]   385   0   0

                                                               Sum 3694 10   0
beside our greate losse where we were plundered of all our sheepe & corne

Lands and other guifts of Father

Sedgford lease by yeare wth the Parsonage cleare	290	0	0
Sedgeford manour belonging to Stranges by the yeare	110	0	0
South Linne land by the year	120	0	0
Land in Hunston given to my sonne Nicholas Le Strange by the yeare	20	0	0
Holme Parsonage given to my sonne Hamon Le Strange by yeare	70	0	0

                                                               Sum   610   0   0

Lands given me at South Linne sold for	880	0	0
Runton Mannor sold for	40	0	0
Lands in Holme given to my sonne Hamon Le Strange sold for	1000	0	0
given to my daughter Jane Le Strange	100	0	0
given to my daughter Elizabeth Le Strange	100	0	0
given to my sonne Roger Le Strange	100	0	0
given to my selfe	50	0	0

                                                               Sum 2270   0   0
given to my chilldren sheepe to 4 of them 140, besides some plate &
beding   116 16   0

[p][69]

Household stuff given to me by my father at his death as they were	£	s	d
prised a greene carpet garded with velvet, a needle worke cupbord carpet, 6 needle worke cushions	6	13	4
/in his Owne Chamber/ a bed, beding and tester	3	0	0
a little table, an olde carpet, a payre of tongs, a payre of dogge irons & an old chayer		8	0
/in the Hall Chamber/ a downe bed, 2 bolsters, a payre of pillows, a payre of blanketts, a covering of Arras, a bedsted wth tester & curtaynes	10	0	0
a payre of andirons & a payre of tonges		8	0
the hangings of Darnix not prised			
/in the little Parlour/ a downe bed, a bolster, a payre of pillows, a payre of blanketts, a rugge, an Arras covering, a bedstead, a tester of flowered damask & an old taffeta curtaynes	10	0	0
a cupbord with a carpett of pentad,[70] a chayer & a payre of dog irons		10	0

---

68. See above, p. 81.

69. List of church repairs follows, but not transcribed.

70. Pintado, decorative Indian cotton, used as table and cupboard cloths, *see* Whittle &
Griffiths, p. 121.

hangings of say	1	10	0
/in the Paynted Chamber/ a bed, a bolster, a payre of pillows, a payre of blanketts, a tapestry covering an olde bedsted with a tester, a livery cupbord with an olde Turkey worke carpett	5	0	0
/in the Dining Room/ a drawing table, a livery cupbord with 2 olde carpetts	2	10	0
2 chayers, 9 buffett stools, 3 formes & 5 olde cushions	2	0	0
an iron cradle, a fyer pan, a payre of tonges & a fyer forke		13	0
/in the Parlour Chamber/ a bed, a bolster and tapistry covering, and olde bedsted & a tester	6	13	0
/in the Brewhouse/ the copper with the mashphatt, the gilephatt[71] & the cooler	10	0	0
the copper in the wash house	1	10	0
Sum	60	16	0
/Plate/ to myself a diamond ring not in the inventory	6	0	0
a mawdlin cup	2	0	0
3 gilt bowles with a cover	12	0	0
to my sonne Nicholas a gilt salt	6	0	0
& a bason & ewer	20	0	0
Sum	46	0	0
& a horse for my husband	10	0	0

---

71. A mash vat: mash is malt plus hot water from which the wort is formed; a gyle vat or tub held the fermenting wort. Yaxley, *Glossary*, pp. 23, 95, 130.

The Sheep Accounts of Alice Le Strange,
1617–1655

Acco[unt]s of Flocks & Foldcourses by the Lady L'estrange for divers yeares[72]
Acco[unt]s of her sonns charges and expenses at Eaton and Cambridge
Acco[unt]s of the charges & profitts of a ship in divers voyages
Inventory of the furniture in Hunstanton anno 1632

[The Children's Sheep Accounts 1618–27][73]

[p][74]	[Nicholas's account 1618–27][75]	£	s	d
[1618]	Page delivered at Midsomer 1618: 13 wether hogges; 20 ewe hogges; of these he had 4 stone 4lb of wooll[76]			
	Received beside 10s for his wooll at Sedgford for the 4 stone 4lb of wooll, for 33 hogges 52s 7d, in all[77]	3	2	7
	Received for 13 wether hogges	4	6	8
	Sum	7	9	3

---

72. The main sheep accounts are found in the second book in LEST/P10. The titles on the cover have been included to show the links between Alice's activities and what she considered appropriate to be included with her sheep accounts. For those doubtful about foldcourses, see above, pp. 37–9.

73. As explained, the sheep accounts do not appear here in the original order; they have been placed chronologically and begin with the children's accounts, see above, pp. 59–60.

74. The folios are not numbered, but the change of page is marked in the LH margin.

75. The LH margin has been narrowed and larger entries have been moved to the LH side of the central text. When absent from the LH margin, the year has been inserted to provide a firm chronology and structure to the accounts. In the original document, sometimes the date has been inserted for this purpose, sometimes not; any resulting repetitions have been retained. The £ s d are as in the account.

76. The long lists of entries for sheep charged, delivered and brought to the clipping has been consolidated with the entries running on. The end of each original entry is marked with a semi-colon.

77. The original entries are retained where money sums exist in the RH columns.

Midsomer 1618 I bought for him 29 wether lambes and 6 ewe   7   0   0
lambes; for greasing his 35 lambes   2   8
for clipping   11

          Sum   7   3   7

Delivered to Page at Midsomer 1618: 20 ewes of one sheare, 29
wether lambes, 6 ewe lambes. Sum 55[78]

1619   Page brought to the clipping at Midsomer: 19 ewes of 2 sheare; 17
lambes; 6 ewe hogges; 27 wether hogges.
Sum beside lambes 52

[p]   [top third of page illegible][79] for 14 lambes   2   0   0
for 20 ewes of 2 sheare   6   0   0

          Sum   11   7   6
so Nicholas oweth 2s

Delivered to Page at Midsomer 1619: 46 ewes; 6 ewe hogges –
one was a wether; 17 of his owne lambes; <23> *22* lambes that
were bought. Sum 91

Received for 2 ewes skinn and 2 hogge skinns 20d which went
toward the clipping. One of the 20 ewes of 2 sheare one did stray
out of the close before Page had them

[1620]   Page delivered at Midsomer 1620: 48 ewes; a 2 sheare wether; 20
ewe hogges; 14 wether hogges; 3 rixey hogges; 18 lambes; 16 ewes
and 5 lambes came to be clipped from Sedgford. Sum <86> *96*
[102][80] beside lambes, of these he had 4 stone and 8lb of wooll
which he *is to allow* for the joycement

[p]   [top third of page illegible] Received for <an ewe> *a wether
skinn* and 8 lamb skinns to goe towards the joyce

[1621]   Page delivered at the clipping 1621: 85 ewes; 62 lambes; 21
wethers whereof 5 proved rixseyes. Sum beside lambes 106, of
these he had 9 stone 5lb of wooll, of these were croned 5 ewes;
5 rixseyes delivered to Crisp; 19 lambes sent to the fayer; a fatt
lamb sold. Crisp delivered the 3 rixseyes home and the wether dyed

---

78. 'sums' of sheep often include lambs, sometimes not.
79. Damage and fading in these early accounts has caused illegible and missing entries.
80. Totals are not always accurate, or what they seem. When the figures differ markedly,
they usually include a shepherd's allowance, which does not appear in Alice's 'sum'.

	£	s	d
/This mony was allowed for joyce /			
Received for 9 stone 5lb of wooll at 8s	3	14	4
Received for 19 pooke lambes	1	4	6½
Received for a fatt lamb		3	0
for 3 rixseyes		12	0
Received for 5 crones		13	4
Sum	6	7	2½

1621 Page his charge at Midsomer: 80 ewes, 16 wethers 2 were
[p] rixseyes, 20 wether lambes, 22 ewe lambes. Sum 138

1622 /Page/ brought to the clipping at Midsomer: 14 wethers *of* 2
sheare; 2 rixseyes of 2 sheare; 15 wether shorlins; 4 rixsey shorlins;
79 ewes and 33 ewe lambes; 28 wether lambes; 20 ewe shorlins.
Sum beside lambes 114 [*134*]. Morte skinns he brought home:
one ewe, 2 ewe hoggs, one wether hogge. Sum 4 mortes, so he
is right.
Of the 114 sheepe he had 12 stone of wooll sold at [?]

/Crisp/ delivered of the 5 rixseyes all and had them againe in
charge to Page

Taken away from Barrett Ringsted: 13 wethers of 2 sheare to
Ringsted; a wether of 2 sheare into the close that is like to dye; 2
rixseyes of 2 sheare to Ringsted; 4 rixsey shorlins to Ringsted; 4
crones to sell; 5 ewe pookes to the fayer; 8 wether pookes to the fayer

/Barkers/ charge at Midsomer 1622: 75 ewes; 20 ewe hoggs; <20
wether lambes> *15 wether shorlins*; 28 ewe lambes. Sum 118 [*138*]

[*Sedgeford North ground*] /Corners/ charge at Midsomer 1622: 15
wether shorlins; 20 wether lambes. Sum 35

[*Barrett Ringstead*] /Page/ his charge at Midsome[r] 1622: 13
wethers of 2 sheare; 2 rixseyes of 2 sheare; 4 rixsey shorlins; 5
rixseys of 3 sheare. Sum 24

[*Barrett Ringstead*] /Barker/ brought to the clipping at Midsomer
1622: 70 mother ewes, skinnes 2; 20 ewes of 2 sheare, 13 wethers
of 2 sheare [*skins*] 2; 27 ewe shorlings [*skins*] 1; 17 wether lambes;
19 ewe lambes; 21 small lambes

[p] Sum beside lambes 133 [*130*]. Barker delivered 5 skinnes, so he is
right, of these sheep he hath 11 stone & 3lb of wooll sold toward
the joyce

[*1623*]   /*Sheepe*/ taken from Barker at Midsomer 1623: 20 crones; 17
wether lambes to Corner; 21 small lambes sold; 1 wether of 2
sheare dyed dizy. Sum beside lambes 21

1623   /*Corner*/ brought to the clipping at Midsomer 14 wether
shorlinges and 6 skinnes. So he is right, of these he had 1 stone
9lb of wooll sold with the other
/*Sheep*/ taken from Corner at Midsomer 1623: 14 wether
shorlinges to Crisp

1623   /*Page*/ brought to the clipping at Midsomer: 12 wether of 3 sheare
& a skinne; 11 rixseys sold. So he is right, of these he had [?]
/*Sheepe*/ taken from Page at Midsomer 1623 when he delivered
the charge to Crisp. 11 rixeseys sold

/*Barkers*/ charge at Midsomer 1623: 73 mother ewes, 27 ewe
shorlings; 39 ewe shorlings that were Leveretts; 12 wethers of 2
sheare; 19 ewe lambes; a lambe from Bircham an ewe lambe.
Sum 171

/*Corners*/ charge at Midsomer 1623: 17 wether lambes from
Bircham. Sum 17

[*Ringstead South flock*] /*Crisps*/ charge at Midsomer 1623: 12
wethers of 3 sheare; 14 wether shorlings from Corner. Sum 26

[*p*]   Sold to Nicholas his sheep this yeare 20 crones; 21 small lambes;
11 rixseyes. With this mony was bought 39 ewe shorlings that
were Leveretts, 18 Bircham lambs bought also. So the flocks
being sett in 1623 the whole sum of Nicholas his sheepe is 214

1624   /*Barker*/ brought to the clipping at Midsomer: 65 mother ewes,
8 skinnes[81] /*19 croned*/;[82] 26 ewes of 2 sheare, 1 [*skin*]; 38 Leverett
ewes of 2 sheare, 1 [*skins*]; 17 ewe shorlins, 2 [*skins*]; 1 ewe shorlin
of Bircham; 11 wethers of 3 sheare, 1 [*skin*]; 15 wether lambes; 15
ewe lambes; 3 fatt lambes; 22 pooke lambes. Sum 138 [*158*] sheep
and 13 skinns, so he is right, of these 11½ stone of wooll which
with the skinnes is allowed for joyce

---

81. Alice sometimes inserted a column on the RH side of the central text recording skins
and sheep lost; these appear after the relevant entry in the consolidated accounts.

82. Alice occasionally used the RH margins to enter details of crones, morts and sold. To
avoid confusion with income and expenditure these have been moved to the central text
after the relevant entry.

1624   [*Sedgeford North ground*] /*Lennard*/ brought to the clipping at
Midsomer 17 wether shorlins, of these 1½ st of wooll for joyce

1624   /*Crisp*/ brought to the clipping at Midsomer: sold 12 wethers of 3
sheare, 12 wethers of 2 sheare skinnes 2, so he is right, of these 2
stone for joyce

		£	s	d
1624	/*solde*/ for 19 crones	2	18	o
	for 12 wethers of 3 sheare	4	16	o
	for 3 fatt lambes		9	o
	for 22 pookes	1	17	8
	Sum	10	o	8
	/*bought*/ for these 22 ewes	5	o	o
	11 ewes	3	13	4
	4 ewes	1	8	o

[*p*]   Sum, £10 1s 4d, so he oweth 8d

[*Barrett Ringstead*] /*Pypers*/ charge at Midsomer 1624: 110 mother
ewes; 22 ewes bought of Martin Smith; 11 ewes bought of Gage;
4 ewes bought of Gregory Willis; 18 ewe shorlins; 11 wethers of 3
sheare; 15 wether lambes; 15 ewe lambes. Sum 186 [*206*]

Lennards charge at Midsomer 1624: 17 wether shorlins

/*Crispes*/ charge at Midsomer 1624: 12 wethers of 2 sheare

The whole summe of Nicholas his sheep the flocks being sett at
Midsomer 1624 is 215

1625   /*Pyper*/ brought to the clipping at Midsomer: 140 mother ewes /*5
morts, 23 croned*/; 13 ewe shorlins /*2 morts*/; wether of 3 sheare /*11
sold*/; 11 wether shorlins /*4 morts*/. Sum 164 and 11 mortes and 11
wethers sold for £4 9s, so he is right, of these 164 sheep he had 12
stone of wooll which with the skinnes is allowed for joyce
/*Lambes 106*/ 24 store ewe lambes; 20 store wether lambes; 4 fatt
lambes sold; 58 pooke lambes sold

[*p*]   /*Lennard*/ brought to the clipping at Midsomer 1625: 15 wethers
of 2 sheare; 2 wethers sold of 2 sheare for 17s. Sum 17, wooll 2 stone for joyce

/*Crisp*/ delivered at Midsomer 1625 [*illegible*] wethers of 3 sheare;
3 rixeyes that went for wethers

	£	s	d
1625 /sold/ 13 wethers for	5	16	0
/Crisps/ 3 rixseyes for		13	6
58 pooke lambes for	4	1	0
4 fatt lambes for		13	4
23 crones	3	12	10
/Lennard/ 5 rixseyes	1	2	6

Sum <£14 15s 8d> *£15 18s 2d*
of this he ought [*owed*] 8d the last year

/Pypers/ charge at Midsomer 1625: 117 mother ewes; 13 ewe shorlins; 27 ewe lambes; 11 wethers of 2 sheare; 19 wether lambes; 1 ramme lambe. Sum 188

/Lennards/ charge at Midsomer 1625: 10 wethers of 2 sheare

/Crisps/ charge at Midsomer 1625: 9 wethers of 3 sheare

The whole summe of Nicholas his sheep the flocks being sett at Midsomer 1625 is 207

1626 /Pyper/ brought to the clipping at Midsomer: 126 mother ewes /4 morts, 20 croned/; 26 ewe shorlins /1 mort/; 11 wethers of 3 sheare; 16 wether shorlins /3 morts/; a ramm shorlin; 29 store ewe lambes; 20 store wether lambes; 8 fatt lambes; 49 pooke lambes. Sum of sheep, beside lambes, is 180 and 8 skinnes

[*p*] Sheepe taken from Pyper 1626

	£	s	d
20 crones sold for	3	6	8
49 pookes sold for	4	6	10
8 fatt lambes sold for	1	4	0
Sum	8	17	6

/Lennard/ delivered to the clipping at Midsomer 1626: 10 wethers of 3 sheare

/Crisp/ delivered at Midsomer 1626: 8 wethers of 3 sheare one

	£	s	d
sold for		9	7
Due to Nicholas the last yeare	15	17	6

Due to him for a wether crones and lambes sold this yeare £9 7s 1d out of which I payd 4s 4d for a wether hogge, so there resteth

	£	s	d
due to him	9	2	9
Sum	25	0	3

/Pypers/ charge at Midsomer 1626: <106> *26* ewe shorlins /4 morts/; 106 mother ewes /12 morts, 16 croned/; 29 ewe lambes

/3 morts/; 17 wether shorlins whereof one bought /1 mort/; 20
wether lambes 2 were rams /2 morts/; 1 ramm shorlin. Sum 199

/Crispes/ charge at Midsomer 1626: 8 wethers of 4 sheare /1 mort/;
10 wethers of 3 sheare from Lennard; 11 wethers of 3 sheare from Pyper

The whole summe of Nicholas his sheep when the flocks were
sett at Midsomer 1626 is 208

[1627]   /Pyper/ brought to the clipping at Midsomer 1627: <116> *117*
mother ewes / <16> *15* morts, 1 sold, 16 croned/; 26 ewe shorlins
/3 morts/, <1 dizy>; 16 wether shorlins /2 morts/;

178   2 ramm shorlins; 16 wethers of 2 sheare /1 mort/; 1 ramm
<shorlin> *of 2 sheare*; 33 store ewe lambes; 24 store wether
lambes; 44 lambes to sell wherof 39 pookes. Sum 178 [besides
lambes] and 21 skinns, so he is right

[p]	/taken/ from Pyper at Midsomer 1627	£	s	d
	16 crones wherof one dyed and 15 sold for	2	12	6
	One gill ewe sold for		7	6
	5 lambes sold		16	8
	39 pooke lambes sold for	3	11	6
	one dizy ewe shorling worth nothing			
	/Taken from Crisp/ 7 wethers sold for	2	16	0
	3 rixseys sold for		12	0
	Sum	10	16	2

which being added to £25 and 3d which was due to Nicholas the
last yeare and there is now due to him £35 16s 5d

1627   /Crisp/ brought to the clipping at Midsomer: 18 wethers of 4
sheare; /sold/ 7 wethers of 3 sheare /1 mort/; /sold/ 3 rixseyes. Sum
28 and one skinne so he is right

Nicholas sold all his sheep to his father at these rates following:

		£	s	d
/in Pypers charge/ 100 ewes at 7s		42	0	0
25 ewe shorlins at 6s		7	10	0
3 rammes			15	0
57 store lambes		10	18	6
/Crisps flock/ 18 wether at 18s		7	4	0
16 wethers of 2 sheare from Pyper at 7s		5	12	0
16 wether shorlins at 6s 8d from Pyper		5	6	8
Sum £79 6s 2d which being added to the £35 16s 5d there is due		79	6	2

to Nicholas £115 2s 7d wherof there is in the sum of £300,
£20 1s 6d written

[*p*]   [*Hamon's account 1619–27*] [*top third of page illegible*][83]

[*1619*]   [*Barrett Ringstead*] Delivered to Page at Midsomer 1619: 6 ewe
hogges; one ewe and 2 lambes. Sum 9
Received for an ewe skinn 5d which went toward to the clipping

[*1620*]   Page delivered at Midsomer 1620: 6 ewes; 2 ewe hogges; 2
lambes; 10 ewes and 5 lambes came to be clipped from Sedgford.
Sum beside lambes 18, of these he had 4½lb of wooll which
goeth for the joycement

Page his charge at Midsomer 1620: 18 ewes; 7 lambes whereof 3
wether lambes; 40 ewes given him by his grandfather Stubbe.
Sum 65. Received for an ewe skinn and 4 lamb skinns

1621   Page delivered at Midsomer: 57 ewes; 42 lambes; one rixsey.
[*p*]   Sum 58 [*besides lambes*] so he wanteth 2 wethers which Page must
allow of these, 5 stone of wooll; of these sheepe croned; 6 croned
ewes; a rixsey sent to Crisp; 7 lambes sent to the fayer, <of the
sheep that was sent to Crisp the last yeare the wether died and
the 2 rixseys proved rams and were delivered to Page – the[*y*]
were Rogers>

Page his charge at Midsomer 1621: 51 ewes; 2 wethers which Page
must allow, he allowed 2 ewes; 18 ewe lambes; 17 wether lambes
– 3 were rixseys and a ramm. Sum 88

	£	s	d
/For joyse/ Received for 5 stone of wooll	2	0	0
Received for 6 crones		16	0
Received for 7 pooke lambes		9	0
Sum	3	5	½

[*1622*]   /Page/ delivered at Midsomer 1622: 53 ewes; 22 wether lambes
and ewe lambes 23; 16 ewe shorlins; 13 wether shorlins; 3 rixsey
shorlins; a ram shorlin. Sum beside lambes 86, he brought 2 ewe
hogge skins, so he is right, of these 86 sheepe he had 6 stone and
2lb of wooll sold at [?]

/Crisp/ had a rixsey and he brought home the skinne

Sheep taken out of the flock: 4 ewes croned; one like to dye
in the close; <19> *17* wether <shorlins> *lambes* to Corner;

---

83. Two blank pages after the previous entry.

3 rixsey shorlins to Ringsted; <1 ram shorlin to Ringsted>,
<6> *5* wether pookes to the fayer; 4 ewe pookes to the fayer.
Sum beside lambes 22

[p] [*Barrett Ringstead*] /Barkers/ charge at Midsomer 1622: 13 wether
shorlins and a ram shorlin; 48 ewes; 16 ewe shorlins; 13 were
wethers; 18 ewe lambes
/of the 16 ewe shorlins, 9 were wethers, & 4 rams/

[*Sedgeford North ground*] /Corners/ charge at Midsomer 1622:
<13 wether shorlins> 17 wether lambes. Sum 30

/Page/ his charge at Midsomer 1622: 3 rixsey shorlins, a ram
shorlin. Sum 30

1623 /Page/ brought to the clipping at Midsomer: 3 rixseys that after
were sold

1623 /Corner/ brought to the clipping at Midsomer: 17 wether
shorlings which he delivered to Crisp, of these 13lb of wooll

1623 /Barker/ brought to the clipping at Midsomer: 47 ewes for store,
1 skinne; 3 ewes of 2 sheare; 22 wethers of 2 sheare; 5 ramms; 15
ewe shorlings, 3 [*skins*]. Sum 92 and 4 skinnes, so he is right.
/lambes 30 and small lambes 27/
/Sheep/ taken from Barker at Midsomer 1623: 16 ewes croned
sold; 22 wethers of 2 sheare to Crisp; 18 wether lambes to
Corner; 27 small lambes sold. Sum beside lambes, of the 92
sheep, he had 7 stone and 10lb of wooll which with the rest was
sold toward the joyce

[*Ringstead South flock*] /Crisps/ charge at Midsomer 1623: 22
wethers of 2 sheare from Barker; 17 wether shorlings from
Corner. Sum 39

/Corners/ charge at Midsomer 1623: 18 wether lambes from
Barker. Sum 18

/Barkers/ charge at Midsomer 1623: 31 mother ewes; 18 ewe
shorlinges and 3 sheare; 27 ewe shorlinges that were Leveretts; 12
ewe lambes; 5 rammes. Sum 93

[p] The 16 crones that were sold and 3 rixseys and 27 small lambes
all these being sold I bought with that mony 27 ewe shorlings

that were Leveretts. So the whole sum of Hamons sheep when
the flocks were sett at Midsomer 1623 is 150

1624   /*Barker*/ brought to the clipping at Midsomer: 31 mother ewes
/*11 crones*/; 18 ewes of 2 sheare; 26 Leverett ewes of 2 sheare, 1
skinne; 11 ewe shorlins; 5 rammes; 18 ewe lambes; 18 wether
lambes; one fatt lambe; 26 pooke lambes. Summ 91 sheepe, of
these 7 stone of wooll for joyce

1624   /*Lennard*/ brought to the clipping at Midsomer 12 wether
shorlins and 6 skinnes; of these a stone of wooll for joyce

1624   /*Crisp*/ brought to the clipping at Midsomer: 22 wethers of 3
sheare, 1 skinne; 16 wethers of 2 sheare, 1 skinn. Sum 38, of these
5 stone of wooll for joyce

/*Sold of*/ Hamons for the yeare 1624	£	s	d
11 crones	1	13	0
1 fatt lambe		3	0
26 pookes	2	4	6
Sum £4 0s 6d to buy sheep the next yeare			

[p]   [*Barrett Ringstead*] /*Pypers*/ charge at Midsomer 1624: 64 mother
ewes; 11 ewe shorlins; 18 ewe lambes; 18 wether lambes; 5 rammes. Sum 116

/*Lennards*/ charge at Midsomer 1624: 12 wether shorlins

/*Crispes*/ charge at Midsomer 1624: 22 wethers of 3 sheare; 16
wethers of 2 sheare

So the whole summ of Hamons sheep at Midsomer 1624 is 146

[*1625*]   /*Pyper*/ brought to the clipping at Midsomer 1625: 74 mother
ewes /*1 mort, 10 croned*/; 5 rammes; 14 ewe shorlins /*4 morts*/;
14 wether shorlins /*4 morts*/; 12 ewe lambes; 9 wether lambes;
2 ramme lambes; 36 pooke lambes sold. Sum 107 sheepe and 9
skinnes, so he is right croned of these 10, so remayne 97, wooll 10
stone for joyce

/*Lennard*/ brought to the clipping at Midsomer 1625: 9 wethers of
2 sheare /*3 sold*/. So he is right of these a stone of wooll for joyce

/*Crisp*/ brought to the clipping at Midsomer 1625: 38 wethers
<Pypers charge at Midsomer 1625>

/*Sold of*/ Hamones at Midsomer 1625

3 wethers of 2 sheare		1	6	0
3 rixseys that went for wether of Lennard			13	6
10 crones sold for		1	11	8
36 pooke lambes for		2	10	6
	Sum	6	1	8

which with the £4 0s 6d that remayned last yeare is £10 2s 2d

[*p*] /*Bought*/ for Hamon at Midsomer 1625 for 29 ewes and a lambe. So there remayneth of the £10 2s 2d, £2 18s 2d to buy sheepe the next yeare   7   4   0

/*Pypers*/ charge at Midsomer 1625: 64 mother ewes; 29 ewes that were bought; 13 ewe lambes wherof one bought; 5 rammes; 14 ewe shorlins; 9 wether lambes; 2 ramm lambes; 14 wethers of 2 sheare. Sum 130

/*Lennards*/ charge at Midsomer 1625: 6 wethers of 2 sheare

/*Crisps*/ charge at Midsomer 1625: 22 wethers of 4 sheare; 16 wethers of 3 sheare. Sum 38

So the whole summe of Hamons sheepe the flocks being sett at Midsomer 1625 is 174

[*1626*] /*Pyper*/ brought to the clipping at Midsomer 1626: 105 mother ewes /*2 morts, 23 crones*/; 13 ewe shorlins; ramm lambes nll /*2 morts*/; 14 wethers of 3 sheare; 9 wether shorlins; 5 rammes; 18 store ewe lambes; 26 store wether lambes; one fatt lambe; 47 pooke lambes. Sum 126 [*146*] and 4 skinnes

/*Sheep*/ taken from Pyper 1626

		£	s	d
14 wethers of 3 sheare to Crisp				
23 crones sold for		3	16	8
A fatt lamb sold for			3	0
47 pooke lambes sold for		4	6	2
	Sum	8	5	10

[*p*] [*top third of page torn off*]
13 ewe shorlins /*4 morts*/; 18 ewe lambes /*2 morts*/; 9 wether shorlins; 26 wether lambes /*4 morts*/; 5 rammes. Sum 133[84]

/*Crisps*/ charge at Midsomer 1626: 4 wethers of 4 sheare;

---

84. Several entries are missing which is reflected in the sum.

14 wethers of 3 sheare from Pyper; 6 wethers of 3 sheare from Lennard. Sum 24.

The whole summe of Hamons sheep at Midsomer 1626 the flocks being sett is 157

[*1627*] /*Pyper*/ brought to the clipping at Midsomer 1627: 82 mother ewes /*13 morts, 10 croned*/; 16 ewe shorlins /*2 morts*/; 5 rammes;

114 9 wethers of 2 sheare; 22 wether shorlins /*4 morts*/; 35 store lambes; 35 lambes to sell wherof 30 pookes. Sum 114 [*134*] and 19 skinnes, so he is right

		£	s	d
/*Crisp*/ brought to the clipping at Midsomer 1627: 16 wethers of 4 sheare & /*8 sold*/				
/*Sold from Pyper*/ 23 crones sold for		1	15	0
5 lambes sold for			16	0
30 pooke lambes sold for		2	15	0
8 wethers from Crisp sold		3	4	0
Sum £8 10s which being added to £27 9s 10d which was due to Hamon the last yeare and it maketh £35 19s 10d of this I payd Hamon £30 so rest due to him £5 19s 10d[85]		8	10	0

[*p*] [*Roger's Account 1618–27*] [*top third of page illegible*] £ s d
[*1618*] [*illegible*] given him by his grandfather

		£	s	d
	Sum	1	9	9
for washing and clipping the 20 ewes [*faded figures*]				
for 7 lambes		1	8	4
for greasing of his 23 lambes [*faded figures*]				

Sum £1 10s 5d, so he oweth 8d

[*Barrett Ringstead*] Delivered to Page at Midsomer 1618: 20 ewes; 23 lambes. Sum 43

[*1619*] Page brought to the clipping at Midsomer 1619: 20 ewes and <18> *17* lambes; 21 ewe hogges; one wether hogge and a ram hogge. Sum 43, beside lambes

Delivered to Page at Midsomer: 21 ewes wherof one he has for his wether hogge; 21 ewe hogges one was a wether; a ramm hogge; 17 lambes of his owne; 1 lambe given him by his grandfather Stubbe. Sum 61

---

85. This entry is followed by 2 blank pages and 'A note of such sheep as the tenants of South Flock of Ringsted' and 2 more blank pages. For the note, see below, p. 191.

[p] Received for 4 ewes skins and 2 hogge skins 2s 6d which went toward the clipping

[1620] Delivered to Page at Midsomer [*top third of page illegible*]

Page his charge at Midsomer 1620: 37 ewes; 9 ewe hogges; a ramm hogge; a ramm of 2 sheare; 21 lambes wherof one wether lamb and 3 ram lambes; 40 ewes given him by his grandfather Stubbe. Sum 113
Received for 7 lamb skinns to goe towards the joyce /ewe lambes all but one wether lamb/

[1621] Page delivered to the clipping 1621: 97 ewes; 67 lambes; 2 ramms; 3 hogge ramms; 4 wethers. Sum beside lambes 106, of these he had 9 stone of wooll

[p] /Abated/ of these croned 11 ewes; sent to the fayer 8 pooke lambes; 23 *wether* lambes to Corner; 4 lambes sold; of the sheepe that Crisp had in charge the last yeare the wether dyed and the 2 rixseyes proved ramms and were brought to Page

Page his charge at Midsomer 1621: 86 ewes; 22 ewes that were Janes; 4 wethers; 2 ramms; 3 ramm shorlins, 2 were rixseyes; 2 ramms from Crisp; 30 ewe lambes; 7 ewe lambes that were Janes; a wether lamb; a rixsey lamb. Sum 158

	£	s	d
/For joyce/ Received for 9 stone of wooll at 8s	3	12	0
Received for 11 crones	1	9	4
Received for 8 pooke lambes		10	4
Received for 4 lambes		12	0
Sum	6	3	8

[1622] /Page/ brought to the clipping at Midsomer 1622: 41 [*of*] 3 sheare wethers; a wether shorlin; 5 ramms; 3 rixseyes; 105 ewes; 55 wether lambes and 44 ewe lambs; 33 ewe hoggs. Sum beside lambes 131 [*188*][86]
He brought 3 ewe skins and 4 ewe hogge skins, so he is right, he had of these 131 sheepe 12 stone and 4lb wooll sold for [?]

/Corner/ brought to the clipping 22 wether shorlins and a skinne, of the 22 he had 2 stone 2lb of wooll

---

86. Alice seems to have missed the 33 ewe hogs at the end; a shepherd's allowance is not included in the sum.

[p]   Sheepe taken out of the number: 39 wether lambes to Corner; 21
crone ewes; one ewe in the close that will dye; 2 dizy ewe hoggs;
4 wethers of 3 sheare to Ringsted; 5 rams to Ringsted; 3 rixseyes
to Ringsted; 26 pooke lambes to the fayer
Sum beside lambes 36

[Barrett Ringstead] /Barkers/ charge at Midsomer 1622: 1 wether
shorlin; 83 ewes; 5 ramms; 34 ewe lambes; 31 ewe shorlins
Sum 134 [154]

[Sedgeford North ground] /Corners/ charge at Midsomer 1622: 22
wether shorlins; 39 wether lambes < 1 wether shorlin>. Sum 61

/Page/ his charge at Midsomer 1622: 4 wethers of 3 sheare; <5
rams>; 3 rixseyes. Sum 7

1623   /Barker/ brought to the clipping at Midsomer: <74> *77* mother
ewes, skinnes 2, lost 4; 31 ewes of 2 sheare; 32 ewe shorlinges,
[skinnes] 2; wether shorlin; 4 rammes, [skinn] 1. /48 lambes and 42
small lambes/
Sum 144 and 6 skinnes, so he hath lost 4 ewes that he must
make good, of these he had 10 stone 10lb of wooll

1623   /Corner/ delivered to the clipping at Midsomer: 21 wethers of 2
sheare, skinnes 1; 29 wether shorlinges, 10 [skins]
Sum 50 and 11 skinns so he is right of these he had 4 stone and a
halfe of wooll which was sold with the rest toward the joyce

/Sheep/ taken from Barker at Midsomer 1623: 14 ewes croned; 19
wether lambes <from>*to* Corner; 42 small lambes sold. Sum
[33] beside lambe

/Sheep/ taken from Corner at Midsomer 1623: 29 wether
shorlinges to Crisp. Sum 29

1623   /Page/ brought to the clipping at Midsomer: 3 rixseyes afterward
sold; 3 wethers of 4 sheare and a skinne, so he is right
[p]   /Sheep/ taken from Page – 3 rixseyes sold

/Barkers/ charge at Midsomer 1623: 98 mother ewes; 32 ewe
shorlins; 10 ewe shorlings of Leveretts; 4 ramms; 29 ewe lambes.
Sum 153 [173]

/Corners/ charge at Midsomer 1623: 21 wethers of 2 sheare; 19
wether lambes from Barker. Sum 40

/Crisps/ charge at Midsomer 1623: 3 wethers of 4 sheare; 29 wether shorlings from Corner; 17 wether shorlings of Leveretts; 6 rixsey shorlings of Leveretts. Sum 55

I did sell 3 rixseyes, 14 crones and 42 small lambes for which Roger had 27 ewe shorlings and 6 rixseyes of Leveretts sheepe. So the whole sum of Rogers sheepe when the flocks were sett at Midsomer 1623 is 268

1624 /Barker/ brought to the clipping at Midsomer: 91 mother ewes, skinnes 7, /19 croned/; 29 ewes of 2 sheare, [skins] 3; 39 Leverett ewes of 2 sheare, [skin] 1; 26 ewe shorlins, [skins] 3; 4 rammes; 25 ewe lambes; 26 wether lambes; 6 fatt lambes sold; 28 pooke lambes sold. Sum 139 [159] sheep and 14 skinnes of these 12½ stone of wooll for joyce

1624 [Sedgeford North ground] /Lennard/ brought to the clipping at Midsomer: 21 wethers of 3 sheare; 16 wether shorlins and 3 skinnes. Sum 37 sheep and 3 skinnes of these 3 stone of wooll
[p] for joyce

1624 /Crisp/ brought to the clipping at Midsomer: sold 3 wethers of 4 sheare skinnes; 29 wethers of 2 sheare; 17 wethers of 2 sheare of Leveretts; 1 rixsey and 5 skinnes. Sum 47 sheep and 5 skinnes, of these 2½ stone for joyce

/sold/ of Rogers for the yeare 1624	£	s	d
3 wethers of 4 sheare	1	4	0
19 crones	2	17	0
6 fatt lambes		18	0
28 pooke lambes	2	8	0
Sum £7 7s bought with this 21 ewes	7	7	0

/Pypers/ charge at Midsomer 1624: 110 mother ewes; 21 ewes bought of Gregory Willis; 26 ewe shorlins; 29 ewe lambes; 4 ramms; 26 wether lambes. Sum 192 [216]

/Lennards/ charge at Midsomer 1624: 21 wethers of 3 sheare; 19 wether shorlins. Sum 37

/Crispes/ charge at Midsomer 1624: 29 wethers of 2 sheare; 17 Leverett wethers of 2 sheare; 1 rixsey of 2 sheare. Sum 47.

So the whole sum of Rogers sheepe the flocks being sett at Midsomer 1624 is <236> 256

[*1625*]   /*Pyper*/ brought to the clipping at Midsomer 1625: 131 mother
ewes /*6 morts, 30 croned*/; 4 rammes; 22 ewe shorlins /*3 morts*/;
17 wether shorlins /*9 morts*/; 13 ewe lambes; 15 wether lambes; 3
ramm lambes; 10 fatt lambes sold; 60 pooke lambes sold.

101   Sum 174 sheepe and 18 skinnes, so he is right, of these croned
[*p*]   30 of these 13 stone of wooll with the skinnes for joyce

1625   /*Lennard*/ brought to the clipping at Midsomer: 10 wethers of 4
sheare /*11 sold*/; 15 wethers of 2 sheare. Sum <35> *25* and 11 solde
and one skinne, so he is right, of these 3 stone of wooll
for joyce

1625   /*Crisp*/ brought to the clipping at Midsomer: 42 wethers of 3
sheare /*4 morts*/; rixsey /*1 mort*/. Sum 42 sheep and 5 skinns

	£	s	d
/*Sold*/ of Rogers at Midsomer 1625			
for 11 wethers from Lennard	4	18	0
for 4 rixseys from Lennard		18	0
for 8 rixseys from Crisp	1	16	0
for 30 crones	4	15	0
for <8> *10* fatt lambes <£1 6s 8d>	1	13	4
for 60 pooke lambes	4	3	6
Sum <£17 17s 2d>	18	3	10
Bought 2 wether hoggs		9	0

<Bought of Rose 9 ewes and a wether £2 13s 4d>
<Remayne to Roger £15 3s 6d> due to Roger £17 14s 10d

[*p*]   /*Pypers*/ charge at Midsomer 1625: 101 mother ewes; 22 ewe
shorlins; 23 ewe lambes; 4 rammes; 3 ramm lambes; 17 wethers
of 2 sheare; 15 wether lambes. Sum 185

/*Lennards*/ charge at Midsomer 1625: 10 wethers of 4 sheare; 11
wethers of 2 sheare. Sum 21

/*Crisps*/ charge at Midsomer 1625: 34 wethers of 3 sheare; 2
wether hoggs bought. Sum 36

So the whole summe of Rogers sheep the flocks being sett at
Midsomer 1625 is 222 [*242*] sheepe

[*1626*]   /*Pyper*/ brought to the clipping at Midsomer 1626: 120 mother
ewes /*3 morts, 20 croned*/; 23 ewe shorlins /*3 croned*/; 16 wethers of
3 sheare /*1 mort*/; <14> *15* wether shorlins /*1 croned*/; 4 rammes;
ramm lambes nll /*3 morts*/; 21 store ewe lambes; 31 store wether
lambes; 13 fatt lambes; 50 pooke lambes. Sum 178 sheep and 7 skinnes

	£	s	d
/Sheepe/ taken from Pyper at Midsomer 1626			
16 wethers of 3 sheare to Crisp			
21 crones sold for	3	8	2
13 fatt lambes sold for	1	19	0
50 pooke lambes sold for	4	11	8
Sum	9	18	10

/Lennard/ delivered at Midsomer 1626: 10 wethers of 5 sheare; 10 wethers of 3 sheare /1 mort/. Sum 20 sheepe and a skinne

/Crisp/ delivered at Midsomer 1626: <2> *10* wethers of 4 sheare; <3> *1* wether of <4> *2* sheare /1 mort/; sold 24 wethers of 4 sheare. Sum 35 sheepe and a skinn

	£	s	d
for 24 wethers	11	6	1
for lambes and crones sold	9	18	10
due to Roger the last yeare	17	14	10
[p] Sum	38	19	9

[*Jane's account 1619–21*][87]

[*1619*] [*Barrett Ringstead*] Delivered to Page at Midsomer 1619: 3 ewe hogges; one lamb ewe; one ewe. Sum 5

[*1620*] Page delivered at Midsomer 1620: 4 ewes and an ewe hogge; 3 lambes of these she had 5lb of wooll

Delivered to Page at Midsomer 1620: 45 ewes wherof 40 were given her by her grandfather Stubbe; 3 ewe lambes. Sum 48

[*1621*] Jane Le Strange dyed and Page delivered to the clipping at Midsomer 1621: 48 ewes, 36 lambes

	£	s	d
of these 4 crones sold for		10	8
for 4 stone of wooll at 8s	1	12	0
to the fayer 2 pooke lambes		2	7
Sum	2	5	3

22 ewes and 7 lambes to Roger
22 ewes and 7 lambes to Bess
[p]   20 lambes to Dorothe Guybon

[**Elizabeth's account 1620–27**][88]

[*1620*] [*Barrett Ringstead*] Page delivered at Midsomer 1620: one ewe and an ewe hogge; a ewe lambe of these shee had 2lb of wooll

---

87. This entry follows eight blank pages after the previous entry.
88. This entry follows nine blank pages after the previous entry.

Delivered to Page at Midsomer 1620: 2 ewes; one ewe lambe; 40
ewes given her grandfather Stubbe. Sum 43.
Received for 2 ewe skinns which goeth toward the joyse

		£	s	d
1621	Page brought to the clipping at Midsomer: 41 ewes; 38 lambes			
	Sum 79 of these delivered to Corner 25 lambes, of these sheepe			
	she had 4½ stone of wooll sold for 8s the stone	1	16	0
	Received for a lamb		3	0
	Received for a crone /goeth for joyse/		2	8
	Sum <38s 8d> *41s 8d*	2	1	8

[p]   /Page/ his charge at Midsomer 1621: 40 ewes; 22 ewes that were
Janes; 7 ewe lambes that were Janes; 8 ewe lambes one was a
rixsey; 3 wether lambes; a ramm lambe. Sum 81

[1622] /Page/ brought to the clipping at Midsomer 1622: 61 ewes; 22
wether lambes and 34 ewe lambes; 13 ewe shorlins; 3 wether
shorlins; a ram shorlin; a rixsey shorlin. Sum beside lambes 79,
he brought a ewe skinne and a ewe hogges skinne so he is right;
of the 79 sheep she had 6 stone 1lb of wooll sold at [?]

/Corner/ brought 2 skins and 23 wether shorlins to the clipping
of these she had 2 st[one] and 9lb of wooll sold at [?]

/Sheep/ taken out at Midsomer 1622: <Barkers charge> 12 pooke
lambes to the fayer; 11 crones; a rixsey to Ringsted; a ram to
Ringsted; 3 wether shorlins to <Corner> *Barker*; 16 wether
lambes to Corner. Sum beside lambes 16

[Barrett Ringstead] /Barkers/ charge at Midsomer 1622: 50 ewes;
13 ewe shorlins; 28 ewe lambes one was a ram; 3 wether shorlins
and a ram shorlin. Sum <94> *95*

[Sedgeford North flock] /Corners/ charge at Midsomer 1622: 23
wether shorlins; 16 wether lambes <3 wether shorlins>

/Page/ his charge at Midsomer 1622: a rixsey shorlin; <a ram shorlin>

1623   /Barker/ brought to the clipping at Midsomer: 49 mother ewes,
lost 1; <23> *13* ewes of 2 sheare; 2 wethers of 2 sheare, 1 [skin]; a
ramme of 2 sheare; a ramm shorling; 21 ewe shorlings, 3 [skins],
2 [lost]; a lame ewe shorling; /lambes 28 and 15 small lambes/. Sum
88 <5> *4* skinnes and 3 [lost] he must
[p]   make good of these she had 6 stone of wooll

1623   /Corner/ brought to the clipping at Midsomer: 21 wethers of 2
       sheare, skinns 2; 12 wether shorlings, [skins] 4. Sum 33 and 6
       skinnes, so he is right, of these she had 3 stone of wooll which
       was sold toward the joyce

       /Page/ brought a rixsey at Midsomer 1623 which was sold

       /Sheep/ taken from Barker at Midsomer 1623: 15 crones and 15
       small lambes; a dizy ewe shorling that dyed. Sum 16

       /Sheep/ taken from Corner at Midsomer 1623: 12 wether shorlins
       to Crisp

       /Barkers/ charge at Midsomer 1623: 48 mother ewes; 23 ewe
       shorlings; 5 ewe shorlings of Leveretts; 2 wethers of 2 sheare; a
       ramme of 2 sheare; a ramm shorling; 11 ewe lambes; 17 wether
       lambes. Sum 108

       /Corners/ charge at Midsomer 1623: 21 wethers of 2 sheare; 17
       wether lambes from Bircham. Sum 38

       [Ringstead South flock] /Crisps/ charge at Midsomer 1623: 12
       wether shorlings from Corner. Sum 12

[p]   I sold 15 crones 15 small lambes and a rixsey for which I bought
       her 5 ewe shorlings that were Leveretts and 17 wether lambes
       from Bircham. So the some of all Elizabeths sheep when the
       flocks were sett at Midsomer 1623 is 158

1624   /Barker/ brought to the clipping at Midsomer: 47 ewes for store,
       skinnes 1 /4 croned/; 23 ewes of 2 sheare; 4 Leverett ewes of 2
       sheare, [skin] 1; 9 ewe shorlings, [skins] 2; 2 rammes; 2 wethers of
       3 sheare; 17 wether shorlins; 11 ewe lambes; 14 wether lambes; 2
       ram lambes; 3 fatt lambes; 12 pooke lambes. Sum 104 sheep and
       4 skinnes, of these 6 stone 12lb of wooll for joyce

1624   [Sedgeford North flock] /Lennard/ brought to the clipping at
       Midsomer: 1 wethers of 3 sheare, skinnes nll; 13 wether shorlins,
       [skins] 4. Sum 34 and 4 skinnes of these she had 4 stone 3lb of
       wooll for joyce

1624   /Crisp/ brought to the clipping at Midsomer 12 wethers of 2
       sheare, of these 1 stone 11lb of wooll for joyce
       /Sold of/ Elizabeths for the yeare 1624   £   s   d
       3 fatt lambes   9   0

4 crones		12	0
12 pooke lambes	1	0	10
Sum	2	1	10
Bought 5 ewes of Gregory Willis. Rest due to her 6s 10d	1	15	0

[*Barrett Ringstead*] /*Pypers*/ charge at Midsomer 1624: 70 mother ewes; 5 ewes from Gregory Willis; 9 ewe shorlins; 11 ewe lambes; 2 rammes; 2 ramm lambes; 2 wethers of 3 sheare; 17 wether shorlins; 14 wether lambes. Sum 112 [*132*]

[*Sedgeford North flock*] /*Lennards*/ charge at Midsomer 1624: 21 wethers of 3 sheare; 13 wether shorlins. Sum 34

/*Crisps*/ charge at Midsomer 1624: 12 wethers of 2 sheare

[*p*] The whole summe of Elizabeths sheepe the flocks being sett at Midsomer 1624 is 158

1625 /*Pyper*/ brought to the clipping at Midsomer: 79 mother ewes /5 morts, 16 crones/; 11 ewe shorlins; 4 rammes; 2 wethers of 3 sheare; 11 wethers of 2 sheare /2 sold, 4 morts/; 12 wethers shorlins /2 morts/; 14 ewe lambes; 10 store wether lambes; 1 store ramme lambe; 3 fatt lambes sold; 42 pooke lambes sold. Sum 119 sheep and 2 sold and 11 skinnes, croned 16, of these 3st and 5lb of wooll with skinnes for joyce

1625 /*Lennard*/ brought to the clipping at Midsomer: 6 wethers of 4 sheare /sold 15/; 13 wethers of 2 sheare. Sum 19 and sold 15, so he is right, of these 2 stone of wooll for the joyce

1625 /*Crisp*/ brought to the clipping at Midsomer [?]

/*Sheep*/ sold at Midsomer 1625	£	s	d
17 wethers for	7	12	0
for 16 crones	2	10	8
for 3 fatt lambes		10	0
for 42 pooke lambes	2	16	4
for 5 rixseyes from Lennard	1	2	6
for 2 rixseyes from Crisp		9	0
Sum to which add 6s 10d due to her the last yeare and the sum is £15 7s 4d	15	0	6

[*p*] /*Bought*/ of Rose 9 ewes and a wether which being taken out rest due to her £12 13s 8d | 2 | 13 | 8

1625   /*Pypers*/ charge at Midsomer: 63 mother ewes; 9 ewes bought of
       Rose; 11 ewe shorlins; 14 ewe lambes; 2 wethers of 3 sheare; 12
       wethers of 2 sheare wherof one bought; 4 rammes; one ramme
       lambe; 10 wether lambes. Sum 106 [*126*]

       /*Lennards*/ charge at Midsomer 1625: 6 wethers of 4 sheare; 8
       wethers of 2 sheare. Sum 14

1625   /*Crisps*/ charge at Midsomer: 9 wethers of 3 sheare

       The whole summe of Elizabeths sheepe the flocks being sett at
       Midsomer 1625 is 129

1626   /*Pyper*/ brought to the clipping at Midsomer: 80 mother ewes /*3
       morts, 21 croned*/; <23> *13* ewe shorlins /*1 mort*/; sold 2 wethers
       of 3 sheare; 11 wethers of 3 sheare /*1 mort*/; 10 wether shorlins;
       nll ramm lambe /*1 mort*/; 4 rammes; 14 store wether lambes; 17
       store ewe lambes; 2 fatt lambes; 29 pooke lambes. Sum 118 and 6
       skinnes and 2 sold

		£	s	d
/*Sheep*/ taken from Pyper at Midsomer 1626				
21 crones sold for		3	10	0
2 fatt lambes sold for			6	0
2 wethers			19	0
29 pooke lambes sold for		2	10	8
[*p*]	Sum	7	6	9

1626   /*Lennard*/ brought to the clipping at Midsomer: 6 wethers of 5
       sheare; 8 wethers of 3 sheare. Sum 14 all to Crisp

		£	s	d
Crisp delivered at Midsomer 1626: 3 wethers of 4 sheare; 6 wethers of 4 sheare sold. Sum 9				
for 6 wethers		2	17	6
for 2 wethers, crones and lambes sold for		7	6	9
due to Elizabeth the last yeare		12	13	8
	Sum	22	17	11
Layd out of this for 60 lambes £10 so there resteth due to her		12	17	11

       /*Pypers*/ charge at Midsomer 1626: 59 mother ewes /*6 morts*/; 13
       ewe shorlins /*3 morts*/; 17 ewe lambes one wether lambe /*4 morts*/;
       11 wethers of 3 sheare /*11 sold*/; 10 wether shorlins; 14 wether
       lambes; 60 wether lambes bought /*6 morts*/; 4 rammes.
       Sum 168 [*188*]

/Crisps/ charge at Midsomer 1626: 3 wethers of 4 sheare; 6 wethers of 5 sheare from Lennard; 8 wethers of 3 sheare from Lennard. Sum 17

[p]   The whole summe of Elizabeths sheepe the flocks being sett at Midsomer 1626 is 185 sheep

1627 /Pyper/ brought to the clipping at Midsomer: 63 mother ewes /9 morts, 2 sold, 11 crones/; 12 ewe shorlins /4 morts/; 4 rammes; 10 wethers of 2 sheare; 11 wethers of 4 sheare; 69 wether shorlins
149 /6 morts/; 32 store lambes; 35 lambes to sell wherof 30 pooke. Sum 149 [169] and 19 skinnes, so he is right

1627 /Crisp/ brought to the clipping at Midsomer: 5 wethers of 6 sheare and /1 sold/; 11 wethers of 4 sheare. Sum 16 and one sold, so he is right

	£	s	d
Sheep sold /from Pyper/ 11 crones sold for	1	18	6
2 gills sold for		15	0
11 wethers of 3 sheare sold for	4	19	0
5 lambes sold for		16	0
30 lambes sold for	2	15	0
/in Crisps flock/ 1 wether sold for		8	0
5 wethers of 6 sheare	2	0	0
Sum £13 11s 6d which being added to £12 17s 11d which was due to Elizabeth the last yeare and it maketh £26 9s 5d	13	11	6

	£	s	d
Elizabeth sold all her sheep to her father at these rates following:			
/from Pyper/ 50 ewes at 7s	17	10	0
12 ewe shorlins at 6s	3	12	0
4 rammes	1	0	0
32 store lambes	6	2	8
10 wethers of 2 sheare at 7s	3	10	0
69 wether shorlins at 6s 8d	23	0	0
/from Crisp/ 11 wethers of 4 sheare at 8s	4	8	0
Sum £59 2s 8d which being added to the £26 9s 5d and there resteth due to Elizabeth £85 12s 1d[89]			

---

89. This entry is followed by 1 blank page, and the Wool Account, 1642–54, see below pp. 185–91, and a further 21 blank pages.

[*p*]   [*Alice Le Strange's sheep account 1617–1625*][90]
        [*top third of page illegible*]

| | | Sum | 51 | 11 | 6 |

[*1617*] [*illegible*] Delivered to Page and Goodman Midsomer 1617: 127
        wether lambes; 77 wether hogges. Sum 204 sheepe
        Received for 7 hogges skinnes and 3 wether skinns 7s 2d which
        was all layd out for tarre

1618   Page delivered to the clipping 1618: 120 wether hogges /*morts 10*/;
        74 wethers of 2 sheare wherof I had 24 stone of wooll. Sum 194

payd for greasing of 129 lambes		11	6
lost by <20> *25* sheep bought of Waters which were stricken			
and so were sold with 12d losse in a sheep	1	5	0
payd for washing 2s 9d and for clipping 4s 10d		7	7
for a dozen hurdles		18	0
for 9lb of pitch		1	6
Sum	3	3	7
Received for 24 stone of wooll at 10s	12	0	0
Received for a dizy wether hogg		3	4
received for 49 wether hogges at 6s 8d	16	6	8
one wether hogge dyed of the gelding			
Sum	28	10	0
The £3 3s 7d taken out of £28 10s remayne	25	6	5

[*p*]   [*top third of page illegible*]
[*1618*] [*illegible*] Midsomer 1618 of 2 sheare sheep 54, for 20 of the 2
        sheare sheepe were sold and 20 ewes bought for them; 89 wether
        hogges; 130 lambes. Sum <173> *274*

for 20 ewes	7	12	4
[*1619*] for the sheppheardes wages for a yeare ending Midsomer 1619	1	13	4
Sum	9	5	8
Received for 20 wethers of 2 sheare	8	0	0
Received for a dizy wether		3	0
Received for 8 hogges skins		15	4
Sum	8	18	4

The £8 18s 4d taken out of £9 5s 8d there remayneth more owing
for sheep 7s 4d which being added to the sum of £57 7s 2d and it

maketh it	57	14	6

90. Alice's own account, found at the end of LEST/P10, is the most damaged and faded.

1619   Page delivered at Midsomer 1619: 54 wethers of 3 sheare; 88
        wethers of 2 sheare; 122 wether hogges; 21 ewes and 22 lambes, of
        these I had 37 stone 9lbs of wooll the cause of having 22 lambes
        of 21 ewes is because sum of the 2 sheare sheep are ewes which
        were reckoned wethers. Sum 264 [*285*]

[*p*]   [*top third of page illegible*]

Received for 6, 2 sheare sheep and 52 wether hogges	19	6	0
Received for the tithe of 140 sheep at 4s the skore wherof I			
allowed to the vicar 1s 6d and I was to have but halfe of the			
remayn so I received		11	6
Received for 20 wethers of 2 sheare	7	0	0
Sum[91]	73	8	2

[*1620*] payd the sheppherds wage for a yeare ending Midsomer 1620   1 18 4
        this 38s 4d being taken out of £73 8s 2d there remayneth so I
        pay my father   71 9 10
        the sum of £71 9s 10d being taken out of £77 13s 8d there remayn 6   3 10
        So there is now layd out for sheep more then I have received but 6   3   0
        I payd my father all his mony agayne that I did borrow of him
        but £30 and that £30 I did take order with my cosen Guybon
        to pay my father, but my father dying before he did pay him he
        forgave me the £30 at this death so my cosen Guybon did repay
        it agayne

[*p*]   [*top two thirds of page illegible*]
        Of the chilldrens sheepe as follows: the first yeare 40 sheep; the
        second yeare 106 sheep; the third yeare 147 of Willyam Guybon
        for which they did allow 9 stone of wooll. The sum of £55 4s 4d
        being added to £6 3s 10d it maketh the sum of £61 18s 2d for
        which I have 253 sheep which were delivered to Page at Midsomer
        1619 and are well worth £67, and the shepherds wages for the yeare
        is payd and the joycement allowed until Midsomer 1620

Delivered to Page at Midsomer 1619: <62 wethers> 90 sheep of	£	s	d
one sheare wherof there is one ram and 4 or 5 ewes and the			
residue be wethers; 62 <90> wethers <hogges> of 2 sheare; 21			
ewes; 22 lambes of my owne, 15 were ewes; 98 wether lambes			
bought at Fring. Sum 253 [*294*]; and delivered to Page of the			
chilldrens sheep 147 at Midsomer 1619			
for 2 dozen and 8 hurdles		10	8

---

91. Sum includes missing figures from the faded top of the page.

	for a barrell of pitch		7	6
	/March 26/ for 2 barrells of tarre	1	12	0
[p]	Received for ewe skinns one hogge skinns and 30 wether hogge			
	skinns and 4 wether skinns		14	7
	/skinns 19s 2d/ and for 11 of the chilldren mort skinns		4	7
	for washing of sheep at 8d the C [120] 92		4	
	for clipping of sheep at 8d the C [120]		8	
	/14s 8d/ for draggers and binders		1	
	Sum		14	8

1620	Page delivered to the clipping: 62 wethers of [illegible] sheare; 78			
	wethers of 2 sheare and a 2 sheare ram and 2 wether hogges for 2			
	that he lost of the 2 sheare wethers; 74 wether hogges and a rixy			
	hogge; 14 ewe hogges; 26 ewes; 21 lambes. Sum 258 beside lambes			
	of these sold 59 wethers of 3 sheare for	22	2	6
	3 wethers of 3 sheare to Ringsted flock; the 78 wethers of 2 sheare			
	to Ringsted; a rixey to Ringsted flock, a crone ewe <sold for> <10 16>			
	was worryed. Sum 142			
	/Received for wooll/ of the 258 sheep I had 18st of wooll and of the			
	chilldrens wooll 9st which was all sold for at 8s	10	16	0

1620	/in Barrett Ringsted/ Page his charge at Midsomer: a ramm; 39			
	ewes wherof 14 are hogges; 79 wether hogges and 2 more that			
	Page allowed for 2 wethers of 2 sheare which he lost; 21 wether			
	lambes; 92 wether lambes bought cost	19	18	8
	Sum <237> 229 beside of the chilldrens sheepe			
	Received for the tithe of 140 sheep at 4s the skore allowing the			
	vickar 2s 6d for the halfe. So I received the residue of the 14s for			
	my halfe and more for tarr		13	6
[p]	for 5 dozen and 8 hurdles	1	4	1
	for greasing of 115 lambes at 18d the skore		8	7
	for a barrell of tarre		16	0
	for oyle			9
	to the shepheardes for their quarter ending at St Michaell		14	2
	to the shepheardes for their quarters wages ending at Christmas		14	2
	to the shepheards for their quarters wages ending at our Lady		14	2
	to the sheppheards for their quarters wages at Midsomer		14	2
	Sum	5	6	7
	Received for 2 dizey wether shorlins		6	8

---

92. The pennies in the next three entries are illegible. The sum provides the total for these items.

Received for 2 wether skins and 17 wether lambe skinns these are
written on the other side with the chilldrens sheep skinns

for washing of all the sheep reckoning the chilldrens being 489	6	9
for clipping of the sheepe	12	2
for dragging of the sheepe	1	2
for 3 dozen and 4 hurdles	14	6

Sum   2   4   7

Received for sheepe, wooll, tithe and skins for this yeare as
heare appeareth   34   17   10
layd out for lambes, hurdles, shepheards wages, tarre washing,
clipping and greasing   30   14   8
this £30 14s 8d taken out of £34 17s 10d there remayn   4   3   2

1621   /Barrett Ringsted/ Page brought to the clipping at Midsomer:
39 ewes; 29 lambes; 72 wethers of 2 sheare; 84 wether shorlins;
9 shorlins <126> that proved rixseyes; one ramm. Sum beside
lambes 205. He delivered 19 skinns, 2 dizy wethers were sold. So
he wanteth 3 wether shorlins for which he must allow, of these
205 sheepe I had 19 stones of wooll

So I have toward the joycements of 3 yeares ending at Midsomer
1620 the wages & hurdles & tarre and other things coming to £7
11s 2d for 1621 are reckoned in   4   3   2

[p]   Sheepe taken from Page at the clipping: 2 ewes croned; 34 ewes
delivered to Sedgford to Woods; 72 wethers of 2 sheare delivered
to Corner; 48 wether shorlins delivered to Corner; 2 rixseyes to
sell; 7 rixseys to Crisp <6>; 4 pooke lambes to the fayer; 6 lambes
sold; 2 dizy wethers turned into the parke which are not like to
live, a rixsey to sell which Page should have delivered to Crisp
last yeare but did not

1621   /Barret Ringsted 1621/ Page his charge at Midsomer: 10 wethers
from Crisp <one was a ramm>; a ram; 3 ewes; 34 wether shorlins
one was a ramm; 3 <4> wether shorlins Page must allow for;
for these he allowed 3 ewes; 9 ewe lambes; 8 wether lambes; 2
ramm lambes. Sum <62> 70 more to Page of the chilldrens 465
Sum in all 535 and 3 sheep from Crisp which he had lost

	£	s	d
Received for 19½ stone of wooll of my own	7	16	0
Received for 32 stone of the chilldrens wooll at 8s toward the feed of the 381 sheepe	12	16	0
Received for 30 pooke lambes of the chilldrens	2	6	6

Received for 25 crones of the chilldrens /<8s 4d>/	3	8	8
Received for 3 rixseyes of my owne		12	0
Received for 3 rixseyes of the chilldrens		12	0
Received for 23 skins of the chilldrens and 19 skins of my own		14	11

Sum of the mony received for the chilldrens sheep: lambes, wooll
and skins is £28 6s 1d which being added to the £4 3s 2d due for
joyse on the other side of this leafe it make the sum

	32	9	3

of the 81 wethers which were delivered to Crisp the last yeare
there dyed one the skinn was [de]stroyed and he delivered 10 at
Midsomer to Page and he hath 10 of those wethers still and there
was 60 of them sold for

	21	0	0
Received for 6 lambes of the chilldrens		18	0

Received for 4 crones wherof 2 of the chilldrens /2 *dyed before
they were sold*/

		5	4

Received for the tithe of 140 sheep at 4s beside 5s due out of it
to Mr Burward

	1	3	0
Received for 4 pooke lambes at 15½d		5	2

[p] Received for skins, sheep, crones, lambes and wooll for the
year ending at Midsomer 1621

	56	0	9
payd for greasing of 170 lambes at 18d the xx [score]		12	9
to the shepheards for their quarters wages ending at St Michael		14	3
to the shepheards for their quarters wages ending at Christmas		14	3

1622 /*Barrett Ringsted sheep*/ Page brought to the clipping at Midsomer:
45 wethers; 6 ewes; 4 lambes; 2 old rams; 2 ram shorlins; 7 ewe
hogs; 7 wether hoggs. Sum 69 beside lambes. He brought a
wether skinne, 2 ewe hoggs skinnes a wether hogge skinn, so his
reckoning is right, of these I had 7 stone and 2lbs of wooll

[p] [*Sedgeford East ground*] /*Woods*/ delivered of his 34 ewes all and
they remayn with him
[*Sedgeford North ground*] /*Corner*/ delivered of his 72 wethers all
to Ringsted flock he brought to the clipping of his 48 [*of*] 2 sheare
wethers, 46 which remayne with him and he delivered 2 skinns
/*Ringsted South flock, Crisp*/ delivered of his 7 rixseyes all and
had them back againe but one that was sold

1622 Sheepe to be taken from Page

1 crone ewe	1	10
2 lambes to kill	6	0
2 pooke lambs to the fayer	2	4

<43> *40* wethers to Ringsted; 4 rams to Ringsted; 7 wether
shorlins to Corner. Sum 52 beside lambes

/Barrett Ring[sted] flock, Barker/ his charge 1622: 33 wethers from
Corner; 5 ewes; 5 wethers and 7 wether shorlins; 7 ewe hogges
and 4 ramms; 12 lambes from Woods. Sum <72>, <76> *73* of
the chilldrens 403 and a wether that Crisp did allow for one he
lost but he delivered an ewe

1622   /Sedgford East ground, Woods/ his charge at Midsomer: 738
mother ewes; 183 ewe shorlings; 14 old rammes; 6 yonge ramms;
2 bell wethers; 104 ewe lambes; 3 ramme lambes. Sum 1080 [*1050*]

1622   /Sedgford North ground, Corner/ his charge at Midsomer:
39 wethers of 3 sheare; 46 wethers of 2 sheare; 150 wether
shorlins; 148 wether lambes
/Nicholas/ 20 wether lambes[93]
/Hamon/ 17 wether lambes
/Rogers/ 22 wether shorlins and 39 wether lambes
[p]   /Elizabeth/ 23 wether shorlins; 16 wether lambes
Sum 520 and 80 joyce [*sheep*]

/Barrett Ringsted, Page/ his charge at Midsomer 1622 for
Ringsted: 100 old wethers that were bought of my brother
Yellverton; 119 olde wether of 4 sheare bought of him; 40 wethers
from Barker; 6 rixseyes <4 rams from Barker>
/Nicholas/ 13 wethers and rixseyes 11 <3>, <6>
/Hamon/ <a ram> and 3 rixseyes
/Roger/ 4 wethers <5 ramms> and 3 rixseyes
/Elizabeth/ <a ramm and> a rixsey. Sum 300

1623   /Barrett Ringsted, Barker/ brought to the clipping: 33 wethers; 3
ewes, skinnes 2; 5 wethers; 7 wethers of 2 sheare; 4 rammes; 7
ewes of 2 sheare; 11 ewe shorlins, [*skin*] 1. /lambes 2 store, 6 pookes/
/Nicholas/ 73 <53> mother ewes, [*skins*] 2; 20 ewes of 2 sheare;
27 ewes of a sheare, [*skin*] 1; 13 wethers of 2 sheare *and a dizy*,
[*skins*] 2; /lambes 36 & 21 small ones/
/Hamon/ 47 mother ewes, [*skin*] 1; 34 ewes of 2 sheare; 15 ewe
shorlins, [*skins*] 3; 22 wethers of 2 sheare; 5 rammes /lambes 30,
27 small ones/
/Roger/ <74>, <76> 77 mother ewes, skinnes 2, lost 4; 31 ewes
of 2 sheare; 32 ewe shorlins, [*skins*] 2; wether shorlin, [*skin*] 1; 4
rammes, [*skin*] 2; /lambes 48, 42 small lambes/
/Elizabeth/ <48> 49 mother ewes, lost 1; 13 ewes of 2 sheare;

---

93. From this point, Alice identified the lambs and sheep belonging to each child;
consolidation of entries respects the individual holdings.

wethers of 2 sheare, [skin] 1; a ramme; a ramme shorlin; 21 ewe
shorlins, [skins] 3, [lost] 2; one lame ewe shorling /lambes 28,
small lambes 15/. Sum 448 [559]

So Barker delivered 22 skinnes and the dizy and poore sheep had
418 more, so he wanteth 7 sheep which he must allow me for. Of
[p]   my owne sheep of Barkers charge I had 7 stone and 5lb of wooll
and of the chilldrens sheep I had 35 stone and 9lb of wooll which
was sold with the rest toward the joyce of there sheep. The whole
sum of Barrett Ringsted wooll is 43 stone
/Sheepe/ taken from Barker 1623: 5 wethers old; 33 wethers sold and
a dizy wether of Nich dyed>; 8 ewes of 3 sheare to Allen; 2 ewes
croned; 2 wether lambes to Corner 6 sold; 11 ewes of 2 sheare to Allen
/Nicholas/ 17 wether lambes to Corner: 21 sold
/Hamon/ 18 wether lambes to Corner: 27 sold 22 wethers of 2 sheare
to Crisp
/Roger/ 19 wether lambes to Corner and 42 sold
/Elizabeth/ 15 lambes sold
/Nicholas/ 20 crones and a wether of 2 sheare dizy
/Hamon/ 16 crones and of Rogers 14 crones
/Elizabeth/ 15 crones and a dizy ewe shorling
Sum 128 beside lambes

1623   /Sedgford East ground, Woods/ brought to the clipping at
Midsomer: 861 mother ewes and ewes of 2 sheare & skinnes 90;
90 ewe shorlings 2 dizy, [skins] 14; 2 bell wethers; 14 old rammes;
3 ramme shorlins; 6 rammes of 3 sheare. Sum 976 and 104 skinns
[1080] so Woods is right, of these I had 58½ stone the tithe payd.
/lambes beside 52 for tithe & 4 marking lambes 462/

/Sheepe/ taken from Woods when he delivered his charge to
Allen: 103 ewes croned *sold*; 22 ewes shorlins croned *sold*; 4
ewe shorlins dizy that dyed; 3 rammes croned; 140 fatt lambes
sold; 108 lambes sold at Kenninghall fayer; 133 lambes sold at
[p]   Coolidg fayer; 107 wether lambes to Corner. Sum of sheepe,
beside lambes, is 110

1623   /Sedgeford North ground, Corner/ delivered to the clipping at
Midsomer: 36 olde wethers, skinns 2, lost 1; 46 wethers of 3
sheare; 237 wethers of 2 sheare & wether shorlins, [skins] 50,
[lost] 1
/Nicholas/ 14 wether shorlings, [skins] 6
/Hamon/ 17 wether shorlings

/Roger/ 21 wethers of 2 sheare, [skin] 1; 29 wether shorlins,
[skins] 10
/Elizabeth/ 21 wethers of 2 sheare, [skins] 2; 12 wether shorlins,
[skins] 4
Sum 433, of these I had of my owne wooll 36½ stone, and of
the chilldrens wooll 10 stone which was sold toward the joyce of
their sheep. The whole sum of the wooll of Corners flock is 46½
stone. Corner brought home 75 skinns and he hath lost 12 sheep
that he must make good, one of the skinnes are stroyed

/Sheepe/ taken from Corner at Midsomer 1623: 63 wethers of 2
sheare to Crisp; one dizy wether of 2 sheare dyed
/Nicholas/ 14 wether shorlings to Crisp
/Hamon/ 17 wether shorlings to Crisp
/Roger/ 29 wether shorlings to Crisp
/Elizabeth/ 12 wether shorlings to Crisp
Sum 136

/Barrett Ringsted, Page/ brought to the clipping at Midsomer
1623: 58 olde wethers, sold 42; 117 olde wethers, skinns 2; 40
wethers that he had of Barker; 6 rixseyes that he had of Barker
/Nicholas/ 11 rixseyes; 12 wethers of 3 sheare
/Hamon/ 3 rixseyes
/Roger/ 3 rixseyes; 3 wethers of 4 sheare, [skin] 1
/Elizabeth/ 1 rixseye

Sum 254, beside 42 sold; of these I had 2 stone of wooll of the
chilldrens & of my owne 24 stone. Page delivered 4 skinns that
[p]   were stroyed and the 42 wethers that were sold, so his reckoning
is right

/Sheepe/ taken from Page 1623 when he delivered his charge to
Crisp at Midsomer: 20 old wethers sold to Edmond Creamer; 30
old wethers sold; 24 rixseyes sold being all his rixseyes. Sum 64 [74]

/Barrett Ringsted, Barkers/ charge at Midsomer 1623: 4 rammes;
12[94]   7 wethers of 2 sheare; 1 ewe lamb
/Nicholas/ 73 mother ewes; 27 ewe shorlings; 39 ewe shorlings
that were Leveretts; 12 wethers of 2 sheare; 19 ewe lambes; 1 ewe
151   lamb from Bircham
/Hamon/ 31 mother ewes; 18 ewe shorlings; 27 ewe shorlings that
93   were Leveretts; 5 rammes; 12 ewe lambes

---

94. Totals for each child appear in the LH margin for the first time; the sum total [555]
includes a shepherd's allowance.

/*Roger*/ 98 mother ewes; 32 ewe shorlings; 10 ewe shorlings that
153   were Leveretts; 4 rammes, 29 ewe lambes
/*Elizabeth*/ 48 mother ewes; 23 ewe shorlings & wethers; a
ramme and a ram shorling; 5 of Leveretts ewe shorlings; 11 ewe
108   lambes; 17 wether lambes. Sum 517 [*555*]

/*Sedgford East ground, Allens*/ charge at Midsomer 1623: 758
mother ewes; 84 ewe shorlins; 6 young ramms and 3 ram
shorlings; 2 bell wethers; 107 ewe lambes; 84 ewe lambes from
Bircham and 6 ramm lambes; 8 ewes of 3 sheare from Barker;
11 ewe shorlings from Barker. Sum [*1069*] 1080 and 9 crones left
with him

/*Sedgford North ground, Corners*/ charge at Midsomer 1623:
82 olde wethers; 153 wethers of 2 sheare and wether shorlins;
12 wether shorlings that he must make good that he lost; 107
wether lambes from Allen; 31 wether lambes from Bircham
[*p*] /*Nicholas*/ 17 wether lambes from Bircham
/*Hamon*/ 18 wether lambes from Barker
/*Roger*/ 21 wethers of 2 sheare; 19 wether lambes from Barker
/*Elizabeth*/ 21 wethers of 2 sheare; 17 wether lambes from
Bircham. Sum [*498*] 520 and 80 joyce sheepe

/*Ringsted South ground, Crispes*/ charge at Midsomer 1623: 8 old
wethers; 157 wethers of 4 sheare; 63 wether shorlings from Corner
/*Nicholas*/ 14 wether shorlings from Corner; 12 wethers of 3 sheare
/*Hamon*/ 22 wethers of 2 sheare from Barker; 17 wether shorlings
from Corner
/*Roger*/ 3 wethers of 4 sheare; 29 wether shorlings from Corner;
17 wether shorlings of Leveretts; 6 rixsey shorlings that were Leveretts
/*Elizabeth*/ 12 wether shorlings from Corner. Sum 360

[*1624*] /*Barrett Ringsted, Barker*/ brought to the clipping at Midsomer
11   1624: 4 rammes; 7 wethers of 3 sheare; Bircham lambes nll, skin 1
/*Nicholas*/ 65 mother ewes, [*skins*] 8 /*croned 19*/; 11 wethers of 3
sheare; 38 Leverett ewes of 3 sheare, [*skin*] 1; 26 ewes of 2 sheare,
[*skin*] 1; 18 ewe shorlins, [*skins*] 2 /*30<36> stores, 3 fatt lambes,*
138   *22 pookes*/
/*Hamon*/ 31 mother ewes, /*croned 11*/; 18 [*of*] 2 sheare ewes; 5
rammes; 26 Leverett 2 sheare ewes, 1; 11 ewe shorlins, [*skin*] 1
91   /*36 stores, one fatt lamb, 26 pookes*/
/*Roger*/ 91 mother ewes, [*skins*] 7 /*croned 19*/; 29 ewes of 2 sheare,
[*skins*] 3; 9 Leverett ewes of 2 sheare, [*skin*] 1; 4 ramms; 26 ewe
shorlins [*skins*] 3 /*51 stores, 6 fatt lambes, 28 pookes*/

[p]

139   /Elizabeth/ 47 mother ewes, [skin] 1, /croned 4/; 23 ewes of 2
      sheare; 4 Leverett ewes of 2 sheare, [skin] 1; 4 ramms; 2 wethers
      of 3 sheare; 9 ewe shorlins; 17 wether shorlins /27 stores, 3 fatt
104   lambes, 12 pookes/
      Sum 443 [485] and 34 skinnes, so he is right, of these 443 sheep I
      had 38 stone and 12lb of wooll: croned 53

1624 /Sedgford East ground, Allen/ brought to the clipping at
      Midsomer: 680 mother ewes, skinnes 70 /40 croned/; 103 ewe
      shorlins, [skins] 68; 2 bell wethers; 8 olde rammes [skins] 3; 9
      yonge rammes; 6 ramm shorlins
      Sum 948 [808] and 121 [141] skinnes, so he is right, and I had
      of these 48 stone 12lb of wooll, croned 40. Of these 680 ewes I
      had 394 lambes, whereof for tithe 45 and for marking lambes 4
      and sold for fatt lambes 14 and there remayneth 331 lambes, of
      these sold at Coolidg 110 lambes, remayne for store delivered to
      Lennard 103 wether lambes. Remayne with Allen for store 110
      ewe lambes and 8 ram lambes. Sum 768 whereof one dyed at the
      clipping and 2 are dizy and are worth nothing remayne 763

1624 /Sedgeford North ground, Lennard/ brought to the clipping at
      Midsomer: 73 olde wethers, skinnes 9; 165 wethers of 3 sheare
      and 2 sheare; 102 wether shorlins, 2 dizy, [skins] 38
      /Nicholas/ 17 wether shorlings
      /Hamon/ 12 wether shorlings, 6
      /Roger/ 21 wethers of 3 sheare; 16 wether shorlins, [skins] 3
[p]   /Elizabeth/ 21 wethers of 3 sheare; 13 wether shorlins, [skins] 4
      Sum 400 [440] and 60 skinnes I had of these 39 stone and 10lb
      of wooll, 2 of the 102 were dizy and Lennard is to deliver to
      Crisp 104 whereof all of 3 sheare and 2 sheare

1624 /Ringsted South ground, Crisp/ delivered to the clipping at
      Midsomer: 107 wethers of 3 sheare and 4 sheare, skinnes 19; 60
      wethers sold; 22 wethers sold
      /Nicholas/ 12 wethers of 4 sheare sold; 12 wethers of 2 sheare,
      [skins] 2
      /Hamon/ 22 wethers of 3 sheare; 16 wethers of 2 sheare, [skins] 1
      /Roger/ 3 wethers of 4 sheare sold; 46 wethers of 2 sheare; rixsey
      of 2 sheare, [skins] 5
      /Elizabeth/ 12 wethers of 2 sheare, [skin] 1
      Sum 216 and 82 sold and 27 skinnes and 15 sold, so he is right.
      I had of these 200 the tithe being payd and also for tithe of the
      sheep sold 19 stone 9½ lb of wooll

/Barrett Ringsted, Pypers/ charge at Midsomer 1624: 4 rammes;
II   7 wethers of 3 sheare
/Nicholas/ 110 mother ewes; 27 ewe shorlings; 22 ewes bought of
Martin Smith; 11 ewes bought of Gage; 4 ewes bought of Gregory
Willis; 18 ewe shorlins; 11<rammes> wethers of 3 sheare; 15 <18>
186   ewe lambes
116   /Hamon/ 64 mother ewes; 11 ewe shorlins; 5 rammes; 18 ewe
lambes; 18 wether lambes
[p]   /Roger/ 110 mother ewes; 21 ewes bought of Gregory Willis; 26
192   ewe shorlins; 25 ewe lambes; 26 wether lambes
/Elizabeth/ 70 mother ewes; 5 ewes bought of Gregory Willis; 9
ewe shorlins; 11 ewe lambes; 11 ewe lambes; 2 ramms; 2 wethers
of 3 sheare; 17 wether shorlins; 14 wether lambes; 2 ramm
112   lambes. Sum [617, 685] 577⁹⁵

/Sedgford East ground, Allens/ charge at Midsomer 1624: 637
mother ewes; 103 ewe shorlins; 2 bell wethers; 8 olde rammes; 9
yonge rammes; 6 ram shorlins; 8 ramme lambes; 110 ewe lambes.
Sum 883

/Sedgford North ground, Lennards/ charge at Midsomer 1624:
73 olde wethers; 61 wethers of 3 sheare; 100 wether shorlins; 103
wether lambes from Allen
/Nicholas/ 17 wether shorlins
/Hamon/ 12 wether shorlins
/Roger/ 21 wethers of 3 sheare; 16 wether shorlins
/Elizabeth/ 21 wethers of 3 sheare; 13 wether shorlins
Sum 417 [437] joyce sheepe 120

/Ringsted South ground, Crispes/ charge at Midsomer 1624: 107
wethers of 3 sheare and 4 sheare; 104 wethers of 3 sheare and 2
sheare from Lennard; 63 wether shorlings from Corner
/Nicholas/ 12 wethers of 2 sheare
/Hamon/ 22 wethers of 3 sheare; 16 wethers of 2 sheare
/Roger/ 29 wethers of 2 sheare; 17 wethers of 2 sheare; 1 rixsey
/Elizabeth/ 12 wether of 2 sheare
Sum 300 [383]

---

95. The actual total of sheep is 685, including 63 bought which subtracted brings it closer
to the margin total of 617 and the sum given of 577, allowing 40 sheep to the shepherd.

[p]   [*top third of the page torn off*][96] /Remayne 97/

192   /Roger/ 131 mother ewes; 4 ramms; 22 ewe shorlins; 17 wether
      shorlins; /Remayn 144/

112   /Elizabeth/ 79 mother ewes; 11 ewe shorlins; 4 ramms; 12 wether
      shorlins; 11 wethers of 2 sheare; 2 wethers of 3 sheare; /Remayn 105/
      Sum 508 sheep, 20 sold and 49 skinnes, so there remayneth,
      beside 80 that are croned, 448 sheep of these 50 stone and 3lb of
      wooll and lambes as followeth

106   /Nicholas/ 24 ewe lambes; 20 wether lambes; 20 wether lambes; 4
      fatt lambes and 58 pooke lambes

59   /Hamon/ 9 wether lambes with 2 ramme lambes; 12 ewe lambes
      and 36 pooke lambes

101   /Roger/ wether lambes 15 and 3 ramme lambes; 13 ewe lambes
      and 60 pooke lambes; 10 fatt lambes
      14 ewe lambes and 3 fatt lambes; 10 wether lambes and a ram
      lamb; 42 pooke lambes. Sum 294 [*336*]

1625 /Sedgford East ground, Allen/ brought to the clipping at
      Midsomer: 707 mother ewes /53 morts, 102 croned/; 119 ewe
      shorlins, /11 morts/; 2 bell wethers; 15 old rammes /2 morts, 1
      croned/; 6 yonge rammes; 6 ramme shorlins. Sum 815 [*855*] and
      68 skinnes, whereof croned 103 and 2 dizy ones sold so remayne 730.

[p]   [*top third of the page illegible*]
      [illegible] wethers /69 sold/; [illegible] wethers of 4 sheare; 94
      wethers of 2 sheare, /2 sold, 4 morts, 2 dizy/; 109 wether shorlins
      /Nicholas/ 15 wethers of 2 sheare /2 sold/
      /Hamon/ 9 wethers of 2 sheare /3 sold/
      /Roger/ 10 wethers of 4 sheare /11 sold/; 15 wethers of 2 sheare /1 mort/
      /Elizabeth/ 6 wethers of 4 sheare /15 sold/; 13 wethers of 2 sheare.
      Sum 296 sheep, 102 sold and 19 skinnes, so he is right, of these I
      had 38 stone of wooll.

	£	s	d
/Sheep/ taken from Lennard at Midsomer 1625			
30 of his oldest wethers	12	15	0
3 rixseys of the 109 that went for olde wethers		13	6
one dizy wether of the 94			
/Nicholas/ 5 rixseyes			
/Hamon/ 3 rixseyes			
/Roger/ 4 rixseyes			
/Elizabeth/ 5 rixseyes			
Sum 51 so Lennard hath 245			

---

96. Entries for Nicholas and Hamon are missing.

/Ringsted South ground, Crisp/ brought to the clipping 1625 198
wethers of 3 sheare and 4 sheare, /31 sold, 2 mort/

/Nicholas/ 12 wethers of 3 sheare	13	15	6
/Hamon/ 22 wethers of 4 sheare; 16 wethers of 3 sheare			
/Roger/ 42 wethers of 3 sheare	4	4	0
rixseys	1	1	0
/Elizabeth/ 11 wethers of 3 sheare		1	0

Sum 281 [301] 31 sold and 8 mortes, so he is right of these 32
stone 12½lb of wooll

[Alice Le Strange's new account from 1625][97]
[top of the page torn off]

[1625] [Pypers charge at Barrett Ringstead]
[Nicholas] [mother] ewes; 3 ewe shorlins; 27 ewe lambes; 11
188   wethers of 2 sheare; 19 wether lambes; 1 ramme lambe
/Hamone/ 64 mother ewes; 14 ewe shorlins; 29 ewes that were
bought; 13 ewe lambes whereof one bought; 9 wether lambes;
130   4 ramme lambes; 14 wethers of 2 sheare; 5 rammes
/Roger/ 101 mother ewes; 22 ewe shorlins; 23 ewe lambes;
4 rammes; 3 ramme lambes; 17 wethers of 2 sheare; 15 wether
185   lambes
/Elizabeth/ 63 mother ewes; 9 ewes bought; 11 ewe shorlins;
14 ewe lambes; 12 wethers of 2 sheare wherof one bought;
<104> 2 wethers of 3 sheare; 10 wether lambes; 1 ramme lambe; 4
106 rammes. Sum <579> 592

/Sedgford East Ground, Allens/ charge at Midsomer 1625:605
[p]   mother ewes; 117 ewe shorlins; 2 bell wethers; 14 olde rammes
[top quarter of page torn off] 106 wether shorlins; 1 stray wether;
110 wethers from Allen
/Nicholas/ 10 wethers of 2 sheare
/Hamon/ 6 wethers of 2 sheare
/Roger/ 10 wethers of 4 sheare; 11 wethers of 2 sheare
/Elizabeth/ 6 wethers of 4 sheare; 8 wethers of 2 sheare
Sum 356 and 100 joyce sheepe

[Ringsted South Ground] /Crisps/ charge at Midsomer 1625 189
wethers of 4 sheare and 3 sheare
/Nicholas/ 9 wethers of 3 sheare
/Hamon/ 38 wethers of 3 sheare and 4 sheare

---

97. This is the end of the children's and Alice's own sheep account; the transcript returns
to the front of the book for the new accounts Alice started in 1625.

/Roger/ 34 wethers of 3 sheare; 2 wether hoggs bought
/Elizabeth/ 9 wethers of 3 sheare
Sum 261 [*281*]

1626 /Sedgford East Ground, Allen/ brought to the clipping at
Midsomer: 686 mother ewes /*36 morts, 133 croned*/; 126 ewe
shorlins /*7 dizy sold, 23 morts*/; 2 bell wethers; 13 olde rammes
819 /*1 mort, 1 croned*/; 12 yonge rammes
500 [*579*] lambes, wanting one, whereof: 60 for tithe lambes; for
marking lambes; 172 store ewe lambes; 80 store wether lambes;
60 store wether lambes to sell; 16 fatt lambes to sell; 174 lambes
to sell; 13 pooke lambes whereof one blinde to sell worth little all
of them. Of the 819 [*839*] sheep I had 64½ stone of wooll the
tithe payd

		£	s	d
[*p*]	[*page damaged*] /Allen/ hath delivered since Midsomer 1625			
	6 skinnes whereof 1 stroyed sold for	1	13	0
	[*illegible*] dizy hogges sold before the clipping			
	[*illegible*] sheep sold at the clipping		17	0
	[*illegible*] sheep brought home from clipping worth little or nothing			
	[*illegible*] crones sold to Watts for 3s 4d a piece [*illegible*] one given into the bargain	22	3	4
	Sold to one of Well[*s*] 20 crones	4	0	0
	169 lambes sold to Watts	17	6	6
	5 lambes sold to others for		8	6
	13 very little pook lambes whereof one blinde		6	0
	16 fatt lambes sold for 3s a piece	2	8	0
	60 wether lambe sold for	10	0	0
	Sum	60	2	10

[*1626*] /Sedgford North Ground, Lennard/ brought to the clipping at
Midsomer 1626

	15 wethers of 5 sheare /*sold 20*/	8	10	0
280	265 wethers of 3 sheare and 2 sheare /*morts 25*/ and of those about 90 wether shorlins	13	10	0

/Nicholas/ 10 wethers of 3 sheare
/Hamon/ 6 wethers of 3 sheare
/Roger/ 10 wethers of 5 sheare; 10 wethers of 4 sheare
/Elizabeth/ 6 wethers of 5 sheare; 8 wethers of 3 sheare
Sum 310 [*330*] so he is right, of these 41 stone and 5½lb the tithe
payd, 2 of these were brought home, dizy worth nothing *sold
for 1s* and 3 dyed a weeke after they were clipped and delivered
to Crisp

/Barrett Ringsted, Pyper/ brought to the clipping at Midsomer
1626: 3 rammes
/Nicholas/ 126 mother ewes /4 morts, 20 croned/; 26 ewe shorlins
/1 mort/; 1 ramm shorlin; <19> *16* wether shorlins /3 morts/; 11
180   wethers of 3 sheare
/20 wether lambes, 29 ewe lambes, 49 pookes, 8 fatt lambes/
[p]   /Hamon/ 115 mother ewes /2 morts, 23 croned/; 13 ewe shorlins; 9
wether shorlins; nll ramm <lambes> *shorlins*; 14 wethers of 3
126   sheare; 5 rammes
/26 wether lambes, 18 ewe lambes, 47 pookes, 1 fatt lambe/
/Roger/ 120 mother ewes /3 morts, 10 croned/; 23 ewe shorlins;
14 wether shorlins; nll ramm shorlins; 16 wethers of 3 sheare;
178   4 rammes
/5 wether lambes//21 ewe lambes//50 pookes//3 fatt lambes/
/Elizabeth/ 80 <shorlin> *mother* ewes /3 morts, 21 croned/; 13
ewe shorlins /1 mort/; 11 wethers of 3 sheare /1 mort/; nll wethers
100   of 4 sheare /2 sold/; 10 wether shorlins; nll ramm lamb; 4 rammes
/14 wether lambes, 16 ewe lambes, 29 pookes, 2 fatt lambes/
Sum 567 [592] and 25 skinnes; of these I had 49 stone 10lbs of wooll
/Sheep/ taken from Pyper 1626:
/Nicholas/ 11 wethers of 3 sheare to Crisp
/Hamon/ 14 wethers of 3 sheare to Crisp
/Roger/ 16 wethers of 3 sheare to Crisp
86 croned; 2 sold. Sum 108 [129] sheepe
[p]   Remayne with Pyper 459 sheepe beside lambes
/Ringsted South Ground, Crisp/ brought to the clipping 1626
139 wethers of 4 sheare /5 morts, 43 sold/
/Nicholas/ 8 wethers of 4 sheare /1 sold/
/Hamon/ 4 wethers of 4 sheare /34 sold/
/Roger/ 10 wethers of 4 sheare /24 sold/; 1 wether of 2 sheare /1 mort/
/Elizabeth/ 3 wethers of 4 sheare
Sum 165 <265> so he is right, of these I had 22 stone [of wool]

/Sheepe/ taken from Crisp since 1625 with mortes [or] 6 skinnes whereof one Rogers	£	s	d
22 wethers of <5> *4* sheare before Midsomer /sold/	9	18	0
20 wethers of 4 sheare before Midsomer	9	10	0
3 wethers of 4 sheare before Midsomer	1	8	9
<5 wethers to the clipping			
/Nicholas/ 1 wether of 4 sheare sold for		9	7
/Hamon/ 34 wethers of 4 sheare	16	5	10
/Roger/ 24 wethers of 4 sheare	11	6	1
6 wethers of 4 sheare	2	17	6

/Sedgford East Ground, Allens/ charge at Midsomer 1626: 547
<549, 586> mother ewes; one stray ewe; 126 ewe shorlins; 2 bell
700   wethers; 12 olde rammes; 12 <yng> yonge rammes
172 store ewe lambes; 80 store wether lambes
Sum 912 [*952*]

/Barrett Ringsted, Pypers/ charge at Midsomer 1626
/of my owne/ 3 ramms
/Nicholas/ 106 mother ewes; 26 ewe shorlins; 29 ewe lambes; 17
199   wether shorlins whereof one bought; 20 wether lambes 2 were
rammes; a ramm shorlin
[*p*] 133 */Hamon/* 82 mother ewes; 13 ewe shorlins; 18 ewe lambes; 9
wether shorlins; 26 wether lambes; 5 rammes
/Roger/ 100 mother ewes; 18 ewes bought; 23 ewe shorlins; 21 ewe
lambes; 14 wether shorlins; 31 wether lambes with 2 ramm
191   lambes; 4 rammes
/Elizabeth/ 59 mother ewes; 13 ewe shorlins; 17 ewe lambes
whereof one bought *a wether*; 10 wether shorlins; 14 wether
<shorlins> lambes; 60 wether lambes bought; 11 wethers of 3
168   sheare; 4 rammes
Sum of Pypers charge is 674 [*694*] and 40 joyce sheepe

1626   */Crisp/* had remaining in his charge at Midsomer: 165 sheep and   £   s   d
he received of Lennard <388> 308 sheep in all 473 sheep of these
sold 45 wethers for   18   0   0
60 to Edmond Cremer for   22 10   0
Sum remayne is 388 [*368*]

/Ringsted South Ground, Crispes/ charge at Midsomer 1626
/of my owne/ 54 wethers of 3 sheare */3 morts, 51 sold/*
15 wethers of 5 sheare, */15 sold/*
163 wethers of 2 and 3 sheare from Lennard */2 morts, 89 sold/*
312   100 wether shorlins whereof 29 rixseys
<28>   */Nicholas/* 8 wethers of 4 sheare */1 mort/*; 11 wethers of 3 sheare
29   from Pyper 3 were rixseys; 10 wethers of 3 sheare from Lennard
/Hamon/ 4 wethers of 4 sheare; 6 wethers of 3 sheare from
24   Lennard; 14 wethers of 3 sheare from Pyper
/Roger/ 10 wethers of 4 sheare; 1 wether of 2 sheare; 10 wethers of
5 sheare from Lennard; 10 wethers of 4 sheare from Lennard; 16
47   wethers of 3 sheare from Pyper
17   */Elizabeth/* 3 wethers of 3 sheare; 6 wethers of 5 sheare from
Lennard; 8 wethers of 3 sheare from Lennard
[*p*]   Sum 409 [*429*]

[*1627*] /*Sedgford East Ground*/ Allen brought to the clipping at
Midsomer 1627: 810 sheep whereof: 632 mother ewes /*33 <43>*
morts, 116 crones, remain 516/; 112 ewe shorlins,/*40 morts, remain*
112, 4 dizy/; [*illegible*] bell wethers; [*illegible*] olde rammes; 12
yonge rammes; 68 wether shorlins
Sum 810 and 93 [73] mortes. So he wanteth 9 sheep for his
charge was 912, in wooll 60 stone and 4lb the tithe payd

/*Allen*/ brought in lambes 461 whereof 54 for tithe; 2 marking
lambes; 22 fatt lambes sold; 214 pooke lambes sold; 100 store
wether lambes; 100 store ewe lambes; 6 lame lambes in East hall;
3 worth nothing in the <east> Park

/*Taken*/ from Allen at Midsomer 1627	£	s	d
116 crones sold at £21	23	16	0
2 fatt ewes sold		16	0
4 dizy sheep worth nothing			
2 fatt lambes sold		10	0
20 lambes sold	3	6	0
214 pokes sold at £11	23	5	8
60 wether shorlins to Crisp			
Sum 182 sheep and 236 lambes			

/*Sedgford East Ground, Allens*/ charge at Midsomer 1627: 514
mother ewes; 108 ewe shorlins; 2 bell wethers; 12 olde rammes;
12 yonge rammes; 9 ewes that Allen must make good; 100 store
ewe lambes; 100 ewe lambes bought; 100 store wether lambes.

[*p*] Sum 917 [*957*] sheepe and a new stray sheepe which was challenged

/*Barrett Ringsted, Pyper*/ brought to the clipping at Midsomer
1627 /*of my owne*/ 3 ramms /*2 croned*/
/*Nicholas*/ 117 mother ewes /*15 morts, 1 sold, 16 croned*/; 16 wethers
of 2 sheare /*1 mort*/; 1 ramm of 2 sheare; 2 ramm shorlins; 16

178 wether shorlins /*2 morts*/; 26 ewe shorlins /*1 dizy, 3 morts*/
/*Lambes*/ 33 store ewe lambes; 24 store wether lambes; 44 lambes
101 to sell whereof 39 pooke
/*Hamon*/ 82 mother ewes /*13 morts, 10 croned*/; 16 ewe shorlins
/*2 morts*/; 22 wether shorlins /*4 morts*/; 5 rammes; 9 wethers of

134 2 sheare
/*Lambes*/ 13 store ewe lambes, 22 store wether lambes; 35 lambes
91 to sell whereof 30 pookes
/*Roger*/ 142 mother ewes /*19 morts, 1 sold, 20 croned*/; 17 ewe
shorlins /*2 dizy, 4 morts*/; 14 wethers of 2 sheare; 4 rammes; 2

206 ramm shorlins; 27 wether shorlins /*2 morts*/

/Lambes/ 28 store ewe lambes; 28 store wether lambes; 48 lambes

83   to sell whereof 43 pookes

/Bess/ 63 mother ewes */9 morts, 2 sold, 11 croned/*; 12 ewe shorlins */4 morts/*; 4 rammes; 10 wethers of 2 sheare; 69 wether shorlins

169   */6 morts/*; 11 wethers of 4 sheare

/Lambes/ 17 store ewe lambes; 15 store wether lambes; 35 lambes to sell whereof 30 pookes

Sum 710 and 84 skinnes. So he is right, of these I had 47½ stone

/Taken/ from Pyper at Midsomer 1627

/of my owne/ 2 rammes croned

/Nicholas/ 16 crones whereof 1 dyed and 15 sold; one ewe sold; one ewe dizy worth nothing; 16 wethers of 2 sheare to Crisp; 16

50   wether shorlins to Crisp; 44 lambes sold

[p]   */Hamons/* 10 crones sold; 9 wethers of 2 sheare to Crisp; 22

41   wether shorlins to Crisp; 35 lambes sold

/Roger/ 20 crones sold; one fatt ewe sold; 2 dizy ewe shorlins worth nothing; 3 wethers of 2 sheare sold; 11 wethers of 2 sheare

64   to Crisp; 27 wether shorlins to Crisp; 48 lambes sold

/Elizabeth/ 11 crones sold; 2 fatt ewes sold; 11 wethers of 4 sheare sold; 10 wethers of 2 sheare to Crisp; 69 wether shorlins to Crisp;

143   38 lambes sold

The sum taken from Pyper is 258. So Pyper hath still 452 sheepe and 180 lambes all sold to Mr Strange at these prises following

Mother ewes of Nicholas 120 and of Hamon 72, of Roger 121, of Elizabeth 50, in all 363 at 7s sold for	127	1	0
Ewe shorlins of Nicholas 25, of Hamon 16, of Roger 15, of Elizabeth 12 in all 68 at 6s	20	8	0
Rammes of Nicholas 3, of Hamon 5, of Roger 6, of Elizabeth 4 at 5s sold for	4	10	0
Store ewe lambes of Nicholas 33, of Hamon 13, of Roger 28, of Elizabeth 17 in all <81> 91 ewe lambes. And wether lambes of Nicholas 24, of Hamon 22, of Roger 28, of Elizabeth 15 in all wether lambes 89 which with the 91 ewe lambes make 180 sold	34	10	0

/Barrett Ringsted, Pypers/ charge at Midsomer 1627: 19 rammes with one of my owne; 363 mother ewes; 68 ewe shorlins; <126>

91 ewe lambes; 89 wether lambes 10 were rams; 8 ewe lambes

[p]   bought; 12 rixey lambes that were gellt. Sum 550 [650] and 40 cullett [sheep]

/Ringsted South Ground, Crisp/ brought to the clipping at Midsomer 1627

/of my owne/ 92 wethers of 3 sheare */5 morts/*; 90 wethers of 2

192   sheare */1 mort/*; 29 rixseys of 2 sheare

/Nicholas/ 7 wethers of 5 shear /1 mort/; 18 wethers of 4 sheare;
3 rixseys
/Hamon/ 16 wethers of 4 sheare

40   /Roger/ 4 wethers of 6 sheare; <19> *17* wethers /1 mort/ 2 rixseys
of 5 sheare; 16 wethers of 4 sheare; 1 wether of 3 sheare

16   /Elizabeth/ 5 wethers of 6 sheare; 11 wethers of 4 sheare

	£	s	d
Sum 271<272> sheepe and 8 skinnes and sold before clipping as followeth			
/of my owne/ 18 crone wethers to George Bastard	5	2	0
1 dizy wether sold for		3	0
121 wether to Mr Hobson	58	9	11
15 wethers sold	6	0	0
/Hamon/ 8 wethers sold for	3	4	0
/Roger/ 6 wethers sold for	2	8	0
/Elizabeth/ 1 wether sold for		8	0

Sum 170 sold which being added to 279 above, it amounteth to
489 [449] which was Crispes charge. So he is right, of these I had
the tithe payd 28 stone 2lb

	£	s	d
/Taken/ from Crisp at Midsomer 1627			
/of my owne/ 29 rixses of 2 sheare sold to George Bastard at 4s	5	16	0
/Nicholas/ 3 rixseys sold for		12	0
7 wethers of 5 sheare	2	16	0
/Roger/ 12 wethers of 5 sheare	4	16	0
2 rixseys		8	0
4 wethers of 6 sheare	1	12	0
/Elizabeth/ 5 wethers of 6 sheare	2	0	0

Sum <60> *62* sheep

Mr Strange bought all the wethers in Crisps and Pypers charge
at the rate following:
/Nicholas/ 18 wethers of 4 sheare in Crisps charge <and 16
wethers of 2 sheare from Pyper>
/Hamon/ 16 wethers of 4 sheare with Crisp and Pyper <and 9
wethers of 2 sheare from Pyper>
/Roger/ 5 wethers of 5 sheare, 16 wethers of 4 sheare and a wether

[p]   of 3 sheare with Crisp <and 11 wethers of 2 sheare from Pyper>
/Elizabeth/ 11 wethers of 4 sheare with Crisp So the sum of
wethers of 3 and 4 and 5 sheare is 67 at 8s   26   16   0
/Nicholas/ 16 wethers of 2 sheare from Pyper
/Hamon/ 9 wethers of 2 sheare from Pyper
11 wethers of 2 sheare from Pyper

10 wethers of 2 sheare from Pyper
So there is 46 wethers of 2 sheare at 7s   16 2 0
/Nicholas/ 16 wether shorlins from Pyper
/Hamon/ 22 wether shorlins from Pyper
/Roger/ 27 wether shorlins from Pyper
/Elizabeth/ 69 wether shorlins from Pyper So there is 134 at
6s 8d all delivered to Crisp   44 13 8

/Ringsted South Ground, Crisps/ charge at Midsomer 1627: 159
wethers of 3 and 4 sheare; 136 wethers of 2 sheare; 134 wether
shorlins; 60 wether shorlins from Allen. Sum 409 [489]

1628   /Sedgford East Ground, Allen/ brought to the clipping at
Midsomer: 601 <602> mother ewes /30 morts, 73 croned, remain
548/; 143 ewe shorlins /32 morts, remain 143/; 2 bell wethers; 12
olde rammes; 12 yonge rammes; 58 wether shorlins /42 morts/
/Lambes 300 the tithe payd/, 18 very little lambes
Sum of sheepe 808 [828] which with 5 ewe hoggs brought home
before clipping and sold for 15s 10d, and 104 mortes, he is right,
of these 52 stone 3lb of wooll the tithe payd

	£	s	d
/Lambes sold/ to Mr Cooper 222 lambes for	26	16	6
sold 20 lambes at 2s 9d	2	15	0
18 little lambes sold for		10	6
2 for marking lambes			
116 store lambes			
/Crones sold/ 73 crones sold to Mr Cooper at 4s 6d	16	8	6
one dizy ewe he brought home & dyed			

112   58 wethers he delivered to Crisp
[p]   So Allen hath remayning old sheep 716 and 116 lambes

/Barrett Ringsted Ground, Pyper/ brought to the clipping at
Midsomer 1628: <370> *415* mother ewes & ewe shorlins /51
morts, 29 sold, 386 croned/; 29 rammes; 76 wether shorlins /15
morts/ /Lambes/ 395 lambes. Sum of sheep 500 [520] which with
the mortes maketh up 546 [586]. So he wanteth 4 sheep to make
up of these I had 43 stone of wooll
/Lambes/ 104 lambes sold to Mr Cooper at 2s 5d   14 19 8
11 lambes sold at 2s 9d   1 10 3
one marking lambe
176 store lambes
3 left in the close that would not drive

/*Crones sold*/ 20 crones sold to Mr Cooper whereof one was given
into the lambes at 4s 6d   4   5   6
2 sold for   5   0
6 crones sold to George Bastard   1   7   0
one dyed worth nothing
9 dizy hoggs brought home whereof 6 sold for 11s 6d and 3 dyed
nothing worth   11   6
76 wethers to deliver to Crisp
Sum <38>114 So Pyper hath, with 4 he should make good, 410
old sheep and 176 store lambes

/*Ringsted South Ground, Crisp*/ brought to the clipping 1628
290 wethers
100 sold for   57   10   0
30 sold for   13   10   0
/*Mortes*/ 9 mortes
Sum 409 [*429*] so he is right, of these I had 31½ stone. So Crisp
hath remaining 290

/*Barrett Ringsted Ground, Pypers*/ charge at Midsomer 1628: 381
<377> mother ewes and ewe shorlins; 29 rammes; 100 store ewe
lambes; 76 store wether lambes; 2 wethers bought; 18 ewes
[p]   bought. Sum 586 [*606*] and 40 joyce sheep

1628   /*Sedgford East Ground, Allens*/ <brought to the clipping at
Midsomer> charge at Midsomer: 690 mother ewes and ewe
shorlins; 2 bell wethers; 12 olde rams; 14 yonge ramms; 66 ewe
lambes; 20 wether lambes 2 were ramms. Sum 812

/*Ringsted South Ground, Crisps*/ charge at Midsomer 1628: 290
wethers of his owne charge; 58 wethers from Allen; 76 wethers
from Pyper. Sum 404 [*424*]

1629   /*Sedgford East Ground, Allen*/ brought to the clipping at
Midsomer: 703 mother ewes and ewe shorlins /*2 dizy, 28 morts,
96 croned, remain 719*/; 2 bell wethers; 48 wether shorlins; 29
ramms /*4 croned*/. Sum 782 which with 2 dizy that were sold for
5s and 28 mortes, his sum of 812 is right, of these I had 68 stone
want 3lb the tithe payd
1629   /*Lambes*/ Allen brought 536 wherof for tithe, because there were   £   s   d
4 od lambes[98] the last yeare, 64. So remayne 492 lambes wherof

---

98. For the payment of the tithe, odd lambs are those left over from division by 10; they
are then added to the next years tally. These calculations became more frequent after 1643.

203 sold to Mr Cooper for   33   2   6
40 sold to Lawes of Wullferton   6   0   0
21 fatt lambes sold at 3s 4d for   3   10
7 suckerell lambes sold for   17   6
109 store wether lambes & ramm lambes; 130 store ewe lambes;
2 marking lambes. Sum 492 [*512*]

/*Sheepe*/ taken from Allen at Midsomer 1629
100 crones wherof 4 rammes sold at 4s 4d   21   13   4
2 dizy aat the clipping nothing worth
a fatt ewe sold for   8   0
48 wether shorlins delivered to Crisp
Sum 131 [*151*] which being taken out of 782, there remayneth 652
which he delivered to Thistle

/*Ringsted South Ground, Crisp*/ brought to the clipping at
Midsomer 1629: 337 wethers /*13 morts*/
sold 50 wethers   22   8   4
[*p*]   Sum with 13 mortes 400. So he wanteth 4 sheep

/*Sheep*/ taken from Crisp at the clipping 30 wethers sold for   12   15   0
So remayne with Crisp with the 4 sheep that he wanteth 311
wethers

/*Barrret Ringsted, Pyper*/ brought to the clipping at Midsomer
1629: 473 mother ewes and ewe shorlins /*21 morts*/; 29 ramms;
59 wether shorlins /*19 morts*/
Sum 541 [*561*] and 40 mortes and 2 dizy sold for 10s so he
wanteth 3 sheep that he is to make good. /*Wooll 48 stone*/

/*Lambes*/ Pyper brought 315 lambes wherof 165 sold to Mr
Cooper for   15   2   6
7 sold at 3s 4d   1   3   4
one markin lambe; 78 store wether lambes; 104 store ewe lambes.
Sum 315 [*355*]

/*Sheep*/ taken from Pyper at Midsomer 1629
64 croned sold for   10   17   0
4 rammes to Thistle; 59 wethers to Crisp
Sum <108> 107 [*127*] which being taken out of 541, there
remayneth with Pyper 434, and the 3 sheep that he wanteth

1629   /*Barrett Ringsted Ground*/ Pypers charge at Midsomer 1629
412 ewes and ewe shorlins and a bell wether; 104 ewe lambes; 25
rammes; 78 wether lambes with 3 ram lambes.

Sum 599 [*619*] and 40 joyce sheep, and 2 crones were left that would not drive

1629   /*Sedgford East Ground*/ Thistles charge at Midsomer 1629
     620 ewes and ewe shorlins; 130 ewe lambes; 27 rammes; 4
     rammes from Pyper; 109 wether lambes and ram lambes.
     Sum 879 [*890*] wherof one is marked for my Lady Yellverton
[*p*]   and one of the ewe lambes

     /*Ringsted South Ground*/ Crisps charge at Midsomer 1629:
     311 wethers; 59 wethers from Pyper; 48 wethers from Thistle;
     16 wethers bought and 10 for Cooper. Sum 419 & 10 wethers
     delivered to Cooper to the North Ground

	£	s	d
1630[99] Crisp brought to the clipping with the 10 wethers which he did not deliver to Cooper – 375 wethers /*11 morts*/ more which he had for a wether, 1 ewe			
sold 51 wethers	22	10	0
Sum 409 [*427*] so he wanteth 5 <6> sheepe with which he hath 371, of these I had 49 stone of wooll the tithe being payd			
1630 Sheepe to be taken from Crisp			
1 dizy sold for 2s			
80 wethers sold for, 21 more sold – 100	44	15	0
A dizy more sold for 2s			
[? 1320] ewe to Pyper			
Sum 103 wethers beside 10 wethers to deliver to Cooper So Crisp hath still of his wethers 288			

1630   Pyper brought to the clipping as followeth: 477 ewes and ewe
     shorlins /*38 morts, 5 dizy*/; 19 ramms and 3 yong rams /*3 morts*/; 1
     bell wether; 64 wether shorlins, /*11 morts*/
     Sum 544 [*564*] of these I had of wooll 51st 3lb the 544 sheepe
     with the 57 morts and dizy maketh 601 so he wanteth no sheep

	£	s	d
1630 Lambes delivered by Pyper as followeth: 70 store wether lambes; 4 store ramm lambes; 87 store ewe lambes			
9 fatt lambes sold for	1	16	0
3 little lambes sold for		15	0
60 small lambes sold at Kenningall at 22d	5	10	0
140 lambes sold to Mr Cooper for	17	15	6
Sum 335 lambes			

---

99. From 1630 the date usually appears in the LH margin.

		£	s	d
1630	Sheep taken from Pyper			
	60 crones at 3s 11d to Mr Cooper	11	15	0
	6 crones to George Bastard	1	4	0
	8 crones poore ones sold for		12	0
	64 wether shorlins delivered to Crisp			
[p]	Sum 118 [138] remayne 426 sheep			

1630 /Sedgford East Ground/ Thistle brought to the clipping: 697 ewes
and ewe shorlins /71 morts, 2 dizy/; a bell wether; 28 rammes; 105
wether shorlins *with a bell wether* /4 morts/
Sum 811 [831] of these I had 80 stone of wooll the tithe payd;
the 811 with the dizy and 75 mortes maketh 868 sheepe & he
delivered more 2 of my Lady Yellvertons.

		£	s	d
1630	Thistle brought lambes as followeth:			
	15 fatt lambes sold for	3	0	0
	2 lambes sold for		6	0
	2 lambes sold at the sheares for		6	8
	100 lambes sold at Kenningale for	9	4	0
	40 lambes sold to Crisp for	6	0	0
	18 lambes sold to Roll	2	14	0
	20 lambes sold to Mr Cooper	2	4	6

2 markin lambes; 57 tithe lambes and 4 od to tithe 1631 160 store
ewe lambes; 108 store wether lambes; 29 wether lambes to Pyper;
1 lambe of my Lady Yellvertons.
Sum 494 [554]

		£	s	d
1630	Sheep taken from Thistle			
	4 rammes delivered to Pyper			
	60 crones wherof 5 rammes sold for	11	15	0
	one fatt ewe sold for		8	0

2 dizy came home at the clipping *sold for 16d* <4 dizy dyed
presently after the clipping>; 106 wether shorlins *with the bell
wether* to Crisp.
Sum 153 [173] so remayne with Thistle

1630 /Sedgford East Ground/ Thistle his charge at Midsomer: 634 ewes
and ewe shorlins; nll bell wether; 24 rammes; 160 ewe lambes for
store; 108 wether lambes *and 20 ramms* for store
Sum 906 [926] and 2 ewes and a lambe of my Lady Yellvertons in
[p]   all 909

1630 /Ringsted South Ground/ Crisps charge at Midsomer: 288 olde wethers; 106 wether shorlins of Thistle; 69 wether shorlins of Pyper. Sum 418 [463]

1630 to Cooper 10 wethers

1630 Pypers charge at Midsomer: 403 ewes and ewe shorlins; 1 ewe from Crisp; 22 rammes; 1 bell wether; 4 rammes from Thistle; 71 store wether lambes; 4 store ram lambes; 86 store ewe lambes; 29 store wether lambes
Sum 600 beside 40 joyce sheepe, the full stock is 600 [621]

1631 Thistle brought to the clipping: 701 ewes and ewe shorlins /113 morts, 60 crones/; 29 olde rams /10 crones/; 16 yonge ramms /4 morts/; 53 wether shorlins /35 morts/; 3 ewes of my Lady Yellvertons. Sum 777 [802] and 132 morts which maketh 909 sheepe, of the 777 sheepe I had 75 stone of wooll the tithe payd, and 5lb of my Lady Yellvertons untithed

1631 Thistle brought lambes as followeth: 405 wherof one is my   £   s   d
Lady Yellvertons, 48 of these for tithe; 4 lambes were odd the
last yeare & 4 odd this yeare, for these 8 lambes and one of my
Lady Yellvertons Mr Loads had 2s 4d for tithe

20 fatt lambes sold for	4	0	0
4 lambes sold to Bassam for		2	8
2 lambes sold to Roll for		6	8
110 lambes sold to Thomson at 2s	9	4	0

2 marking lambes; 238 lambes reserved for store; 1 lambe of my

377 Lady Yellvertons
[p] 20 lambes sold for   3   0   0

1631 Sheep taken from Thistle

4 dizy came sold for	4	6
one dizy wether hogge sold for	5	0

52 wether shorlins to Crisp; 70 croned wherof 3 dyed and Thistle hath skins to add to his next morts
Sum 107 [127] So remayne with Thistle 670

1631 /Barrett Ringsted, Charge 600/ Pyper brought to the clipping 569 ewes and wether shorlins and rams /31 morts/
Sum 569, beside mortes, of these I had 53½ stone of wooll

1631   Pyper brought as followeth in lambes 350
48 store wether lambes; 82 store ewe lambes; 1 markin lambe for the sheppheard

2 lambes sold for		6	0
6 lambes sold for		14	0
220 small lambes sold to Thomson for	25	16	0
11 pooke lambes sold for		3	4

Sum 350

/Sheepe/ taken from Pyper 1631

80 crones sold for 3 dyed Pyper hath the skins	11	13	8

101 wether hoges delivered to Crisp
Sum 161. So remayne with Pyper olde sheepe 408

1631   /Charge 428, Crisp/ brought to the clipping 369 wethers
<30 for the kitching none of his charge>
<30 more for the kitching none of his charge>

66 wethers sold for	31	1	6

<1 dizy sold none of his charge>
1 he sayeth he left with Thistle which dyed /not true/
11 mortes. Sum 427 so he wanteth one sheep, of the 369 wethers I had 49 stone 6lb

/Sheep/ taken from Crisp 1631

26 rixseys sold for	6	1	4

30 wethers for the kitching; 40 wethers for the kitching
Sum 96. So Crisp hath still in his charge beside one 2 he is to make good 293 wethers

1631   /Ringsted South Ground/ Crisps charge 1631: 293 wethers; 2 wethers which he was to allow; 101 wether hoggs from Barrett Ringsted; 52 wether hoggs from Sedgford East Ground.

[p]   Sum 408 [448]

1631   /Sedgford East Ground/ Thistles charge 1631: 640 ewes and ewe shorlins; 30 ramms; 100 wether lambes store; 158 store ewe lambes. Sum 908 [928] and more 3 ewes and a lamb of my Lady Yellvertons

1631   /Barrett Ringsted Ground/ Pypers charge 1631: 408 ewes, rams and ewe shorlins; 68 store wether lambes; 62 store ewe lambes; 30 store ewe lambes. Sum 548 [568]

1632 /Barrett Ringsted/ Pyper delivered to Cooper 1632 clipped: 431
ewes and ewe shorlins /45 morts/; 24 ramms; 53 wether hogs /15
morts/. Sum 508 and 60 mortes, so Pyper delivered right 548, but
he wanteth 3 crones skins, of these 508 I had 44½ stone of wooll
/Pyper/ delivered lambes 310 as followeth 1632
70 store wether lambes; 70 store ewe lambes

6 twinn lambes sold for	1	0	0
11 lambes sold for	1	16	8
90 lambes sold at Kennigale for 15½d	6	4	0
102 lambes sold at Coolidg for 17¼d	7	8	0

1 marking lambe
Sum 310 [350]

1632 /Sheepe/ taken from Cooper 1632
53 wether hoggs delivered to Crisp

52 crones sold for 2s <5d ½ > at Coolidg	5	4	0

Sum 105 sheepe. So remayne with Cooper 403 sheepe

1632 /Sedgford East Ground [charge] 900/ Thistle delivered to
Greenwood and clipped 1632: 696 ewes ramms and ewe shorlins
/132 morts/; 73 wether hoggs /27 morts/. Sum 749 [769] and 159
skinns, so he is right, of these 749 sheep I had 55 stone of wooll;
more Thistle delivered to Cooper 4 ewes and 2 lambes of my
Lady Yellvertons and 3 crone skinnes of 1631

[p]

1632 /Sedgford/ Thistle delivered lambes 333 as followeth:
83 store wether lambes; 95 store ewe lambes

	£	s	d
93 lambes sold at Coolidge for	6	19	0
65 lambes sold at Kenningale for	4	8	5
16 lambes sold for	2	17	10

2 markin lambes; 39 tithe lambes and 3 to goe on the next yeare.
Sum 333 [393]

1632 /Sheepe/ taken from Greenwood 1632
73 wether hogges to Crisp

65 crones sold for	6	10	0
11 crones sold for	1	9	4

Sum 129 [149] So there remayneth with Greenwood 620

1632 /Ringsted South Ground/ Crisp brought to the clipping:
289 wethers

100 wethers sold for	46	3	4
6 wethers sold for	2	14	0

/*May*/ 20 wethers sold for   9   0   0
5 crone dizy wethers sold for 8s   8   6
Sum 400 [*420*] and 24 skinns. So he wanteth <3> *4* sheepe of
the 289 wethers I had 33½ stone

Sheepe taken from Crisp 1632
/*Septem 8*/ 20 wethers sold for   8 10   0
/*Septem 29*/ 20 wethers sold for   9   0   0
Sum 40. So there remayneth with Crisp 249 and 3 *4* for those
he lost

1632   /*Ringsted South Ground*/ Crisps charge 1632: 249 wethers; <3>
       4 wethers he is to allow; 73 wether hoggs from Greenwood; 53
       wether hoggs from Cooper; 53 wether lambes bought of Robert
       Segon; 1 ewe lambe bought of Segon. Sum 413 [*433*]

1632   /*Sedgford East Ground*/ Greenwoods charge 1632: 610 ewes and
       ewe shorlins; 28 ramms; 2 bell wethers; 83 store wether lambes;
       95 store ewe lambes; 19 ewe lambes bought of Robert Segon.
[*p*] Sum 797 sheepe [*837*]

1632   /*Barrett Ringsted*/ Coopers charge 1632: 399 ewes and ewe
       shorlins *with* <and> 3 crones; 24 ramms; 3 ewes from Pyper
       for 3 he lost; 70 store ewe lambes; 70 store wether lambes. Sum
       <527> *526* [*566*] more to Cooper 4 ewes and 2 lambes of my
       Lady Yellvertons

1633   /*Barrett Ringsted*/ Cooper brought to the clipping 1633: 445 ewes
       rams and ewe shorlins /*19 morts*/; 48 wether hoggs /*32 morts*/.
       Sum 493 sheepe and 51 skins. So he wanteth 2 sheep to make
       526, of these 493 sheepe I had 37 stone and a halfe of wooll

1633   Cooper brought lambes as followeth: £   s   d
       60 store ewe lambes; 60 store wether lambes
       4 lambes sold for   13   4
       150 lambes sold at 22d   15 11   8
       5 little lambes sold for   2   6
       1 markin lambs. Sum 260 [*280*] lambes

       /*Sheepe*/ taken from Cooper 1633: 48 wether shorlins to Crisp
       49 crones sold for 2s 6d a piece   6   2   6
       Sum 97. So remayne with Cooper 416 beside the 2 sheep that he
       wanteth, and my Lady Yellvertons 6 ewes and 4 lambes

1633   /Sedgford East Ground/ Greenwood brought to the clipping 1633:
        650 ewes, ramms and ewe shorlins /99 morts/; 46 wether shorlins
        /14 morts/. Sum 696 and 113 skins. So he wanteth to make up 797
        [817] 8 sheep, of these 696 sheepe I had 55 stone of wooll the tithe payd

1633   Greenwood brought lambes as followeth:

			£	s	d
80 store ewe lambes; 60 store wether lambes					
20 lambes sold for			3	6	8
170 lambes sold for at 22d			17	8	4
2 little lambes				2	6
2 markin lambes					
8 little lambes left in the flock to sell: solde				12	0
[p] 40 tithe lambes. Sum 342 [382] lambes					

1633   /Sheepe/ taken from Greenwood 1633: 46 wethers to Crisp

65 crones sold for at 2s 6d			8	15	0

        Sum 111 sheep. So Greenwood hath remayning 605 wherof 5 are
        crones to sell beside 8 which he wanteth

1633   /Ringsted South Ground/ Crisp brought to the clipping 1633
        277 wethers /<36> 40 morts, wherof 3 had no eares/; 16 wether
        hoggs /32 morts/; 5 wether hoggs after

/December/ 20 sold for			9	0	0
/January/ 20 sold for			9	0	0

        Sum 318 [338] and <68> *72* skinns, which maketh <386> *390*
        sheep, so he wanteth 23 sheepe, of 298 sheepe I had 31 stone

/Sheepe/ taken from Crisp 1633					
/August/ 20 wethers sold for			9	0	0
/October/ 5 wethers sold for			2	0	0
2 dizy sold for				4	0
a dizy sold for				2	0

        Sum 28 sheepe. So remayne with Crisp beside 23 which he wanteth

1633   /Ringsted South Ground/ Crisps charge 1633: 270 wethers;
        23 wethers which he was to make good; 46 wethers from
        Greenwood; 48 wethers from Cooper. Sum 367 [387]

1633   /Sedgford East Ground/ Greenwoods charge 1633: 600 ewes,
        ramms and ewe shorlins; 5 crone ewes left to sell; 8 ewes for 8 he
        wanted; 70 store wether lambes; 70 store ewe lambes

10 small lambes to sell sold for				14	6

[p]   Sum 713 [763] sheepe

1633   /*Barrett Ringsted*/ Coopers charge 1633: 416 ewes, ramms &
        hoggs; 2 ewes for 2 he wanted; 60 ewe lambes for store; 60
        wether lambes for store. Sum 418 [*438*] more 6 ewes & 4 lambes
        of my Lady Yellvertons

1634   /*Barrett Ringsted*/ Cooper brought to the clipping 1634: 45 wether
        shorlins, /*15 morts*/; 426 ewes, ramms and ewe shorlins /*29 morts*/.
        Sum 471 sheepe and 44 mortes which maketh 515, so he wanteth
        3 sheepe, of these 471 sheepe I had 47 stone of wooll

1634   Cooper brought lambes as followeth:
        100 store ewe lambes; 47 store wether lambes
        140 sold to Thomson at 2s 4d   18   13   4
        2 fatt lambes sold for   8   0
        3 little fatt lambes sold for   9   0
        10 lambes sold for   1   3   4
        1 markin lambe; 2 pooks worth nothing. Sum 305 lambes
        Sheepe taken from Cooper 1634: 82 crones sold for [?]; 45 wethers
        to Goodman
        3 ewes sold for   1   4   0
        Sum 110 [*130*] sheepe. Remayne with him 361

1634   /*Ringsted South Ground*/ Crisp brought to the clipping 1634
        [*charge*] /*367*/ 304 wethers /*8 morts*/
        21 wethers sold in January; 20 wethers sold in Aprill
        1 wether sold for   8   0
        1 wether sold   7   4
        3 dyzy wethers like to dye
        Sum 350 and 8 skinnes, so Crisp wanteth 9 sheepe, of the 304
        wethers I had 31 stone of wooll, for the 9 sheepe that he wanted
[*p*]   he payd 57s, and delivered his charge to Goodman

1634   /*Sedgford East Ground*/ Greenwood brought to the clipping:
        [*charge*] /*713*/ 613 ewes, ramms and shorlins /*59 morts*/; 60 wether
        shorlins /*2 morts*/; 4 of the 5 crones were delivered home and they
        were lost. Sum 657 [*677*] which with 61 mortes maketh 718, so he
        wanteth 15 sheepe, of these 653 sheepe I had 60 stone of wooll

1634   Greenwood brought lambes as followeth: £   s   d
        99 store wether lambes; 137 store ewe lambes
        2 fatt lambes sold for   8   0
        138 sold to Thomson at 2s 4d   18   8   8
        2 markin lambes and 6 pookes worth little
        Sum 364 [*384*]

Sheep taken from Greenwood
75 crones sold for [?]; 60 wether shorlins to Goodman
4 wethers sold   1   12   0
Sum <118> 119 [139] Remayne still with him <435> 535

1634   /Sedgford East Ground/ Greenwoods charge 1634: 534 ewes,
ramms and ewe shorlins; 15 ewes for 15 which he lost; 106 ewes
from Bircham; 99 wether lambes for store; 137 ewe lambes for
store. Sum 871 [891] sum now 801 <802> sheepe

[1634]   /Barrett Ringsted/ Coopers charge 1634: 361 ewes, ramms and ewe
shorlings; 30 of Bircham ewes; 3 ewes for 3 he wanteth; 100 ewe
lambes for store; 46 wether lambes for store
[p]   Sum 520 [540] beside: 20 ewes of little Nicholas Lestranges;[100] 10
ewes of the Lady Yellvertons; 5 lambes of the Lady Yellvertons; 1
lambe for little Ham.[101] The whole sum is *557* <557> [556]

[1634]   /Ringsted South Ground/ Goodmans charge 1634: 304 wethers; 60
shorlings from Greenwood; 45 wether shorlins from Cooper; 2
wethers from Greenwood. Sum 411

/Ringsted North Ground/
70 wether lambes to Richardson from Greenwood

The whole number of sheepe layd 1634
At Sedgford East Ground, /802/
At Ringsted South Ground, <521> [411]
At Barrett Ringsted Ground, [557]

1634   /charge 520, Barrett Ringsted/ Cooper delivered to Goodman
1635: 327 store ewes and rammes /morts 134; 34 wether shorlins to
Francis Crisp; 45 crones sold at 3s 6d for   7   17   6
Sum 406, which with 134 mortes do make 520 of the 407 sheepe
I had 27½ stone of wooll

1635   /Lambes/ 100 store lambes
32 fatt lambes sold for
66 pooke lambes sold for   20   0   0
2 marking lambes. Sum 200 lambes

---

100. Sheep given to grandchildren make an appearance. Nicholas Le Strange was born
in 1632.

101. Hamon was born in 1631. He died early in 1656, and it may be that he was impaired
in some way. His younger brother Nicholas was favoured from the outset with more sheep.

1635   Goodmans charge for Barrett Ringsted 327 store ewes and
rammes; 30 ewes bought; 100 store lambes. Sum 457 beside 20
ewes of little Nicholas Lestranges; 20 lambes of little Nicholas; 1
ewe shorling of little Hamms; 11 ewes of my Lady Yellvertons to
Sedgford; 4 lambes of my Lady Yellvertons to Sedgford. Sum 56

1634   [charge] /70/, *Ringsted North Ground/* Thomas Crisp received of
Richardson 1635, 46 wether shorlings /24 morts/ of these I had 2
[p]   stone 8lb of wooll

[1635]   /Sedgford East Ground/ Greenwood dyed and Osburn delivered
of his charge being 801 at Midsomer 1635: 606 store ewes and
ramms /123 morts/; 90 crone ewes; 20 wether shorlings to Francis
Crisp; 2 wethers Ringsted Flock before Midsomer. Sum 696
which with 123 mortes doe make 800 <700 5xx and 18> [819] so
he hath lost 1 of the 695, I had 45 stone of wooll the tithe payd

1635   /Lambes/ 153 store lambes beside 32 for tithe; 2 marking lambes;
114 pooke lambes sold for   4   0
6 little lambes worth nothing. Sum <258> 255 [275] the tithe payd
and 7 lambes to be tithed the next year

1635   Osburns charge of Sedgford East Ground 606 store ewes and
rammes; 153 store lambes; 32 lambes of the tithe bought of Mr
Waters. Sum <769> *771* [791] more which he wanted one

1635   /Ringsted South Ground/ Goodman delivered of his charge being
411 at Midsomer 1634
200 wethers for stock and 112 /morts 19/
30 crone wethers sold for   14 15 0
20 wethers sold for   9   0 0
30 wethers sold for   13 10 0
20 wethers sold for   9   0 0
Sum 392 [412] which with 19 mortes make 411, of the 311 sheep
I had 39 stone of wooll the tithe payd

1635   /Charge/ Francis Crisp for Ringsted South Ground: 312 store
wethers; 34 store wether hogges from Barrett Ringsted; 20
wether shorlings from Sedgford. Sum 346 <366> wethers

1635   /Ringsted North Ground/ Thomas Crisps charge 1635: 46 wethers
[p]

[1636] /Sedgford East Ground/ Osburn delivered 1636 as followeth, his
charge being at Midsomer 1635: <779> *772* sheepe, 608 store
sheep /morts III/; 40 wether shorlins to Crisp

50 crones to sell *sold for*   10   0   0

Sum 678 [698] and III mortes so he doth want 3 sheep which he
will deliver, of these 678 sheep I had 58 stone of wooll the tithe payd
/Lambes/ 210 small lambes wherof for tithe 25; 217 store lambe
wherof for tithe 24. Sum the tithe payd 378 of these: 187 store
lambes; 2 markin lambes

205 small lambes sold for   28   2   6

4 fatt lambes sold for

Sum 278 [298] of the 7 lambes left to tithe the last yeare 3 were
tithed with the 117 lambes and remayne to be tithed 1637, 4 lambes

1636   /Barrett Ringsted/ Goodman delivered 1636 his charge being at
Midsomer 1635: 457 and one of Hams and 40 of little Nicholas
he delivered as followeth

350 store sheep /morts 23/; 68 wether shorlins to Crisp

36 crones sold for   7   4   0

Sum 434 and 23 mortes so right of these 434 sheepe I had 42
stone & 4lbs of wooll of these I dizy worth nothing and one
sold, more he delivered of one ewe and a lambe of little Hams
and 34 ewes and 6 crones and 28 lambes of little Nicks.
/Lambes/ 115 store lambes wherof to Crisp *58*
2 markin lambes

30 fatt lambes sold for   6   0   0

11 fatt lambes sold for   2   4   0

160 small lambes beside sold for   22 10   0

Sum 290 [318] lambes beside 29 of the little boyes

1636   /Ringsted South Ground/ Francis Crisp delivered 1636, his charge
being <306> *346* wethers *1635*, 266 wethers /mortes 15/

80 wethers sold for <20 wethers sold £9>   36   0   0

5 crone wethers sold for   2   0   0

Sum 346 [366] with 15 mortes of the 266 wethers I had the tithe
payd 42 stone of wool; and 30 of the 266 were sold for   13 10   0

1636   /Ringsted North Ground/ Thomas Crisp delivered 1636, his charge
being 46 wethers as followeth 40 wethers, /4 morts/; 1 wether
dizy worth nothing; 1 lambe.

[p]   Sum 42 I had in wooll 4 stone 4lb

[1636] /Sedgford East Ground/ Osburns charge at Midsomer 1636: 611
charge store sheep; 187 store lambes; 24 lambes bought of Mr Waters.
Sum 802 [822] sheepe beside of my Lady Yellvertons 16 [sheep]

1636   /Barrett Ringsted/ Goodmans charge at Midsomer 1636: 350 store
charge sheep *and 60 bought*; 165 store lambes *wherof 28 bought*
Sum 475 [515]
Ham   2 wherof one lambe
Nick   62 wherof 28 lambes
Sum of all 519 [539]

[1636] /Ringsted South Ground/ Francis Crisps charge at Midsomer 1636:
£14[102] 236 wethers; 40 wether shorlins from Osburn; 68 wether shorlins
from Goodman. Sum 324 [344]

[1636] /Ringsted North Ground/ Francis Crisps charged with 1636:
41 received of Thomas Crisp wherof 40 are wethers and one a
lambe; 58 wether lambes from Goodman. Sum 99

[1637] /Sedgford East Ground/ Osborne delivered 1637 as followeth,   £   s   d
his charge being 1636: 802 sheepe
731 store sheep ewes and rammes /morts 69/
1 ewe sold for   8   0
1 ramm sold for   2   0
Sum 733 & 69 mortes, so he is right, of these clipped 731 of
which I had 74 stone of wooll and a halfe the tithe payd
65 of these croned sold for   13   0   0
49 wether shorlins to Ringsted South Ground
32 wether shorlins to Ringsted North Ground
Sum 126 [146] Remayne 605

/Lambes/ 200 pookes sold to Thomson for   28   8   4
40 lambes sold for   7   0   0
4 lambes sold for   13   4
2 markin lambes; 202 store lambes
Sum 428 [448] wherof due for tithe of 420   50   0   0
I payd Mr Waters for his odd lambes at 3½d the lambe and for
[p]   50 lambes at 2s 10d   7   1   8

─────────────────

102. It is not clear what this sum refers to, possibly the sale of 40 wether shorlins @ 7s
each.

1637	/Barrett Ringsted Ground/ Goodman delivered 1637 as followeth, his charge being 1636: 475, and of the little boyes 64, in all 519 [539]; 406 store ewes and rams /morts 14/		
	53 crones sold for	11 10	3
	2 ewes sold for	14	0

Sum 461 <2> and 14 mortes, of these I had 59 stone of wooll
/of Hams/ 2 ewes & 2 lambes one sold
/of Nicks/ 55 store ewes /1 mort/
6 crones 15s. Sum 63 a mort & a lambe

		£ s	d
	/Lambes/ 100 store wether lambes to Ringsted South Ground	£ s	d
	100 store ewe lambes		
	46 lambes sold for	7 13	4
	164 lambes sold to Thomson for	23 15	4
	2 markin lambes. Sum 366 [412] lambes		
Nick	15 store lambes		
	15 lambes sold to Thomson for	1 19	0
Ham	2 lambes one for store & one sold		
	Sum 32 lambes		

/Ringsted South Ground/ Francis Crisp delivered 1637 as doth follow his charge being 1636: 324 [sheep]

244 store wethers /20 morts/	
80 wethers sold for	36 0 0

Sum 304 [324] and 20 mortes, of these 39 stone of wool and the tithe payd

/Ringsted North flock/ Francis Crisp delivered 1637, his charge being 1636: 99 wethers and lambes; 89 wethers /10 morts/. Sum 99 of these 11 stone of wooll

/Sedgford East Ground/ Osburns charge 1637: 605 store ewes and rammes; 202 store lambes. Sum 807 and 21 of Mrs Gurneys

1637   /Ringsted South Ground, charge/ Francis Crisps charge 1637: 244 store wethers; 49 wether shorlins from Osburne; 100 wether shorlins from Goodman. Sum 393

1637   /Ringsted North Ground, charge/ 89 store wethers to Francis Crisp; 32 wether shorlins from Osburn. Sum 101 [121]

1637   /Barrett Ringsted/ Goodmans charge 1637: 406 store ewes and rammes; 75 store lambes. Sum 481 and a stray ewe & a lambe
/of Hams/ 2 store ewes; 1 store lambe

|of Nicks| 55 store ewes; 15 store lambes
Sum 73. Sum of all is 536 [556]

1638	/Sedgford/ <Barrett Ringsted> Osborne delivered 1638 as			
	followeth his charge being 1637: 807			
	702 store ewes and rammes /morts 44/			
	100 crones sold for	20	0	0
	<3 sheep sold to Sallis for £1 3s 7d>			
	Sum 806 with 44 mortes, so he wanteth one, of these I had 74			
	stone of wooll the tithe payd			
196	/Lambes/ of store beside 24 tithe			
156	small lambes sold *inde*[103] 6 given in	36	7	6
36	more sold	5	8	0
2	more sold	6	8	0
12	more sold	2	4	0
2	marking lambes			
	Sum beside the tithe 384 [404]; 96 wether shorlins Osburn			
	delivered to Ringsted flock so remayne in his charge with one he			
	wanted the sum of 607			

1638	/Barrett Ringsted /Goodman delivered 1638 as followeth, his			
	charge being 1637: 536; 463 sheep of my owne /20 morts/; 68 of			
	little Nicks sheep, /2 morts/; 3 of little Hamms sheep. Sum 536, so			
	he is right, of my 463 I had 64 stone of wooll			
	58 of my owne croned sold for	11	4	0
	15 more sold by Cobble	3	18	4
	3 rammes sold	1	3	6
	Sum 76. Remayne 407, 6 of little Nickes croned, rem[ain] 62			

1638	/Lambes/ 100 store lambes to Ringsted			
	102 store lambes for Barrett Ringsted			
	162 small lambes sold	22	15	0
	2 markin lambes			
	31 fatt lambes sold	5	13	8
[p]	Sum 377 [397] <356>			

Hamm 3 store lambes
Nick 16 store lambes
27 lambes sold. Sum 46

---

103. Latin 'of which'.

1638   /Ringsted South Ground/ Francis Crisp delivered 1638 as
        followeth, his charge being 393 and in the North <South> Flock
        101. Sum 494
        380 wethers, /mortes 18/; 110 sold.
        Sum 470 [490] which with 18 skinns make 488, so he wanteth 6
        sheep, of these 380 sheep I had 61½ stone of wooll

1638   Remayne in his charge with 6 that he wanteth 386; 386 wethers;
        96 wether hogges from Osburn; 100 wether lambes from
        Goodman. Sum 562 [582]

1638   /Sedgford East flock/ Osburns charge at Midsomer: 607 store
        ewes and rammes; 200 store lambes. Sum 807

1638   /Barrett Ringsted/ Goodmans charge at Midsomer: 407 store
        ewes and rammes; 85 store ewe lambes. Sum <468> 472 [492]
Ham   3 store sheep; 3 store lambes
        /Nicholas/ 62 store sheep; 16 store lambes. Sum 84

1638   /Ringsted/ Francis Crispes charge at Midsomer 1638 in the North
        and South flocks 386 wethers: 96 wether shorlins from Osburne;
[p]   100 wether shorlins from Goodman. Sum 562 [582]

1639   /Sedgford East flock/ Osburn delivered his charge 807 as
        followeth: 640 sheepe to the clipping for store /72 morts/; 100
        crones. Sum 740 which with 72 skinnes maketh 800 [812]
        wanting 8 so he wanteth 15 sheep [827] of these 740 sheep I had
        the tithe payd 60 stone 4lb

        /Lambes/ 200 store <beside> lambes *with 4 ram lambes &* 24
        for tithe; 6 lambes sold for   2 0 0
        119 small lambes beside 14 tithe lambes sold at Gissing for   11 8 1
        2 markin lambes. Sum 307 [327] beside tithe; 100 wether shorlins
        Osburn delivered to Ringsted flock, so there remayneth in his
        charge, with 15 he is to make good, 575

1639   /Barrett Ringsted flock/ <Goodman delivered his charge being
        553 as follow: 400 <<341>> store ewes and ramms /23 morts/; 66
        crones; 68 of little Nick /4 morts/; 6 crones of little Nicks; 6 of
        little Hamms. Sum 526 which with 27 mortes>

1639   Goodman delivered at Midsomer his charge being 536 as follow:
        401 store ewes and ramms /23 morts/; 66 crones; 60 store sheep
        of little Nicks /4 morts/; 14 crones of little Nicks; 6 store sheep of

little Hamms. Sum 507 and 27 mortes make 534, so he wanteth 2
sheepe, of the 447 I had 53 stone of wooll.

/Lambes/ 104 store ewe lambes
40 store wether lambes to go to Sedgford

100 lambes sold for	12	0	0
69 lambes sold at Gissing fayer	6	12	3
5 lambes sold for		8	0
33 lambes sold for	5	7	0

2 marking lambes. Sum 313[353] lambes

Ham   3 store lambes; /of Nicks/ 30 store lambes

29 small lambes sold for	2	15	0

[p]   [top quarter page faded and illegible]

1639   /Ringsted South & North flock/ Francis Crisp delivered his charge
being 562 as followeth: 350 he brought to the clipping /32 morts /

40 sold	18	0	0
88 sold	40	0	0
60 sold	27	0	0

Sum 530 [570] with 32 mortes So he wanteth 32

1639   /Sedgford East flock/ Osburnes charge at Midsomer: 575 store
ewes and rammes; 196 store lambes; 28 store lambes; 40 lambes
from Goodman. Sum 819 [839] & 2 crone skinns

1639   /Barrett Ringsted/ Goodmans charge at Midsomer: 402 <one>
store ewes and rammes; 1 ewe that Thomas Cobble is to allow;
104 store lambes. Sum 487 [507] & 4 crone skinns
60 of little Nicks store sheep; 30 store lambes of little Nicks; 6
store ewes of little Hams; 3 store lambes of little Hams; 2 store
lambes of little Jacks.[104] Sum 101

1639   /Ringsted South & North flocks/ Francis Crispes charge at
Midsomer: 382 store wethers; 100 wether shorlins from Osburn.
[p]   Sum 462 [482]

1640   /Sedgford East Ground/ Osborn delivered as followeth, his charge
being 801: a bell wether sold 9s; 767 store ewes and wether
hogges /52 morts/. Sum 800 [820] with 52 mortes, so he wanteth 1
sheep, of these 768 sheep I had 69 stone 12lb of wooll

---

104. John was born in 1636.

1640 /*Lambes*/ 183 store lambes; 2 markin lambes

12 lambes sold   1 10 0

205 sold at Kippon   17 12 11

45 to Mr Waters for tithe

Sum 407 [*447*] 92 croned wherof 2 dyed and were stroyed and 90

sold to Mr Dusgate[105]   10 8 6

67 wether shorlins to Willis

Sum 139 [*159*] Remayne with one he wanteth 629

1640 /*Barrett Ringsted*/ Goodman delivered as followeth, his charge
being of my owne 491 & 101 of the childrens, in all 572 [*592*]: 465
store ewes and rams /*24 morts*/; 9 store sheep of little Hamms;
78 store sheep of little Nicks /*2 morts*/; 10 crones of little Nicks; 2
store sheep of little Jacks.

Sum 544 [*564*] and 26 morts & one ewe sold /*7s*/. Sum 571, so he
wanteth one, of the 465 sheep I had 46½ stone of wooll
Croned 61 sold to, 43 to Willis of wether shorlins

1640 /*Lambes*/ 101 store lambes

31 lambes sold   4 13 0

189 small lambes sold   17 5 0

303   2 marking lambes

20 store lambes of little Nicks; 36 small lambes of little Nicks
sold; <9> *3* of little Hams store lambes; 3 small lambes of little

66   Hams sold; [*illegible*] store lambe of little Jacks

[*p*]   Sum <359, 354> *349* [*389*]

1640 /*Ringsted South & North Ground*/ Francis Crisp delivered as
followeth, his charge being 462

350 store wethers /*21 morts*/

30 wethers sold   13 0 0

20 wethers sold   8 15 0

20 wethers sold   9 0 0

17 wethers sold   8 0 0

20 wethers sold   8 15 0

3 wethers sold   6 0

1 wether brought home & dyed

Sum 462 with 21 skinns

1640 /*Sedgford East Ground*/ Osburns charge at Midsomer 1640:
629 store ewes and rammes with one he wanted; 25 store ewes
bought; 183 store lambes. Sum 817 [*837*]

---

105. Thomas Dusgate of Heacham, son of William Dusgate of Cockley Cley, *see*
Blomefield & Parkin, *Norfolk*, X, p. 312.

1640   /Barrett Ringsted/ Goodmans charge at Midsomer 1640: 382 store
        ewes and ramms with one he wanted at the clipping; 30 ewes

493   bought; 101 store lambes
        78 of store ewes of little Nicks; 20 store lambes of little Nicks; 9
        store ewes of little Hams; 3 store lambes of little Hams; 2 store

113   ewes of little Jacks; 1 store lambes of little Jacks.
        Sum 586 [606]

1640   /Ringsted South Ground/ Willis his charge at Midsomer 1640:
        350 store wethers from Francis Crisp; 67 wether shorlins from
        Osburn; 43 wether shorlins from Goodman. Sum 440 [460]

		£	s	d
1641	Willis delivered as followeth, his charge being 440			
	320 store wethers /10 morts/			
	40 sold	17	10	0
	20 sold	9	0	0
	10 sold	4	15	0
	20 sold	9	0	0
	20 sold	9	0	0
	20 sold	9	0	0
[p]	Sum 440 with 10 morts of the 320 sheep I had 49 stone & 9lb			

1641   /Sedgford East Ground/ Osborn delivered as followeth his charge
        being 817: 605 store ewes and rams /70 morts/; 111 wether shorlins
        to Willis; 85 crones sold; 2 ewes sold for   16 0
        Sum 763 [803] and 70 mortes in all 811, so he wanteth 4 sheep
        wherof 3 dyed at Hunston so want one, of the 761 sheep I had 70
        stone of wooll
        /Lambes/ 195 store lambes

	£	s	d
15 lambes sold	2	5	0
130 lambes sold to Hawkins	15	13	6
60 lambes sold at Kippen	4	0	0

        2 marking lambes; 48 tithe lambes to Mr Waters
        Sum 410 [450]

[1641]   /Barrett Ringsted/ Goodman delivered as followeth, his charge
        being 493 & of the childrens 113, in all 586 [606]: *352* store ewes
        and ramms /39 morts/; 71 wether shorlins to Willis; 49 crones
        sold; 85 store sheep of little Nicks /4 morts/; 10 store ewes of little
        Hams /1 mort/; 3 store ewes of little Jacks; 9 crones of little Nicks
        sold; 1 crone of little Hams sold. Sum *440*[106] [580] and 44

---

106. The first two insertions in this entry are patches pasted over the old figures.

morts which make <584> *580*, so he wanteth 2 sheepe, of the
448 sheep I had 48½ stone

1641	/*Lambes*/ 100 store lambes			
	17 lambes sold	2	11	0
	166 lambes sold to Hawkins	19	15	6
	45 lambes sold at Kipon	8	5	0
	2 markin lambes /<347, 351>/			
	7 store lambes of little Hams			
	1 lamb of little Hams sold		2	1
	31 store lambes of little Nicks			
	15 lambes sold of little Nicks	2	15	0
	33 lambes sold of little Nicks	3	8	9
	2 lambe of little Jacks			
	Sum 400 [*419*] lack one			

1641   [*Ringsted South Ground*] Willis his charge at Midsomer: 320
        store wethers; 111 wether shorlins from Osburn; 71 wether
[*p*]   shorlins from Goodman. Sum 482 [*502*]

1641   /*Sedgford East Ground*/ Osburns charge at Midsomer 1641: 606
        store ewes and ramms; 195 store lambes; 34 store ewes bought.
        Sum 815 [*835*]

1641   /*Barrett Ringsted*/ Goodmans charge at Midsomer: 354 store ewes
454   and ramms; 100 store lambes; 10 store ewes of little Hams; 7
        store lambes of little Hams; 85 store ewes of little Nicks; 31 store
        lambes of little Nicks; 3 store ewes of little Jacks; 2 store lambes
118   of little Jacks.
        Sum 572 [*592*] beside a stray ewe. Bought since 21 ewes

        /*Cullett [sheep]*/ 17 ewes 7 lambes of Megge Guybon
        30 of George Bastard
        20 of Robert Banyards

1642	Willis delivered as followeth his charge being 482			
	392 store wethers *clipped 482* /20 morts/	£	s	d
	20 wethers sold	9	0	0
	30 wethers sold	13	0	0
	20 sold of wethers	9	0	0
	20 wethers sold	9	0	0
	Sum with 20 morts 482 of these I had 47 stone & 11lb of wooll			
	12 of these sold of olde wether			
	20 wethers sold August 6	8	10	0
	Remayne in charge 360			

1642   /Sedgford East flock/ Osborne delivered as followeth, his charge
being 815 ewes: 582 store ewes and rammes /186 morts/; 34 wether
hogges to Willis; <5> *4* 9 crones sold
Sum 645 [665] & 186 mortes, so he wanteth 4 sheep, of the 645
sheep I had 48 stone of wooll
/Lambes /160 store lambes; 6 lambes sold   18   0
117 lambes sold at Gissing at 22d   12   13   4
15 small lambes sold at home; 2 marking lambes; 37 tithe lambes

[p]   Sum 317 [337] lambe so there is 7 lambes to pay tithe for

1642   /Barrett Ringsted/ Goodman delivered as followeth, his charge
being 455 & 21 bought and 118 of the childrens, in all 594; 359
of store ewes and ramms /41 morts/; 80 crones sold & 2 dizy; 16
wether shorlins to Willis. Sum 476 [with 41 morts 496] of these
435 sheepe I had 45 stone and 13lb of wooll
17 of little Hammes; 88 of little Nicks /10 morts/; 18 crones of
little Nicks sold; 3 of little Jacks
Sum with 10 morts 118 [128]
/Lambes/ 109 store lambes
36 fatt lambes sold at 30 & 6   5   8   0
117 lambes sold at Gissing at 22d   10   16   8
43 lambes small ones sold; 2 marking lambes. Sum 267 [307]
6 store lambes of little Hames; 32 store lambes of little Nicks
37 of small lambes of little Nicks sold   3   8   0
2 store lambes of little Jacks. Sum 77 lambes

1642   /charged/ Goodmans charge 1642 at Midsomer: 359 store ewes
and rammes; 1 stray ewe from Ringsted; 119 store lambes; 10
store lambes bought. Sum 459 [479]
17 store ewes of little Hams; 6 store lambes of little Hammes;
5 store ewes of little Jacks; 2 store lambes of little Jacks; 1 store
lambe of little Wills;[107] 82 store ewes of little Nicks; 32 store
131   lambes of little Nicks; 6 wether hogges of little Nicks
/100 bought to add to the 459/ Sum 590 [610]
/Cullett [sheep]/ 30 of George Bastard, 20 of Robert Banyards

1642   Willis his charge at Midsomer 1642: 360 store wethers; 34 wether
shorlins from Osborne; 16 wether shorlins from Goodman.
[p]   Sum 410 sheep

---

107. William was born in 1639. Dorothy who was born between John and William got
no sheep.

1642 /Sedgford East flock/ Osbornes charge at Midsomer 1642: 586
store ewes and ramms with 4 was to make good; 160 store <ewes
and> lambes. Sum 726 [746]

1643 /Sedgford East Ground/ Osborne delivered as followeth, his
charge being 726: 613 store ewes and rams /39 morts/; 61 wether
hoggs to deliver to Willis; 2 ewes which were sold; 50 crones
that were sold. Sum 706 [726] and 39 mortes. So he wanteth a
sheep, of these 706 sheep I had the tithe payd 60 stone of
wooll

	/Lambes/ 180 store lambes *inde* 35 to Goodman	£	s	d
419	/inde/ 190 sent to Gissing wherof 4 dyed	19	16	3
50	/for tithe/ 34 sold at home	3	6	8
	3 sold more		10	0
	50 tithe lambes; 2 marking lambes. Sum 419 [459]			

1643 /Barrett Ringsted/ Goodman delivered as followeth, his charge
being 590: 404 store ewes and rams /26 morts/; 89 crones sold; 78
wether hogges to deliver to Willis
Sum 531 [571] and 26 morts. So he wanteth 2 sheep, of the 531, I
had in wooll 53 stone
[Wool] /3 stone/ 21 store ewes of little Hams /2 morts/
[Wool] /7lb/ 7 store ewes of little Jacks
[Wool] /2lb/ 1 ewe hogge of little Wills
Sum with 2 morts 31
/Lambes/ 134 store lambes

15 lambes sold at Gissing fayer	1	8	9
151 lambes sold at Home	15	7	8
36 lambes sold	5	8	0

2 marking lambes. Sum 318 [338]
12 lambes of little Hamms; 3 lambes of little Jacks

1643 /Ringsted South Ground/ Willis delivered as followeth, his charge
being 410 wethers: 300 store wethers /9 morts/

110 wethers sold	48	13	0
10 crone wethers sold	2	14	9
1 wether worried sold		4	0

[p] Sum 400 [421] with 9 morts, of the 300 I had 42 stone

/Sedgford East Ground/ Osbornes charge at Midsomer 1643: 614
store ewes and ramms with 1 which he is to make good; 145 store
lambes; 35 lambes which he should deliver to Goodman. Sum
774 [794] of these Captayne Poe took 753.

Rest 21 wherof mortes & stroyed 13. Remayne 5 ewes and 3 lambes & 4 rammes out the Parke in all 12

1643   /Barrett Ring[sted]/ Goodmans charge at Midsomer 1643: 404 store ewes and ramms; 134 store lambes; /not delivered/ 35 store lambes from Sedgford. Sum 553 [573]
21 store ewes of little Hamms; 12 store lambes of little Hammes; 7 store ewes of little Jacks; 3 store lambes of little Jacks; 1 store lambe of little Neds. Sum 45
Sum of all <598> *563*
/Cullett sheep/ 40 George Bastard, 20 Robert Banyards

1643   /Ringsted South Ground/ Willis his charge at Midsomer: 300 store wethers; 78 wether hogges from Goodman; 61 wether hogges from Osborne. Sum 419 [439]

753   Captayn Poe tooke of Osburns charge[108]
410   Captayn Poe tooke of Willis his charge
483   Captayn Poe tooke of Goodmans charge of my owne
 45   Captayn Poe tooke of the little boyes
  2   Captayn Poe tooke at Sedgford for Anne Guybons instead of ours. Sum 1653 [1693] sheepe

  8   more his trooper stole of the fatt sheep in the close
  2   they stole of Goodmans sheep in the close
  5   they stole fatt lambes in the close
  2   they stole 2 rammes in the parke
  5   they worried 5 ramms [word illegible] with setting of dogges to kill the deare
[p]   Sum 22 sheep and lambes beside those they eate in the house

1643   Goodmans charge after plundering: 16 rammes out of the Parke /1 mort/; 20 ewes out of the Close; 5 ewes from Osborn; 20 ewes bought at Bircham; 60 ewes hogges bought with Will Guybon; 3 ewes bought of Constable with 3 lambes; 6 lambes out of the close inde 2 rams; 8 tithe lambs from Heacham /5 morts/; 3 lambes from Osburn; 5 wether shorlins from Willis; 60 wether hoggs bought of Mr Drury; 11 wethers bought of Richard Giles;

---

108. These entries refer to the plundering of sheep by Captain Poe of the parliamentary forces in the summer of 1643. At this stage Alice wrote a 'A note of the tenants sheep on the South Flock of Ringstead in 1643' and some notes on the flocks, foldcourse and shepherds covenants, which she inserted on a spare page between Nicholas and Hamon's accounts, 1618–1627; these have been placed at the end, pp. 191–3.

40 wether hoggs bought of Edmund Taylor; 30 wether hogges bought of Richardson; 60 ewe hoggs bought of Mr Drury; one ewe lambe of little Wills; one ewe lambe of little Neds. Sum 309 [*349*]

1644   Goodman delivered at Midsomer 1644: 15 rammes /*1 mort*/; 40 ewes; 113 ewe shorlins; 121 wethers and wether shorlins; one ewe shorlin of little Wills; one ewe shorlin of little Neds
Sum 291 and 13 mortes and 4 were worried, so he wanteth one sheep, of these 289 sheepe I had 38 stone 7lb of wooll
/*Lambes*/ 40 store lambes & 8 hoggs lambes; 2 sold for fatt lambes

Sheep taken from Goodman: 5 rammes sold; 121 wethers and wether shorlins to Gates

1644   /*Barrett Ringsted*/ Goodmans charge at Midsomer 1644: 10 store rammes *sold 5 beside the 10*; 40 store ewes *inde* one bell wether*; 113 ewe shorlins *sold 98 rem 35*; /*inde 9 of Heacham*/ 27 ewe lambes *& wether lambes*; 30 wether lambes *& ewe lambes to Gates*; one ewe lambe of little Jacks; one ewe shorlin of little Wills; one ewe shorlin of little Edwards. Sum 203 [*223*]
[*p*]   Sold 98. Remayne 125 wherof to Gates 30. Rem[*ain*] 115

[*1644*] Cullett sheep in Barrett Ringsted 1644[109]	£	s	d
120 My sonne Hamon	7	0	0
100 Thomas Goodman	6	0	0
60 Mr Dusgate	3	0	0
60 Robert Banyard	3	0	0
62 Edmond Taylor & John Woodrow	3	2	0
20 Willyam Makement	1	0	0
20 Robert Harrison	1	0	0
20 Thomas Wallker	1	0	0
20 Richard Sutton	1	0	0
20 Will Rawlins	1	0	0
Sum 462 [*502*]	1	0	0
John Woodrow, Edmond Taylor & Goodman payd for joyce of 103 sheep bought of me at 9d for 3 quarters	3	17	3
[*Sum*]	30	19	3

109. These refer to the cullett sheep placed by neighbours to stock the foldcourses. Numbers of sheep have been moved from the RH columns to the LH margin; details of payments have been moved to RH columns.

[*1644*] /*Ringsted North Ground*/ Gates his charge at Midsomer 1644: 10 wethers of 2 sheare; 111 wether shorlins; 30 wether lambes & ewe lambes. Sum 151

1644	Cullett [*sheep*] in Ringsted North Ground			
100	Mr Nash	4	10	0
18	Robert Banyard		12	0
40	Nicholas Markant	1	10	0
40	Willyam Holly	1	10	0
20	Willyam Rawlins		15	0
20	Anne Guybon		15	0
60	Robert Ling	2	0	0
	Sum 280 [*298*]: in all want 2 /*to accompt 1645*/	11	12	0

1644   [*Charge*] /*115, Barrett Ringsted*/ Goodman delivered at Midsomer 1645: 10 rammes /*4 morts*/; 71 ewes; 24 ewe shorlins & wether shorlins /*3 morts*/; 1 ewe shorlin of little Jacks; 1 ewe shorlin of little Wills; 1 ewe shorlin of little Edwards.[110] Sum 108 sheep & 7 skinnes, of these I had 9 stone of wooll 4lb

/*Lambes*/ 35 store lambes & one for little Roger

8 solde   1   6   8

1 lambe of little Willyams; 1 lambe of little Edwards

Sum 46 beside 2 markin lambes

/*Sheepe*/ taken from Goodman 1645: 1 wether for the kitching; 1 ramme to be corded[111] *& ramm lambe*; 1 ewe that was Osborns

[*p*]   worth nothing; 8 wether shorlins to Willis; 1 wether hogg nothing worth

1645   [*Charge*] /*151, Ringsted North flock*/ Gates his charge at Midsomer 1645: 123 wethers & wether shorlins to Willis /*7 morts*/; 3 wethers of 3 sheare to the kitching; 30 ewe shorlins to Goodman. Sum 140 [*156*] & 7 skinnes so he wanted 4 sheepe of these 140 sheepe I had 16 stone of wooll and 4lb

[*1645*] Willis his charge 1645 Ringsted North flock: 123 wethers & wether shorlins to Willis; 8 wether shorlins from Goodman; 12 wether lambes from Godwin; 58 wether lambes from Docking

Sum 201 & 243 cullett [*sheep*]

---

110. Edward was born in 1640, Roger in 1644.

111. No explanation has been found, but as 'corded' refers to a ram, the most likely meaning is castrated.

		£	s	d
[*1645*]	Barrett Ringsted tithe 1645			
	my cosen Dusgate for 60 at 2d		10	0
	Goodman for 234 with his covenant 100	2	5	8
	/*Lambes*/ 7 John Woodrow & Edmond Taylor [112]			
	1 Thomas Wallker			
	1 Willyam Makemid			
	1 Robert Harrison			
	1 Richard Sutton			
	1 Willyam Rawlins			
14	2 Robert Banyard			

		st	lb
1645	/*Tithe wooll*/ John Woodrow & Edmond Taylor[113]	1	0
	Thomas Wallker		2
	Robert Harrison		2
	Willyam Makemid		2
	Robert Banyard		2
	Will Cooke		1
	Richard Sutton		1

at 10s a stone £10 sold part of 11 stone
Goodmans charge 1645: 9 rammes; 70 store ewes; 27 ewe shorlins
& ewes *inde* £14 from Gates; 23 store lambes; 14 tithe lambes of
Hunston; a tithe lambes of Heacham; a lambe out of the close.
Sum 125 [*145*]
1 ewe shorlin of little Jacks; 1 ewe of little Willyams; 1 lambe of
little Willyams; 1 ewe of little Edwards; 1 lambe of little

[*p*]	Edwards; 1 lambe of little Rogers. Sum 6 [*in all*] 131 [*151*]			

		£	s	d
	Cullett sheepe layd in Barrett Ringsted 1645			
180	My sonne Hamon	10	0	0
60	Robert Banyard	3	0	0
65	John Woodrow	3	5	0
65	Edmond Taylor	3	5	0
60	Thomas Goodman	3	0	0
20	Richard Sutton	1	0	0
20	Willyam Makemid	1	0	0
20	Robert Harrison	1	0	0
20	Willyam Harrison	1	0	0
20	Robert Bastard	1	0	0

112. Reference to the payment of tithe for lambs; over the next few years, Alice developed a system for calculating these lambs.

113. Alice used the RH columns to record quantities of wool; this method has been retained.

			£	s	d
30	Thomas Wallker		1	10	0
10	Willyam Rawlins			10	0
	Sum [*of cullett sheep*] 510 [*560*]				

1645	Cullett sheepe layd in Ringsted North flock				
100	Willyam Holly		4	10	0
60	Nicholas Markant		2	5	0
20	Robert Banyard		0	13	4
10	Thomas Wallker		0	9	6
20	Willyam Springall		0	15	0
20	Willyam Rawlins		0	15	0
33	Megge Fisher		1	2	6
	/to accompt 1646/ Sum 243 [263]		10	8	4

1645 /*Charge 125 & 6, Barrett Ringsted*/ Thomas Goodman delivered at Midsomer 1646: 8 rammes /*18 morts*/; 100 ewes & ewe shorling; 3 wether shorlins. Sum 111 with 14 mortes, wherof 5 were worried wch maketh 125 & of these I had 12 stone and 0lb.

1646	/*Lambes*/ 39 store lambes	£	s	d
	16 lambes solde	3	4	0
	6 lambes solde	1	4	0
	7 pooke lambes solde at 2s 6d		1	6
	2 marking lambes; 1 lambe of little Jacks; 1 lambe of little Willyams. Sum 73			

	Sheepe taken from Goodman 1646: 14 ewes croned sold; 3 wether shorlins to Ringsted Flock; 1 ewe stroyed in the close	2	16	0
[*p*]	Sum 18. Remayne with him 113 and of the chilldrens 6			

/*Charge 20, Ringsted North flock*/ Willis delivered his charge at Midsomer 1646: 130 wethers /*4 morts*/; 65 wether shorlins Sum 195. So he wanteth 2 sheepe, of these I had 24 stone & 5lb of wooll /*the 2 he did want, he delivered to Goodman*/; 2 of these were smothered at the clipping. Remayne 213 delivered to Strett

1646	Barrett Ringsted tithe for wooll & lambe			
	Thomas Goodman for tithe of his covenant sheepe 20s & for the tithe of 60 more 10s	1	10	0
	/*Lambes*/ 4 of John Woodrow			
	4 of Edmond Taylor			
	3 of Robert Banyard			
	1 of Robert Bastard			
	1 of Willyam Makemid			

1 of Robert Harrison
2 of Thomas Wallker
wooll of divers persons, my sonne Hamon paying no tithe, 3
stone sold   2   3   8

1646	Heacham tithe wooll & lambe 1646	£	s	d
	of divers of Massingham at 2d the sheepe		18	4
	of Thomas Goodman for tithe at 2d a piece		5	0
	of Thomas Crampe for 9 odd lambes at 4d[114]		3	4
	of James Cock for 4		1	4
	of Thomas Cornell for 3		1	0
	of John Jenner for one			4
	of John Sallter for one			4
	of Robert Partridg for 6		2	0
	of Willyam Woods for 6		2	0
	of Willyam Woods for 2			8
	/36s 4d/ of Thomas Burnham for 6		2	0

/Lambes/ 8 of my cosen Dursgate
11 of Thomas Crampe & his sonnes
3 of Thomas Burnham
2 of John Fisher
3 of Willyam Woods
1 of his Page
30   2 of Thomas Goodman
      /of these 3 dyed & were stroyed & 26 to Goodman/
[p]   of divers of Heacham men of wooll in all 6 stone & a halfe sold
      for   4   7   9

1646   /Barrett Ringsted/ Thomas Goodman his charge at Midsomer
       8 rammes; 1 ramme cott[115] out of the close; 105 ewes & ewe
       shorlings; 39 store lambes; 16 lambes of Barrett Ringsted tithe;
       26 lambes of Heacham tithe; 30 lambes bought of Goodman;
       7 ewes bought of Strett; 2 ewes of Willis for the 2 wethers he
       wanted. Sum 214 [234]

       1 ewe, 1 lambe: 2 of John Le Strange
       2 ewes, 2 lambes: 4 of Will Le Strange

---

114. Odd lambes are those left over from division by 10; they are then added to the
next years tally.

115. This is the first reference to the word 'cott' used with sheep i.e. cott ram, lambs,
ewes, or just cotts; also 'cott wool' in the wool account. No explanation has been found,
but the way it is used suggests that it might be related to a sheep-cot, i.e. those sheep living
with access to cover, see below pp. 172, 184–91.

2 ewes of Edward Le Strange
1 ewe of Roger Le Strange
Sum 203 & cullett [*sheep*] 440

[*1646*] Henry Strett his charge at Midsomer 1646: 193 wethers & wether
shorlins; 3 wether shorlins for Goodman to deliver; 60 wether
lambes bought of Mr Johnson. Sum 236 [*256*] & 3 from Birch &
cullett 455 so short 21

	[*1646*] Cullett [*sheep*] in Ringsted North flock 1646	£	s	d
260	the fearmours of the South flock			
80	Willyam Holly	3	6	8
20	Robert Banyard		13	4
15	Robert Harrison		12	6
14	Robert Bastard		11	8
20	Thomas Wallker		16	8
20	Willyam Springall		16	8
20	Willyam Rawlins		16	8
36	Thomas Farror	1	1	8
20	Megge Fisher		16	8
205	[*245*] Sum [*in all*] 465 [*505*] at 9d & 8d /to accompt 1647/	9	12	6

	[*1646*] Cullett in Barrett Ringsted flock 1646			
180	my sonne Hamon	10	0	0
60	Robert Banyard	3	0	0
60	John Woodrow	3	0	0
60	Thomas Goodman	3	0	0
20	Willyam Makemid	1	0	0
20	Willyam Harrison	1	0	0
20	Robert Harrison	1	0	0
20	Robert Bastard	1	0	0
30	Thomas Wallker	1	10	0
5	Will Rawlins	0	5	0
[*p*]	Sum <495> 440 [*470*]			

[*1647*] Thomas Goodman delivered at Midsomer 1647: 9 rammes /17
morts/; 175 ewes & ewe shorlins & a ramm; 13 wether shorlins.
Sum 197 which with 17 mortes maketh 214, of the 197 sheepe I
had 18 stone & 12lb of wooll

/Lambes/ 63 store lambes; 23 fatt lambes solde; 1 pooke lambe
putt into the parke; 2 marking lambes. Sum 89 lambes

1647   2 ewes of little Jacks, 1 lambe of little Jacks – 3
        4 ewes of little Willyams, 3 lambe of little Willyams – 7
        2 ewes of little Edwards, 1 lambe of little Edwards – 3
        1 ewe of little Rogers – 1

        Sheepe taken from Goodman 1647: 4 crones sold at Kippon   1   0   0
        13 wether shorlins to Henry Srett; 16 crones putt into the close
        for lambes 1648. Sum 23[33]

        [Charge] /239, *Ringsted North Ground*/ Henry Strett delivered at
        Midsomer 1647: 166 wethers & wether shorlins, /16 morts/
        36 wethers sold before Midsomer   15   5   0
        20 wethers sold   10   0   0
        20 wethers sold   10   0   0
        Sum 222 [242] which with 16 morts maketh 238. So he wanteth
        one, of the 166 wethers I had the tithe payd of wooll 19 stone &
        12lb sold before St Michael 1647 – 40 at twise[116]

1647   Henry Strett his charge at Midsomer: 126 wethers & wether
        shorlins beside 40 sold; 13 wether shorlins from Goodman;
        lambes wherof 100 from Thomas Wasy of Bircham & 20 of
        Goodman. Sum 249 [259] & one he wanted

1647   /*Cullett in Ringsted North flock*/
        260 the fearmours of the South flock[117]
        80 Willyam Holly
        30 Robert Bastard
        20 Robert Bastard
        20 Thomas Wallker
        20 Megge Fisher
        20 Willyam Rawlins
[p]   Sum 410 [450] so short 60

1647   Thomas Goodman his charge at Midsomer: 13 rammes & a
        ramme lambe out of the close; 161 ewes & ewe shorlings; 63 store
        lambes; 19 lambes of Barrett Ringsted tithe lambes; 20 lambes
        bought of Goodman. Sum 257 [276] & one out of the parke that
        was a pooke & after a good sheepe
        2 ewes of little Jacks, 1 lambe of little Jacks – 3
        4 ewes of little Willyams, 3 lambe of little Willyams – 7

---

116. The meaning of 'twise' is unclear, but it may possibly be 'twice' relating to the
payment of the tithe.

117. New placing for numbers of the cullett sheep.

2 ewes of little Edwards, 1 lambe of little Edwards – 3
1 ewe of little Rogers, 1 ewe shorlin of little Rogers – 2 /15/

1647 Barrett Ringsted tithe wooll & lambe
/Lambes/ 3 of the tithe of 26 of my owne
4 of John Woodrow over 3[118]
3 of Robert Banyard
2 of Robert Bastard over 3
2 of Thomas Wallker
1 of Willyam Makemid over 1
1 of Willyam Harrison over 4
1 of Robert Harrison over 3
2 of Katherin Crampe
19 Sum 19 lambes

	£	s	d
Heacham tithe wooll & lambe 1647			
/Lambes/ 2 of Thomas Crampe senior & 6 over			
2 of Thomas Crampe junior & 1 over			
1 of John Crampe & 4 over			
1 of John Fisher & 1 over			
2 of Thomas Burnham & 2 over			
1 of Woods the Shepheard			
1 of Thomas Goodman			
3 of my cosen Dusgate			
1 of Mr Gurling			
Sum 14 sold for	3	3	0

	st	lb	di
Hunston [Hunstanton] tithe wooll 1647			
John Woodrow		7	½
Willyam Harrison		3	0
Robert Banyard		6	0
Robert Bastard		3	¼
Willyam Makemid		2	¼
Thomas Wallker		3	½
Robert Harrison		2	½
of my owne		5	0
Sum	2	5	0

[p]

	lb	di	qr
Heacham tithe wooll 1647			
My cosen Dusgate	10	1	
Thomas Crampe senior	7		
Thomas Crampe junior	4		

---

118. 'over' means left over after division by ten for tithe.

John Crampe	2	I	
John Fisher	3		
Thomas Burnham	6		
Willyam Woods	6		
Edward Woods	6		
Willyam Pennock junior		I	I
Henry Duck of Massingham	2		I
Henry Ducks page	I		
Willyam Gravelin	I		
Thomas Goodman	I	I	
John Buckenham	3	I	I
olde Duck of Massingham	8	I	

Sum 4 stone 5lb 3qr[119]

1647	Cullett in Barrett Ringsted in Goodmans charge	£	s	d
100	My sonne Hamon	6	0	0
60	John Woodrow	3	0	0
60	Robert Banyard	3	0	0
60	Thomas Goodman	3	0	0
30	Thomas Wallker	1	10	0
20	Willyam Makemid	1	0	0
20	Robert Harrison	1	0	0
20	Willyam Harrison	1	0	0
20	Robert Bastard	1	0	0
10	Willyam Murton		10	0
4	Thomas Farror		4	0
52	of my owne 29 ewes & 23 lambes	2	12	0
	Sum 416 [456]	23	16	0

1647	Cullett in Ringsted North foldcorse beside 260 layd by the fearmours of the South flock	£	s	d
80	Willyam Holly at 10d the sheepe	3	6	8
30	Robert Bastard	1	5	8
20	Thomas Wallker		16	8
20	Megge Fisher		16	8
20	Willyam Rawlins		16	8
20	Robert Banyard Baylife of Ringsted		13	4
	/to accompt 1648/	7	15	0

1648 [Charge] /258/ Thomas Goodman brought to the clipping: 10 rammes /4 morts/; 231 ewes & ewe shorlins /13 morts/. Sum 258

---

119. 'qr' appears to be a quarter of a lb.

with 17 mortes, so right, of these I had wooll 26 stone & 12lb,
sold with other wooll at 12s 4d in 1649

1648   /Lambes/ 63 store lambes; 23 fatt lambes sold; 1 pooke lambe putt
into the parke; 2 marking lambes. Sum 89 lambes
/of John Le St/ 3 of John Le Stranges
/of Willyams/ 7 of Willyam Le Stranges
/of Edwards/ 3 of Edward Le Stranges
[p]   /of Rogers/ 2 of Roger Le Stranges

1648	Goodman brought at Midsomer: 121 *inde*	£	s	d
	/Lambes/ 2 for marking lambes			
	20 sold for	6	0	0
	1 for to sell sold for		5	0
	35 pookes sold at Kippon for 35 /4 dyed/	4	13	9
	8 store lambes			
	Sum 119 more he brought /of lambes/			
	2 of John Le Stranges			
	3 of Willyam Le Stranges			
	2 of Edward Le Stranges			
	1 of Roger Le Stranges			

1648	Sheep taken from Goodman	£	s	d
	6 crones sold at Kippon for			
	2 dizy sheepe sett to the close		2	4
	66 wether hogges to Strett 26 & to Sedgford 40			
	1 bell wether		14	0
	So remayne in Goodmans charge 116			

	Henry Strett brought to the clipping 206	£	s	d
	20 sold for	12	0	0
	13 sold for	8	9	0
	Mortes *inde* one stroyed			

Sum 249. So he is right, of the 206 I had of wooll 27 stone. Sold
with other wooll at 12s 4d in January 1649

	Sheepe taken from Henry Strett 1648: 2 dizy putt into the close		2	4
	40 wethers to sell	24	0	0

2 rammes to Goodman; a wether stroyed after clipping. Sum 45.
Remayne in Stretts charge 1648, 181

1648   Barrett Ringsted wooll & lambes
/Tithe Lambes/ 3 of my owne sheepe allowed for tithe
5 of Robert Banyard

5 of John Woodrow
2 of Robert Harrison
2 of Thomas Wallker
1 of Willyam Makemid
1 of Willyam Harrison
Sum 19 lambes

		st	lb	di
1648	/*Tithe wooll*/ of my owne tithe wooll		7	o
	John Woodrow		6	½
	Robert Banyard		o	o
	Robert Bastard		4	½
	Thomas Wallker		3	o
	Willyam Makemid		2	½
	Robert Harrison		2	½
	Willyam Harrison		2	½
[*p*]	Sum 2 stone & halfe a pound sold at 12s 4d with other wooll in January 1649	2	o	½

Heacham tithe wooll & lambe 1648
5 /*Lambes*/ My cosen Dusgate for tithe
4 Thomas Crampe junior
2 Thomas Crampe senior
1 John Fisher
Sum 12 sold at Kippon for 40s

	st	lb	di
/*Wooll*/ Thomas Crampe junior & John Crampe	1	2	o
Thomas Crampe senior		5	o
My cosen Dusgate	1	7	o
John Fisher		3	o
Francis [*illegible*]		2	½
Sum	3	5	½

		st	lb	di
	/*In mony*/ Thomas Thornely for tithe of sheepe		5	o
1648	John Duck for tithe of sheepe		15	6
	of divers men for odd parcells of wooll received by my cosen Dusgate of Simon Waynesford, John Buckenham, Thomas Matchin, Danyell Crosse & Willyam Gravelin	1	o	o
	Received of Thomas Burnham for tithe of 36 ewes & 26 hogges all sold at our Lady		7	6
	Sum[120]	2	9	8

---

120. Sum should read £2 8s od.

1648   Thomas Goodman his charge at Midsomer: 10 rammes *inde* 2
        from Strett; 178 of ewes & ewe shorlins; 83 store lambes with 2
        from the Close; 19 of Barrett Ringsted tithe lambes; 60 wether
        lambes bought of Thomas Wasy. Sum 308 [*350*] & a bell wether
        /*Charles Le Strange*/ ewe lambe twinnes – 1
        /*John Le Strange*/ 3 ewes & ewe shorlins, 2 lambes – 5
        /*Will Le Strange*/ 7 ewes & ewe shorlins , 3 lambes – 10
        /*Edward Le Strange*/ 3 ewes & ewe shorlins, 2 lambes – 5
        /*Roger Le Strange*/ 2 ewe & ewe shorlins, 2 lambes – 4
        [*in all*] 25

1648	/*Cullett in Barrett Ringsted* /	£	s	d
100	of my sonne Hamon Le Stranges	6	0	0
69	of my owne	3	9	0
11	*Thomas Farrors*		11	0
40	Robert Banyards	2	0	0
40	John Woodrowes	2	0	0
20	Robert Bastards	1	0	0
20	Willyam Makemid	1	0	0
20	Robert Harrisons	1	0	0
20	Willyam Harrisons	1	0	0
20	Thomas Wallkers	1	0	0
10	Willyam Murtons		10	0
[*p*]	Sum £18 19s *11s* for 330 [*370*] writt			

1648   /*Ringsted North flock*/ Henry Strett his charge at Midsomer 181
        wethers; 26 wether shorlins part of 66; 20 wether lambes from
        Thomas Wasy. Sum 208 [*227*]

	Cullett in Ringsted North flock 1648	£	s	d
200	my sonne Hamon Le Strange			
80	Robert Thurlow besides 160 in the South flock			
20	Robert Banyard as Baylife		13	4
20	Thomas Wallker		16	8
100	Willyam Holly	5	0	0
60	John Cole	2	10	0
20	Robert Bastard		16	8
14	Willyam Rawlins		11	8
20	Megge Fisher		16	8
	Sum 500 [*534*] writt for 1649	11	5	0

1649   Payd which was reserved of Robert Birch his lease now layed
        there 40 wether hogges part of 66 of Goodmans; these 40

wethers were clipped at Midsomer whereof I had wooll the tithe
payd 4 stone 5¼lb sold with other wooll at 12s 4d in
January 1649

Hunston [*Hunstanton*] tithe wooll 1649	st	lb	di
Robert Harrison		3	0
Willyam Makemid		2	0
Willyam Harrison		2	0
John Woodrow		7	4
Robert Bastard		2	3
Murton		2	0
Thomas Wallker		2	4
for my owne tithe		8	0
Sum 2 stone 1lb sold at 12s 4d in 1649	2	1	0

Barrett Ringsted Tithe lambes 1649
3 of Robert Banyard
0 of John Woodrow layd moste hogges od 6
1 of Willyam Harrison & 6 odd
1 of Robert Harrison & 8 odd
1 of Willyam Makemid & 6 odd
1 of Thomas Wallker & 4 odd
1 of Willyam Murton for 2 yeare & 2 odd
5 of my owne sheepe allowed for tithe
Sum 13 *inde* 4 pooke sold for £1
/*Robert Bastard sold his sheepe & payd for tithe lambe 4s, 4 sold
for pookes*/

Heacham Tithe wooll & lambes 1649	£	s	d
/*Lambes*/ Received of Buckenham of Massingham		10	0
Received of Thomas Thornely		5	0
4 lambes of my cosen Dusgate sold at Kipon		20	0
3 lambes of Thomas Crampe he payd		15	0
Sum	2	10	0
/*Wooll*/ a stone & 8lb of my cosen Dusgate he payd		18	0

12lb of wooll others sold & written wth the wooll of 1648 in 1650

[*p*] at 10s in all 4 stone & 2lb

1649 [*North flock*] Henry Strett delivered at Midsomer as followeth:

	£	s	d
175 wethers & wether shorlins; 20 wethers sold for	12	0	0
20 wethers sold for	14	0	0
1 bell wether to Goodman before clipping			
10 morts wherof 3 were stroyed		1	6

Sum 206 [*226*] so he wanteth one payd /3s 6d/. Of these 175
sheepe I had wooll the tithe being payd 20 stone & 8lb. Sold at
12s 4d with other wooll in January 1649

Sheepe taken from Strett 1649: 19 wethers sold for	13	6	0
156 wethers & wether shorlings to Goodman. Sum 175			

1649 /*Barrett Ringsted*/ Thomas Goodman delivered as followeth:
310 rammes, ewes & ewe shorlins
30 morts wherof 3 were stroyed   13   2
Sum 311 [*331*] so he is right, of these I had wooll 32 stone & 9lb,
sold at 12s 4d with other wooll in January 1649

1649 /*Lambes*/ he brought lambes 126 as followeth:

	£	s	d
23 lambes sold for	6	18	0
2 suckerell lambes sold for		10	0
46 pooke lambes sold for one dyed 45 sold	11	6	0

2 lambes dyed after clipping; 2 marking lambes; 70 store lambes.
Sum 125 [*145*]

1649 Sheep taken from Barrett Ringsted charge

	£	s	d
11 crones sold for at 7s 6d	4	2	0
2 dizy sheepe left in the close sold for		2	0

95 wether shorlings to Ringsted North flock
Sum 108 remayne 213

1649 Thomas Goodmans charge of Barrett Ringsted: 213 rammes,
ewes & ewe shorlings; 70 store lambes; 5 tithe lambes from me; 4
tithe lambes of Barrett Ringsted. Sum 272 [*292*]
/*of John LeStrange*/ 5 ewes & ewe shorlings, 3 lambes – 8
/*Will LeStrange*/ 10 ewes & ewe shorlings, 6 lambes – 16
[*p*] /*Edward LeStrange*/ 5 ewes & ewe shorlings, 3 lambes – 8
/*Roger LeStrange*/ 3 ewes & ewe shorlings, 2 lambes – 5
/*Charles LeStrange*/ 2 ewe shorlings – 2
Sum of the chilldrens 39 & of the stock 272 [*is*] 311

1649 /*Cullett in Barrett Ringsted*/

	£	s	d
80 of my sonne Hamon[121]	4	0	0
110 of my owne	5	10	0
40 of Robert Banyards	2	0	0
40 of John Woodrowes	2	0	0

---

121. Standardized format achieved with money in the RH columns.

		£	s	d
20 of Willyam Makemids		1	0	0
20 of Robert Bastards		1	0	0
20 of Robert Harrisons		1	0	0
20 of Willyam Harrisons		1	0	0
20 of Thomas Wallkers		1	0	0
10 of Willyam Murtons			10	0
/for 1650/ Sum 320 [380] £19 written		19	0	0

1649	/Cullett in Ringsted North flock/	£	s	d
200	my sonne Hamon Le Strange			
60	Robert Thurlow			
60	Thomas Goodman	2	10	0
60	John Cole	2	10	0
20	Robert Banyard as Baylife		13	4
20	Robert Bastard		16	8
20	Thomas Wallker		16	8
20	Henry Coppin		16	8
20	John Clerke		16	8
	/for 1650/ Sum 440 [480] £9 written	9	0	0

1649   Thomas Goodmans charge of Ringsted North foldcorse at
Midsomer 1649: 156 wethers & wether shorlins of Strett; 95
wether shorlins from Barrett Ringsted; 60 wether lambes from
Mr Partridg; 40 wether lambes bought of Goodman.
Sum 311 [351]

1649   /Sedgford East Ground/ 40 wethers of 2 sheare layd there being
reserved wth Robert Birch, of these I had 4 stone & 5½ lb sold at
12s 4d amongst other wooll to Thomas Allyard in January 1649

1650	/Sedgford East Ground/ Robert Birch his shepheard brought to	£	s	d
	the clipping 39 wethers of 3 sheare, 1 wether was dizy & sold for			
	/8s/. Sum 40 of these 39 I had 5 stone & 3lb the tithe payd			
	these 39 wethers were sold for	12	0	0
[p]	and 19 wethers for	11	8	0

1650   Thomas Goodman delivered of Barrett Ringsted as followeth:
252 rammes, ewes and ewe shorlins & wethers; 1 ramme hogge
was stolen out of the close; 2 dizy were drowned in the parke &
stroyed, 17 morts. Sum 272 of these 252 sheep I had 29 stone &
3lb of wooll

		£	s	d
1650	/Lambes/ in all 173 lambes wherof as followeth: 18 lambes sold for	4	10	0
	5 pooke lambes clipped & putt into the parke			
	76 pooke lambes sold 16 at 3s & 60 at 5s	17	8	0
	2 marking lambes; 93 store lambes 2 dyed remayne 90			
	Sum 173 [*194*] lambes			

		£	s	d
1650	Sheep taken out of Barrett Ringsted charge			
	8 crones sold at Kippon at 6s 8d	2	13	4
	5 wether hogges to Ringsted North Ground			
	70 wether lambes to Ringsted North Ground			

		£	s	d
1650	Thomas Goodman delivered of his charge of Ringsted North flock as followeth: 237 wethers and shorlings			
	81 wethers sold for	54	7	0
	2 dizy brought home dyed & was stroyed; 11 morts brought home. Sum 311 [*331*] So he is right: one for the kitching & 40 to Sedgford of these 238 sheepe I had wooll /*33 stone and 7lb*/ the tithe payd of these 40 to Sedgford & one sold 11s			

		[*tithe lambs*]	
	Barrett Ringsted tithe wooll & lambe 1650		
	of my owne for tithe of 59	6	odd
	Robert Banyard 38	4	0
	John Woodrow 6 odd & now 41	4	7
	Robert Harrison 8 odd & now 18	2	6
	Willyam Makemid 6 odd & now 17	2	3
	Thomas Wallker 4 odd & now 16	2	0
	Willyam Harrison 6 odd & now 14	2	0
	Willyam Murton 2 odd & now 7		9
	Sum	22	

		st	lb	di
1650	/*Tithe wooll*/ of my owne for 109 sheepe	1	4	0
	Thomas Wallker		3	0
	John Woodrow & Robert Bastard		5	½
	Willyam Makemid		1	½
	Robert Harrison		2	¾
	Willyam Harrison		2	½
	Willyam Murton		1	0
[*p*]	Sum	2	6	¼

		£	s	d
1650	Heacham tithe lambe & wooll 1650			
	of my cosen Dusgate tithe lambes	7	35	0
	Thomas Crampe senior & junior	2	10	0

of Thomas Matchin for tithe of 52 sheepe at 1½d[122]	6	6
of John Buckenham for tithe of 40 sheepe	5	0
of Richard Buckenham for tithe of 20 sheepe	2	6
of my cosen Dusgate for 100 hogges that went away at our Lady	12	0

[section pasted over] /15s, 12s/
/written/

Sum £3 11s 0d beside

/written/ James Cock payd for a lambe 1651 for 1650		4	0
/wooll/ my cosen Dusgate for a stone 7lb of wooll payd		15	0
divers men payd wooll 2 stone 7lb which was sold to John Bently			
with the wooll of 1651 at 10s	1	5	0
Sum[123]	1	14	0

1650   Thomas Goodmans charge of Barrett Ringsted: 239 ewes & ewe
     shorlins & rammes; 6 cott rammes out of the parke & close; 8
     cott hogges; 20 store lambes; 22 tithe lambes wth 6 of mine. Sum 295
13   /John LeStrange/ 8 ewes & ewe shorlins, 5 lambes
26   /Will LeStrange/ 16 ewes & ewe shorlins, 10 lambes
13   /Edward LeStrange/ 8 ewes & ewe shorlins, 5 lambes /1 mort/
7   /Roger LeStrange/ 5 ewes & ewe shorlins, 2 lambes /1 mort/
7   /Charles LeStrange/ 2 ewes & 2 lambes
     3 lambes out of the parke
     Sum of the stock 295 [and] sum of the chilldrens 66: 341 [361]

/Cullett in Barrett Ringsted/ 122 of my owne	7	2	0
60 of my sonne Hamon Le Strange	3	0	0
30 of Robert Banyard	1	10	0
20 of John Woodrow	2	0	0
20 of Robert Bastard	1	0	0
20 of Willyam Makemid	1	0	0
20 of Robert Harrison	1	0	0
20 of Willyam Harrison	1	0	0
20 of Thomas Wallker	1	0	0
10 of Willyam Murton		10	0
Sum 302 [342] £18 2s written	18	2	0

1650   /Sedgford East Ground/ 40 wethers delivered from Ringsted
[p]   North flock

---

122. Tithe paid by head.
123. Sum should read £2 4s.

Thomas Goodmans charge of Ringsted North Ground 1650 216
wethers of the last yeares stock; 5 wether hogges from Barrett
Ringsted; 70 wether lambes from Barrett Ringsted; 94 wether
lambes bought at Bircham & Goodman. Sum 345 [385]

1650	/Cullett in Ringsted North Ground/	£	s	d
200	my sonne Hamon Le Strange			
60	Robert Thurlow			
60	John Cole	2	10	0
40	Henry Coppin	1	13	4
20	Robert Banyard as Baylife		13	4
20	John Woodrow		16	8
20	Thomas Wallker		16	8
	Sum 400 [420] £6 10s written			

1651 Thomas Goodman delivered of Barrett Ringsted sheepe as
followeth: 269 rammes, ewes & ewe shorlins; 1 ramme hogge
stolen out of the close; 2 rammes drowned in the Mill River, /23
morts/. Sum 295 so he is right, 19 croned, of these 269 sheepe I
had 25 stone of wooll

1651	/Lambes/ in all 117 lambes wherof as followeth	£	s	d
	20 lambes sold for	5	0	0
	3 lambes sold for		18	0
	52 lambes sold at Kippon for	7	12	0

40 store lambes; 2 marking lambes. Sum 117. Sheep taken from
Barrett Ringsted flock, crones 19 sold, with 2 crones left the last
year, at 4s 6d to my cosen Dusgate

1651	Thomas Goodman delivered his charge of Ringsted North flock			
	as followeth: 10 wethers sold for £6; 10 wethers sold for £6; 20			
60	wethers sold for £11; 20 wethers sold for £11	34	0	0

2 dizy he brought home that dyed in the close; 1 weake wether
was putt into the close and was eaten with wormes; 1 wether a
dogge worried; 30 morts brought home; 271 wether & wether
shorlins clipped. Sum 345 [365] So he is right, of these I had
[p]   33 stone & 12lb of wooll the tithe payd

1651	Sheepe taken from Ringsted North flock			
	1 wether to Robert Banyard for one I had of Strett			
	20 wethers sold for	10	0	0

1 wether to Sedgford East flock. Sum 22. Remayne in charge
249, wherof delivered to Sedgford 20, rem[ain] 229

1651 /Sedgford East flock/ 39 wethers brought to the clipping, 1 mort –
40 so he is right, of these I had 4 stone 1 of wooll the tithe payd

1651		st	lb	di
Barrett Ringsted tithe wooll & lambe				
of my owne for 10½ stone of 119 sheepe		1	1	0
Robert Bastard & John Woodrow			3	1
Willyam Makemid			1	1
Robert Harrison & Willyam Harrison			3	0
Robert Banyard &			5	0
	Sum	2	0	0

1651 /Barrrett Ringsted tithe lambes/		[tithe lambs]	
of my owne tithe of 97 lambes		10	odd
Robert Banyard 20		2	0
Robert Harrison 6 odd & now 16[124]		2	2
Willyam Harrison 10		1	0
John Woodrow 7 odd & now 16		2	3
Willyam Murton 9 odd & now 7		1	6
Thomas Gotterson for Robert Bastard 10		1	0
Thomas Wallker 14		1	4
Willyam Makemid 3 odd & now 5		0	8
	Sum	20	

Heacham tithe lambe & wooll 1651			
/Lambes/ of my cosen Dusgate 8 & his sonne in lawe one		9	odd
Thomas Crampe senior & junior		3	9
Simon Loke		2	0
Willyam Banyard of Sedgford /7 odd/		1	7
Wattson of Docking		1	0
James Cock junior		1	5
James Cock senior [father and son] /pd 8s/		0	6
Willyam Newman		0	9
John Fisher		0	8
Sum 17 [lambs] inde 16 to Goodman		17	

	st	lb	di
/Wooll/ My cosen Dusgate	1	7	
John Partridg		3	½
Thomas Crampe		13	
Katherin Foster		1	
Simon Loake		5	

124. This new table shows how odd lambs are added to the current year and a new calculation made.

James Cock /pd 2s 2d/				3	
Wattson				3	
Willyam Banyard				4	½
Robert Constable				5	½
	Sum		4	3	½
Sum 4 stone [*illegible words*] Cock oweth[125]		£	s	d
				15	0
/*Sedgford East flock*/ Robert Birch his shepheards charge		1	5	0
39 wethers remayning in his charge			5	6
1 wether from Ringsted North flock			11	0
[*p*] Sum 40			11	3

1651   Thomas Goodmans charge of Barrett Ringsted: 250 rammes,
ewes & ewe shorlins; 2 ewes out of the Close *that were hoggs*;
50 store lambes *inde 10 tithe*; 26 tithe lambes *inde 16 of
Heacham*; 6 cott lambes. Sum 334 wherof to Ringsted 14

16   /*John Le Strange*/ 13 ewes & ewe shorlins, 3 lambes
32   /*Will Le Strange*/ 26 ewes & ewe shorlins, 6 lambes
16   /*Edward Le Strange*/ 12 ewes & ewe shorlins, 4 lambes
11   /*Roger Le Strange*/ 7 ewes & ewe shorlins, 4 lambes
 8   /*Charles Le Strange*/ 6 ewes & ewe shorlin, 2 lambes one of those
       in the close of Spurne
16   /*Tho. Le Strange*/ 11 ewes, 5 lambes
       Sum of the stock 300 & sum of the chilldrens 98 [*is*] 398

		£	s	d
1651	/*Cullett in Barrett Ringsted*/			
	35 of my owne	1	15	0
	40 of my sonne Hamon Le Stranges	2	0	0
	20 of Robert Banyards	1	0	0
	20 of Robert Bastards	1	0	0
	20 of John Woodrows	1	0	0
	20 of Willyam Makemids	1	0	0
	20 of Robert Harrisons	1	0	0
	20 of Willyam Harrisons	1	0	0
	20 of Thomas Wallkers	1	0	0
	10 of Willyam Murtons		10	0
	Sum 205 [*225*] & £11 5s writt			

125. The figures below in the RH column relate to Cock's debt, rather than Robert
Birch's shepherds charge.

1651   Thomas Goodmans charge of Ringsted North Flock: 249
        wethers & wether shorlins; a stray wether shorling; 100 wether
        lambes from Bagthorpe; 14 wether lambes from Barrett
        Ringsted. Sum 324 [*364*]

1651	/Cullett in Ringsted North flock/			
200	my sonne Hamon Le Strange			
60	Robert Thurlow			
60	John Cole	2	10	0
40	Henry Coppin	1	13	4
20	Robert Banyard		13	4
20	John Woodrow		16	8
20	Thomas Wallker		16	8
20	Thomas Goodman		16	8
[*p*]	Sum 400 [*440*] & £7 6s 8d writt	7	6	8

[*1651*]   /Sedgford East foldcourse/ Robert Birch his shepheards charge: 39
        wethers remayning in his charge; 1 wether from Ringsted North
        flock; 20 wether from Ringsted North flock. Sum 60

1652   Robert Birch his shepheard delivered 59 wether /1 mort/; wherof I
        had wooll 5 stone & 9lb tithe payd

[*1652*]	Heacham tithe wooll & lambes 1652	£	s	d
	/Lambes/ of my cosen Dusgate, 6 & odd 2	1	0	0
	Thomas Crampe, 6	1	0	0
	John Crampe [*odd*] 5		1	3
	Francis Cock			
	John Fisher [*odd*] 8			
	Willyam Allen [*odd*] 6			
	Willyam Banyard, 1 [*& odd*] 1		3	8
	Henry Rutland [*odd*] 6			
	John Ellgar 2 [*odd*] 1		0	0
	/2 to Goodman/			
	/15/ Mr Thomas Thornly for tithe of 89 sheepe		8	7
	Mr Boning for tithe of 54 hoggs		6	9
	John Duck for tithe of 20 sheepe, 10 at Midsomer, 10 at our Lady			
	Mr Rawlings for tithe			
	The widow Partridg for 18 sheep for 2 yeares	0	6	0

		st	lb	di
1652	/Wooll/ My cosen Dusgate	2	0	0
	Thomas Crampe	1	3	0

Divers others for small parcells of wooll	I o ¼
Sum	4 3 ¼

/Mony for wooll/ John Crampe for 14 sheepe /2s 4d/
Henry Rutland for 20 sheepe
Willyam Wattson for 48 sheepe
Francis Cock for 5 sheepe
Augustin Waters for 19 sheepe
Willyam Allen for 7 sheepe

		tith	odd
Barrett Ringsted tithe wooll & lambe 1652		tith	odd
1651	/Lambes/ Robert Banyard odd nll 1652 21	2	I
	Robert Harrison odd 2 now 12	I	4
	Willyam Harrison odd nll now 12	I	2
	John Woodrow odd 3 now 19	2	2
	Willyam Murton odd 6 now 8	I	4
	Gotterson for Robert Bastard odd nll now 8	o	8
	Thomas Wallker odd 4 now 16	2	o
	Willyam Makemid odd 8 now 13	2	I
	Sum 11 lambes to Goodmans charge		

	st	lb	di
/Wooll/ Of my owne 35 hogges	o	6	½
Of divers townes men for small parcells of wooll	I	12	½
[p] Sum	2	5	o

	£	s	d
1652 Thomas Goodman delivered at Midsomer of Barrett Ringsted sheepe as followeth: 296 ewes, rammes & ewe shorlins; 24 morts. Sum 300 [320] so he is right, of these 296 sheepe I had 23 stone & 1lb of wooll; 2 of these were pricked at the sheares & dyed & 28 were croned. Remayne of the stock 266	5	12	o

1652 /Lambes/ in all 164 lambes wherof as followeth:			
9 lambes sold for	2	10	o
87 pooke lambes sold for	12	1	o
44 store ewe lambes; 40 store wether lambes to goe to Ringsted; 2 markin lambes; 2 pooke lambes putt into the Parke little worth. Sum 164 [184]			

/Delivered of the chilldrens/
/John Le Strange/ 16 ewes & ewe shorlins, 6 store lambes, 7
pooke lambes sold
/Will Le Strange/ 29 ewes & ewe shorlins & mortes 1 & croned 2,
15 store lambes, 8 pooke lambes sold

/*Edward Le Strange*/ 16 ewes & ewe shorlins, 4 store lambes, 7
pooke lambes sold
/*Roger Le Strange*/ 11 ewes & ewe shorlins, 1 store lambe, 6
pooke lambes sold
/*Charles Le Strange*/ [?] ewes & ewe shorlins, 1 store lambe, 5
pooke lambes sold
/*Thomas Le Strange*/ 15 ewes, 10 store lambes

1652	Thomas Goodman delivered of Ringsted North flock as followeth			
	30 wethers sold for 18s October, 10 wethers sold for 6s			
	Novem[*ber*], 20 wethers sold for 10s Aprill	34	0	0
	44 morts, 1 dizy wether putt into the close that dyed; 239 wether			
	& wether shorlins clipped.			
	Sum 324. So he is right, of these 239 wethers I had the tithe payd			
	24 stone 9lb, 20 of the 239 wethers were solde.			
	So remayne, 219 in charge			

1652	Thomas Goodmans charge of Ringsted North flock: 219 wethers			
	& wether shorlins; 59 wethers from Sedgford East Gound			
	39 wethers bought 20, & 17, & 2	13	9	4
[*p*]	40 wether lambes from Barrett Ringsted. Sum 337 [*357*]			

1652	Cullett in Ringsted North foldcourse			
200	Mr Thomas Raymond			
50	Robert Thurlow			
60	Henry Coppin	2	0	0
20	Robert Banyard		13	4
20	John Woodrow		16	8
20	Thomas Wallker		16	8
	Sum 100 – 4[126]			

1652	Thomas Goodmans charge of Barrett Ringsted: 266 rammes
	ewes, 7 ewe shorlins; 44 store lambes; 11 tithe lambes of Barrett
	Ringsted; 2 store lambes of Heacham. Sum 303 [*330*]

1652	/*John Le Strange*/ 16 ewes & ewe shorlins, 3 ewes bought, 6 store
25	lambes
48	/*Willyam Le Strange*/ 29 ewes & ewe shorlins, 4 ewes bought, 15
	store lambes

---

126. This sum appears inaccurate, but it was inserted later and refers to just those '4'
paying a charge.

23 /*Edward Le Strange*/ 16 ewes & ewe shorlins, 3 ewes bought, 4 store lambes

15 /*Roger Le Strange*/ 11 ewes & ewe shorlins, 3 ewes bought, 1 store lambe

18 /*Charles Le Strange*/ 7 ewes & ewe shorlins, 3 ewes bought, 2 ewes out of the close, 1 store lambe, 5 lambes out of the close

25 /*Thomas Le Strange*/ 15 ewes & ewe shorlins, 10 store lambes
Sum of the stock of ewes 266 & of lambes 57 [*is*] 303 [*323*]
Summ of chilldrens ewes 112 & of lambes 42 [*is*] 134 [*154*]
Sum [*in all*] 437 [*477*]

		£	s	d
1652	Cullett in Barrett Ringsted flock			
	58 of my owne /my husband/	<2	18>	0
	20 of Robert Banyard	1	0	0
	20 of Robert Bastard	1	0	0
	20 of John Woodrow	1	0	0
	20 of Willyam Makemid	1	0	0
	20 of Robert Harrison	1	0	0
	20 of Willyam Harrison	1	0	0
	20 of Thomas Wallker	1	0	0
	10 of Willyam Murton		10	0
	Sum £7 10s for <188> *130* [*150*] sheepe	7	10	0

1652 /*East Hall shepheard*/ had in charge of my ewes 60, he delivered after our Lady 5 skinnes & 55 ewes & 30 lambes all which my husband had toward the mony I lost & owe upon my accompt & 5 ewes from Docking

[*p*]
A Reckoning of the sheepe of Nicholas Le Strange
my grandchilde[127]

1652 I bought for him of my sonne Hamon Le Strange 100 ewes & layd them at Docking Summer Flock they cost me £48

		£	s	d
1653	Wattson, Docking sheppheard delivered morts 6 & ewes 114 in all /100/ [*120*] of these there was wooll the tithe payd /6 stone & 10lbs/ Watson delivered lambes the tithe payd 71			
	/whereof/ 45 lambes sold at Coolidg at 23¼d	4	7	8
	7 pooke lambes sold for		14	0
	19 store lambes sold for	3	6	6
	11 crones sold out of the 114 ewes at 3s	1	13	0
	Sum	10	1	0

---

127. Consolidation of entries continued where appropriate.

1653	payd to Mr Drury for joyce of 100		6	0	0

1653   payd to Mr Drury for joyce of 100   6   0   0

payd for washing 1s & for clipping of them 4s & for dragging
of them 1s   6   0

payd for 17 ewes to make up the 100   5   13   4

Sum   11   19   4

the £10 1s that I received as above being deducted out the £11 19s
4d that disbursed remayne due from Nicholas to me   1   19   4

1653   John Willis his charge in Docking Summer flock
Wattson delivered to John Willis 103 ewes 17 ewes bought
delivered to him 100 [*120*]

1654   Willis brought to the clipping as followeth:
5 morts, 115 ewes [*is*] 100 [*120*], of these there was wooll *16 stone &*
1lb/
75 lambes the tithe payd wherof

1654   /*whereof*/ 12 store lambes delivered to Wills Hall
2 store lambes to Barrett Ringsted

54 lambes sold to my cosen Bagge[128] at 2s 2d   5   17   0

5 pooke lambes sold to Goodman   6   8

30 crones out of the 115 ewes sold to Robert Thurlow at 3s 4d   5   0   0

Received for 6 skinns of 1653   1   6

Received for 5 skinns of 1654   1   4

Sum   11   6   6

Due to me from Nicholas as appeareth by the reckoning 1653   1   19   4

1654   payd to Mr John Drury for joyce of 100   6   0   0

for washing of the 115 ewes   0   8

for clipping of the 115 ewes   4   0

for dragging of those sheepe   0   4

Sum   8   4   4

payd for 23 ewes to lay at East hall   7   13   4

Sum   15   17   8

1654   The £11 6s 6d that I received as above being deducted out of the
[*p*]   £15 17s 8d I disbursed remayne due from Nicholas to me   4   11   2

1654   Ewes remayning with John Willis beside 30 crones sold, 85 ewes
whereof

1654   /*Summerflock*/ 25 ewes delivered to East Hall & 60 ewes remayne
in John Willis his charge

---

128. Francis Bagge, ancestor of Sir Jeremy Bagge, 7th bt of Stradsett Hall, Downham,
Norfolk.

1654 /*East Hall flock*/ 23 ewes bought delivered to East Hall, 25 ewes delivered by Willis, 12 store lambes. Sum 60

1654 /*Barrett Ringsted*/ 2 store lambes delivered by Willis

1655 John Willis brought to the clipping
2 morts, 56 ewes of these there was wooll the tithe payd /*4 stone & 7lb*/. So he wanteth 2 sheepe
47 lambes of the tithe payd whereof

1655 51 ewes delivered to Robert Crisp; 30 store lambes delivered to Robert Crisp; 17 pooke lambes sold; 5 crones sold.

1655 East Hall shepheard delivered as followeth: 2 morts, 58 ewes – 60
36 lambes the tithe payd whereof
1655 12 store lambes remayne in his charge; 9 store lambes delivered to Robert Crisp; 15 pooke lambes sold, 11 crones whereof 2 dyed soone after the clipping & 9 crones sold

1655 /*East Hall shepheards charge*/ 47 ewes, 12 store lambes – 59

1655 /*Robert Crisps charge*/ 51 ewes delivered by Willis; 2 ewes Willis is to make good that he wanted; 2 ewe hoggs from Barrett Ringsted; 9 store lambes from East Hall; 30 store lambes delivered by Willis.

[*p*] Sum 94 whereof one Willis did not deliver to Crisp /*not payd*/ 4 morts whereof 2 crones at East Hall, 2 morts with Willis

		£	s	d
1655	/*crones & pooke lambes*/ 5 crones from Willis			
	9 crones from East Hall 14 sold for	2	2	0
	sold 17 pooke lambes from Willis			
	15 pooke lambes from East Hall 32 sold for	3	0	0
1655	Due from Nicholas to me as apeareth by his reckoning in 1654	4	11	2
	to Mr John Drury for joyce of 60 sheepe	3	0	0
	for washing & clipping of Docking sheepe		3	4
	for washing & clipping of East Hall sheepe		2	6
	Sum	7	17	0
1655	The £5 2s which I received as above being deducted out of £7 17s that I layd out. Remayne due from Nicholas to me	2	15	0

1655 Nicholas his whole stock of sheepe is as followeth:
47 ewes, 12 lambes – 59 with East Hall shepheard

55 ewes, 39 store lambes - 94 wth Robert Crisp wth 1 Willis oweth. [*Sum*] 133 [*153*]

		st	lb
/*Wooll to sell*/ 6 stone & 10lb of Docking wooll of 1653, 6 stone & 1lb of Docking wooll of 1654		12	11
1655	4 stone 7lb of Docking wooll, 4 stone 7lb of East Hall wooll	9	0
	Sum	21	11

/*of this*/ I have Docking wooll of 1655		4	7
My cosen Bagge hath East Hall wooll 1655		4	7
& Thomas Butterell is to accompt for 1653 & 1654		12	11

A Reckoning of the profit of my grandchilde Nicholas Le Stranges sheepe[129]

		£	s	d
1634	I gave him store ewes 20			
1637	I received for 15 small lambes	1	19	0
1636	Received for 6 crones		15	0
1637	Received for 3 stone of wooll	1	4	0
1638	Received for 27 small lambes	1	16	0
	For 6 crones		15	0
	For 4 stone of wooll	1	12	0
1639	Received for 29 small lambes	2	15	7
	Received for 14 crones	1	15	0
	Received for 5 stone of wooll	2	0	0
1640	Received for 36 small lambes	3	0	0
	Received for 10 crones	1	5	0
	Received for 5 stone of wooll	2	0	0
1641	Received for 48 small lambes	6	3	9
	Received for 9 crones	1	3	0
	Received for 6 <crones> stone of wooll	2	8	0
1642	Received for 37 small lambes	3	8	0
	Received for 18 crones	2	5	0
	Received for 10 stone of wooll	3	0	0
	Sum	41	4	4

/*Remayne*/ 82 store ewes, 32 store lambes, 6 wether hoggs – 100 [*120*] These 100 sheep his grandfather bought of him 1642 after

	£	s	d
they were clipped for which he payd	31	4	0
to which add the mony received above by me	41	4	4
Sum payd by me	72	8	4

---

129. Three pages after the previous entry.

A note of what sheep were layd upon Barrett Ringsted
ground these the losse[130]

			/morts/
1631	The charge 548 sheep delivered	1632	60
1632	The charge 552	1633	51
1633	The charge 508	1634	44
1634	The charge 557	1635	134
1635	The charge 513	1636	23
1636	The charge 524	1637	14
1637	The charge 537	1638	22
1638	The charge 536	1639	27
1639	The charge 568	1640	26
1640	The charge 586	1641	44
1641	The charge 647	1642	51
1642	The charge 630	1643	28

[p]

		£	s	d
1653	/Ringsted North flock/ Thomas Goodmans charge 1652 was 337 he delivered at Midsomer 1653[131]			
	20 wethers in October, 20 wethers in November, 20 wethers in March, 20 wethers in Aprill sold for	39	10	0
	23 morts with one stroyed, 1 dizy dyed in the close – 24 morts 253 clipped whereof I had 27 stone 2lb of wooll. Sum 337 [357] so he is right.			
	So remayne wethers in Goodmans charge 253, of these sold before the flock was sett 23 wethers.	10	7	0
	Remayne in his charge wethers 230			
1653	Thomas Goodman delivered of his charge for Barrett Ringsted being 303 & 59 that were mine & 30 from Docking & East Hall were mine in all 388 as followeth: 348 ewes & ramms & shorlins; 40 morts wherof 4 eaten wth wormes & 3 stroyed Sum 388 whereof I had 30 stone 2lb of wooll /of these sheepe/ 43 croned whereof one dyed in driving to the fayer, 3 ewes were worried wth Hamon Powlls dogge. Sum 46. So remayne in Goodmans charge sheepe 337			
1653	/Lambes/ in all [illegible] delivered as followeth: 174 lambes & 88 lambes of mine delivered to him a little before clipping for mony that I did owe my husband upon my accompt. Sum 245 /of these/ 22 lambes sold for fatt lambes	4	14	0

---

130. A page after the previous entry.
131. A page after the previous entry.

2 marking lambes

128 lambes sold at Coolidg fayer wth 2 stolen	14	3	0
18 lambes sold at Kippon	7	8	0
/£26 5s/ Sum 170	[26	5	0]

95 store lambes remayne, 19 lambes, 8 lambes, 5 of Hunston
lambes, 3 of Heacham tithe lambes – 110 [130] store
6 of these were worried with Hamon Powlls dogg, 3 of the 100
dyed before greasing. So remayne [?]
/Lambes store/ 49 store lambes to Barrett Ringsted
71 store wether lambes to Ringsted flock
1 lambe in the parke in all – 101 [121]
/Remayne sheepe 392/ 38 crones to Coolidg whereof 1 dyed on
the way, 11 crones sold to Henry Coppin, 10 wether shorlins to
Ringsted Flock, 3 ewes worried with Hamon Powlls dogge.
Sum 62. /Remayne/ 310 ewes & rammes & 49 store lambes.

[p]   Sum 339 [359]

1653   Mony received for Caly tithe wooll & lambes[132]

	£	s	d
/Wooll/ My cosen Dusgate payd for 2 [stone]		18	0

Thomas Crampe payd wooll 1 [stone]
John Crampe payd wooll ¾[lbs]
Katherin Foster payd wooll 2[lbs]
Robert Constable payd wooll 3½[lbs]
Robert Banyard payd wooll 1½[lbs]
Sum 3 stone 8¾lbs

/Lambes to Barrett Ringsted/ John Duck payd 1
John Ellgar payd 1

	£	s	d
Robert Constable payd 1			
my cosen Dusgate payd 3	0	7	6
Thomas Crampe payd 4	0	10	0
Katherin Foster payd 1	0	2	6
Robert Banyard payd for the tithe of 9	0	2	3
/22s 3d/	1	2	3
/10s for sheepe all written /of Mr Thornly for tithe of 100	10	0	

---

132. Five pages after the previous entry (the ship account fits in between, see below, pp. 195–8).

A note for laying of sheepe in Ringsted
before the agreement with the townesmen of Ringsted
for laying the North Flock intire[133]

/Southflock & North/ 400 the Lord layd
300 the towne layd in all 800
100 the shepheard layd} & so in the North
/now/ 700 the Lord layeth in the North flock
100 the shepheard layeth in the North flock
/South flock/ 100 the Lord layeth in the South flock
66 the Lord layeth for Reads & Whittles
55 the towne layeth
100 the shepheard layeth

[p]   Sum 800

A Reckoning for sheepe beginning from Midsomer 1653

1653   /Barrett Ringsted charge/ Remayning in Thomas Goodmans
charge after the crones & other sheepe were taken off as
appeareth by this booke as followeth: 200 ewes & ramms &
shorlins; 30 ewes bought of John Woodrow; 14 ewes bought of
Thomas Walker; 6 ewes bought of Willyam Murton; 24 ewes
bought of Edward Lawes; 23 ewes bought of Thomas Goodman;
[346]   49 store lambes *inde* on marked for Kempe. Sum beside Kemps
411, bought of Cr [*illegible*] 7, kitching lamb, lose 2 [*is*] 420

1653   Thomas Goodmans charge of the childrens sheepe

/morts, crones 1654/

31   /Jo Le Strange/ ewes & ewe shorlins 22, store lambes 9

/2 crones, remayne 29/

58   /Will Le Strange/ ewes & ewe shorlins 43, store lambes 15

/2 morts, 6 crones, remayne 50/

30   /Edw Le Strange/ ewes & ewe shorlins, 21 store lambes 9

/1 mort, 2 crones, remayne 27/

20   /Rog Le Strange/ ewes & ewe shorlins 13, store lambes 7

/1 crone, remayne 19/

23   /Char Le Strange/ ewes & ewe shorlins 15, store lambes 8

/remayne 23/

31   /Tho Le Strange /ewes & ewe shorlins 25, store lambes 6

/1 crone, remayne 30/

the chilldrens sheep 119, the chilldrens lambes 54 [*is*] 173 [*193*] the
whole charge is 585

---

133. This is a summary of an agreement dating from 1650, LEST/Q37.

		£	s	d
1653	/Barrett Ringsted cullett/			
	20 Robert Banyard	1	0	0
	20 Henry Coppin	1	0	0
	7 Margaret Guybon		6	0

1653   Thomas Goodmans charge of Ringsted North flock 1653: 230 wethers remayne as appeareth by this booke; 10 wether shorlins

341   from Barrett Ringsted; 50 wether shorlins bought of Robert Dunham; 71 wether lambes from Barrett Ringsted. Sum 341 [361]

		£	s	d
1653	/Cullett in Ringsted/			
200	Mr Reymond			
50	Robert Thurlow			
60	Henry Coppin	2	10	0
20	John Woodrow	0	16	8
20	Robert Banyard	0	13	4
20	Thomas Walker	0	8	4
20	John Cooke	0	16	8
[p]	Sum 359 [390]			

1653   /Sedgford East Ground/ 51 ewes that my husband had of me for debt, 10 lambes that my husband had of me for debt. Sum 61

1654   Sedgford shepheard brought to the clipping: 60 ewes & /1 mort/ of these 60 ewes there was wooll the tithe payd 4 stone 7lb; /Sedgford sheepe/ 12 crones & sold; 48 ewes delivered to Barrett Ringsted /Sedgford lambes/ the tithe payd; 39 of these 27 sold to my cosen Bagge at 2s 2d; 12 delivered to Barrett Ringsted

1654   /Barrett Ringsted/ Thomas Goodman delivered at Midsomer his charge being 420 beside one marked for Kempe as followeth: 411 ewes & ramms & shorlins and /5 morts/; of these there was wooll 32 stone 7lb
/Lambes/ he brought 310 whereof: 2 for marking <ing lambes>; 34 for fatt lambes to the closes; 83 for store lambes; 206 sold to my cosen Bagge; 5 pooke lambes little worth 3 dyed & 2 were putt into the parke. Sum 310

1654   Sheepe taken from Thomas Goodman
84 ewes croned sold at Kipon fayer
1 ewe dyed at the clipping
/Remayne 1654/ 346 remayne still in his charge

1654   /Ringsted North Ground/ Thomas Goodman delivered at
        Midsomer his charge being 341 as followeth: 60 wethers brought
        home for the kitching; & 289 wethers & wether shorlins & /12 morts/
        Sum 341[134] of these there was wooll the tithe payd 36 stone 4lb

1654   /Remayne/ 289 wethers & wether shorlins wherof brought home
        for the kitching the 31 of July 20 wethers. So remayne 269
[p]   wethers & wether shorlins doe remayne in his charge

1654   Thomas Goodmans charge in Ringsted North foldcourse: 269
        wethers & wether shorlins; 40 wether shorlings brought of
        Goodman; 81 wether lambes from Barrrett Ringsted.
        Sum 370 [390]

1654   Thomas Goodmans charge of Barrett Ringsted flock: 346 ewes,
        rammes & shorlings as by his accompt after the crones abated;
        48 ewes brought from East Hall; 2 store lambes part of 83
        lambes; 12 lambes from East Hall; 2 lambes of Barrett Ringsted
        tithe; 1 stray ewe; 2 lambes of Nicholas brought from Docking.
        Sum 413 & lambes out of the Sheepe Close 7, in all /400 wanting one/

1654   Thomas Goodman charge of the chilldrens sheepe
        /John Le Strange/ ewes & ewe shorlins 29, lambes 10 – 39
        /Willyam Le Strange/ ewes & ewe shorlins 50, lambes 20 – 70
        /Edward Le Strange/ ewes & ewe shorlins 27, lambes 10 – 37
        /Roger Le Strange/ ewes & ewe shorlins 19, lambes 7 – 26
        /Charles Le Strange/ ewes & ewe shorlins 23, lambes 9, more out
        of the close 3 – 35
        /Thomas Le Strange/ ewes & ewe shorlins 30, lambes 12 – 42
        Sum 206 whereof: sheepe 158, lambes 68 - 206 [226][135]
        more as above 419 & /7/ *608*<119>/
        /more of Kemps /2/ of Mr Raymonds /20/ of Robert Banyards /20/
[p]   Sum 648 [667]

        A Reckoning of the Kitching Sheepe 1654
1654   /June 3/ Cotts remayning the third of June wth a kitching ewe   6
        /July 31/ wethers remayning then   50
        /Septembe[r] 25/ more in the park a ramme hogge   1
        wethers received of Goodman before his charge   20

---

134. The actual figure is 349, plus 12 morts, makes 361, which hides a shepherd's
allowance; after 36 stone and 4lb '20' is entered, which may relate to ounces.

135. In fact, the children's totals show a further 23 sheep – the 3 lambs in the close and
a further shepherd's allowance of 20 sheep.

wethers received bought of John Cooke	18
Sum [*sheep*]	95

/more/ 4 of the crones taken out of Barrett Ringsted which were apoynted to be sold being the best of them were left unsolde & remayne in the close with the fatt sheepe

A Reckoning of Lambes 1654

1654	/June 3/ Cotts lambes remayning in the close	4
	Received out of Goodmas flock to fatt	36
	Sum [*lambs*]	40
	/of these/ sold to Wadelow the bucher, cotts lambes	4
	sold to Wadelow of the other lambes	4
	/in October/ delivered to Goodman to Barrett Ringsted	6
	remayne lambes for the kitching	25
	Sum [*lambs*]	38
	killed of the 25 lambes at the 23th of October	19
	kitching lambes remayne to kill the 27 of October	3
	Cott ewes remayne whereof olde	6
	/Charles/ hath remaining in the close & in the parke 2 cott ewes	
[p]	& 2 cott lambes whereof one is a ramme lambe	

All the wooll of 1642 was sent into Holland and there sold[136]

1643	/Wooll/	st	
	Sedgford wooll	60	
	Barrett Rinsgted wooll	53	
	Ringsted wooll	43	
	Kitching wooll	4	
	Heacham wooll	4	
	Sum	164	
	/£ s d/		
	/39 0 0/ of this sold to Thomas Mego at 6s	130	
	/10 0 0/ sold to divers others at 8s	25	
	/3 4 0/ sold more to others at 8s	8	
	more spunn for hose yarn	1	
	Sum 164 stone – £52 4s		

1644	/Wooll after plunder/	st	lb
	Barrett Ringsted wooll	39	0
	Kitching wooll	14	0
	Heacham Tithe wooll	3	7
	Sum	56	7

---

136. The wool account is located after Elizabeth's account and before Alice's own account, see above, pp. 59–60.

1644 /£ s d/
    /5 17 0/ of this sold to divers men at 9s   13   0
    /13 0 0/ sold more to others at 10s   26   0
    /7 0 0/ sold of kitching wooll at 11s   14   0
    /1 8 0/ sold Heacham wooll at 10s   3   7
                 Sum 56 stone 7lb – £27 5s

1645 /Wooll/   st   lb
    Barrett Ringsted wooll with the tithe   13   0
    Ringsted wethers wooll   16   0
    Kitching wooll   10   0
    Heacham wooll* tithe*   4   7
                 Sum [43]   41   7

1645 /£ s d/
    /5 10 0/ of this sold to divers men at 10s   11   0
    /8 16 0/ sold at 11s to others at 11s   16   0
    /5 10 0/ sold of kitching wooll at 11s   10   0
    /1 5 0/ sold Heacham tithe wooll at 10s   2   0
    /1 0 0/ of Heacham wooll to sell now *sold to Ellgar* 2   7
£22 1s   Sum   41   7

1646 /Wooll/   st   lb
    Barrett Ringsted wooll   12   0
    Ringsted wethers wooll   24   5
    Kitching wooll   8   2
    Barrett Ringsted tithe wooll   3   0
    Heacham tithe wooll   6   7
                 Sum   54   0

    /£ s d/
    /1 17 0/ of this sold to Ellgar of Heacham tithe   3   0
    /2 10 9/ sold to Harrison of Heacham tithe at 14s 6d   3   7
    /17 13 0/ sold to Harrison of Ringsted wooll at 14s 6d   24   5
    /8 14 0/ sold to Harrison of Barrett Ringsted wooll at 14s 6d   12   0
    /2 3 6/ sold to Harrison of Barrett Ringsted tithe at 14s 6d   3   0
    /5 18 0/ sold to Harrison of kitching wooll at 14s 6d   8   2
    /2 8 6/ sold to Harrison that did sett out in all this wooll   3   5
£41 4 9   Sum   57   5

[p]   st   lb
1647 /Wooll/ Kitching wooll   7   4   0
    Wooll of 5 cotts   7   7   0

Ringsted wooll	19	12	0
Barrett Ringsted wooll	18	12	0
Barrett Ringsted tithe wooll	2	5	4
Heacham tithe wooll	4	7 4/3	
Sum[137]	53	5 4/3	

1647 /£   s   d   Wooll/

/5   9   0/ sold to Willyam Harrison of A[y]lsham of the kitching
wethers wooll at 15s   7   4   0

/0   7   6/ sold to him of cotts wooll at 15s   7   0

/14 18   0/ sold to him of Ringsted wethers wooll at 15s   19 12   0

/14   3   0/ sold to him of Barrett Ringsted wooll   18 12   0

/1 15   0/ sold to him of Barrett Ringsted tithe wooll   2   5   0

/2 14   0/ sold to him of Heacham tithe wooll at 12s   4   7   3

[illegible] sold to him that did set out in all this wooll 1647 at 15s
beside [illegible]

Sum   55   9   0

1648 /Wooll/ Ringsted wethers wooll[138]   27   0   di

Barrett Ringsted wooll   26 12   0

Barrett Ringsted tithe wooll   2   0   1

Kitching wooll 7 stone 10lb & cotts wooll a stone 4lb   9   0   0

Sum   64 12   1

1648 Heacham tithe wooll 3 stone 5lb

1649 /Wooll/ Ringsted wethers wooll   20   8   0

Barrett Ringsted wooll   32   9   0

Sedgford wooll   4   5   1

Barrett Ringsted tithe wooll   2   1   0

Kitching wooll 5 stone 10lb & cotts wooll 13lbs   6   9   0

Sum   66   4   1

1649 Heacham tithe wooll 2 stone 6lb

1649 /Wooll/ sold to Thomas Alyard all the wooll of 1648 but   st   lb   di

/£40 10s/ Heacham wooll at 12s 4d the stone & 10s over all   64   12   ½

/£40 18s/ sold to him all the wooll of 1649 but Heacham   66   4   ½

/£17s 3d/ sold to him at the same rate part of out setts   2   3   0

---

137. Alice started to enter portions of a pound in the final column, 4/3 probably
indicates ¾ of a lb.

138. In the final RH column, Alice entered 'di' or dimidus, indicating halves as in the
perches column, but still ½ and 4/3 appear.

		l	s	d
/£5/ sold to him more which was hurt with lying neare the wall at 10s part of out setts, so the 2 yeare wooll did sett out 12 stone & 3lb /£87 15s 7d/		10	0	0
	Sum	143	6	0

<table>
<tr><td>1650
[p]</td><td>/£3 8s sold 1650/ Heacham sold to my cosen Dusgate; sold by
John Partridg both these being the wooll of 1648 & of 1649</td><td>1</td><td>8</td><td>0</td></tr>
<tr><td></td><td></td><td>4</td><td>3</td><td>½</td></tr>
</table>

[1650]	Wooll of 1650 as by the sheepe booke		st	lb	di
	Ringsted wethers wooll		33	7	0
	Barrett Ringsted wooll		29	3	0
	Sedgford wooll		5	3	0
	Barrett Ringsted tithe wooll		2	6	1
	Heacham tithe wooll		4	2	1
	Kitching wooll		5	4	1
	Cotts wooll that went in the parke & closes		2	9	0
		Sum	82	7	0

1651	/Wooll/ Ringsted wethers wooll		33	12	0
	Barrett Ringsted wooll		25	0	0
	Sedgford wooll		4	1	0
	Barrett Ringsted tithe wooll		2	0	0
	Heacham tithe wooll		4	0	0
	Kitching wooll		6	10	0
	Cotts wooll		0	9	0
		Sum	76	4	0
	The sum of wooll 1650 & 1651		158	11	0

		st	lb	di
sold to Willyam Harrison at 10s		15	0	0
/£73 for 146 stone/ sold to John Bently at 10s, 2 stone of wooll and 2 stone of locks given him into the bargayne		148	0	0
sold to my cosen Dusgate *of Heacham wooll*		3	0	0
Sum 166 stone with the 2 stone given in so the wooll set out in these 2 yeares		7	3	0

	Wooll of 1652 as by the sheepe booke apeareth		st	lb
1652	Ringsted wethers wooll the tithe payd		24	0
	Barrett Ringsted wooll		23	1
	Sedgford wooll the tithe payd		5	9
	Barrett Ringsted tithe wooll		4	5
	Heacham tithe wooll		4	4
	Kitching wooll		7	4
	Cotts wooll		0	8
		Sum	67	3

/£	s	d/			
/3	19	0/ sold to Simon Ellgar at 11s	7	3	
/0	10	0/ sold to Kirby	1	0	
/0	10	0/ sold to Richard Jolls	1	0	
/28	16	0/ sold to John Bently at 9s	64	0	

Sum 73 stone 3lbs £33 15s   73   3

So the wooll did sett out this yeare beside a stone & 8lb used to

[p]¹³⁹ make 2 wooll twillts and socks were spunn to make a coverlet   6   0

[1653]   /June 8/ Wooll remaining in the wooll chamber of 1653 for

	st	lb	di
Thomas Butterell to accompt			
of Nicholas his wooll from Docking	6	10	0
of John Le Strange wooll	2	8	0
of Willyam Le Strange wooll	4	12	0
of Edward Le Strange wooll	2	4	0
of Roger Le Strange wooll	1	6	0
of Charles Le Strange wooll	2	4	0
of Thomas Le Strange wooll	2	10	0
[sub-total]	22	12	0
of kitching wooll with 6 stone	6	10	0
of Barrett Ringsted wooll	30	2	0
of Ringsted the tithe payd	27	12	0
of Sedgford wooll the tithe payd	3	6	0
of Heacham tithe wooll beside 2 stone of 1653 sold	1	8	3
Sum 69 stone 10lbs & 3 quarters beside the 22 stone & 12lbs of the chilldrens	69	10	4/3

		st	lb	di
1654	/Wooll sold of/ Kitching wethers wooll	6	9	0
	of cotts wooll 9lb & a ramm in the parke 1lb		10	0
	of Barrett Ringsted ewes clipped with the kitching sheepe	2	7	0

Sum 9 stone 12lb this was solde to Simon Ellgar with 5lb of little
     Charles his wooll which made it up 10st & 3lb sold for £4 17s
Other wooll in the wooll chamber:
of Barrett Ringsted wooll beside 2 stone 7lb sold to Simon Ellgar

as above	30	0	0
Ringsted wooll the tithe payd	36	4	1
Sedgford wooll the tithe payd	4	7	0
Robert Banyards tithe wooll		2	1
Henry Copins tithe wooll		1	1

---

139. Twilt is a quilt, see Yaxley, Glossary, p. 225.

Heacham tithe wooll

		st	lb	di
1653	Wooll in the wool chamber of 1653	69	10	¾
1654	Wooll in the wool chamber of 1654 beside Heacham wooll	71	1	½
	Sum 140 stone 12¼ lbs beside 22 stone 12lbs of the chilldrens			
	& a fleece of a stray sheepe taken up in the closes 1654	140	12	¼

		st	lb	di
1654	Received of Heacham tithe wooll 2 stone 12¼lbs which being			
	added to 71 stone 1½lbs it maketh the wooll of 1654	73	13	¾
[p]	More my cosen Dusgate tithe wooll of 1654	2	5	0
	Sum	76	4	¾

	st	lb	di
Wooll for Thomas Butterell to accompt 1654			
of 1653 of Nicholas his wooll from Docking	6	10	0
of John Le Strange wooll	2	8	0
of Willyam Le Strange wooll	4	12	0
of Edward Le Strange wooll	2	4	0
of Roger Le Strange wooll	1	6	0
of Charles Le Strange wooll	2	4	0
of Thomas Le Strange wooll	2	10	0
[Sub-total]	22	12	0
of 1653 of kitching wooll with 6 stone of cotts wooll	6	10	0
of Barrett Ringsted wooll	30	2	0
of Ringsted wooll the tithe payd	27	12	0
of Sedgford wooll the tithe payd	3	6	0
of Heacham tithe wooll beside 2 stone of 1653 sold	1	8	3
[Sub-total]	69	10	¾
of 1654 of the kitching wethers wooll	6	9	0
of cotts wooll		9	0
of Barrett Ringsted ewes clipped with the wethers	2	7	0
of a ramme hogge in the parke		1	0
[Sub-total]	9	12	0

this 9 stone 12lbs with 5lbs of little Charles his wooll did make
10 stone & 3lbs and was sold to Simon Ellgar for £4 17s

		st	lb	di
1654	Barrett Ringsted wooll beside 2 stone 7lb sold as above	30	0	0
	Ringsted wooll the tithe payd	36	4	1
	Sedgford wooll the tithe payd	4	7	0
	Henry Copins tithe wooll		1	1
	Robert Banyards tithe wooll		2	1
	Heacham tithe wooll	2	12	4
	[Sub-total]	73	13	¾
	Sum beside the 22 stone 12 lbs of the chilldrens wooll			
	& a fleece of a stray sheepe is to accompt for	142	1	½

When the wooll be sold I am to be allowed for 6 stone & 10lbs of
Nicholas wooll 1653 & of Nicholas wooll of 1654 which was layd
into the wooll chamber beside wooll as above reckoned 6 stone
& 1lb in all   12   11   0

A note of such sheepe as the tenants
layd on the South Flock of Ringsted 1643[140]

Sheep		£	s	d
22[141]	Mr Hodson for Gillions 4 for Northall 12 for Chants severalls 6: in all		3	8
4	Mr Loades for Crisp			8
30	George Bastard		5	0
26	Edward Gitting		4	4
6	John Draper		1	0
20	Robert Thurlow		3	4
8	Edward Crisp		1	4
10	Francis Flack		1	8
15	Thomas Cornell		2	6
4	Christopher Bennett			8
15	Robert Constable senior		2	6
15	Robert Constable junior		2	6
15	Robert Constable junior		2	6
5	Robert Constable for Gages			10
20	Jebeliah Wallden for		3	4
20	John Cademan		3	4
5	Francis Levett for Crisps			10
6	John Hancell		1	0
4	John Grange			8
8	Robert Stevenson for Mr Hocknell		1	4
12	Mathew Jolls		2	0
24	Robert Browne		4	0
4	Richard Constable the smith			9
7	John Kirby		1	2
10	Richard Jolls		1	8
10	Mr Read		1	9
5	Richard Constable senior			10
15	Robert Woodton		2	6
7	Robert Woodison for Plafords		1	2
4	John Stokely for Seborns			8
3	James Creed for Seborns			6

140. This note comes after Hamon's account, 1618–25.

141. To avoid confusion between sheep and money, the sheep have been moved to the
LH margin.

3	John Smith for Seborns			6
4	Willyam Benit			8
5	Richard Draper			10
	[Sum]	/£3	10s	2d/

Sum 311 [371] so there is 11 sheepe more then they ought to
have for they are to lay but 300 for which they are to pay 2d
the sheepe at Midsomer and the shepheard is to lay 100 and his
wages is 3s 6d and his bellweather fleece and the tenants & the
shepheard is to lay the like in Ringsted North flock

the Lord is to lay 400 sheepe in the North & South flock

/Ringsted North & South/ the shepheards of the North and South
Ground are to have 3ac in every breck paying 12d the acre and
for tath 12d 1ac

fol. 185   it appeareth by my fathers booke that he tooke in joyce sheepe
1619   at 10d the sheepe in Ringsted North foldcorse and for the tath
fol. 230   that yeare Thomas Gitting had but 3ac amongst the brecklands
1608   Thomas Gitting had 3ac wherof 2ac for the Baliwick & 1ac for
the parke so in the North & South Breck 6ac

fol. 230   the Lord is to find hurdles pitch & tarre for the whole flocks and
[p]   to pay the shepheards wages

Sedgford East Ground
fol. 191   it appeareth by my fathers booke that the Lord ought to lay on
1603   the East Ground /940/; by the same booke that Thomas Lock
fol. 204   did owe for the tath 2ac, 2s, this sheweth the shepheard payd
1606   for tathing his covenant land
So Sedgford East Ground is to used as followeth
the Lord to lay sheepe /940/
/Shepheards covenants/ the shepheard to lay sheepe /120/
the shepheard his wages and livery   3   12   8
the shepheard to have 2ac in every breck and to pay for the
tath; he is to have 2 marking lambes & his bellwethers fleece

Sedgford South Ground
fol. 191   it appeareth by my fathers booke that the Lord should lay in sheep
1603   /549/
the shepheard should lay in sheepe /100/
the shepheards wages   3   6   8
the shepheard to have 2ac in every breck and to pay for the
tath; he is to have a marking lambe and the bellwethers fleece

Sedgford North Ground
the usuall laying of that ground hath been /550/
the shepheard for his covenants layeth /100/
the shepheards wages   3   6   8
he hath 2ac in every breck and payeth for the tath
he hath the bellwethers fleece

Barrett Ringsted foldcorse
the usuall lay of this flock of the Lord /700/
the shepheard for his covenants layeth /100/
the shepheards wages   3   6   8
he hath [2ac] in every breck [to pay for the tath]
he is to have 2 marking lambes and the bell-wethers fleece, he
is to pay for the tithe of his 100 sheep 2s

The Ship Account, 1618–1622

**[*Accounts of ye charges & profitts of a shipp in divers voyages,*
c. 1618–1622]**[142]

	£	s	d
[*top third of page illegible*]			
the summ of 21s taken out of £5 16s 7½d[143] *17s 7½d* there			
will remayne of the gayne of the 4 voyages above, but <£4 16s			
7½d>	4	16	7½
gayned in a voyage to Wells		11	1½
gayned in a voyage to Heacham		15	1½
Sum	1	6	3
for our part of tarr and deales for the shippe 12s which being			
taken out of the 26s 3d there remayneth 14s 3d			
the gayne of the 6 voyages these abatements taken out is	5	10	4½
his £5 10s 4½d being taken out of the £7 18s 4d which was of			
purse the first voyag[e] these remayneth still out of purse	2	7	11½

		£	s	d
[p]	[*top third of page illegible, including detail of other voyages*]			
	gayned in a voyage to Hunstanton	4	1	1
	Sum	12	8	2
	Lost in a voyage to Rotterdam	1	1	4
	The 47s 11½d and 21s 4d taken out of £12 8s 2d gayne, there is			
	remaining which the ship hath gayned	8	18	10½

---

142. The ship account occurs towards the end of the second book in LEST/P10 before the children's sheep accounts. The account is very faded and there is no date until the third page with dates of voyages from 1620 to 1622. The enterprise started in c. 1618 alongside the children's sheep accounts. At the bottom of the second page, we find Alice spending some of the profits on sheep.

143. In the document, the ½ comes after the 'd'.

	gayned in a voyage to Amstrelldam		4	4½
	gayned in a voyage to France	4	4	8½
	gayned in a voyage to [New]Castle	1	18	1½
	gayned in a voyage to Castle	1	18	5
	gayned in a voyage to Castle	2	2	0
	gayned in a voyage to Castle	2	0	2
	gayned in a voyage to Holland		16	4
	gayned in a voyage to Holland	2	8	0
	gayned in a voyage to Holland	3	4	11
	gayned in a voyage to Castle	2	10	3
	gayned in a voyage to Castle	3	14	6
	Sum	25	1	9½
	Layd out for a boate, sayles, ropes and other things and £5 5s for the carpenters bill the halfe cometh to	16	13	8
	the whole gayne of the shippe is	34	0	7½
	whereof take out £16 13s 8d there remayneth	17	6	11½
	whereof sold in a voyage to Colchester		1	6

[p]		[top third of page illegible]			
July		[gayned] in a voyage to Castle[144]	3	0	0
	/August/	gayned in a voyage to Castle	1	19	0
	/September/	gayned in a voyage to Castle	2	3	0
	/October/	gayned in a voyage to Castle		18	0
	/October/	gayned in a voyage to Castle	4	2	6
	/December/	gayned in a voyage to Holland	3	0	9
	/February/	gayned in a voyage to Holland	2	6	1
March		gayned in a voyage to Holland	2	0	8
Aprill		gayned in a voyage to Holland	3	16	0
May		gayned in a voyage to Holland £3 5s and coming home by Castle gayned by the coals 37s 1d	5	2	1
May		gayned in a voyage to Hunstanton	3	16	9
		gayned when the ship was lett	3	0	0
	/August/	gayned in a voyage to [New]Castle	2	1	0
		Sum	37	15	8
		So there remayneth of the gayne of the ship beside the £6 3s 10d that was layed out for sheepe	46	17	3½
		/the halfe/[145] Layd out as appeareth by divers bills for new building of the shippe and bringing of her from Linne	23	5	6

---

144. Figures in the pennies column not clear; this accounts for the missing shillings and pennies in the total.

145. The Le Stranges owned only half the boat; sharing was a recognised method of reducing risk in the absence of reliable insurance.

this £23 5s 6d being taken out of the £46 17s 3½d of the 2 sums
above which the ship hath gayned and their doth remayne the

[p]	gayne of the ship		23	11	9½
1620	/January/ gayned in a voyage to Holland		3	5	1
	/February/ gayned in a voyage to Holland		3	19	6½
March	a voyage to Holland wherin there was bought a cable cost £11				
	2s, so we were out of purse for the voyage 55s 11d and gayned in				
May	a voyage to Holland £6 16s 11d the 55s 11d being taken of the				
1621	£6 16s 11d there remayneth £4 1s to be devided, the halfe of it is	2	0	6	
June	gayned in a voyage to Castle		2	17	7½
July	gayned in a voyage to Castle		2	13	1
	/August/ gayned in a voyage to Castle		3	1	5
	/August/ gayned in a voyage to Wells			17	11½
	/September/ gayned in a voyage to Castle		1	6	4
	/October/ gayned in a voyage to Castle		1	6	4
	/November/ gayned in a voyage to Castle beside the halfe of				
	£3 2s 9d that was layd out fir graining of the ship		2	4	6

/£23 12s 4½d written/

	/January/ gayned in a voyage to Castle		2	9	8½
April	Lost in Thornham the sayles, cable and ancre in a storme so				
	wee were out of purse in a voyage to Castle for our part £7 13s 3d				
May	gayned in a voyage to Castle		1	5	6
June	gayned in a voyage to Castle		1	11	½
July	gayned in a voyage to Castle		1	15	11
July	gayned in a voyage to Castle		1	9	8½
	/August/ gayned in a voyage to Castle		1	6	2½
1622	/October/ gayned in a voyage to Castle nll because he was in a				
	stress and lost the mayne mast and the toppe sayle, so we were				
	out of purse for our part 2s 7d	[9	18	1]	

/£9 15s 6d/

	/December/ saved in a voyage to Collchester		2	14	5
	/February/ saved in a voyage to Collchester		1	5	7
April	saved in a voyage to Castle		1	1	4
April	Lost in a voyage to Castle because the graving of the shippe				
	came to £3 19s 7d, so lost of our part 2s 6½d				
May	gayned in a voyage to Castle 13s ½d, the 2s 6½d lost the				
	voyage before being taken out of the 13s ½d there remayneth			10	6
June	gayned in a voyage to Castle		1	17	9½
July	gayned in a voyage to Castle		2	13	9

/£10 3s 4d/   [10   3   4½]

of the £9 15s 6d there is to be abated for October voyage
£7 13s 3d, so there will remayne of that some 42s 3d.
Sum 312 5s 7d written

[*p*]   The ship was wracked upon the coast of France having in the
          £12 2s 9d, all which was lost, so heare endeth the reckoning

Sedgeford Sheep Account, 1620–1622

A Table [*of Contents*] for this end of the book[146]

[*p*] 3[148]

/*1620*/ A booke mentioninge the profits of sheepe & corne in Sedgford £   s   d
Bought of my brother Yellverton at Midsomer 1620, 1331 sheepe at
£32 the hundred wherof 463 wethers and 870 [*1333*] which cometh to   355   14   8
more allowed to them for <20> *16* dozen of hurdles   3   3   7

[*East Ground*]
of these sheepe delivered to Woods 557 ewes

---

146. LEST/BK7. Random notes occupy the first two pages with this table of contents inserted later by Sir Nicholas Le Strange in the 1680s. For this volume the first two items, the sheep account 1620–1622 and the rental of 1634, have been transcribed with the remaining list to illustrate the range of Alice's activities. At the other end of the book, Alice entered her Sedgeford Account 1621–1635 which is closely linked to the rental of 1634.

147. The first account refers to corn as well as sheep; in fact no entries to corn were made. The account only lasted for two years when the Sedgeford sheep were absorbed into the general sheep accounts.

148. From fol. 3 only the facing pages and odd numbers are recorded on the document, but the even numbers have been inserted to draw attention to the page breaks.

/*Joyce sheepe 313*/ of Willyam Guibons 73 sheepe; of Francis Guybons 240
Sum 870

[*South Ground*]
Rose his charge: Rose hath 310 ewes
of Francis Guybons 139, whereof 120 is in lew of 120 that I have of
wethers going in his part of Ringsted flock
/*Joyce sheepe 132*/ of Gorge Framingham 36 sheepe; of Robert
Banyardes 28 sheepe; of Willyam Crisps 6 sheepe; of Edmond
Banyards 4 sheepe; of Thomas Longstrawes 4 sheepe; of Willyam
Greenes 10 sheepe; of John Elgars 20 sheepe; of Pennocks 5 sheepe[149]
Sum 560 [*581*][150]

[*p 4*]
Sedgford Sheep 1620
[*North Ground*] Corner hath, beside 32 wethers which were sent to
Ringsted ground, 432 wethers
/*Joyce sheepe 51*/ of Francis Guybons 39 sheepe; of Gorge
Framinghams 12 sheepe. Sum 483
the whole some of the joyce sheepe is 496

	£	s	d
to Woodes for his quarters wages ending at St Micheall		16	8
to Rose for his quarters wages ending at St Micheall		16	8
to Corner for his quarters wages ending at St Micheall		16	8
to Rose for his quarters wages at Christmas		16	8
to Rose for his halfe yeares allowance for 60 sheep which we are to lay at 6d the sheepe which are not layd this yeare		15	0
to Corner for his quarters wages at Christmas		16	8
to Woods for his quarters wages at Christmas		16	8
to Rose for his quarters wages at our Lady		16	8
to Corner for his quarters wages at our Lady		16	8
to Woods for his quarters wages at our Lady		16	8
[*p*] 5 to Rose for his quarters wages at Midsomer		16	8
to Rose for his allowance for 60 sheepe for halfe a yeare		15	0
to Rose for his livery		6	0
to Woods for his quarters wages at Midsomer		16	8
to Woods for his livery		6	0
to Corner for his quarters wages at Midsomer		16	8
to Corner for his livery		6	8

---

149. As in the sheep accounts, entries have been consolidated, separated by a semi-colon, where appropriate.

150. The actual total is in brackets. Alice's totals seem to include the allowance for the shepherd, see pp. 21–2.

for 2 barrells of tarre and a barrell of pitch	2	1	0
Sum	14	9	8
Received for tath due at St Michaell last[151]	1	9	3
Received for 14 mort sheep skins wherof from Woods 12 from Corner 7 from Rose 6 and from Crisp one		11	0
	[2	0	3]

the 100 wethers are reconed heare because they went for 100 of my cosen Guybons that he had in Roses flock so Crisp brought them to Sedgford to be washed and clipped
the charge of sheppheards wages and pitch and tarre is £14 9s 8d out of which take 40s 3d received for tath and skinns: there remayneth that I have layd out   12   9   5

[*North Ground*] Corner brought to the clipping at Midsomer 1621: 425 [*sheep*], of these there [*were*] 55 stone and the tithe payd. Of these 425 wethers there shall go to Ringsted 305 and 3 wethers from Woods. So with the 32 wethers that went to Ringsted the last yeare there shall be of Sedgford sheep at Ringsted 340 wethers Corner delivered 7 skinns, so his reckoning is right

[*Ringsted South Flock*] Crisp brought to the clipping 114 wethers of which came 15 stone and a halfe and the tithe payd, of these there was 32 Sedgford wethers and <6> *7* of the chilldrens and 81 that came from Barrett Ringsted; of these *3 of the rixeys were sold and 2 that proved rams of the chilldrens were brought home and* 60 of the Barrett Ringsted wethers. So he hath remayning of the 32 that came from Sedgford 29 and 20 of Barrett Ringsted for he lost 3 of Sedgford sheep for which he must pay. /3 skinns of Ringsted sheep 2 were stroyed/

[*p 6, South Ground*] Rose brought to the clipping 303: [*of these*] ewes 302, *8*rams and a wether, of these there came 25½ stone and the tithe payd. He brought lambes the tith payd for all but 6 of which shall be tithed with Woods his lambes 228 lambes wherof 11 small lambes were sent to the fayer and there remayneth still 217, wherof 118 be ewe lambes and 99 wether lambes, whereof to Corner's flock all the wether lambes and all the ewe lambes to Woods his flock. Rose delivered 6 skinns so Rose wanteth one which he must allow

[*East Ground*] Woods brought to the clipping 530 ewes & rams and 4 wethers, and of these came 45 stone of wooll the tithe payd, he

---

151. This entry has been moved from its position amongst the shepherds' wages above.

brought lambes 331, wherof small lambes sent to the fayer 61 the tithe
paid. So there remayneth 270 the tithe payd, wherof 113 [are] wether
lambes and 157 ewe lambes, wherof to Corners flock 93 wether
lambes and 20 small wether lambes sold. Woods delivered 12 skinns
so Woods wanteth one which he must allow
Croned out of Woods and Roses flock 39 ewes and a ram, of these
ewe lambes were taken out for the shepherds 6 marking lambes and
29 lambes to sell /of these 29 lambes 2 dyed/ so Woods had remayning
122 lambes

	£	s	d
Layd out in charges as appeareth on the other side more then was received for tath and skinns	12	9	5
payd for washing of 1320 and a halfe and odd sheepe at 12d		11	6
payd for clipping of 1320 and a halfe of sheepe at 3s 6d	2	0	2
to Fisher and Bockin for a day ½ a peice dragging of sheep		2	6
to Lipkin for a day ½ dragging of sheep		1	3
to Matthew for 2½ dayes dragging of sheep and putting the sheepe into the pitt		2	1
to 4 winders for a day ½ a peice winding of wooll		4	0
to Salter for a day ½ branding		1	3
for hurdles 10 dozen	2	3	4
for 4 dozen and 11 hurdles for Ringsted	1	1	0
the whole sum of charges layd out is[152]	18	17	2

	£	s	d
[p] 7 the whole sum of Sedgford and Ringsted wooll is 141 stone this 144 stone was sold at 8s it did sett out 3 stone	57	12	0
Received for 72 small lambes all charges abated	4	13	4
Received for 20 wether lambes and <29> *27* ewe lambes	5	7	4
Received for 40 crones out of Woods and Rose his flock	5	6	8
Received for the joyce of 496 sheepe for the yeare	24	16	0
Sum	40	3	4
the sum of £18 17s 2d above written being taken out of £40 3s 4d there remayneth of the profit of Sedgford sheepe corses beside wooll	21	6	2

The charge delivered to Corner, Woods and Crisp at Midsomer 1621:

[North Ground] /1621 Corner/ had 100 wethers remayning in his
charge more out of Woods and Roses flock 192 wether lambes and
from Barrett Ringsted 48 wether <lambes> *shorlins* and <100>
72 wethers *of 2 sheare* and of Rogers 23 and of Besses *25 wether
lambes* for which they must allow /Joyce sheep 120/

---

152. Actual figure is £18 16s 6d.

[*Ringsted South Flock*] /*1621 Crisp*/ hath remayning with him 29 Sedgford wethers and 20 of Barrett Ringsted wethers and more he received from Corners flocks 305 wethers and from Wood 3 wethers and from Page 13 rixseys and he shall deliver home 10 wethers to Page <and 60 wethers to fell. Summ> So he hath 360

[*p 8, East Ground*] /*1621 Woods*/ had remayning in his charge 492 ewes, <10> *9* rammes and <4> *a* wether and <118> *122* lambes, and he received of Rose 295 ewes, 8 ramms, a wether and 118 lambes and <35 lambes> *34* ewes from Barrett Ringsted. So he hath in his charge 601 ewes, 17 ramms, 2 wethers and 240 lambes in all 1080 [*860*]

[*South Ground*] Rose his flock being 500 is letten to my cosen Guybon for £18 a yeare and his to discharge the sheppeard and hurdles and tarre

	£	s	d
to Woods for his wages at St Micheall for a quarter		16	8
to Corner for his quarters wages at St. Micheall		16	8
for a Spannish staffe[153] for Woods		3	4
for greasing of 480 hogges at 9s the 100	1	15	9
to Crisp for his halfe yeares wages	1	5	0
to Woods for his quarters wages ending at Christmas		16	8
to Corner for his quarters wages at Christmas		16	8
to Woods for his quarters wages ending at our Lady		16	8
to Corner for his quarters wages ending at our Lady		16	8
to Woods for his quarters wages at Midsomer		16	8
to Corner for his quarters wages at Midsomer		16	8
to Woods for his livery		6	8
to Corner for his livery		6	8
for a barrell of tarre	1	0	0
Sum	11	10	9

[*p*] 9 [*East Ground*] /*1622 Woods*/ brought to the clipping 1041 sheep wherof as followeth

782 ewes [154]	and 19 skinns, croned 34, rem[*ain*] 768 ewes
214 ewe hoggs	and 20 skinns, croned 25 and 6 dizy, remay[*n*] 183
6 ramm hogs	remayne still
17 olde rams	croned 3, remayne 14 rams
2 bell wethers	remayne still

---

153. A Spanish staff was a tool or implement, *see* Yaxley, *Glossary*, p. 195.
154. Alice experimented with the layout.

of these 1041 he had the tithe payed 93 stone of wooll sold at [?]
of the 802 ewes he had 682 lambes: wherof for tithe 68 and for
marking lambes 4 so there remayned 609 lambes: of these ewe
lambes for store 104 and wether lambes for store 148 and 3 ramme
lambes. So there remayneth lambes to sell 355 lambes to sell, which
sold one with another I received from them all but 12 that he
delivered to Barker

[North Ground] /1622 Corner/ brought to the clipping 432, of these
that follow: 119 wethers of 4 sheare and one skinne, to Ringsted, all
72 wethers of 3 sheare, skinns nll, all these to *Barrett* Ringsted
but 39; 46 wethers of 2 sheare and skinns 2, remayne 16; 150 wether
shorlins and 42 skinns, remayne 150; 22 wether shorlins of Rogers
and one skinne, remayne 22; 23 of Elizabeths wether shorlins and
2 skinns, remayne 23; of these 432 sheepe he had the tithe payd of
Rogers 2 stone and 3lb and of Elizabeths 2 stone and 9lb which they
allow for joyce and of my owne 41 stone and 13lb. So in all 46 stone
and 9lb sold at [?]

[p 10, Ringsted South Ground] /1622 Crisp/ brought to the clipping
182 as followeth: 161 Sedgford sheepe and 6 skinns and there was
sold before clipping 170 for £60 2s 10d. So there doth remayne of
Sedgford sheepe 161; 9 wethers of Barrett Ringsted and a skinne,
remayne 9; 12 rixseys and a rixsey skinne of Hamons; of these 183
he had the tithe payed 23 stone and 9lb, wherof allowed for tithe of
the 170 wethers that were sold before the clipping 2 stone and 6lb,
so there remayned 21 stone and 3lb sold at [?]; 5 rixseys of Nicholas
delivered to Page; 7 rixseys of my owne sold one for 6s; 9 of Barrett
Ringsted wethers sold for £3 3s; 61 Sedgford wethers sold for £21 7s;
and one wether that Crisp did allow of the 3 that he lost sold for 6s.
Remayne 100 Sedgford wethers delivered to Page

	£	s	d
Layd out for the shepherds wages and tarre and gresing as appeareth on the other side	11	10	9
for washing of 1387 sheepe at 12d		13	8
for casting them into the pitt		0	6
for clipping of 1387 sheepe at 3s 6d the 100	2	8	1
for 5 draggers of sheepe for 2 dayes a piece & one for a day at 10d		9	2
for 4 wooll winders & 2 gatherers for 2 dayes eyther of them at 8d		8	0
to Salter for 2 dayes branding		1	8
for 16 dozen of hurdles	3	8	0
for [?] dozen hurdles for Ringsted nll because the 2d a sheep will pay it			
the whole sum layd out is	[18	19	10]

[*p*] 11 The whole sum of Sedgford wooll is 139 stone 11lb Ringsted wooll is 21 stone 3lb

Received for tath at Hollowmas last	1	12	0
Received for 87 mortes			
Received of my cosen Guybon for the South foldcourse	18	0	0
Received for 100 joyce sheepe of the North grownde	6	0	0
Received for 25 ewe hoggs 25s and for 37 crones £3 7s 10d	4	12	10
Received for 6 dizy sheep skinns of Woodses that were taken out at the clipping			
Received for 16 fatt lambes of Woodes	2	8	0
Received for 200 lambes at £14	28	0	0
Received for 87 lambes at 20d	7	5	0
[*Sum*	*67*	*17*	*10*]

[*p 12, East Ground*] /1622/ Woods his charge at Midsomer: 768 mother ewes; 163 ewe shorlins; 6 ramme shorlins; 14 olde rams; 104 ewe lambes; 3 ram lambes; 2 bell wethers. Sum 1080 [*1059*]

[*North Ground*] /1622/ Corner his charge at Midsomer: 46 [*of*] 2 sheare wethers; 150 wether shorlins; 148 wether lambes; 7 wether shorlins from Hu[*n*]ston; 15 wether shorlins of Nicholas *from Hunston*; 19 wether lambes of Nicholas; 13 wether shorlins of Hamons *from Hunston*; 17 wether lambes of Hamonds; 22 wether shorlins of Rogers; a wether shorlin of Rogers from Hunston; 39 wether lambes of Rogers; 23 wether shorlins of Elizabeths; 3 wether shorlins from Hunston of Elizabeths; 16 wether lambes of Elizabeth. /*Whereas there is heare written 39 wether shorlins from Hunston he had 39 of his wethers for them of 3 sheare*/
Sum 520 [*525*] wherof of the childrens 149 [*174*]; /*Joyce*/ sheepe 80

/1622/ Page his charge at Midsomer when he tooke Ringsted ground: 100 olde wethers that were bought of my brother Yellverton; 119 wethers of 4 sheare also bought of my brother; <72 wethers of 3 sheare from Corner>; <49> *40* wethers from Barker; 4 ramms from Barker
[*p*] 13 wethers of Nicholas; 6 rixseyes of Nicholas; 3 rixseys of Hamonds; a ramme of Hamonds; 4 wethers of Rogers; 5 ramms of Rogers; 3 rixseyes of Rogers; a rixsey of Elizabeths; a ram of Elizabeths
        Sum 240½ [*300*] wherof of the chilldrens 31
Page had again in exchange 11 rixseyes for 11 rams wherof 6 were my owne and 5 were Nicholas

	£	s	d
for greasing of 340 lambes at 18d	1	5	6
for 10lb of sope for them		2	6
to Woods for his quarters wages at St Michaell		16	8
to Corner for his quarters wages at St Michaell		16	8
for a barrell of tarre		17	4
to Woods for his quarters wages ending at Christmas		16	8
to Corner for his quarters wages ending at Christmas		16	8

The Sedgeford Estate Account, 1621–1635

A table for this end of the book

Particular of lands wch wee had of Wm Guybon in exchange for the
North Pasture 1634 pa[*ge*]   1
An acco[*unt*] of the profitts of Sedgford for one year ending Mich 1621   3
& so for divers year to 1631
Outpaym[*en*]ts to the Dean & Chapter, Mr Cobb &c   7
The rest are particulars of lands letten some for money rent, some for
barly rent at 2 bushell per acre in the severall yeares

Sedgford North Brecks

		a	r	p		a	r	p
1	Breck was	38	1	25	it is now	28	1	14
2	Breck was	12	0	18	it is now	28	0	28
3	Breck was	68	0	20	it is now	27	2	27
4	Breck was	5	3	20	it is now	28	2	27
5	Breck was	27	0	30	it is now	37	0	10
6	Breck was	33	3	0	it is now	25	0	14
7	Breck was	2	2	5	it is now	27	0	20
8	Breck was	27	3	0	it is now	26	0	34
	Sum	215	2	38	Sum	228	1	14

Sedgford South Brecks

		a	r	p		a	r	p		a	r	p
1	Breck was	27	1	0	and for barly	3	0	0	all	30	1	0
2	Breck was	15	2	20	and for barly	0	0	0		15	2	20
3	Breck was	32	0	0	and for barly	4	0	10		36	0	10
4	Breck was	53	0	0	and for barly	10	0	0		63	0	0
5	Breck was	24	2	0	and for barly	19	3	0		44	1	0

---

155. LEST/BK7.

6 Breck was	32	0	0	and for barly	13	1	20	45	1	20
7 Breck was	37	2	30	and for barly	34	1	0	71	3	30
8 Breck was	49	1	30	and for barly	14	1	0	63	2	30
						[Sum]		370	0	30

Quere if these brecks could be reduced to 46a in a breck

[p] 1[156] Land which we had of Will Guybon in Eaton in exchange 1634

		a	r	[p]	
q 25[157]	n 1689	3	0	0	at Bishops Crowne
q 25	n 1690	2	0	0	there next called Wrenns Parke
q 25	n 1691	5	0	0	there next and south
q 25	n 1692	0	3	1	there next and south[158]
q 25	n 1693	2	0	0	there next and south
q 25	n 1694	0	1	1	there next and south
q 25	n 1695	0	2	0	there next and south
q 25	n 1696	0	2	1	there next and south
q 27	n 1712	1	0	0	at Heasellsty
q 27	n 1713	0	3	0	there next and east
q 27	n 1714	2	1	0	there next and east
q 27	n 1716	3	0	0	there next and east with a goare in the North Corner
	Sum	21	1	3	

Lands which Will Guybon had for these in exchange in the North Pasture 1634 as followeth

			a	r	[p]	
2 pre	q 14	n 280	0	2	0	late Sedgfords in the 1 Breck
	q 14	n 280	2	0	0	part of 5ac[159] in the 1 Breck – now exchange
	q 14	n 280	3	0	0	the other part of 5ac in the 2 Breck – now exchange
	q 16	n 292	9	0	0	late Sedgfords in the 2 Breck – now exchange
3 pre	q 20	n 527	3	0	0	late Sedgfords in measure 3ac 1r 17p in the 3 Breck
2 pre	q 11	n 253	4	0	0	part of 14ac in the 4 Breck

---

156. Only odd/facing pages are numbered, but reverse/even page numbers are inserted.

157. Quarentia is abbreviated to 'q' with numbers 'n'. The numbers from 1–1759 identify the strips and closes, superseding the system of precincts and quarentia.

158. There are 40 perches in a rood, which usually appear as 10, 20 or 30 as above, but sometimes, they are abbreviated, as in folio 1, where there is no title to the column, 1 = one half of rood or 20p. From p. 226 below, 20p is shown as 1 or ½ to show 30 perches, the rather clumsy format ½ 10p or 1 10p was used; this has been simplified to 30 in the text; 1 15p to 25. For clarity [p] has been inserted in the untitled columns. In the document, the word rod is used unformily, but in this context it should be rood. Rod is a linear measurement, while rood refers to ¼ acre ie 40 square rods/perches, see Yaxley, Glossary, pp. 172–3.

159. Abbreviations for acre, 'rod', perch, are shown as 'ac', 'r', 'p' when used with figures.

	q 11 n 256	2	1	0	part of 9ac in the 4 Breck
	q 11 n 253	10	0	0	part of 14ac in the 5 Breck
	q 17 n 307	3	0	0	late Sedgfords in the 5 Breck
1 pre	q 5 n 20	2	0	0	late Sedgfords in the 6 Breck
	q 5 n 25	1	1	0	part of 2ac 2r late Sedgfords the south side in the 6 Breck

Sum 40 0 0

[*p*] 3 **An accompt of the profitts of Sedgford for the yeare ending at St Michaell 1621 when wee entered none but my cosen Guybons fearme and the foldcorse. My brother Yellverton had the ferme and tithe so he payd the Deane St Martins rent**[160]

	£	s	d
Of my cosen Guybon for 153ac 1r of infield lande and 106ac and halfe of inclosed ground at 5s the ac[*re*] in all 259ac and a halfe and 1r more for 35ac of wintercorne in the brecks by \<Storm\> Stormhill, and barley and oates there 82ac, and summerlay there 41ac, and in the south feild breck 79ac of barley *and 29ac of rey* and summerlay there 13ac, the sum of acres cometh to 279ac at 5s cometh to £69 15s of this I abate 45s for Hall Bottome Close because the yeare was so hard; as the sheep had it so long as he could reape no proffit of it. So I received of my cosen Guybon for these lands[161]	67	10	0
Received for Sedgford rents at our Lady[162]	8	11	4
Received for Sedgford rentes at Midsomer	8	10	1½
Received for Sedgford rentes at St Martin	8	12	9
Received for Easthall fearme for a yeare	6	19	6
Received for Costens fearme for a yeare		16	0
Received for the house and the hempland by the dovehouse for a yeare		13	4
Received for Sallters fearme for a yeare	1	10	0
Received for the widdow Masons fearme for a yeare	4	17	0
Received of the widdow Mason for divers persell of ground		13	1
Received for the tithe of Sawers mill		5	0
Received for the tithe of Lawes his mill		6	8
the tithe barley at 1 bushell[163] the acre besides pease and fitches is 304 comb and 3 pecks. Sold at severall prises for	126	2	8
the fearme barley at 2 bushell the acre is 227 comb 2 bushell and was sold at severall prises for	87	6	9

---

160. The narrow LH margin has been removed as it is only used intermittently.

161. Noughts are inserted after the final figure, but not before.

162. Capital letter used for 'Received' but rarely elsewhere at the start of a line. Although inconsistent, the format has been left in place as it may have had some significance to Alice.

163. Combs, bushells and pecks all extended.

the tithe pease and fitches my cosen Guybon had in lew of pease that
I had of him for the sheepe the last yeare all but 2½ bushell sold for
10s the comb   6   3

               Sum [*sub-total*][164]   387   19   2½

[*p 4*] Received for lambes and crones and tath and skinnes and joyse
sheepe beside £18 17s 2d disbursed for tarre, pitch, hurdles, washing,
clipping, greasing and sheppheards wages and liveryes. I received
beside these   21   6   2
Received for 125 stone and a halfe of wooll at 8s   50   4   0
Received of Humphrey Cooper for landes in Shernburn   4   0
Received for fines   1   18   9
Received for proffits of courtes nll more then the fines
Received for haywardshipp   15   0
Received for Amy Ellgar the Idiotts Land nll because her land was
driven
Received of Sallter 2 comb of barley sold for   16   0
Received of Willyam Crisp 10 bushell of barley sold for   1   0   0
Received for rents of assize [*nill*]

               Sum [*sub-total*]   76   3   11
the whole sum of the receipts for Sedgford this yeare 1621 is   464   3   1½

/*Payments*/[165] payd to the Deane of Norwich at our Lady   25   19   0
payd to the Deane of Norwich at Midsomer   25   19   0
<payd to the Deane of Norwich at St Martin>   5½
for acquittance   4½
to the poore for 8 moneths   2   2   8
to the poore for 2 moneths   10   8
for repayring of the houses   9   0
for repayring the chancel 17s and for glasing of all the windowes and
mending the barres £3 5s 8½d   4   2   8½
for cutting of a tree and sawing of boarde   19   8
for mending of the bearne and the house   18   8
to Martin Cobbe for a [? *missing word*][166]

[*p*] 5 to the Kinges dyett and the Kinges oates   19   0
for rates to the poore after they were agreed of the rates   1   2   0
to the baylif for his fee   2   0   0

---

164. Sub-totals of accounts appear at the bottom of each page. Unmarked change of
page noted.

165. Alice started to utilize the LH margin inserting titles and annotations
intermittently.

166. For Martin Cobbe the entry was always nill.

to \<the\> Thomas Creamer for Strange 1s and for the Mannour 7s 6d   8   6
/6s-11-8½/

An accompt of the profitt of Sedgford for the yeare 1622 ending at St Michaell

Of my cosen Guybon for 153ac and 1r of infeild lande and 106½ac of   £   s   d
inclosed ground at 5s the acre in all 259 ac and 1r and halfe an acre   64   18   9
for 35 acres at Stormhill with winter corne the last yeare and now
sowne with barley[167]
of the 82 acres at Stormhill the last yeare sowne with barley and oates
he layeth now downe 48 acres so he holdeth still of that 34 acres
he taketh up this yeare at Stormehill for summerlay 15 acres
summerlay the last yeare at Stormhill now sown with rey
41 acres in the south[168] feild toward Fringg the last yeare with rey
now sowne with barley 29 acres
in the south feild with barley the last yeare 79 acres of this he layeth
downe 41 acres so he holdeth with barley and pease 38 acres
he taketh up in south feild for summerlay 33 acres
summerlay the last yeare in the south feild now sowne with rey 13 acres

[p 6] the whole sum of breck lands this yeare in my cosen Guybons
use is 238 acres which at 5s the acre is   59   10   0
Received for Sedgford rents at our Lady   8   11   4
Received for Sedgford rents at Midsomer   8   10   1½
Received for Sedgford rents at St Martin   8   12   9
Received for Easthall fearme for the yeare   6   19   6
Received for Costens fearme for the yeare   16   0
Received for the house and the hempland by the dovehouse for
the yeare   13   4
Received for Sallters fearme for the yeare   1   10   0
Received for the widdow Masons fearme for a yeare   4   17   0
Received of the widdow Mason for divers percells of grownd   13   1
Received for the tithe of Laweses mill   6   8
Received for the tithe of Sawers mill   5   0
the tithe being lett for 1 bushell the acre of barley for all kinde of
graynes except pease and fitches which are payd in kinde: the tithe
cometh to 346 comb and halfe a peck. And the fearme barley at 2
bushell the acre doth come to 216 comb 1 bushell and halfe a peck.
In all the tithe and fearme cometh to 562 comb 1 bushell and halfe a
peck which sold at severall prises cometh to   295   19   0

---

167. Alice started to organise the layout of Guybons brecks to show the rotations
followed. Also, she abandoned abbreviations and used 'acres' and 'rods' in the body of the
text.

168. Alice dropped the capital letter for South field.

Received for the tithe of 12 acres lying in Heacham 6 comb sold for	2	14	0
Received of Thomas Creamer for the tith of 6 acres nll because it was sowne with \<sowne with\> peas and so it was payd in kinde			
Received of Sallter 2 comb of barley that he is to pay for his lease sold for nll it is reckoned into the fearme			
Received of Willyam Crisp which he is to pay more then 2 bushell the acre for 5 acres \<10\> 5 bushell sold for		12	6
Received for the tith pease 14 comb sold for £6 13s 6d and 3 comb for 31s 6d	8	5	0
Received for heywardshipp		15	0
Received for rents of assize [nill]			
Received of Cooper for fearme of landes in Sherborne		4	0
Received of my cosen Guybon for the fearme of the South foldcourse for the yeare	18	0	0
Sum [sub-total]	427	14	3

[p] 7 Received for the profits of the East and North foldcorses all charges allowed

the whole sum received for Sedgford this yeare at St Michael 1622 is[169] 492 13 0

Disbursements for Sedgford for the yeare ending at St Michael 1622	£	s	d
/payments/ to the Deane of Norwich at St Martin	20	9	5½
for an accquittance			4½
to the Deane of Norwich at our Lady	25	19	0
for an accquittance			4
payd to the Deane at Midsomer for Sedgford	25	19	0
for an accquittance			4
to Mr Martin Cobbe [nill]			
to Thomas Creamer for Stranges 1s and the Mannor 7s 6d		8	6
to the poore for 7 monthes	1	17	4
payd to 8 bills for the poore	2	2	8
for 4 bills for repayring the church	2	1	4
for 16 load of carre 16s and for the masons worke of the fence wall about the yarde £9 13s	10	9	0
/917 4/ [sub-total] for the baylifs fee	2	0	0
[p 8] for cutting of reed, more then I received for segge, the reed being all layd up about the bearne		1	11
to Horne for finishing the chancell windowes		8	6
for mending the keelhouse to Costen		7	6
for 2 windles the masons had			6
for 15 challder of lime used about the walls at 6s	4	10	0

169. This figure includes the £64 18s 9d for Guybon's infield lands.

/6 13 5/ [*sub-total*] for 30 deales to make the bearne dores   1 5 0

The sum of layings out is   [*98* *0* *9*]

[*p*] 9 **An accompt of Sedgford for the yeare ending at St Michael 1623 the corne being due at the time when the yeare endeth allthough it be not all payed until Candlemas**

	£	s	d
Of my cosen Guybon for 153 acres and 1 rod of infield land and 6½ acres of inclosed grownd at 5s the acre in all 259 acres and a halfe and 1 rod	64	18	9

For 35 acres at Stormhill with barley the last yeare now with barley pease and oates

the 34 acres at Stormhill the last yeare he now layeth downe

the 15 acres of summerley the last yeare at Stormhill he soweth now with rey

the 41 acres at Stormhill with rey the last yeare he now soweth with barley

he taketh up this yeare at Stormhill for summerley 18 acres

In the south feild toward Fring with barley the last yeare and it is againe with barley this yeare 29 acres, whereof the widdow Mason hath ½ an acre, so my cosen Guybon hath 27½ acres in the south feild with barley and pease, the last year 38 acres which this yeare he layeth downe

in the south feild summerley the last yeare now sown with wintercorne, 33 acres in the south feild with rey the last yeare, now sowne with barley 13 acres, he taketh in south feild for summerley 53 acres

The whole sum of breck land this yeare in my cosen Guybons use is			
235½ acres at 5s the acre cometh to	58	17	6
Received for Sedgford rents at St Martin	8	13	6½
Received for Sedgford rents at our Lady	8	19	9
Received for Sedgford rents at Midsomer	8	8	11
Received for Easthall fearme for the yeare	6	19	6
For Costens fearme for the yeare		16	0
Sallters fearme for the yeare	1	10	0
the widdow Masons fearme for the yeare	4	17	0
for the fearme of diverse percells of land used by the widdow Mason		13	1
Sum [*sub-total*][170]	164	14	½

[*p 10*] Received for the house and the hempland by the dovehouse for the yeare		13	4
Received for the tithe of Laweses mill		6	8
Received for the tithe of Sawers mill		5	0

---

170. Sub-total includes Guybon's infield lands.

the tithe being lett for 1 bushell the acre of barley for all kinde of graynes
except pease and fetches which are payd in kinde. The tithe cometh to
355 comb and 2 pecks, and the ferme barley at 2 bushell the acre.
Sallters barley being cast in cometh to 205 comb 2 bushell 2 pecks:
and for 12 acres at Hecham 6 comb, and of Willyam Crisp for 5 acres
more then this tith and fearme 5 bushell, all of which cometh to 568

comb, sold at several prises for	238	4	2
Received of Thomas Creamer for the tith of 6 acres nll sown pease			
Received for the tithe pease nll for the sheep did eate them			
Received for tath	1	11	0
Received for profitts of courtes	3	3	8
Received for the heywardshipp for the yeare		15	4
Received for rents of assize nll			
Received of my cosen Guybon for the yeares fearme of the South foldcourse for the yeare	18	0	0
the East and North foldcourse and the dovehouse reserved			
Sum [*sub-total*]	262	19	2
the whole sum received for the yeare at St Michael 1623 is	427	3	2½

[*p*] 11 Received for the profitt of the North and East foldcourse all
charges deducted

Disbursements from St Michaell 1622 unto St Michaell 1623 for Sedgford	£	s	d
/*payments*/ to the Deane for his rent at St Martin	20	9	5½
for an acquittance			4½
to the Deane of Norwich at our Lady	25	19	0
for an acquittance			4
payd to the Deane of Norwich at Midsomer	25	19	0
for an acquittance			4
to Mr Martin Cobbe [*nill*]			
to Thomas Creamer for Stranges 1s and the Mannor 7s 6d		8	6
for the baylifs fee	2	0	0
to Costen and his men for worke about the house		12	0
to the masons for walling the gardin wall £3 8s and for 1500 brick 16s 6d	4	4	6
for making of a new pump 14s 6d and for lether for the pump 8d		15	2
for diging of clay and covering of the yarde wall		7	8
for planchering of the corn chamber		16	0
for repayring the church	1	5	8
more for repayring the church	2	11	4
payd for 11 bills to the poore £2 18s 4d; and to the Kinges dyet 19s	3	17	4
/89-6-8/	[89	6	8]

[*p 12*] payd in mony to buy corne for the poore at a reasonable rate   3   4   0
to the masons and carpenters for wages and for new glasing the
windowes and for stone and brick to repayre the kitching and
pastery with the chambers over the   20   11   9
for mending the backhouse chimbney   4   0
for 1500 brick and for the masons and carpenters wages and for
nayles and digging of clay to mend part of the backhouse and the
larder   8   1   4
for shooting the lead[171] of the chancell £4 16s and for 1200 of leade
for the chancell 12s   5   8   0
for 20 challder of lime   6   0   0

                               Sum   43   9   1

[*p*] 15[172] **An accomp of Sedgford for the yeare ending at St Michael 1624 the tithe and fearm corne being then due but not all payed untill Candlemas**
of my cosen Guybon for 153 acres and 1 rod of infield land and 106½   £   s   d
acres of inclosed grownd at 5s the acre. In all 259 acres and a halfe
and 1 rod   64   18   9
of my cosen Guybon for 5 acres late *taken out of exchange with*
Hargates at 5s   1   5   0
the 35 acres at Stormhill the last yeare now layd downe
the 15 acres at Stormhill with rey the last yeare now with barley
the 41 acre at Stormhill the last yeare with barley now with barley
pease and oates
the 18 acres at Stormhill for summerley the last yeare now with
wintercorne /102ac/ 28ac taken up at Stormhill for summerley
the 27½ acres in the south feild toward Fring layd downe
22½ acres in the south field toward Fring taken up
the 33 acres in the south feild the last yeare wintercorne now with barley
the 13 acres in the south feild the last yeare with barley and now with
barley whereof the widow Mason hath 1½ acre so my cosen Guybon
hath 11½ acres the 53ac summerley in the south feild now with wintercorne
So the whole summe of breck land this yeare in my cosen Guybons
use is 222 acres at 5s the acre is   55   10   0
Sedgford rents at St Martin   8   12   5
Received for Sedgford rentes at our Lady   8   10   9
Received for Sedgford rentes at Midsomer   8   8   11

           Sum [*sub-total*]   147   5   10

---

171. Laying the lead on the church roof.
172. Pages 13 and 14 are blank.

[p 16] Received of my cosen Guybon for the South foldcourse	18	0	0
Received of him for Easthall fearme for the yeare	6	19	6
For a close of Allen toward Docking		10	0
Received for the widdow Masons fearme for the yeare	4	18	0
Received of the widdow Masons other grounds		13	1
Received for the house and the hempland by the dovehouse nll because it is sold			
Received for Sallters fearme for the yeare	1	12	0
Received of Costen for his house for the yeare		16	0
Received for the heywardshipp for the yeare		15	4
Received for rents of assize *nll*			
Received for the tithe of Sawers mill		5	0
Received for the tithe of Laweses mill		6	8
Received for profitts of courtes	3	11	½
Received for that	1	4	8

the tithe being lett for 1 bushell the acre of barley for all kinde of graynes except pease and fetches which are payd in kinde. The tithe cometh to 276 combs 2 pecks, and the fearme at 2 bushell an acre. Sallters and Heacham being cast in. All which amounteth to 448 comb 2 pecks being sold at severall prises cometh to *beside 5 bushell brewed for the carters*

	222	9	0
Received for 10 comb 1 bushell of pease	4	2	0
Sum [Sub-total]	266	2	3½
the whole sum recived for this yeare ending at St Michael 1624 is	413	8	1½

the North and East foldcourses are in our owne hand and
the dovehouse

[p] 17[173] Disbursements for Sedgford for the yeare ending			
St Michaell 1624	£	s	d
to the Deane for his rent at St Martins	20	9	5½
for the acquittance[174]	0	0	6½
to the Deane for his rent at our Lady	25	19	0
for the acquittance	0	0	4
to the Deane of Norwich at Midsomer	25	19	0
for an acquittance	0	0	4
to Mr Martin Cobbe [nill]			
to Thomas Creamer	0	8	6
for the King's oates	0	6	9
payd to 7 bills for the poore	1	17	8
payd to the church wardens for 7 bills	4	9	10

---

173. Pages 18–20 blank.

174. Alice started to insert noughts in disbursements, possibly to clarify payments.

	£	s	d
payd to the constables *for 3 bills*	2	10	0
payd to the King for task	0	0	0
for the East and North foldcourse	3	14	9½
payd for buylding as appeareth by my booke page 124	33	19	11
more for buylding as appeareth by my booke page 125	23	14	4
to the baylif for his fee	2	0	0

/145 10 5/

[p] 21 An accompt for Sedgford for the yeare ending at St Michaell 1625 the corne being then due but not all payed untill Candlemas

	£	s	d
Received of my cosen Guybon for 153 acres 1 rod of infield land and 106½ acres of inclosed ground at 5s the acre, in all 259 acres and a halfe and 1 rod	64	18	9
of him for 8 acres and 3 rod late Thomas Hargates	2	3	9

the 15 acres at Stormhill last yeare with <rye> barley *& pease* now oates
/15/[175] the 41 acres at Stormhill with oates and pease the last yeare
now <he layeth downe with barley> *he layeth downe*
/18/ the 18 acres at Stormhill with winter corne the last yeare now
with barley
/28/ the 28 acres at Stormhill summerley the last yeare
/47/ now with rey
/108ac/ the 47 acres at Stormhill this yeare taken up
/22/ the 22 acres south toward Fring summerley last yeare now with rey
/33/ the 33 acres in the south feild last yeare with barley, the widow
Mason hath 1½ acres, so 31½ acres now barley, the 11½ acres in the
south field with barley the last yeare he now layeth downe
/53/ the 53ac in the South field with rey the last yeare now with barley
/21/ 21 acres in the South feild taken up this yeare
the whole sum of breckland in my cosen Guybons use this yeare is

	£	s	d
235½ acres which at 5s the acre is	58	17	6
Sum [sub-total]	125	19	6

	£	s	d
[p 22] Received of my cosen Guybon for Easthall fearme for the yeare	6	19	6
Received for Sedgford rents at St Martin	8	10	4
Received for Sedgford rentes at our Lady	8	9	7
Received for Sedgford rentes at Midsomer	8	6	11
Received for the widdow Masons fearme	5	11	1
Received of Sallters fearme	1	12	0
Received for Costens fearme		16	0
Received for the fearme of the South foldcorse	18	0	0
Received for reed	1	18	0

---

175. Alice used the LH margin to highlight the structure of Guybon's brecks.

Received for the tithe of Sawers mill		5	0
Received for the tithe of Lawes his mill		6	8
Received for rents of assize for part last yeare		10	4
Received for profetts of courtes	9	14	4½
Received of the townes men for 213 comb 3 pecks of barley at 8s and 192ac and 3r of pease at 12d	102	7	6
Received of Mr Loades for tithe pease and the haywardshipp		15	4
Received for 302 comb of fearme and tith barly of my cosen Guybons at severall prises	155	16	6
Received of Costen for 4ac and of the widdow Mason for one ac all which were bought of Hargate	1	0	0
/331 13 3/ Received for the tithe of Byrds mill	0	6	8
Sum [sub-total]	331	13	3½
the whole summ for Sedgford received this yeare at St Michaell 1625 is	457	12	9½
out payments £75 10s 10d so the cleare value of Sedgford is	382	1	11½

the East and North foldcorse in our owne hands being for 1400 sheep
this last yeare Mr Strange bought the dovehouse of Hargate and
had his 5ac land in exchange again and Mr Strange bought lande of
Hargate for which the rents at St Martin, our Lady and Midsomer
abated this yeare

[p] 23[176]

Disbursements for Sedgford from St Michaell 1624 unto St Michaell 1625	£	s	d
to the Deane of Norwich for his rent at St Martins	20	9	5½
for the acquittance	0	0	6½
to the Deane for his rent at our Lady	25	19	0
for the acquittance	0	0	4
to the Deane of Norwich at Midsomer	25	19	0
for an acquittance	0	0	4
to Mr Martin Cobbe [nill]			
to Thomas Creamer [nill]			
to the baylife for his fee	2	0	0
for the Kings oates	0	9	2
for 2 tasks for the 2 foldcorses	7	9	7
for 11 bills for the poore	2	18	8
to the constables for 7 bills	5	6	2
to the church wardens for 3 bills	1	18	8
layd out for buylding as appeareth in my booke page 132	7	1	2
layd out for buylding as appeareth in my booke page 140	60	3	0

---

176. Pages 24–6 blank.

/215 1 7/ layd out for buylding as appeareth page 142 in my booke   55 6 6

                                             [Sum   215 1 7]

[p] 27 An accomp of Sedgford for the yeare ending at St Michaell 1626 the corne being then due but not all payed untill Candlemas

Received of my cosen Guybon for 153 acres and 1 rod of infield land   £   s   d
and 106½ acres of inclosed ground at 5s the acre. In all 259 acres
and 3 rod   64 18 9
of him for 8 acres and 3 rod late Thomas Hargates   2   3 9
the 15 acres at Stormhill last yeare with pease and oates he layeth
down
/18/ the 18 acres at Stormhill the last yeare with barley: now with
barley and oates
/28/ the 28 acres at Stormhill last yeare with wintercorne now barley
/47/ the 47 acres at Stormhill Summerley last yeare: now with wintercorne
/48/ [total] /141ac/ 48 acres at Stormhill taken up for summerley this yeare
/22/ 22½ acres south toward Fring with rey last yeare: now with barley
the 33 acres in the south feild last yeare with barley he now layeth downe
/40/ 40 acres in the south field he taketh up for summerley
/53/ the 53 acres in the south feild last year with barley now with
barley, whereof the widow Mason hath an acre and a halfe
/21/ 21 acres in the south feild last yeare <rey> summerley now rey
[total] /135/ The whole summ of breck landes in my cosen Guybons
use is 276 acres at 5s the acre cometh to   69 0 0
                          Sum [sub-total]   136 2 6

[p 28] Received of my cosen Guybon for the South foldcorse   18 0 0
Received of my cosen Guybon for Easthall fearme   6 19 6
Received for Sedgford rents at St Martin   8 10 4
Received for Sedgford rentes at our Lady   8 9 7
Received for Sedgford rentes at Midsomer   8 6 11
Received for rents of assize   8 1
Received for profetts of courtes and haywarshipp   8 2 7
Received for the widdow Masons fearme with an acre late purchased
of Hargate at 4s   5 15 1
Received for Costens fearme and 4ac late Hargates   1 12 0
Received of Sallter for his fearme   1 12 0
Received for the tithe of Lawes his mill   6 8
Received for the tithe of Byrds mill   6 8
Received for the tithe of Sawers mill   5 0
Received of the townes men for their tithe barley at 2s the acre and
pease at 12d   103 18 0

	£	s	d
Received for 310 comb 3 bushell of ferme and tithe barly of my cosen Guybons at severall prises	122	10	10
Received of Mr Loades for tithe pease		7	1
Sum [*sub-total*]	285	7	4
the whole summ for Sedgford received this yeare 1626 is	421	9	10
out payments £75 10s 10d so the cleare value of Sedgford is	345	19	0

the East foldcorse and dovehouse is in our owne hand and the North foldcorse is letten the last Midsomer to Mr John Creamer

[p] 29[177]

Disbursements from St Michaell 1625 unto St Michaell 1626 for Sedgford	£	s	d
to the Deane of Norwich for his rent at St Martins	20	9	5½
for the acquittance	0	0	6½
to the Deane for his rent at our Lady	25	19	0
for the acquittance	0	0	4
to the Deane of Norwich at Midsomer	25	19	0
for an acquittance	0	0	4
to Mr Martin Cobb			
to Thomas Creamer	0	8	6
to the baylyfe for his fee	2	0	0
payd for the Kings oates	0	9	6
payd for 9 bills for the poore	2	8	0
to the constables for a bill	0	9	6
to the church wardens for 6 bills	3	11	2
for crying of a stray sheep that proved a stray	0	0	4
layd out for buylding page 149 – £62 6s 9d and page 153 – £34 16s 9d and page 154 – £25 0s 4d as appeareth by my booke, in all for building	122	3	10

/203 19 2/

[p] 33 **An acompt of Sedgford for the yeare ending at St Michaell 1627 the corne then due but not payed until Candlemas**

	£	s	d
Received of my cosen Guybon for 162ac[178] of infield with 8ac 3r late Hargates and 106½ ac of inclosed ground at 5s in all 268½ ac	67	2	6

/East Breck/[179] the 18ac in East feild last barly now <barly & oats>
he layeth down
the 28ac last barley, now barley and oates
the 47ac last winter corne now barly
the 48ac last summerley now winter corne

---

177. Pages 30–2 blank.

178. Abbreviations for acres return.

179. More insertions in LH margin as Alice becomes more specific about rotations.

/158ac/ the 35ac taken up for summerley
/South Feild/ the 53ac last with barly now he layeth downe
22½ac last barly now barly wherof Longstreth hath 1½ acre
21ac last rey now barly
/38 2/ the 40ac last sommerly now winter corne wherof 1½ acre
layd for /127/ covert
46½ac taken up for summerly wherof 9ac late Hargates
the whole summ of brecklands this yeare in my cosen Guybons use

is 285ac which at 5s the acre cometh to	71	5	0
Received of my cosen Guybon for the South foldcorse	18	0	0
Received of my cosen Guybon for Easthall fearme	6	19	6
Received for the widdow Masons fearme with 1ac late Hargates *now letten to Thomas Longstreth*	5	15	1
Received for Costens fearme with 4ac late Hargates	1	12	0
Received for Sallters fearme	1	12	0
Received for Sedgford rents at St Martin	8	10	4
Received for Sedgford rentes at our Lady	8	9	7
Received for Sedgford rentes at Midsomer	8	8	11
Received for rents of assize nll			
Sum [sub-total]	197	12	11

[p 34] Received of Mr Creamer for the North foldcourse	25	0	0
Received for profetts of courtes and haywardshipp	14	14	4½
Received for the tithe of Lawes his mill		6	8
Received for the tith of Byrds mill		6	8
Received for the tithe of Sawers Mill		5	0
Received of the townes men for their tith barly at 2s the acre and pease at 12d	101	6	0
Received for 353 comb 3 bushell of fearme and tith barley of my cosen Guybons at severall prises	106	3	0
Sum [sub-total]	248	1	8½
the whole summ received of Sedgford for the yeare ending at St Michaell 1627 is	445	14	7½
out payments £75 10s 10d so the cleare value of Sedgford is	370	2	9½

the East foldcorse is in our owne hand

[p] 35[180]

Disbursements from St Michaell 1626 unto St Michaell 1627 for Sedgford	£	s	d
to the Deane of Norwich for his rent at St Martins	20	9	5½
for the acquittance	0	0	6½

---

180. Pages 36–8 blank.

to the Deane for his rent at our Lady	25	19	0
for the acquittance	0	0	4
to the Deane of Norwich at Midsomer	25	19	0
for an acquittance	0	0	4
to Mr Martin Cobbe [*nill*]			
to Thomas Creamer for Stranges 1s and the Manour 7s 6d	0	8	6
to the baylife for his fee	2	0	0
payd for 11 bills to the poore	2	18	8
to the constables for 5 bills	2	15	2
to the church wardens for 3 bills	1	18	9
payd to the Kings oates	0	9	10
layd out for buylding page 162	9	8	1
layd for buylding page 168	28	16	6
/121 4 2/			

[p] 39 **An accompt of Sedgford for the yeare ending at St Mich[*ael*] 1628**
the corne then due but not payed untill Candlemas

	£	s	d
Received of my cosen Guybon for 162ac of infield and 106½ac of inclosed ground at 5s	67	2	6
/East Breck/ the 28ac last barly and oates now he layeth downe			
the 47ac last barly now pease and barly			
the 48ac last winter corne now barly			
the 35ac last summerley now wintercorn			
/164ac/ 34ac taken up for summerly			
/South Breck/ the 21ac last barly now he layeth downe			
/19½ac/ the 21ac last barly now barly & oates wherof Longstreth hath 1½ ac the 38½ac last winter corne now barly			
the 40ac last sommerly now winter corne wherof ½ac layd for covert			
the 46½ac last summerly now winter corn			
28ac taken up for summerly. The whole summe of brecklands in my cosen Guybons use is 296½ac which at 5s the ac is	74	2	6
Received of my cosen Guybon for the South foldcorse	18	0	0
Received of my cosen Guybon for Easthall fearme	6	19	6
Received of Mr John Creamer for the North foldcourse	25	0	0
Received for Sedgford rents at St Martin	8	10	4
Received for Sedgford rentes at our Lady	8	9	7
Received for Sedgford rentes at Midsomer	8	6	11
Received for rents of assize		9	10
Received for profetts of courtes and haywardshipp	5	1	½
Received for Sallters fearme	1	12	0
Received for Costens fearme	1	12	0
Received for Longstreths fearme	5	15	1
Received for the tithe of Lawes his mill	0	6	8

Received for the tith of Byrds mill	0	6	8
Received for the tithe of Sawers mill	0	5	0
Sum[*sub-total*]	231	19	7½

[*p 40*] Received of the townes men for their tithe barly at 18d the acre and their pease at 12d	74	18	11½
Received for 309 comb 1 bushell of fearme barly and my cosen Guybons tithe sold at severall prises	125	5	0
Received for Mr Loads his tith pease	0	5	3
Received for Sallters tith pease	0	4	6
Received for my cosen Guybons tithe pease in the straw	2	0	0
Sum [*sub-total*]	202	13	8½
/*1628*/ the whole summ received of Sedgford for the yeare ending at St Michaell is	434	13	4

the East foldcorse is in our owne hand

/*Out payments*/ to the Deane at St Martins & the accquittance 6½d	20	10	0
to the Deane at our Lady with 4d for the accquittance	25	19	4
to the Deane at Midsomer with 4d for the accquittance	25	19	4
to Thomas Creamer for sute entry and shreifeshott for the Pryor		7	6
to him for sute of Sedgford Stranges 1s		1	0
to Mr Martin Cobbe for free rent out of Stranges lands in Eaton 12s and 16d more for lands there and 4d for a decayed messuage there late Rusts in all	13	8	
the baylifs fee	2	0	0
Sum beside reparations and towne charges	75	10	10
the cleare value of Sedgford beside the East foldcorse for the yeare 1628 is	359	2	6

[*p*] 41[181]			
Disbursements from St Michaell 1627 unto St Michaell 1628 for Sedgford	£	s	d
to the Deane of Norwich for his rent at St Martins	20	9	5½
for an acquittance	0	0	6½
to the Deane for his rent at our Lady	25	19	0
for an acquittance	0	0	4
to the Deane for his rent at Midsomer	25	19	0
for an acquittance	0	0	4
to Mr Martin Cobbe [*nill*]			
to Thomas Creamer for Stranges 1s and for the Manour 7s 6d	0	8	6
to the baylife for his fee	2	0	0

---

181. Pages 42–4 blank.

	£	s	d
payd to the Kings oates	o	9	10
payd to 8 bills for the poore	2	2	8
payd to the constables for 3½ bills	1	16	1
payd to the church wardens for 3 bills	2	o	o
layd out making the parlour stayers and jemmalls and altering the parlour seeling	3	10	4

/84 16 1/

[p] 45 An accompt of Sedgford for the yeare ending at St Michaell 1629 the corne then due but not payed untill Candlemas

	£	s	d
Received of my cosen Guybon for 162ac of infield and 106½ac of inclosed ground at 5s	67	2	6
/East Breck/ the 47ac last pease and barly now he layeth downe			
the 48 ac last barly, now barly and oates			
the 35ac last winter corne now barly			
34ac last summerly, now winter corne			
/154ac/ 37ac taken up for summerly			
/South Breck/ the 19½ac last pease and barly now he layeth downe			
/37ac/ the 38½ac last barly, now barly wherof Longstreth hath 1½ac			
the 46½ac last winter corne now barly			
the 28ac last summerly now winter corne			
/128½ac/ 17ac taken up for summerly. The whole summ of brecklands in my cosen Guybons use is 282½ac which at 5s the ac is	70	12	6
Received of my cosen Guybon for the South foldcorse	18	o	o
Received of my cosen Guybon for Easthall fearme	6	19	6
Received of Mr John Creamer for the North foldcourse	25	o	o
Received for Sedgford rents at St Martin	8	10	4
Received for Sedgford rentes at our Lady	8	9	7
Received for Sedgford rentes at Midsomer	8	6	11
Received of Mr John Creamer for an arrerage of a rent of assize of 2s 9d the yeare due from Robert Stone for 11 yeares and 2s 9d for the release in all	1	13	o
Received for rents of assize		10	9
Sum [sub-total]	215	5	1

	£	s	d
[p 46] Received for Longstreths fearme	5	15	1
Received for Sallters fearme	1	12	o
Received for Costens fearme	1	12	o
Received for the tithe of Sawers mill	o	5	o
Received for the tithe of Lawes his mill	o	6	8
Received for the tith of Byrds mill	o	6	8
Received for profetts of courtes and haywardship	4	11	4

Received of the townes men for their tithe barly at 2s the acre and their pease at 12d	94	19	3
Received for 312 comb of fearme barly and my cosen Guybons tithe barly sold at severall prises	154	0	0
Received for 5 comb of tithe pease	2	10	0
Sum [*sub-total*]	265	18	0
the whole received for Sedgford for the yeare ending at St Michaell 1629 is	481	3	1
the East foldcorse is in our owne hand			
out payments as appeareth by the accompt 1628 is	75	10	10
so the cleare value of Sedgford 1629			
beside the East foldcorse all but towne charges	405	12	3

[*p*] 47

Disbursements from St Michaell 1628 unto St Michaell 1629 for Sedgford

	£	s	d
to the Deane of Norwich for his rent at St Martins	20	9	5½
for an acquittance	0	0	4
to the Deane for his rent at our Lady	25	19	0
for the acquittance	0	0	4
to the Deane for his rent at Midsomer	25	19	0
for the acquittance	0	0	4
to Mr Martin Cobb [*nill*]			
to Thomas Creamer for Stranges 1s and for the Manour 7s 6d	0	8	6
to the bayly for his fee	2	0	0
payd for 11 bills to the poore	2	13	8
payd to the Kings dyett	0	9	10
payd to the constables for 4 bills	1	19	4
payd to the church wardens for 3 bills	1	19	4
layd out as appeareth by my booke page 200 and 202 and 216 for buylding	25	4	7

/107 3 8½/

[*p 48*] Longstreths lands with the house 1630 [*for which he pays farm rent*]

	a	r	[*p*]
3 furlong in Eaton[182]	0	2	20
3 furlong	2	2	
4 furlong	1	0	
5 furlong	0	3	20
9 furlong	1	0	
9 furlong	0	2	
9 furlong	0	2	
9 furlong	1	0	
9 furlong	0	2	
10 furlong	0	2	
10 furlong	0	3	
10 furlong	0	3	
11 furlong	1	1	
13 furlong	3	0	20
22 furlong	0	2	
27 furlong	1	0	
27 furlong	0	2	
27 furlong	1	0	
27 furlong	1	2	20
Minkt furlong at Sedgford	0	2	
more there *Masons land*	0	0	
Minkt furlong in Snetsham,	0	3	
more there	0	3	
Sum	21	2	

more he hath 1½ac in the south field of the last crop to sow barly on for [*all*] these lands he payeth

	£	s	d
	4	18	0
3ac more called the Ash yard[183]	0	13	10
1ac in the Ashe yarde late Tho Hargates	0	4	0
Sum	5	15	10

	a	r
Burton 17 furlong in Eaton	1	1
Heacham men at Cattgore	1	1

Longstreths lands for which he payeth barly 2s the acre 1630

	a	r	[*p*]
8 furlong in Eaton	0	3	
8 furlong	0	2	
8 furlong	0	1	
8 furlong	0	1	20
10 furlong	0	3	20
10 furlong	1	1	20
11 furlong	2	0	20
12 furlong	0	2	
15 furlong	1	0	
16 furlong	0	2	
18 furlong	0	3	
18 furlong	0	1	20
18 furlong	0	3	20
19 furlong[184]	0	2	30
19 furlong	0	1	
19 furlong	1	0	30
19 furlong	0	1	
27 furlong	1	1	20
Sum	12	1	

Thomas Creamer			
8 furlong in Eaton	0	1	20
8 furlong	0	3	20
Sum	1	0	

| 15 furlong John Crisp | 0 | 2 | |

My cosen Guybons landes beside the great fearme

4 furlong 2 precinct	5	0
16 furlong 3 pre[*cinct*]	3	0
13 furlong 5 pre	2	3
13 furlong 5 pre	6	0
Sum	16	3

---

182. 20 perches appears as ½ [*rood*] in the document, see fn. 158.

183. 10 perches appears as ¼ [*rood*] in the document.

184. 30 perches appears as 1 10p or ½ 10p in the document.

[p] 49 **A note of all Sedgford Infield lands to whom they are letten for [Barley Rent] the yeare ending at St Michaell 1630**

Willyam Guybon	a	r [p]	
1 furlong 5 precinct	1	2	
1 furlong 5 pre	3	1	
1 furlong 5 pre	2	2	
1 furlong 7 pre	9	0	
5 furlong 5 pre	2	0	
7 furlong 4 pre	0	2	
7 furlong 4 pre	1	0	
7 furlong 4 pre	1	1	
10 furlong 2 pre	1	2	
10 furlong 4 pre	0	3	
11 furlong 4 pre	1	1	
11 furlong 4 pre	1	1	
13 furlong 4 pre	3	0	
13 furlong 3 pre	0	3	20
14 furlong 3 pre	0	3	20
15 furlong 5 pre	1	0	
16 furlong 3 pre	1	2	
17 furlong 3 pre	1	2	
20 furlong 7 pre	5	0	
22 furlong 1 pre *Mr Lo*	1	2	
20 furlong 7 pre *Mr Lo*	0	3	
Sum	41	0	

Mr Loades			
2 furlong 5 precinct	0	0	20
5 furlong 4 pre	2	0	
6 furlong 4 pre	3	2	
6 furlong 4 pre	4	3	
9 furlong 4 pre	1	0	
10 furlong 4 pre	1	1	
10 furlong 2 pre	0	3	
22 furlong 1 pre	2	1	
1 furlong in Eaton	2	2	
10 furlong in Eaton	0	2	20
16 furlong in Eaton	0	3	
Sum	19	1	

20 furlong 7 pre	0	2
Framingham useth		

Martin Smith	a	r [p]	
2 furlong 7 precinct	3	1	
3 furlong 7 pre	1	0	
5 furlong 4 pre	2	2	
8 furlong 4 pre	10	0	
9 furlong 4 pre	2	0	
9 furlong 6 pre	0	1	
9 furlong 7 pre	5	0	
10 furlong 6 pre	3	0	
10 furlong 7 pre	1	3	
13 furlong 5 pre	16	0	
15 furlong 5 pre in 5p	5	0	20
16 furlong 5 pre in 2p	2	1	20
17 furlong 5 pre	9	0	
18 furlong 5 pre	1	1	
20 furlong 5 pre	3	0	
20 furlong 7 pre	1	2	
20 furlong 7 pre	1	0	
4 furlong in Eaton	4	3	
Sum	72	3	

Richard Banyard			
5 furlong 4 precinct	0	2	20
3 furlong 4 pre *Mr Loads*	1	0	
7 furlong 4 pre	0	2	
8 furlong 4 pre	5	0	
9 furlong 4 pre	1	0	
10 furlong 4 pre	3	0	
10 furlong 2 pre *WG*185	0	3	20
13 furlong 4 pre	1	0	
13 furlong 4 pre	0	3	
16 furlong 3 pre	1	2	
17 furlong 3 pre	1	2	10
24 furlong 4 pre	0	2	
Sum	17	1	10

Richard Byrd			
20 furlong in Eaton	0	1	30

---

185. William Guybon.

[p 50] Lionell Bankes	a	r [p]
4 furlong in Eaton S[outh]	1	1
4 furlong S	0	2
4 furlong S	2	0
7 furlong S	0	1 20
7 furlong S	0	1 30
7 furlong S	1	1
7 furlong S	0	2
10 furlong *Lon*186	1	1
11 furlong S	0	2
11 furlong S	0	1 20
11 furlong S	0	3
11 furlong S	1	1
7 furlong 4 pre Addams	0	1
9 furlong 4 pre Ri Bay		
Mr Lo187	2	0
10 furlong 4 pre Addams	0	3
11 furlong 4 pre WG	1	0
11 furlong 4 pre W Acres	1	0 20
13 furlong 4 pre WG&RB	2	0
Minkt furlong Lon	1	2
Sum	19	0 10

Widdow Acres		
5 furlong 4 precinct	0	2
7 furlong 4 pre WG	0	3 20
9 furlong 4 pre	2	0
8 furlong 4 pre	3	0
10 furlong 4 pre	0	3
11 furlong 4 pre	1	0
13 furlong 4 pre	0	3
16 furlong 3 pre	5	0
Sum	14	0 20

John Adams		
1 furlong 4 precinct	5	0
3 furlong 4 pre	4	1
4 furlong 4 pre	1	2
5 furlong 4 pre	2	2
7 furlong 4 pre	0	2
24 furlong 4 pre	1	0
Sum	14	3

Vickers		
2 furlong 5 precinct	0	3
Costen 1 furlong 4ac beside		
his house	4	0
Costen 5 furlong in Eaton	0	3
18 furlong in Eaton	3	0

Sallters Lands 1630	a	r [p]
1 furlong with the house	1	1
9 furlong with the house	0	2
Sum	1	3

for his he payd 32s *p ann*
[*Farm Rent*]

1 furlong in Eaton Mr Lo	1	0
1 furlong Mr Lo	0	2
9 furlong F G188	0	1 20
4 furlong S FC189	1	1
4 furlong S FC	0	1 20
4 furlong S FC	0	1 20
4 furlong S FC	1	1 20
4 furlong S FC	0	3
Sum	5	2

1 furlong in Eaton BC190	0	2
1 furlong BC	0	3
<2 furlong F. Costen	0	0>
3 furlong Thom Long191	0	2 20
3 furlong Long	0	2 20
3 furlong Long	2	2
4 furlong FC	1	1
5 furlong FC	0	2 20
5 furlong FC	1	1
6 furlong FC	0	1 20
6 furlong FC	0	1 30
6 furlong Mr Lo	2	2
7 furlong FC	0	3
8 furlong Long	0	3 20
8 furlong Long	0	3 20
9 furlong 2 precinct WG	1	1

---

186. Longstreth. Insertion marks omitted for initials and abbreviated names.
187. Richard Baynard, Mr Loades.
188. Francis Guybon.
189. Francis Costen.
190. Bartholomew Crisp.
191. Thomas Longstreth.

10 furlong Long	4	0		more by John Ellgar FC	1	0
10 furlong Long	0	2 20		more there FC	0	1
11 furlong FC	1	0		Sum	26	3 10
11 furlong FC	0	1				
11 furlong FC	0	2 20		the whole summ of acres		
17 furlong FC	0	1 20		to pay barly for is	32	1 30
Minkt furlong FC	1	2				

[p] 51 **An accompt of Sedgford for the yeare ending at St Michaell <1623> *1630* the corne then due but not payed untill Candlemas**

	£	s	d
Received of my cosen Guybon for 162ac of infield and 106½ ac of inclosed ground at 5s	67	2	6

/East Breck/ the 48 ac last pease and oates now he layeth downe
the 35ac last barly now pease and barly
34ac last winter corne now barly
37ac last summerly now winter corne
/120ac fearm, 16ac Fen/ 14ac taken up for summerly and 16ac to the Fenes
/South field/ the 37ac last now he layeth downe
the 46½ac last barly, now barly and oates, whereof Longstreth 1½ac
the 28ac last winter corne now barly
the 17ac last summerly now winter corne
30ac taken up for summerly

	£	s	d
The whole summ of brecklands in my cosen Guybons use is 240ac at 5s is	60	0	0
Received of my cosen Guybon for the South foldcorse	18	0	0
Received of Mr John Creamer for the North foldcourse	25	0	0
Received of my cosen Guybon for Easthall fearme	6	19	6
Received for Costens fearme	1	12	0
Received of Sallters sonne for his fearme 32s whereof he had 10s to leave the fearme so received	1	2	0
Received for Sedgford rents at St Martin	8	10	4
Received for Sedgford rentes at <St Martins> *our Lady*	8	9	7
for 47 <acquittances> *loade of whinnes*	2	7	0
for Sedgford rentes at Midsomer	8	6	11
for the <acquittances> *tithe of Sawers mill*	0	5	0
Received for profetts of courtes and haywardship	9	18	6
Received for rents of assize	0	12	2½
/For the Duke of Suffolk/[192]			
Sum [sub-total]	218	5	6½

---

192. Title of the duke of Suffolk extinct in 1551; this is probably Theophilus Howard, 2nd earl of Suffolk.

[*p 52*] Received for the tithe of Lawes his mill	0	6	8
Received for the tith of Byrds mill	0	6	8
Received for the tith of Heacham Mill	0	5	0
Received of the townes men for their tithes at 2s the acre for all			
grayne but pease, fitches and lentils and those at 12d	116	2	6
Received for the fearme barly being 205 comb 2 bushell and for			
my cosen Guybons tithe and Mr Loades being 90 comb 0 bushells			
all sold at severall rates being in all 275 comb 2 bushell at 16s & 17s			
& 10s	249	10	0
Sum [*sub-total*]	366	10	10
the whole sum received for Sedgford 1630 is			
beside the East foldcorse is in our owne hand	584	16	4½
outpayments as appeareth by the accomp 1628 is	75	10	10
so the cleare value of Sedgford 1630			
beside the East foldcorse all but towne charges	509	5	6½
<the whole sum received for Sedgford 1631 is> <the out payments>			

[*p*] 53 **An accompt of Sedgford for the yeare ending at St Michaell 1631 the corne then due but not payed untill Candlemas**

	£	s	d
Received of my cosen Guybon for 162ac of infield and 106½ac of			
inclosed ground at 5s	66	16	10
/East Breck/ the 35ac *5 breck* last barly and pease now he layeth			
downe 34ac 1r last barly now barly and pease			
the 29ac last winter corne now barly			
14ac last summerly now <barley> *winter corne*			
/South Breck 26½ac/ 15ac taken up for summerly			
the 46½ac last barly, now he layeth downe			
the <28> *27ac* 1r last barly now barly and oates whereof Longstreth			
1½ac			
the <14> *15ac* 2r last winter corne now barley			
the 32ac last summerly now winter corne			
53ac taken up for summerly 4 Breck. So the whole summ of			
brecklands in my cosen Guybons use is 218ac 3r at 5s is	54	13	9
Received of my cosen Guybon for Easthall fearme	6	19	6
Received of Thomas Longstreth for his fearme £4 18s and for 4ac 17s 1d	5	15	1
Received of Costen for 4ac		16	0
Received of Thomas Creamer for 1ac ½r		6	8
Received for the South foldcorse of my cosen Guybon	18	0	0
Received for the North foldcorse of John Creamer	25	0	0
Received for the tithe of Lawes his mill		6	8
Received for the tithe of Byrds 6s 8d and for the tithe of Heacham			
Mill 5s		11	8
Received for rents of assize to the Pryor	25	17	4
Received of the tithe of the townes men at 2s the ac and 12d	110	10	2

Received for fearme barly being 203c 2b and for Mr Loades and my
cosen Guybons tithe barly being 84 comb in all 287c 3bush   146   7   2
Received more for 10 bushell of tithe pease   1   2   0
Received for the heywardship 15s 4d and for profitts of courtes 10s 8d   1   6   0
                                              Sum [*sub-total*]   465   3   5½

[*p 54*] the whole sum received for Sedgford 1630 beside the East
foldcorse is   465   3   5½
outpayments as appeareth by the accompt for the yeare ending at
St Michaell 1628   75 10 10
so the cleare vallue of Sedgford for the yeare 1630 is   389 12   7½

Beales Crofft by the field booke sett out

8 precinct	[a	r	p]		a	r	[p]
q 1	1379	1	1	0	sold to Costen	1	1
q 1	1378	0	1	30			
q 1	1379	6	0	0			
q 1	3880	0	1	20			
q 4	1448	0	3	20	this was an Headland next Henry Lawes &		
q 5	1449	0	1	20	now is inclosed with the other piece following		
q 9	1513	0	3	20			
q 9	1514	0	1	20			
q 9	1515	0	3	0			
q 9	1516	3	1	0	letten to Costen that is inclosed with his house 1ac		
q 9	1517	0	2	0	sold to Costen the North Ende of this 2r	0	1
q 9	1518	0	2	0	sold to Costen the North Ende of this 2r	0	1
q 9	1519	1	0	0	sold to Costen	1	0
q 9	1520	2	0	0			
	Sum	18	0	20	wherof sold to Costen	2	3
					and letten to Costen	1	0

Remayne inclosed in Beales Crofft 14ac 3r 20p
it is butt small measure and may be letten for   13   2

[*p*] **55 Infield lands letten to my cosen Guybon with the greate fearme 1632
beside the site of the Mannour**

	a	r	[p]
/*Inclosed*/ Church Meddow, Ingolls acres and grasse Croft with the hedg and 7r of Stranges in all by measure	12	2	0
West fenn part of 10ac *pr[*ecinct*] 1 quar[*entia*] 27*[193]	9	0	0
Water Hall yards *pr 1 q 27	1	0	0
the pightle by Dingles in 2 pieces *1ac & 2r pr 8 qu 28*	1	2	0
by Olde Mill Brigge *pr 8 q 27 2a called Sedgfords & the Alder Carr 2r & Sed Dam*	6	2	0

---

193. Insertions are in different handwriting, possibly Sir Hamon's. Full stops omitted.

& the more by Olde Mill Brigge *a pightle q 27*	I	I	O
Sedgford yarde *pr 1 q 27*	4	2	O
Nether Jeyberd *pr 2 q 27*	7	O	O
Reed Damme Meddow *pr 7 q 31*	I	O	O
South Close *pr 7 q 13*	II	O	O
Hall Bottome Close *pr 2 q 10*	9	O	O
Easthall yards part of 6ac *with one bearne pr 4 q 3*	4	O	O
The Whinne Close *pr 5 q 11, 12*	34	O	O
/102ac not inclosed pr 8 q 9/ Beales his crofft by the bookes 18ac 2½r			
but by measure 15ac 1½r wheroff sold to Costen 2ac 1r and letten to			
Costen 1ac so my cosen Guybon hath	12	O	20
late bought of Hargate *pr 8 q 1*	4	I	O
/by Sedgford Hill/ more that Hargate had in exchang for the			
dovehouse *pr 1 q 26*	5	O	O
Sedgford Hill *pr 1 q 22 **7ac** et 24 **14ac** in 2 peeces*	21	O	O
Upper Jeyberd *pr 2 q 3*	18	O	O
Chappel Crofft *pr 6 q 3*	7	O	O
Morland East Hall *pr 4 q 4*	7	O	O
by the Whinne Close *pr 5 q 4*	14	O	O
by Easthall greene in 3 pieces *pr 4 q 2, q 3*	33	O	O
Black Land *pr 3 q 11*	5	O	O
Wines piece *pr 3 q 9*	12	O	O
Flint Hill *pr 5 q 1*	20	O	O
/165a 1½r/ Fickles Crofft *pr 3 q 6*	7	O	O

Sum of all is 267ac 1½r at 5s is £66 16s 10d

	a	r	[p]
[p 56] **Landes letten in Sedgford for mony 1631**			
/East Hall fearme/ the house with the bearne, stable and yarde	2	O	O
1 furlong 4 precinct inclosed	5	O	O
2 furlong 4 pre in 3 pieces	3	I	O
4 furlong 4 pre in 3 pieces	14	2	O
11 furlong 6 pre by Chappell Crofft	14	O	O

Sum for this 38ac 3r he payeth £6 19s 6d

/Longstreths fearme in lease/			
3 furlong in Eaton beside the house, bearne and stable	O	2	20
3 furlong	2	2	O
4 furlong *this Costen is to have at St Michaell 1631*	I	O	O
9 furlong	I	O	O
9 furlong	O	2	O
9 furlong	O	2	O
9 furlong	I	O	O
9 furlong	O	2	O
10 furlong	O	2	O
10 furlong	O	3	O

	£	s	d
10 furlong	0	3	0
13 furlong	3	0	0
22 furlong	0	2	20
27 furlong part of 10ac called the West fenne	1	0	0
27 furlong	1	0	0
27 furlong	0	2	0
27 furlong	1	0	0
27 furlong	1	2	0
Minkt furlong in Sedgford	0	2	20
more there 5 rod \<this was Masons owne land\> *11 furlong*	1	1	0
Minkt furlong in Snettsham	0	3	0
more there	0	3	0

Sum 20a 1½r and 1a 2r in the South field for these he payeth yearely £4 18s

[p] 57 **Lands letten for mony 1631**

	£	s	d
Thomas Longstreth for 3 acres called the Ashe yard		13	1
more of him for one acre there late Hargates		4	0
Francis Costen in the first furlong late Hargates [4 acres]		16	0
Thomas Creamer in the 8 furlong in Eaton 1r and more there 3½r			
/1 19 9/ in all 1a ½r for this he payeth		6	8

Summ of all the lands letten for mony [336a 3r] beside the brecks
used by my cosen Guybon and Stormhill Close when it is sowne is £80 14s 1d

My cosen Guybons Breck lands 1631 letten for mony

	a	r	[p]
/East Field/ the 35ac last barly and pease now he layeth downe			
/5/ [Breck] the 34ac 1r last barly now on the last cropp	34	1	0
/6/ [Breck] the 29ac ½r now on the second croppe	29	0	20
/7/ [Breck] the 14ac last summerly now on the first cropp	14	0	0
/8/ [Breck] 15ac taken up for summerly	15	0	0
/South Field/ the 46½ac last cropp now he layeth downe			
/1/ [Breck] the 27ac 1r last barly now Longstreth hath 1½ ac and 25ac 3r is now on the last cropp	25	3	0
/2/ [Breck] the 15ac 2½r last barly now on the second cropp	15	2	20
/3/ [Breck] the 32ac last summerly now on the first cropp	32	0	0
/4/ [Breck] 53ac taken up for summerly	53	0	0

	£		
Sum 218ac 3r [of Guybons Breck lands] at 5s the acre cometh to	£54	13	9
This add the sum above of	80	14	1
The totall summ in mony is \<£133 8s 1d\>	135	7	10
/500/ the South foldcorse letten to my cosen Guybon for	18	0	0
/500/ the North foldcorse letten to Mr John Creamer for	25	0	0

/Reserved/ the East foldcorse reserved and stocked with 900;
Sherborn Close of 1ac and a little close of 3ac by South Close; the
Reed Damme 8 acres; 6ac by measure called Stormhill Close

Sum	178	7	10

[p 58] Infield landes letten for 2 bushell of barly the acre 1631

Mr Loades his lands	a	r	[p]
1 furlong with 2r late Sallters	3	0	0[194]
5 furlong late Sallters	1	0	0
6 furlong late Sallters	2	2	0
10 furlong	0	2	0
16 furlong *FG to Jo Ell*[195]	0	3	0
5 furlong 4 pre of Ri Banyard	1	0	0
9 furlong 4 pre of Li Bankes	1	0	0
10 furlong 4 pre of WG	0	3	0
22 furlong 1 pre of WG	1	2	0
22 furlong 1 pre	2	1	0
22 furlong 1 pre of WG	0	3	0
5 furlong 4 pre	2	0	0
6 furlong 4 pre	3	2	½
6 furlong 4 pre	4	3	0
9 furlong 4 pre	1	0	0
10 furlong 4 pre	1	1	0
Sum	27	2	½

Martin Smith			
2 furlong 7 pre in 2 pei[ces]	3	1	0
3 furlong 7 pre	1	0	0
5 furlong 4 pre	5	0	0
8 furlong 4 pre	10	0	0
9 furlong 4 pre	2	0	0
9 furlong 6 pre	0	1	0
9 furlong 7 pre in 2 peices	5	0	0
10 furlong 6 pre	3	0	0
10 furlong 7 pre to Collen	0	0	0
13 furlong 5 pre	16	0	0
15 furlong 5 pre in 5 pieces	5	0	20
16 furlong 5 pre in 2 pieces	2	1	20
17 furlong 5 pre of fring land	9	0	0
18 furlong 5 pre of fring land	1	1	0
20 furlong 5 pre	3	0	0

20 furlong 7 pre	2	0	0
20 furlong 7 pre	1	0	0
Sum <68ac 2r, 71ac>	69	1	0

My cosen Guybons lands	a	r	[p]
4 furlong 2 precinct	5	0	0
16 furlong 3 precinct	3	0	0
13 furlong 5 precinct	2	3	0
13 furlong 5 precinct	6	0	0
Sum	16	3	0

Willyam Guybon his lands	a	r	[p]
first furlong 5 precinct	1	2	0
1 furlong 5 pre	3	1	0
1 furlong 5 pre	2	2	0
1 furlong 7 pre	9	0	0
7 furlong 4 pre	0	2	0
7 furlong 4 pre	1	0	0
7 furlong 4 pre with 3r of Wid[ow] Acres	2	0	0
5 furlong 5 pre	2	1	0
9 furlong 2 pre	1	2	0
10 furlong 2 pre	1	3	0
10 furlong 2 pre of Mr Loads	0	3	0
10 furlong 2 pre of R Bany	0	1	0
11 furlong 4 pre	1	1	0
11 furlong 4 pre	1	0	0
11 furlong 4 pre of Bankes	1	0	0
13 furlong 4 pre	3	0	0
13 furlong 4 pre of Bankes	1	0	0
13 furlong 3 pre	0	3	0
14 furlong 3 pre	0	3	20
15 furlong 5 pre	1	0	20
16 furlong 3 pre	1	2	0
17 furlong 3 pre	1	2	10
20 furlong 7 pre	5	0	0
Sum	44	1	10

194. Noughts appear in the final column; perches shown as 10, 20, 30 rather than, 1, 2, 3 or ½ etc.

195. Francis Guybon, John Ellgar. Insertion marks omitted for names and initials.

[*p*] 59 **Infield lands letten for barly 2 bushell the acre 1631** [*continued*]

Francis Costens lands	a	r	[*p*]
5 furlong in Eaton	0	3	20
18 furlong in Eaton	3	0	0
for 10 years n 1516	1	0	0
9 furlong to enclose his house			
2 furlong of Sallters	1	1	0
4 furlong of Bankes	1	1	0
4 furlong of Bankes	0	2	0
4 furlong of Longstreths	1	0	0
Lease land/*1632 to pay*/			
4 furlong of Sallters	2	0	0
4 furlong of Sallters	1	1	0
4 furlong of Sallters	0	1	20
4 furlong of Sallters	0	1	20
4 furlong of Sallters	1	1	20
4 furlong of Longstreths	0	3	0
5 furlong of Sallters	0	3	20
5 furlong of Sallters	0	2	20
5 furlong of Sallters	1	1	0
6 furlong of Sallters	0	1	20
6 furlong of Sallters[196]		1	30
4 furlong of Martin Smith	4	3	0
7 furlong of Bankes	0	1	20
7 furlong of Bankes		1	30
7 furlong of Bankes	1	1	0
7 furlong of Sallters	0	3	0
7 furlong of Bankes	0	2	0
10 furlong of Sallters	4	0	0
11 furlong of Sallters	0	1	0
11 furlong of Longstreths	1	1	0
11 furlong of Bankes	0	2	0
11 furlong of Sallters	0	2	20
11 furlong of Bankes	0	1	20
11 furlong of Sallters	0	1	20
11 furlong of Bankes	0	3	0
11 furlong of Longstreths	0	2	20
11 furlong of Bankes	1	1	0
17 furlong of Sallters	0	2	0

Minked furlong of Sallters

	a	r	p
1ac & 5 rod and 3 rod in all	3	0	0
Sum<38a, 39a 3r, 40a ½r>	39	0	20

Letten for 21 yeares and
one acre for 10 yeare

Thomas Longstreth his lands	a	r	[*p*]
3 furlong in Eaton of Sallters	0	2	20
3 furlong of Sallters	0	2	20
3 furlong of Sallters	2	2	0
8 furlong of Sallters	0	3	20
8 furlong of Sallters	0	3	20
10 furlong of Sallters	0	2	20
10 furlong of Sallters	1	0	0
10 furlong of Bankes	1	1	0
8 furlong in Eaton	0	3	0
8 furlong	0	1	0
8 furlong	0	2	0
10 furlong	0	3	20
10 furlong	1	1	0
12 furlong	0	2	20
10 furlong	0	0	0
16 furlong	0	2	0
18 furlong	0	3	0
18 furlong	0	1	0
18 furlong	0	3	20
19 furlong	0	2	20
19 furlong		1	30
19 furlong	1	0	0
19 furlong		1	30
27 furlong	1	1	0
Mixt furlong of Bankes	1	2	0
Sum	21	1	0

Allen Collen 10 furlong			
7 pre	1	3	0

---

196. Entry simplified from 1½r 10p to
1r 30p.

Mr Gurling useth for exchange
as lands bought of Will Guybon
which land olde Longstreth sold
to Mr John Lestrang in the

15 furlong 5 pre	1	0	0
more after the 16 furlong			
5 pre	0	2	20

[p 60] Infeild lands letten for 2 bushell of barly the acre 1631 [continued]

Richard Banyards lands	a	r	[p]
5 furlong 4 precinct	0	2	20
7 furlong 4 pre	0	2	0
8 furlong 4 pre	5	0	0
9 furlong 4 pre	1	2	0
9 furlong 4 pre of Bankes	1	0	0
10 furlong 4 pre	3	0	0
13 furlong 4 pre	1	0	0
13 furlong 4 pre	0	3	20
13 furlong 4 pre of Bankes	1	0	0
16 furlong 3 pre *WG*[197]	1	2	0
17 furlong 3 pre	1	2	10
24 furlong 4 pre	0	2	0
Sum	18	0	10

John Addams his lands	a	r	[p]
1 furlong 4 precinct FG	5	0	0
3 furlong 4 pre FG	4	1	0
4 furlong 4 pre	1	2	20
5 furlong 4 pre Mar Smith	0	0	0
7 furlong 4 pre	0	2	0
7 furlong 4 pre of Bankes	0	1	0
10 furlong 4 pre of Bankes	0	3	0
24 furlong 4 pre	1	0	0
Sum	13	1	20

Richard Byrd 20 furlong	0	1	30

Thomas Vickers

5 furlong 5 pre	0	3	0

Bart Crisp			
1 furlong of Sallters	0	2	0
Bart more there of Sallters	0	3	0
John Crisp 15 furlong	0	2	0
Heacham men at Catt gove	12	0	0
Sallter of Heacham of			
Burtons			
17 furlong in Eaton	1	1	0
q 16 2 more at Eaton	1	1	0
Sum	16	0	30

the widdow Acres her lands	a	r	[p]
5 furlong 4 precinct	0	2	20
11 furlong 4 pre of Bankes	1	0	20
11 furlong 4 pre	1	0	0
8 furlong 4 pre			
9 furlong 4 pre	2	0	0
10 furlong 4 pre	0	3	0
13 furlong 4 pre	0	3	20
16 furlong 3 pre	5	0	0
Sum	14	1	20

The summ of infield lands letten for
mony is as followeth:

my cosen Guybon in	a	r	[p]
fearme	267	1	20
East Hall fearme	38	3	0
Longstreths fearme	20	1	0
Longstreth the Ashe yarde	4	0	0

---

197. William Guybon. Insertion
omitted for names and initials.

Costen	4	0	0
Thomas Creamer	1	0	20
Sum	335	2	0

The summ of infeild [lands] letten for barly:

	a	r	[p]
Mr Gurling	1	2	20
my cosen Guybon	16	3	0
Willyam Guybon	44	1	10

Mr Loads	27	2	20
Martin Smith	68	2	0
Richard Banyard	18	0	10
Widdow Acres	14	1	20
John Addams	15	3	20
Francis Costen	38	3	20
Thomas Longstreth	21	1	0
Heacham men in small percells	16	0	10
Sum	283	1	30

	a	r	[p]
[p] 61 **Infield lands whereof no fearme is payed**			
The site of *the* Mannour	7	0	0
13 furlong 4 precinct *for 1ac at Potthow 1 furlong 5 pre* the heyres of Henry Lawes in exchang[e]	0	3	20
1 furlong 5 precinct for 2ac in the 13 furlong 5 precinct	0	0	0
Mr Gurling hath in exchange	1	3	0

/1631/ Brecklands written as appeareth by a note letten to the tennants in the breck for 2 bushell of barly the acre 217ac 3½r

/1632/ **An accompt of Sedgford for the yeare ending at St Michaell 1632 the fearme barly being then due but not payd until Candlemas**

	£	s	d
Received of my cosen Guybon for 102ac of inclosed ground and 165ac 1½r of in feilde in all 267ac 1½r at 5s	66	16	10
/East Field/ last crop in the 6 breck 29ac ½r; second cropp in the 7 breck 14ac; first crop in the 8 breck 15ac: summerley in the first breck 16ac; in all 84ac ½r			
/South Field/ last crop 2 breck 14ac ½r; second crop 3 breck 32 acs; first crop 4 breck 53ac; summerly 5 breck 24ac 2½r; the sum of all is 207acs 3r at 5s	51	18	9
Received of my cosen Guybon for East Hall fearme	6	19	6
Received of John Creamer for the North foldcourse	25	0	0
Received of my cosen Guybon for the South Foldcourse	18	0	0
Received of Thomas Longstreth for his fearme £4 18s and for 4a, 17s 1d	5	15	1
Received of Costen for 4ac		16	0
Received of Thomas Creamer for 1ac ½r		6	8
Received of the townes men for their tithe at 2s the acre 12d for pease all but my cosen Guybon and Mr Loads	105	10	9
Received for fearme barly being 233 comb 2 bushell 3 pecks and for my cosen Guybon and Mr Loads his tithe being 85 comb 1 bushell 1 peck in all 279 comb sold for	183	0	3

Received for Sedgeford rents now altered and payd at our Lady and
St Michaell £25 17s ½d and 2s 5d for Sedgford Stranges and 2s of
Longstreth which was usually payd to Thomas Creamer for a piece
of ground wheron his parlour is builded and 2d the yeare more due
out of Ringsted, which 2s 2d by agreements in now extinguished, for
2s 7½d due from the Mannor of Rustins to Sedgford Stranges so the
rent now to Stranges Mannour is 4s 5d: received in all   26   1   5½
Received for the Duke of Suffolks rents   12   2½
Rec of the tithe of the 3 mills: 6s 8d, 6s 8d and 5s   18   4
                                    Sum [*sub-total*]   491 15 10

[*p 62*] Received for the haywardshipp and profitts of courtes
the whole sum received for Sedgford 1632 beside the East foldcorse is 491 15 10
                            outpayments £75 10s 10d deducted
                    rest of the cleare value of Sedgford 1632   416   5   0

/*1633*/ An accompt of Sedgford 1633 the fearme barly being then due

/*Francis Guybon*/ for 102ac of inclosed ground and 173ac 3r (wherof   £   s   d
8ac was formerly letten for barly) of infield. In all 275ac 3r at 5s   68   18 9
/*South Field*/ last cropp and 3 breck 32 ac; second cropp and 4 breck
53 ac; first cropp 5 breck 24ac 2r; summerly 6 breck 21ac: in all in the
South field 130ac
/*East Field*/ last cropp 7 breck 14ac; second cropp 8 breck 15ac; first
cropp first breck 26ac; summerley 2 breck 44ac; in all in the East
field 99 acs.
Sum of both brecks are 229ac 2r at 5s the acre is   57   7   6
/*Willyam Guybon*/
for first cropp of the new breck in the East Foldcourse at 10s 33ac   16   10 0
of Willyam Guybon for the North foldcourse   20   0   0
of Francis Guybon for South Foldcourse   18   0   0
of Thomas Longstreth for his fearme £4 18s and for 4ac, 17s 1d   5   15 1
of Francis Costen for 4ac   0   16 0
of Edmond Creamer for 1ac ½r   0   6   8
rents of assize to the Pryor   25   17 5¼
for rents of Stranges Mannour   0   4   5
for rents to the Duke of Suffolk   0   12   2½
for the tithe of the 3 mills as in accompt 1629   0   18   4
of the townes men for their tithes at 2s the acre for all graine but
pease and fitches and those at 12d   104   18   0
Received for tithe of Willyam Guybon and Francis Guybon and Mr
Loades 101 comb 1 bushell 2 pecks and for fearme barly 229 comb 1
bushell 1 peck being in all 301 comb 1bushell 3 pecks sold for   193   4   1
Received for Easthall fearme   6   19   6

Received for the haywardship 15s 4d and for profitts of courtes

			£	s	d
[*attached note*] the sum before due corne be written is £215 6s 4¾			215	6	4¾
the tithe and fearme barly 1633 cometh near to 300 comb					
which at 9s the comb will be £162 0s					
the tithe if it be nott altered is £106 7s			268	7	0
[*Sum*]			483	13	4¾

[*p*] 63 **A note of all the infield landes letten for mony to Willyam Guybon 1634 beginning at St Michaell 1633**

	a	r	£	s	d
/q 1/ The site of the manour with the houses	7	0			
Sedgeford yarde at 7s *furlong 27*	4	2			
Church Medow with other grownde within the hedg at 7s	12	2	5	19	0
Dingles Pightle and waterhall yards at 9s	2	2			
the meadow by Olde Mill Brigge at 9s	7	2			
/q 2 £10 18s/ Reed Damm Meadow with the feed of the Reed dam at 9s	1	0	4	19	0
*28ac*198	[35	0]	10	18	0
/q 27/ West fenne *2 precinct q 27*	9	0			
/q 7/ Nether Jayberd *2 pre q 2*	7	0			
/q 18/ Upper Jayberd *2 pre q 3*	18	0			
Beales his croffte *pre 8 q 9*	12	2			
Land in Eaton bought of Hargate first furlong 8 precinct 2 pieces 2a & 9r*	4	1			
/q 22/ Sedgeford Hill *1 pre q 22 7ac; q 24 14ac*	21	0			
exchanged for the dovehouse 26 furlong first precinct	5	0			
in the 4 furlong 2 precinct	5	0			
in the 16 furlong third precinct	3	0			
at Black land *3 pre q 11*	5	0			
Windes piece *3 pre q 9*	12	0			
Fickles Croft *3 pre q 6*	7	0			
[*Sum*] at 6s 4d	108	3	34	8	9
South Close *at 5s 4d 13 furlong 7 precinct*	11	0			
Whinne Close *at 5s 4d the 11, 12 furlong 5 precinct*	34	0	12	0	0
Hall Bottom Close *at 5s 2 pre q 10*	9	0	2	5	0
	[54	0]			
the North foldcourse			20	0	0
the South foldcourse			20	0	0
In the South field first cropp *6 breck*	21	0			
Second cropp *5 breck*	24	2			
Last cropp *4 breck*	53	0			

---

198. Less the 7 acres for the site of the manor.

Summerley *7 breck 10 ac of this is Sherborn Close*		37	2		
Sum at 5s	136	0	34	1	6
The summ of this yeares fearme is			133	13	3
More for first cropp of 29ac of newe broken ground			14	10	
More for second cropp of 33ac of new broken ground in the East foldcorse			16	10	
[Sum]	396	0	164	13	3]

[p 64] **Lands letten in Sedgford for mony 1634**

Francis Guybons fearme of East Hall

	a	r	[p]
/The first fearme/ The house with a bearn, stable and yarde *4 pre 3 furlong*	2	0	0
first furlong 4 precinct inclosed *in 3 pieces*	5	0	0
2 furlong 4 precinct in 3 pieces	3	1	0
4 furlong 4 precinct in 3 pieces	14	2	0
11 furlong 6 precinct by Chappell Crofft	14	0	0
Sum 38ac 3r letten by olde lease for £6 19s 6d			
/The new fearme/ Easthall yardes with a bearn *4 precinct 3 furlong*	4	0	0
Chappell Croft *12 furlong 6 precinct*	7	0	0
Morland Easthall *4 furlong 4 precinct*	7	0	0
by the Whinn Close *4 furlong 5 precinct*	14	0	0
by Easthall Greene in 3 pcs	33	0	0
Flint Hill *first furlong 5 precinct*	20	0	0
Sum 85ac letten for 5s the acre £21 5s			
Last cropp in the East Breck 8 breck	15	0	0
Second cropp there first breck	26	0	0
First cropp there 2 breck	44	0	0
Summerley there 3 breck	42	0	0
Sum 127acs at 3s 6d the acre /£22 4s 6d/			

the whole sum of Francis Guybons 2 farmes for 1634 at St Michaell
is £50 9s 0d

[p] 65 Thomas Longstreths lease lands	a	r	[p]
/N 6/[199] 3 furlong in Eaton <with the house and stable>	0	2	20
3 furlong more east	0	2	20
/N 11/ 3 furlong	2	2	0
8 furlong <this Costen hath> *in 2 pieces at Long howe*	0	3	0
9 furlong	1	0	0
9 furlong	0	2	0

---

199. Unclear as to what N refers to; not to the Sedgeford maps, with their precincts, quarentia and numbers, or the Sedgeford rental of 1634. From that rental they appear to refer to lands of Sedgefords Manor held in Heacham.

	£	s	d
9 furlong *for this he payeth 2s to Barrett Ringsted*	o	2	o
9 furlong	I	o	o
9 furlong *Beck Pightle not in the lease*	o	o	o
10 furlong *an headland*	o	2	o
/4/ 10 furlong *next Henry Creamer*	o	3	20
/6/ 10 furlong	o	3	20
15 furlong *neare Snettsham Border the last piece of the furlong*	I	I	o
13 furlong *John Ellgar south*	3	o	o
22 furlong *next Deane late Suncton*	o	2	½
27 furlong *part of 10ac called the west fenne*	I	o	o
27 furlong *late Creamer on both side*	I	I	o
27 furlong *q Shettington and Rust with the house and stable*	I	o	o
27 furlong *next q Rust a messuage decayed*	o	2	o
27 furlong *next q Rust next Mill Lane*	I	o	o
27 furlong *a pightle called Dovehouse Croft*	I	2	o
<q 22> Mixt furlong in Sedgford *q Rust, Creamer on both sides*	o	2	20
Mixt furlong in Snetsham <3r stett and 3r q Linne q if in Snetsham>	I	2	o

Sum 23ac or for this he payeth £4 18s
of this Costen hath 1a 3r <in the> 4 furlong and Longstreth hath
usually had it in his lease; for this he shall have 4r in the 27 furlong
the pieces thus allowed and this 3 in <Mixt> *the 27* furlong is
meddow

	£	s	d
Thomas Longstreth for 3ac called the Ashe Yarde		13	I
of him for 1ac there late Hargates		14	o
Francis Costen in the first furlong late Hargates 4a *1a; 3r; 2a 1r* in 3 pieces		16	o
In the 8 furlong in Eaton and the same furlong 3½r in all 1a ½r		6	8
[Sub-total	I	19	9]

Sum [of money rent for 1634] £222 [£220 19s 9d]

[p 66] **Sedgford landes letten for barly 1634**

	a	r	[p]
/Thomas Longstreth/ 3 furlong in Eaton *lease*	o	o	o
3 furlong *Richard Byrd west*	o	2	20
3 furlong *John Ellgar east*	2	2	o
/1/ 8 furlong *an headland*	o	3	o
/3/ 8 furlong	o	3	20
/4/ 8 furlong <lease>	o	3	20
/2/ 8 furlong *lease*	o	o	o
9 furlong called Becks Pightle	o	2	o
/7 N5/ 10 furlong	o	3	20
/10 N7/ 10 furlong	o	2	o
/8 N14/ 10 furlong *next Robert Rose*	o	2	10
/3 N17/ 10 furlong *next Robert Rose*	I	I	o

	a	r	p
/9 N20/ 10 furlong *Henry Lawes west*	1	1	0
/9 N 21/ 10 furlong *an headland q Willis*	1	0	0
12 furlong *Martin Cobbe sout*	0	2	0
16 furlong *John Ellgar on both sides*	0	3	0
16 furlong *John Ellgar on both sides*	0	2	0
27 furlong *q Beales next 9 rod late Hargates at Woodcocks*	1	1	0
18 furlong	0	3	0
18 furlong	0	1	0
18 furlong	0	3	20
19 furlong	0	2	20
19 furlong	0	1	30
19 furlong	1	0	0
19 furlong	0	1	30
mixt furlong *q Linne q 29 next Awdly*	1	2	0
Sum	20	1	0

[p] 67 Sedgford landes letten for barly 1634 [continued]

/Francis Costen/	a	r	[p]
2 furlong in Eaton	1	1	0
/N 1/ 4 furlong	1	1	0
/N 3/ 4 furlong	1	1	0
/N 7/ 4 furlong	0	2	0
/N 8/ 4 furlong	2	0	0
/N 11/ 4 furlong	0	1	20
/N 13/ 4 furlong	0	1	20
/N 14/ 4 furlong <of Thomas Longstreth>	1	1	20
/N 15/ 4 furlong *of Thomas Longstreth lease*	1	0	0
/N 17/ 4 furlong	0	3	0
/N 18/ 4 furlong	4	3	0
5 furlong	0	3	20
5 furlong	0	3	20
5 furlong *lease*	0	2	20
5 furlong	1	1	0
6 furlong	0	1	20
6 furlong	0	1	30
7 furlong	0	1	20
7 furlong	0	1	30
7 furlong	1	1	0
7 furlong	0	3	0
7 furlong	0	2	0
9 furlong to inclose to his house for 10 yeares to expire 1640 *now 6s*	1	0	0
10 furlong	4	0	0
11 furlong	0	1	0
11 furlong *long lease*	1	1	0

	a	r	p
11 furlong	0	2	0
11 furlong	0	2	20
11 furlong	0	1	20
11 furlong	0	1	20
11 furlong	0	3	0
11 furlong	0	2	20
11 furlong *this is sett an acre by John Fisher*	1	1	0
17 furlong	0	2	0
mixt furlong 1ac 5r and 3r in all	3	0	0
18 furlong	3	0	0

Sum 40ac ½r which because the measure is small goeth for 40ac
and is letten 39ac for 21 yeares and expireth 1651

[p 68] **Landes letten for barly 1634 of infield in Sedgford** [*continued*]

/Willyam Guybon/	a	r	[p]
first furlong 7 precinct	9	0	0
7 furlong 4 pre	0	2	0
7 furlong 4 pre	1	0	0
7 furlong 4 pre	2	0	0
9 furlong 2 pre	1	1	0
10 furlong 2 pre	1	2	0
10 furlong 2 pre	0	3	0
10 furlong 2 pre	0	3	0
11 furlong 4 pre	1	1	0
11 furlong 4 pre	1	1	0
11 furlong 4 pre	1	0	0
13 furlong 4 pre	3	0	0
13 furlong 4 pre	1	0	0
13 furlong 3 pre	0	3	0
14 furlong 3 pre	0	3	20
15 furlong 5 pre	1	0	20
16 furlong 3 pre	3	0	0
17 furlong 3 pre	1	2	10
20 furlong 7 pre	5	0	0
Sum	36	2	10

/Francis Guybon/ *first* furlong 5 precinct	1	2	0
first furlong 5 pre	3	1	0
first furlong 5 pre	2	2	0
5 furlong 5 pre	2	0	0
13 furlong 5 pre	2	3	0
13 furlong 5 pre	6	0	0
first furlong 4 pre of John Addams	5	0	0
Sum	23	0	0

	a	r	[p]
[p] 69 **Landes letten for barly 1634 of Sedgford infield** [*continued*]			
/*Mr Loades*/ first furlong in Eaton to Willyam Guybon 1635	3	0	0
first furlong in Eaton to John Crisp Grosser 1635	1	0	0
5 furlong 4 precinct to John Crisp Grosser 1635	2	0	0
6 furlong 4 precinct to Francis Guybon 1635	3	2	20
6 furlong 4 precinct to Francis Guybon 1635	4	3	0
6 furlong in Eaton to Thomas Longstreth 1635	2	2	0
10 furlong in Eaton to Thomas Longstreth 1635	0	2	0
16 furlong in Eaton to John Ellgar 1635 *to Tho Longstreth*	0	3	0
9 furlong 4 precinct to Francis Guybon 1635	1	0	0
9 furlong 4 preceinct to Francis Guybon 1635	1	0	0
10 furlong 4 precinct to Francis Guybon 1635	0	3	0
10 furlong 4 precinct to Francis Guybon 1635	1	1	0
22 furlong first precinct to John Lawes 1635	1	2	0
22 furlong first precinct to John Lawes 1635	2	1	0
22 furlong first precinct to John Lawes 1635	0	3	0
Sum	26	2	20
/*Richard Banyard*/ 5 furlong 4 precinct	1	0	0
5 furlong 4 precinct	0	2	20
7 furlong 4 precinct	0	2	0
8 furlong 4 precinct	5	0	0
9 furlong 4 precinct	1	2	0
9 furlong 4 precinct	1	0	0
10 furlong 4 precinct	3	0	0
13 furlong 4 precinct	1	0	0
13 furlong 4 precinct	0	3	20
13 furlong 4 precinct	1	0	0
17 furlong 3 precinct	1	2	10
24 furlong 4 precinct	0	2	0
Sum	17	2	10
[*p 70*] **Lands letten for barly of infield in Sedgford 1634** [*continued*]			
/*John Addams*/ <first> 3 furlong 4 precinct to Francis Guybon 1635	4	1	0
4 furlong 4 precinct	1	2	20
7 furlong 4 precinct	0	2	0
7 furlong 4 precinct	0	1	0
10 furlong 4 precinct	0	3	0
24 furlong 4 precinct	1	0	0
Sum	8	1	20
/*Widdow Acres*/ first furlong 4 precinct	0	2	20
8 furlong 4 precinct	3	0	0
9 furlong 4 precinct	2	0	0
10 furlong 4 precinct	0	3	0

11 furlong 4 precinct	1	0	20
11 furlong 3 precinct	1	0	0
13 furlong 4 precinct	0	3	20
16 furlong 3 precinct	5	0	0
Sum	14	1	20
/*Allen Collen*/ 10 furlong 7 precinct in 2 pieces	1	3	0
/*Martin Henry Lawes*/ second furlong 7 precinct in 2 pieces	3	1	0
3 furlong 7 precinct	1	0	0
5 furlong 4 precinct	5	0	0
8 furlong 4 precinct	10	0	0
9 furlong 4 precinct	2	0	0
9 furlong 6 precinct	0	1	0
9 furlong 7 precinct in 2 pieces	5	0	0
10 furlong 6 precinct	3	0	0
13 furlong 5 precinct	16	0	0
[p] 71 15 furlong 5 precinct in 5 pieces	5	0	20
16 furlong 5 precinct in 2 pieces	2	1	20
17 furlong 5 precinct of fring land	9	0	0
18 furlong 5 precinct of fring land	1	1	0
20 furlong 5 precinct	3	0	0
20 furlong 7 precinct	2	0	0
20 furlong 7 precinct	1	0	0
Sum	69	1	0

/*Sum of Infield letten for barly*/	a	r	[p]
Thomas Longstreth	20	1	0
Francis Costen	40	0	20
Willyam Guybon	36	2	10
Francis Guybon	23	0	0
Mr Loades	26	2	20
Richard Banyard	17	2	10
John Adams	8	1	20
Widdow Acres	14	1	20
Martin Smith	69	1	0
Allen Collen	1	3	0
Sum[200]	257	3	0
/*Mr Gurling*/ in the 15 furlong 5 precinct 1ac and after the 16 furl 5 pre 2½r	1	2	20
Widdow Vickers 2 furlong 5 precinct	0	3	0
Bartholomew Crisp first furlong in Eaton 2r and more there 3r	1	1	0

---

200. The sum in the book reads 12xx 17ac 2rod ½ 20 perches.

Richard Byrd 20 furlong in Eaton	0	1	30
John Crisp 15 furlong in Eaton	0	2	0
Sallter of Heacham 17 furlong 5r and at Catt gore 3ac *and 162 q[201] 5r*	5	1	0
Giles Estwick at Catt Gore	3	0	0
Willyam Hill at Catt Gore	3	0	0
Willyam Segon at Catt Gore	3	0	0
Sum	19	0	10

the whole sum of infield lands letten at 2 bushell of barly an acre is the
30 perches not reckoned 276ac 2½r in barly 138 comb 1 bushell 1 peck

/Infield not rented/ The site of the mannour	6	0	0
13 furlong 4 precinct *n 733* the heyres of Henry Lawes in exchange			
n 870 for 1ac at Pott How *n 781* in the first furlong 5 precinct	0	3	20
1 furlong 5 precinct Mr Gurling in exchange for 2ac *n 870* in the 13			
furlong 5 precinct Mr Gurling hath the Lord 7r n 788	1	3	0
Sum	9	2	20

[p 72] Breck lands letten for barly 1634

/North Pasture/	a	r	[p]
First cropp Mr Loads 8 breck	5	0	0
First cropp Willyam Guybon 8 breck	35	1	0
First cropp Widdow Vickers 8 breck	1	0	0
First cropp John Crisp 8 breck	2	3	0
[Sum]	44	0	0
Second cropp Mr Loads 7 breck	2	2	0
Second cropp Willyam Guybon 7 breck	4	1	5
[Sum]	6	3	0
Last cropp Willyam Guybon 6 breck	16	3	20
Last cropp Richard Banyard 6 breck	4	2	20
Last cropp Leonard Vile 6 breck	5	2	0
Last cropp John Addams 6 breck	6	0	0
Last cropp Widdow Vickers 6 breck	2	0	0
Last cropp Richard Bankes junior 6 breck	1	0	0
Last cropp Richard Bankes senior 6 breck	1	0	0
Last cropp Thomas Banyard 6 breck	3	0	0
Last cropp Robert Crisp 6 breck	5	0	0
Last cropp Peter Eade 6 breck	1	0	30
Last cropp Lingey 6 breck	2	0	0
Last cropp Thomas Outlaw 6 breck	1	0	0
Last cropp Spalding 6 breck	2	0	0
[Sum]	51	0	0

---

201. Several Heacham men were farm barley tenants, LEST/DI17.

	a	r	[p]
Summerly Willyam Guybon first breck	41	3	25

Sum of the North Pasture 143ac 2½r barly 71 comb 3 bushell 1 peck

/South field/

	a	r	[p]
First cropp Allen Collen 6 breck	4	0	20
First cropp George Framingham 6 breck	1	3	0
First cropp lyeth wast by South Close 6 breck	7	2	0
[Sum]	13	1	20
Second cropp Willyam Guybon 5 breck	10	0	0
Second cropp Osburn 5 breck	1	1	0
Second cropp Allen Collen 5 breck	6	2	20
Second cropp Thomas Longstreth 5 breck	1	2	0
Second cropp Robert Rose 5 breck letten for 18d		1	20
[Sum]	19	3	0
Last cropp Willyam Guybon 4 breck	7	0	0
Last cropp Osburne 4 breck	1	0	0
Last cropp Martin Smith 4 breck	2	0	0
[Sum]	10	0	0
Summerly 7 breck Willyam Guybon	34	1	0

Sum of the South field for barly 69a 2r barly 34 comb 3 bushell 0 peck

/East Brecks/

	a	r	[p]
First cropp Francis Guybon 2 breck	16	0	0
Second cropp Francis Guybon first breck	20	0	0
Last cropp Francis Guybon 8 breck	0	0	0
Summerly Francis Guybon 3 breck	25	2	0

Sum 61ac 2r barly 30 comb 3 bushell

the whole sum of barly for Breck lands 1634 is 147 comb 1 bushell 1 peck

[p] 73 Sedgford fearme lands letten for mony 1635

		a	r	p		£	s	d
precinct 2	[a	r	p]		Willyam Guybon the scite of the mannor			
q 1					of Westhall conteyning 7ac			
precinct 1		1	0	0	of Corse Medow the river parteth it by			
q 19					Old Mill Bridge	0	5	0
pre 1 q 27		4	2	0	called Sedgford yarde			
pre 8 q 28		12	2	0	wherof Church Medow is 6a 3r, of Stranges 7r			
N 20–25		0	0	0	part of grasse crofft 3ac and 1ac Ingolls acre			
					at 7s	5	19	0
pre 1 q 27		1	0	0	called Waterhall yardes			
pre 8 q 27		4	0	0	/N 17/ called Sedgfords *1729*			
pre 8 q 27		2	0	0	/N 19/ called Sedgford Damme *1731*			
pre 8 q 27		1	1	0	/N 18/ next q Bennett late Richard Stubbe			
					1730			

	a	r	p		£	s	d
pre 8 q 27	0	2	0	/N 20/ next Sedgford Damme late Allder Carre *1732*			
*this	7	3	0	is inclosed but is small measure & goeth for 7ac 3r*			
pre 8 q 28	1	0	0	/N11/ a pightle q Linne			
	0	2	0	/N12/ a pightle next q Willis called Dingles Pightle			
pre 7 q 31	1	0	0	called Reedamm Medow left out of the booke by Mr Sheppard at 9s	4	19	0
				Sum of medow and pasture			

precinct 1	[a	r	p]		£	s	d
q 22 q 24	21	0	0	called Sedgford Hill in 2 pieces: 7ac and 14ac *q 24*			
q 26 165	5	0	0	sometime exchanged with Hargate for a dovehouse			
pre 2 q 2	7	0	0	called nether Jeyberd			
q 3	18	0	0	called Uper Jeyberd			
q 4 204	5	0	0	*by Walldins*			
pre 1 q 27	9	0	0	part of 10ac called the West fenne			
pre 3 q 6	7	0	0	/n 381/ called Fickles Crofft			
q 9 419	12	0	0	called Windes piece			
q 11 428	5	0	0	called Black land			
q 16 476	3	0	0	*by long Cleylands 5r of this for a close 7s 2d*			
pre 8 q 1	12	2	0	called Beales his croffte *et q 4 et 5*			
q 1 1383	4	1	0	in Eaton late Hargates in 2 pieces: 2a and			
1384				2a 1r part of *5ac 1r*			
				Sum 108ac 3r at 6s 4d the acre is	34	8	9
2 pre q 10	9	0	0	called Hallbottom Close at 5s *243*	2	5	0
5 pre q 11	34	0	0	called the Whinn Close at 5s 4d	9	1	4
				The North foldcorse	20	0	0
				The South foldcorse	20	0	0
				Summ for infield and inclosed and the foldcorses abate 7s 2d for 5r q 16	96	18	1
				Remayne beside the foldcorses	56	10	11

			a	r	[p]
[p 74]	**Willyam Guybons fearme in mony 1635**				
South	Summerly in the 8 breck		49	1	30
Brecks	First crop in the 7 breck whereof 10ac is Shernborn Close		37	2	30
	Second cropp in the 6 breck		21	0	0
	Last cropp in the 5 Breck		24	2	0
	Sum 132ac 2½r at 5s is £33 3s 2d				

		£	s	d
	more for the last cropp of 29ac broken up in the East foldcorse at 10s	14	10	0
	more for the first cropp of 40ac in the East foldcorse	20	0	0
	the whole summ of Willyam Guybons fearme 1635	144	11	3
	with the 2 foldcorses is	169	11	3

	/Francis Guybons Newe fearme/	a	r	[p]
607	3 furlong 4 precinct called Easthall yardes with a bearn	4	0	0
606	3 furlong 4 precinct part inclosed	18	0	0
565	2 furlong 4 precinct called Knattington greene	5	0	0
566	2 furlong 4 precinct	10	0	0
	[Sub-total]	33	0	0
620	4 furlong 4 precinct called Mareland	7	0	0
802	1 furlong 5 precinct called Flint Hill	20	0	0
823	4 furlong 5 precinct by the Whinne Close	14	0	0
1043	12 furlong 6 precinct Chappell Crofft	7	0	0
	Sum 85ac letten for 5s the acre £21 5s 0d			

	/his Olde fearm/			
607	3 furlong 4 precinct the house, bearnes, stable and yarde	2	0	0
	1 furlong 4 precinct in 3 pieces inclosed *n 550, 551, 522*202	5	0	0
	2 furlong 4 precinct in 3 pieces by Bulls Whinnes	3	1	0
	4 furlong 4 precinct in 3 pieces: 12ac; 1ac & 1ac 2r	14	2	0
1037	11 furlong 6 precinct above Chappell Crofft	14	0	0
	Sum 38ac 3r letten by olde lease for £6 19s 6d			
The East	Summerly 4 breck	36	0	0
Brecks	First cropp 3 breck	42	0	0
	Second cropp 2 breck	44	0	0
	Last cropp first breck	26	0	0
	Sum 148ac at 3s 6d the acre is £25 18s 0d			
	So Francis Guybons fearme 1635 is £54 2s 6d			

[p] 75	/Thomas Longstreths/ lease lands	a	r	[p]
	3 furlong 8 precinct in Eaton with the house and stable203	0	2	20
	3 furlong next and east	0	2	20
1426	3 furlong there an headland	2	2	0
N10	8 furlong at Long How in 2 pieces	0	3	0

---

202. Numbers from the new map have been inserted, but insertion marks omitted.

203. At this point, the perches column is titled 'di' short for dimidus, i.e. half. For 20 perches or ½, Alice entered 1 i.e. 1 half, but for clarity and consistency we have converted this to 20p, as before.

		l	s	d
	4 furlong 1ac which Costen hath for which he hath in 27			
171	furlong first precinct a spong part of 10ac called West fenne	1	0	0
N2	9 furlong 8 precinct in Eaton 1499, 1501	1	0	0
N3, 4, 5	9 furlong there *2r 1502 and 2r 1503 & 4r 1504 of Barrett Ringsted*	2	0	0
N8	9 furlong there 2r *a Hempland in Barrett Ringsted account called little Beckyarde not in the lease *			
N1, 4, 6	10 furlong 2r and 3½r and 3½r	2	1	0
N3	13 furlong John Ellgar south *1573*	3	0	0
N11	15 furlong *the last piece of the furlong*	1	1	0
N10	22 furlong *next Deane late Suncton*	0	2	20
N4	27 furlong at Heasall Stye Creamer on both sides	1	1	0
N7	27 furlong q Shettington and Rust *with the house and stable*	1	0	0
N8	27 furlong next q Rust	0	2	0
N9	27 furlong next q Rust next Mill Lane	1	0	0
N10	27 furlong a pightle called Dovehouse Crofft	1	2	0
N20 q 29	Mixt furlong in Sedgford q Rust: Creamer on both sides *1779*	0	2	20
N23, N24	/q 29/ Mixt furlong in Snetsham 3rod and 3rod *1784 & 1786*	1	2	0
	Sum 23ac by lease letten for payeth £4 18s 0d and 2s to Barrett Ringsted for 2r			

8 precinct	Thomas Longstreth at Heasall Stye q Creamer & Hargate being:	£	s	d
q 27	3 0 0 1716 lying next Creamer letten at 8s the acre	1	4	0
N18 & 20	1 0 1 in 2 pieces: 3½r and 1r last used by Thomas			
q 8	Creamer		6	5
N11 q 9	3 0 0 called the Ashe Yarde		13	1
N12 q 9	1 0 0 there next late Hargates		4	0
	Sum £2 7s 6d his whole fearme is £7 5s 6d			

N3 8 pre	Willyam Overman and Thomas Watton for lande late Creamer	a	r	[p]
N4 q 25	and Willyam Guybon neare Bishops Crown, Ri. Byrd north	3	0	0
167 q 25	there next and more south q Bangate	2	0	0
N5	there next and more south q Brigges	5	0	0
N6	there next and more south q Brigges *bond of Sedgford*		3	20
N7	there next and more south q Brigges	2	0	0
N8	there next and more south q Brigges		1	20
N9	there next and more south q Brigges		2	0
N10	there next and more south q Brigges		2	20

		£	s	d
N1 q 27	at Heasall Stye *q* Edmond Creamer *1712*	1	0	0
N2 q 27	there next and more east *q* Alowe *1713*		3	0
N3 q 27	there next and more east *q* Creamer *1714*	2	1	0
	Sum 18ac 1½r letten at 8s the acre £7 7s			

8 pre q 1	Francis Costen late Hargates in 2 pieces 1ac *1385* and 5r *1386*	2	1	0
q 1	more there late Hargates	1	3	0
	Sum 4ac letten for 16s			

		£	s	d
[p 76]	/1635/ Robert Rose for 1½r in the South pasture last cropp		1	6
	The whole sum of fearme lands and 2 foldcorses letten for mony beside the East foldcorse in the Lords hand is	214	3	9

1635 Infield lands letten at Sedgford for 2 bushell of barly the acre

		a	r	[p]
547	1 furlong 4 precinct late Addams	5	0	0
598–600	3 furlong 4 precinct late Addams	4	1	0
636, 648	5 furlong 4 precinct	3	2	20
659–661	6 furlong 4 precinct	3	2	20
665	6 furlong 4 precinct	4	3	0
697	8 furlong 4 precinct *part of 18ac*	5	0	0
700	{9 furlong 4 precinct	2	0	0
	{9 furlong 4 precinct	2	2	0
704	{10 furlong 4 precinct	2	0	0
	{10 furlong 4 precinct	3	0	0
	13 furlong 4 precinct	2	3	20
491	17 furlong 3 precinct	1	2	10
664	24 furlong 4 precinct	0	2	0
794	1 furlong 5 precinct	1	2	0
805	1 furlong 5 precinct	3	1	0
807	1 furlong 5 precinct	2	2	0
826	5 furlong 5 precinct	2	0	0
875	13 furlong 5 precinct	2	3	0
877	13 furlong 5 precinct	6	0	0
	Sum	58	2	30

[p] 77 **Infield landes letten for barly 1635** [continued]

		a	r	[p]
	/Willyam Guybon/			
	1 furlong 8 precinct in Eaton of Mr Loads	0	0	0
14[204] 1061	1 furlong 7 precinct	9	0	0

---

204. Numbers on LH side should probably bear the prefix N.

		a	r	p
[N]7,681	7 furlong 4 precinct *FG*	1	0	0
683	7 furlong 4 precinct	1	0	0
[N]8,689	7 furlong 4 precinct	2	0	0
[N]1,238	9 furlong 2 precinct	1	1	0
[N]2,247	{10 furlong 2 precinct	1	2	0
	{10 furlong 2 precinct	0	3	0
	{10 furlong 2 precinct	0	3	0
[N]9,714	11 furlong 4 precinct	1	1	0
[N]10,717	11 furlong 4 precinct	1	1	0
[N]11,715	11 furlong 4 precinct	1	0	0
[N]12,736	13 furlong 4 precinct	3	0	0
[N]13,737	13 furlong 4 precinct <part of 3ac to Ro Birch 1642 att now>	1	0	0
[N]3,460	13 furlong 3 precinct	0	3	0
[N]4,462	14 furlong 3 precinct	0	3	20
891	15 furlong 5 precinct *to Ro Birch*	1	0	20
[N]5,473	16 furlong 3 precinct	3	0	0
[N]6,488	17 furlong 3 precinct *to Ro Birch 1642*	1	2	10
[N]15,1243	20 furlong 7 precinct	5	0	0
	Sum <36ac 2r 10p>	37	0	10

/Francis Guybon/	a	r	[p]
1 furlong 4 precinct late Adams	5	0	0
3 furlong 4 precinct late Adams	4	1	0
5 furlong 4 precinct late Mr Loads 2ac & 1ac 2r Ri Banyard	3	2	20
6 furlong 4 precinct late Mr Loads	3	2	20
6 furlong 4 precinct late Mr Loads	4	3	0
8 furlong 4 precinct late Ri: Banyard	5	0	0
9 furlong 4 precinct late Mr Loades	2	0	0
9 furlong 4 precinct late <Mr Loads> *Ri Banyard*	2	2	0
10 furlong 4 precinct late Mr Loades	2	0	0
10 furlong 4 precinct late <Mr Loads> *Ri Banyard*	3	0	0
13 furlong 4 precinct late Ri Banyards 2ac & 3½r	2	3	20
1 furlong 5 precinct	1	2	0
1 furlong 5 precinct	3	1	0
1 furlong 5 precinct	2	2	0
5 furlong 5 precinct	2	0	0
13 furlong 5 precinct	2	3	0
13 furlong 5 precinct	6	0	0
17 furlong 3 precinct <Sum 39ac 2r ½ > *late Ri Ban[yard]*	1	2	10
24 furlong 4 precinct		2	0
[Sum	58	2	30]

Lands letten for barly 1635 [continued]

[p 78]

/Thomas Longstreth/

		a	r	[p]
N5	3 furlong 8 precinct in Eaton *in his lease*	0	0	0
N7	3 furlong *Richard Bird west 1422 now lease*	0	2	20
N8	3 furlong 8 precinct < John Ellgar east> *1426 Cremer west now lease an headland*	2	2	0
N5	6 furlong 8 precinct of Mr Loades *1468*	2	2	0
N1	8 furlong 8 precinct *an headland 1478*	0	3	0
	8 furl 8 pre *in 2 pieces Cremer south, late Bird north 1487 1488*	0	3	0
N13	8 furlong 8 precinct *1491*	0	3	20
N14	8 furlong 8 precinct *1492*	0	3	20
N8	9 furlong 8 precinct *called little Beckyarde 1507 pasture now lease*	0	2	0
	furlong 8 precinct *an headland in Rolls Close*	0	0	0
N6	10 furlong 8 precinct <an headland> *1526*	0	3	20
N7	10 furlong 8 precinct *of Mr Loades 1527*	0	2	0
N14	10 furlong 8 precinct *next Robert Rose 1533*	0	2	20
N17	10 furlong 8 precinct *next Robert Rose 1536*	1	1	0
N20	10 furlong 8 precinct *Henry Lawes west 1539*	1	1	0
N21	10 furlong 8 precinct *the last piece of the furlong 1540*	1	0	0
N4	12 furlong 8 precinct *Martin Cobbe south 1569*	0	2	20
N11	16 furlong 8 precinct *John Ellgar on both sides 1596 lease*	0	2	0
N6	16 furlong 8 precinct of Mr Loades *John Ellgar on both sides 1601 [lease]*	0	3	0
N2	18 furlong 8 precinct *1610*	0	3	0
N3	18 furlong 8 precinct *1611*	0	1	0
N4	18 furlong 8 precinct *1612*	0	3	20
N3	19 furlong 8 precinct *1618}*	0	2	20
	19 furlong 8 precinct *1619} 2ac 2r sold to Cremer*	0	1	30
N5	19 furlong 8 precinct *1620}*	1	0	0
N6	19 furlong 8 precinct *1620}*	0	1	30
	22 furlong 1669	0	2	20
N4 lease	27 furlong 8 precinct q Beales at Woodcocks next 9r late Hargates	0	0	0
N13	Mixt furlong in Sedgford q Linne next Thomas Awdly *1772*	1	2	0
n10	In Heacham Booke in Greengate furlong als Barley Mere			
q 152[205]	Creamer north	2	0	0
	Sum <23ac 1r>	23	3	20

---

205. Reference to Heacham map LEST/OB2 and Heacham Book.

/Edward Lawes/

		a	r	
1384	1 furlong 8 precinct in Eaton of Mr Loades *part of 5ac 1r*	3	0	0
	22 furlong first precinct of Mr Loades *143*	1	2	0
	22 furlong first precinct of Mr Loades *145*	3	0	0
	Sum <4ac 2r>	7	2	0

[p] 79 /Francis Costen/

		a	r	[p]
	2 furlong 8 precinct in Eaton *next Snetsham Bordure Markett Way goeth over it 1415*[206]	1	1	0
N1	4 furlong 8 precinct *neare Sallters dike an headland 1427*	1	1	0
N3	4 furlong 8 precinct *more north John Ellgar north 1429*	1	1	0
N7	4 furlong 8 precinct *more north Cremer south 1433*	0	2	0
N8	4 furlong 8 precinct *next Cremer north 1434*	2	0	0
N11	4 furlong 8 precinct *more north Cremer on both sides 1437*	0	1	20
N13	4 furlong 8 precinct *more north Henry Lawes south 1439*	0	1	20
N14	4 furlong 8 precinct <of tho Longstreth> *next 1440*	1	1	20
N15	4 furlong 8 precinct *of Thomas Longstreth next Cremer north 1441*	1	0	0
N17	4 furlong 8 precinct *more north Cremer south 1443*	0	3	0
N19	4 furlong 8 precinct *more north at Calkhill, Bird north 1445*	4	3	0
N3	5 furlong 8 precinct *Henry Lawes north Bird south 1451*	0	3	20
N7	5 furlong 8 precinct *more south Lipkin north Bird south 1455*	0	3	20
N9	5 furlong 8 precinct *more south Bird north Henry Lawes south 1457*	0	2	20
N11	5 furlong 8 precinct *more south Cremer south Hen Lawes north 1459*	1	1	0
N1	6 furlong 8 precinct *1464 an headland Bird south 1464*	0	1	20
	6 furlong 8 precinct *1466 more south Bird on both sides 1466*	0	1	30
N1	7 furlong 8 precinct *an headland 1470*	0	1	20
N2	7 furlong 8 precinct *next & west 1471*	0	1	30
N3	7 furlong 8 precinct *next & west John Ellgar west 1472*	1	1	0
N6	7 furlong 8 precinct *more west Bird east 1475*	0	3	0
N7	7 furlong 8 precinct *next John Ellgar west 1476*	0	2	0
N16	9 furlong 8 precinct to inclose his house for 10 yeares to expire 1640	1	0	0

---

206. In this entry of Francis Costen, the detail after the word 'precinct' is more of an addition than insertions in the two previous entries of Tho Longstreth and Edward Lawes, showing Alice developing her method.

		a	r	[p]
N13	10 furlong 8 precinct *1532 at Suddele, Rose west 1532*	4	0	0
N4	11 furlong 8 precinct *at Suddele John Ellgar west 1544*	0	1	0
N6	11 furlong 8 precinct *more west John Ellgar west 1546*	1	1	0
N7	11 furlong 8 precinct *next & west Bird west 1547*	0	2	0
N9	11 furlong 8 precinct *more west Ro Rose west 1549*	0	2	20
N11	11 furlong 8 precinct *more west Rose east, Minnes west 1551*	0	1	20
N16	11 furlong 8 precinct *more west at Littlehowe Jo Ellgar east 1556*	0	1	20
N19	11 furlong 8 precinct *more west late Bird east 1560*	0	3	0
N20	11 furlong 8 precinct *next John Ellgar west 1561*	0	2	20
N22	11 furlong 8 precinct by John Fisher 1ac by the booke *at Coachland foveva*	1	1	0
N6 post	17 furlong 8 precinct *an headland at Calkpitt 1608*	0	2	0
N7	18 furlong 8 precinct *an headland at Sharnborn Way 1615*	3	0	0
N4, 6, 8.	mixt furlong in Sedgford *1763* 1ac 5r *1765* and 3r *1767* in all q 29	3	0	0
	Sum 40ac ½r letten for 40ac	[40	0	20]

Whereof 39ac is letten for 21 yeares and expireth 1651
and 1ac for 10 yeares and expireth 1640

[p 80]	**Lands letten for barley 1635** [continued]			
	/Martin Smith/	a	r	[p]
1063	2 furlong 7 precinct in 2 pieces: 2r and 2ac 3r	3	1	0
1075	3 furlong 7 precinct	1	0	0
642	5 furlong 4 precinct in 2 pieces	5	0	0
697	8 furlong 4 precinct	10	0	0
699	9 furlong 4 precinct *part of 4ac*	2	0	0
880	13 furlong 5 precinct	16	0	0
913	17 furlong 5 precinct *of Fring land*	9	0	0
916	18 furlong 5 precinct *of Fring land*	1	1	0
934	20 furlong 5 precinct	3	0	0
1010	9 furlong 6 precinct	0	1	0
1024	10 furlong 6 precinct	3	0	0
1106–7	9 furlong 7 precinct in 2 pieces	5	0	0
	20 furlong 7 precinct in 3 pieces	3	0	0
900	15 furlong 5 precinct in 5 pieces	5	0	0
907–8	16 furlong 5 precinct in 2 pieces	2	1	20
	521 Sum 69ac 1r 1 *Robert Rose all but the pieces FG*			

	/Richard Banyard/	a	r	[p]
	5 furlong 3 precinct	1	2	10
	5 furlong 4 precinct	1	0	0

5 furlong 4 precinct *called Wrongland*	0	2	20
7 furlong 4 precinct *to Will Guybon*	0	2	0
8 furlong 4 precinct *part of 18ac*	5	0	0
9 furlong 4 precinct *part of 4ac di*	1	2	0
9 furlong 4 precinct *part of 4ac di*	1	0	0
10 furlong 4 precinct	3	0	0
13 furlong 4 precinct	1	0	0
13 furlong 4 precinct	1	0	0
13 furlong 4 precinct	0	3	20
24 furlong 4 precinct	0	2	0

Sum 17ac 2 rod 10p all these but 2 rod to Francis Guybon

/John Crisp Grosser/	a	r	[p]
1 furlong 8 precinct in Eaton	1	0	0
15 furlong 8 precinct in Eaton of Mr Loades	0	2	0
5 furlong 4 precinct of Mr Loades *to Franck Guybon*	0	0	0

[p] 81   **Lands letten for barly 1635** [continued]

	/John Adams/	a	r	[p]
619	4 furlong 4 precinct *FG*	1	2	20
671	7 furlong 4 precinct in 2 pieces: 1r and 2rd *FG*	0	3	0
707	10 furlong 4 precinct *FG*	0	3	0
758	24 furlong 4 precinct *FG*	1	0	0
	Sum <5ac 0r>	4	1	20

	/John Adam's wife/			
	16 furlong 3 precinct	5	0	0
638	5 furlong 4 precinct		2	20
697	8 furlong 4 precinct *part of 18ac*	3	0	0
699	9 furlong 4 precinct *part of 4ac*	2	0	0
709	10 furlong 4 precinct		3	0
720–21	11 furlong 4 precinct *in 2 pieces*	2	0	20
	13 furlong 4 precinct *part of 7r*		3	20
	Sum	4	0	20

/Mr Gurling/			
15 furlong 5 precinct 1ac }	a	r	[p]
16 furlong 5 precinct 2r di } *FG*	1	2	20
/Allen Collen/ 10 furlong 7 precinct in 2 pieces *FG*	1	3	0
/Widow Vickers/ 2 furlong 5 precinct *FG*	0	3	0
/Bartholomew Crisp/ 1 furlong 8 precinct in Eaton 2r and 3r *FG*	1	1	0
/Richard Byrd/ 20 furlong in Eaton 8 precinct	0	1	30

	/*Willyam Hill*/ 164 furlong at Catt Gore[207]	3	0	0
	/*Willyam Segon*/ 164 furlong at Catt Gore	3	0	0
	/*Giles Estwick*/ 164 furlong at Catt Gore	3	0	0
	/*John Sallter*/ 17 furlong in Eaton in Heacham	1	1	0
N4 q 172	162 furlong in Eaton in Heacham next Cattgore	1	1	0
N3	164 furlong at Cattgore	3	0	0
	Sum 5ac 2r letten for 2 bushell of barly the acre			

---

207. Cattgore and parts of Eaton (Sedgfords Manor) lay in Heacham, furlong numbers refer to Heacham map, LEST/OB2.

The Sedgeford Rental, 1634[208]

[p] 15		a	r	[p]
pre 5	Henry Creamer his [bond] rent to Sedgford 1634[209]			
q 14	2ac[210] a headland at Olde Downe knoll q[211] Smith /Rose/[212]	2	0	0
q 15	at Leakeland q Gogney /Rose/	2	2	0
q 18	at Mouse hyde q Willyam Guybon	0	1	20
q 19	at Mouse hyde q Willyam Guybon	0	3	20
	there more q Willyam Guybon	0	3	20
	there more q Willyam Guybon	0	1	20
q 20	at Wrongland q Willyam Guybon	1	1	0
	there more q Willyam Guybon	3	2	0
	there more q Brock q Willyam Guybon	9	0	0
q 21	there more q Willyam Akers q Willyam Guybon /Rose/	5	0	0
q 21	at [?] next Fring Border q Longstreth	1	3	0
pre 6	/q 6/[213] at Oldowneknoll q Simon Smith q Longstreth /Rose/	0	2	0
q 6	at Fring Border a messuage *part of 13 ac* q Orwell q Thomas Longstreth q Willyam Guybon	12	2	10
q 12	more there q Orwell q Willyam Guybon /Rose/	2	0	0

---

208. From LEST/BK7. The Sedgeford Rental follows on from the Sheep Account 1620–22, but chronologically it comes after the Sedgeford Accounts, 1621–35, so it has been placed in that order.

209. LH margin has been halved in size and restricted mainly to pre[cinct] and q[uarentia] (furlongs) figures. For entries concerning perches, as before, all converted to numbers, i.e. 20, 30 rather than fractions i.e. ½ or numbered halves, i.e. 1, see above, fn. 129. Missing noughts have also been inserted.

210. As before, for acres, roods and perches, abbreviations 'ac', 'r', 'p' used.

211. In the central text 'q' the abbreviation of quondam, meaning formerly, appears in almost every line, and needs to be distinguished from 'q' quarentia in the LH margin.

212. To accommodate margin size, and to avoid confusion, irregular entries in RH acreage/rent columns have been moved to the central text. The insertion of 'Rose' indicates the sale of these lands to Robert Rose; note they are omitted in Henry Creamer's entry for 1637 which follows.

213. Where 'pre' and 'q' compete for space in LH margin, 'q' has been moved to the central text.

		a	r	p
q 7	at the end east of the 6 furlong *q* Longstreth *q* Willyam Guybon /Rose/	0	2	0
	there more east *q* Longstreth *q* Willyam Guybon /Rose/	0	2	0
	there more east and next *q* Longstreth *q* Willyam Guybon /Rose/	0	0	0
	there more east *q* Longstreth *q* Willyam Guybon Robert Rose	0	0	0
q 8	at Oldowne knoll *q* Willyam Rose *q* Willyam Guybon /Rose/	1	1	0
q 8	there more North *q* Thomas Gogney *q* Willyam Guybon /Rose/	1	1	0
q 9	at Stowell Stye *q* Thomas Gogney *q* Willyam Guybon /Rose/	1	1	0
pre 7	/q 3/ at Whipplegate *q* Thomas Orwell *q* Willyam Guybon /Rose/	1	3	0
q 6	at Bungeystile *q* Longstreth *q* Willyam Guybon	3	2	0
q 6	there *q* Orwell *q* Willyam Guybon	3	2	0
	[Sum]²¹⁴	/56	0	10/
pre 8	*q* Thomas Hargate and Edmond Creamer betwixt Henry Lawes			
q 2	and Richard²¹⁵ Bird	1	1	0
q 14	at Overcrowne Crosse *q* Thomas Hargate and Edmond Creamer	0	2	20
q 14	1r and 30p next *q* Thomas Hargate and Edmond Creamer, John Ellgar south *this 1r and 30p now Godfrey Hargate hath*	0	1	0
pre 6	*q* Ralph Hargate and Edmond Creamers with a messuage			
q 12	*q* Brightmeres	2	1	0

[p 16]

		a	r	[p]
pre 5	Henry Creamers bond rents to Sedgford 1637²¹⁶			
q 18	at Mousehide *q* Willyam Guybon an headland	0	1	20
q 19	at Mowsehide *q* Willyam Guybons the first peice of the furlong	0	3	20
q 19	there next *q* Willyam Guybon	0	3	20
q 19	there next *q* Willyam Guybon	0	1	20
q 20	at Wrongeland *q* Willyam Guybon the first peice of the furlong	1	1	0
q 20	next and South *q* Willyam Guybon	3	2	0
q 20	there more South *q* Willyam Guybon	9	0	0
q 21	next Fring Border next Lingsty *q* Willyam Guybon	1	3	0
	at Oldowne knoll a messuage part of 13a *q* Orwell and Martin Smith	12	2	10
	more there *q* Orwell and Martin Smith	2	0	0
	/q 6/ near Bungaystile Gogney and Willyam Guybon	3	2	0
	there next and west *q* Orwell and Willyam Guybon	3	2	0
	at Chappell Crofft *q* Ralph Hargate and Edmond Creamer a messuage	2	1	0

---

214. Sub-totals in LH margin have been moved to RH columns in the same format.

215. Abbreviations for tenants' names have been extended once and then followed as in the text.

216. As before only the facing/odd pages are marked in the text; those for the reverse side have been inserted. In this single example, the perches column has been titled 'di'[midius] signifying half a rood, probably reflecting the later date of the entry, but the entries have all been rationalized to 10, 20, and 30 perches.

		a	r	[p]
	in Eaton *q* Thomas Hargate and Edmond Creamer, Henry Lawes east, Bird west	1	1	0
q 14	at Overcrowne Crosse *q* Hargate and Edmond Creamer	0	2	20
	[Sum]	/43	2	30/
	10 Car[217] Will Guybon to Henry Creamer 2ac 1r q 12 & not the 5r q 2 and but 1r 30p q 14			
	for free rent of 1½r in Heacham feild	0	1	½

[p] 17   Willyam Guybons bond rents to Sedgford 1634

		a	r	[p]
pre 1	at Greengate in 2 pieces *q* \<Burnham\> Allen Clerke *q* Thomas			
q 5	Hargate	2	0	20
q 8	at Greengate an headland *q* Thomas Hargate	1	1	0
q 21	at Hangingwonge *q* John Bird *q* Thomas Hargate	0	3	0
	there more east at Hangingwonge	4	0	0
q 22	at Skotts Croft *q* Thomas Hargate	3	0	20
	there more east *q* Willyam Crisp *q* Thomas Hargate	4	2	0
	there more east called Wards acre *q* John Bird	1	0	0
	there more east *q* Simon Ellgar	5	1	20
q 24	next Skotts yard bounded by itselfe *q* Simon Ellgar	1	1	0
q 25	next West fenne *q* Simon Ellgar	1	3	0
q 26	at the east ende of the 7r next the fenne *q* Simon Ellgar	1	1	0
q 27	next the fenne *q* Ogle *q* Simon Ellgar	1	3	0
pre 2	/q 1/ at \<Linghouse\> Walters Croft *q* Thomas Hargate an headland	1	2	0
	there in exchange for lands in Linghouse *q* Simon Ellgar	1	1	0
q 8	neare Over Jaybert *q* Rust *q* Thomas Hargate	1	0	0
	there more north *q* Folkes *q* Thomas Hargate	3	0	0
	there next an headland *q* John Lawes	1	1	0
q 9	at Heacham gate sometime in 4 pieces *q* Simon Ellgar	9	1	30
	there more West *q* Simon Ellgar at Peter Pitt	3	3	20
q 14	at Ringsted gate *q* Simon Ellgar	1	0	0
q 19	next Hallbottome *q* Thomas Hargate	1	1	0
pre 3	/q 1/ at Docking Way *q* Henry Drake *q* Thomas Hargate	1	3	0
	there more inclosed *q* Thomas Hargate *free 7r } these pay a*	0	0	0
	there more north *q* Thomas Hargate *free 6r } Red Rose*	0	0	0
	there more north *q* John Fox *q* Thomas Hargate	2	1	0
	there more north *q* Thomas Hargate	0	1	0
q 2	neare Heacham gate *q* Thomas Hargate a headland	1	3	0
	there more east *q* Thomas Hargate	1	0	20
q 3	a messauge *q* Robert Chosell *q* Thomas Hargate	0	2	30
	there more east a Messauge *q* Gogney *q* Thomas Hargate	1	3	10

---

217. i.e. Mar 1634–Mar 1635, Regnal years indicate dates of admissions and surrenders.

q 4	at Bishops Croft *q* John Rust *q* Thomas Hargate	1	3	0
	there more east a pightle a hemp land *q* Thomas Hargate	0	2	0
q 8	at nether Heacham gaate *q* John Fokes *q* Thomas Hargate	0	3	0
q 9	at Windes gate *q* John Fokes *q* Thomas Hargate	0	3	20
	there more west *q* John Collen *q* Thomas Hargate	1	3	30
q 11	at Brancaster gate *q* Thomas Hargate	0	2	20
	there more south *q* Thomas Hargate	1	1	20
	there more south at Cleyland *q* Thomas Hargate	1	1	0
	there more south the last piece of the furlong *q* Thomas Hargate	2	2	0
q 12	at Good Acre *q* John Fokes *q* Thomas Hargate	0	2	0
	there more north *q* Thomas Hargate	1	1	0
	there more north *q* Thomas Hargate	1	3	0
	there more north *q* Thomas Hargate	0	1	0
	/79 3 ½/			
[*p 18*]	Sum <79a 3½r, 78a 2r di> [*sub-total*]	76	2	[*p*]
pre 3	/*q 13*/ neare Cheswick an headland *q* Thomas Hargate	1	1	0
	there more next *q* Thomas Hargate	0	2	0
	there next *q* Thomas Hargate	1	3	0
	there next in Cleyland *q* Thomas Hargate	1	1	0
	there more west *q* Thomas Hargate	0	3	0
	there more west *q* Willyam Crisp *q* Thomas Hargate	0	2	0
	there more west *q* Gogney *q* Thomas Hargate	0	2	20
	there more west with a cley pitt in the middest *q* Tho. Hargate	3	0	0
	there more west *q* Thomas Hargate	0	2	20
	there more west *q* Smith *q* Thomas Hargate	1	0	20
	there more west *q* Robert Chosell *q* Thomas Hargate	1	3	0
	there more *q* Thomas Hargate	1	2	0
	there more west *q* John Ellgar *q* Thomas Hargate	1	0	0
q 15	at Goodacre *q* Simon Ellgar an headland	1	1	0
	there next *q* Simon Ellgar	0	1	20
	there next *q* Simon Ellgar	0	1	20
	there next *q* Simon Ellgar	0	2	20
	there next *q* Simon Ellgar	0	2	20
	there next an headland *q* Simon Ellgar	1	1	0
q 16	at Longe Cleyland *q* Thomas Hargate	1	2	0
	there more east *q* Thomas Hargate	2	3	20
	there next *q* Henry Clarke *q* Thomas Hargate	2	3	20
q 18	at Oxeland *q* Thomas Hargate	1	1	20
q 19	at Micklehowe gate *q* Thomas Hargate	0	3	0
q 23	at Ringsted heaves *q* Simon Ellgar	1	2	0
pre 6	in a close of 7ac 2r wherof free 7½r *q* Thomas Hargate 5ac 3r 10p			
q 12	bond	0	1	20
	more part of the same close more west	1	2	0

		1	0	0
more part of the same close with a spong		1	0	0
more part of the same close		1	1	20
more part of the same close with a messuage		1	2	0
	[sub-total]	/36	3	10/

pre 1	/q 25/ at Clowsen Bridg q Lionell Bankes	0	2	20
pre 8	/q 28/ a pightle q Thomas Hargate next Kime Bridg	0	1	0
	there next q Thomas Hargate	0	3	0
pre 1	neare Heacham Way q Edmond Bird q Mr Wallis			
q 6	*3½ by the booke*	0	3	20
q 17	called Tankerd acre q Edmond Bird q Mr Wallis	1	0	0
pre 2	/q 19/ at Hallbottom q Edmond Bird	1	0	0
	[Total] /	121	0	30/
pre 8	part of a decayed messuage q Hargate next 3½r called Colles	0	2	25
q 28	there q Hargate a piece of Marrish next Kime Cawsey /43a or 15p/[218]	0	2	20
pre 6	at Fringe Border a cottage late Willyam Made part of 13a			
q 6	q Orwell	0	2	0

[p] 19
pre 2[219]

	num	fur	[a	r	p]	
Hen Minn	206	5	1	0	0	Ralph Lawes south, Ri Bird north, west upon greengate
[pre] 3	389	6	5	0	0	10p Tho Hargate east, Tho Acres west
Hen Minn	390		0	0	0	South upon Heacham gate
Fra[ncis] Guyb[on]	395	6	1	3	0	Ri Bird east, Tho Hargate west, south upon Heacham gate
Hen Minn	399	7	2	0	0	Ri Bird west, Edw Hargate east, north upon Cheswick
Arnold *Lawes*	416 417	9	1	0	0	Li[onel] Bankes east, Rob Collen east, north upon Brancaster gate
Hen Minn	486	17	0	2	0	Hen Lawes south, Jo Crisp north, east upon Streetgate
Arnold	492	17	0	2	0	10p the Lord south
Fra Guy [pre] 4	575 576	2	1	3	0	The Lord east, Edward Hargate west, south upon Broadgate
Dey now q Alin	594	3 0	2 0	3 0	0 0	Richard Banyard east, Thomas Hargate west, east upon Over Summergate

---

218. Total found by adding the sub-total 36a 3r 10p to the next 6 entries 6a 1r 5p = 43a or 15p.

219. This table contains some innovation with 'fur' for furlong and numbers for each piece which run from 1–1759. The table is not written in Alice's hand and its purpose is not entirely clear.

Fra Guy	622	4	3	1	0	Ri Banyard east, Tho Hargate west, south upon over Sumergate
Arnold	726	11	3	1	0	Thornham Way pertra[n]sit, Jo Crisp west, Fran Guybon east
Fra Guy	626	4	1	0	1	The Lord east & west, south upon Sumergate
Fra Guy	631	5	1	1	0	The Lord east, Jo Crisp west, north upon Brancastergate
Hen Minn	9	5	2	2	0	Parcell of 5ac the Lord south, the residue north,
[pre] 1		0	0	0		east upon greengate
Jo Rose	1138	12	0	1	0	Forera [headland] next Snetsham Border

q Minns 7

Ro Rose	1166	12	1	2	0	There the Lord east & west, south upon
q Fra Guy						Snettisham field
Hen Minn	1171	13	1	0	0	The Lord east & west, north upon Ro Rose
Hen Minn	1345	32	1	0	0	John <Lingey> *Le Strange* north & south, east upon Sherbon way
Ro Rose	1325	31	0	3	0	Ro Lawes south, Jo Ellgar north, west upon
Fra Guy						Maydesty
[Sum]		32	1	0		Sum 136ac 1r 14p[220]
						Lands of Simon Ellgars left out of this admittance
Fra Guy	188	1	1	3	0	with the messuage

[p 20]

<table>
<tr><td>pre 1</td><td>Willyam Guybons free rent to Sedgford 1634</td><td>a</td><td>r</td><td>[p]</td></tr>
<tr><td>q 5</td><td>at Greengate in 2 pieces q Burnham q Bullwer q Thomas Hargate</td><td>3</td><td>0</td><td>0</td></tr>
<tr><td></td><td>there q Henry Drake q Thomas Hargate</td><td>1</td><td>1</td><td>0</td></tr>
<tr><td>q 6</td><td>at Heacham gate q Henry Drake q Thomas Hargate</td><td>0</td><td>3</td><td>20</td></tr>
<tr><td>q 7</td><td>at Cote Stye an headland q Henry Drake q Thomas Hargate</td><td>0</td><td>2</td><td>0</td></tr>
<tr><td></td><td>there more North q Drake q Thomas Hargate</td><td>0</td><td>1</td><td>20</td></tr>
<tr><td>q 9</td><td>neare greengate q Henry Drake q Thomas Hargate</td><td>0</td><td>2</td><td>20</td></tr>
<tr><td>q 10</td><td>neare Kimballdins q Henry Drake q Alowe q Thomas Hargate</td><td>1</td><td>1</td><td>0</td></tr>
<tr><td></td><td>there more south q Drake q Thomas Hargate</td><td>0</td><td>2</td><td>20</td></tr>
<tr><td></td><td>there more south q Drake q Thomas Hargate</td><td>1</td><td>2</td><td>0</td></tr>
<tr><td>q 13</td><td>at Heydownes q Allowe q Thomas Hargate an headland</td><td>0</td><td>2</td><td>0</td></tr>
<tr><td>q 14</td><td>neare Heacham Border q Allowe q Thomas Hargate</td><td>1</td><td>0</td><td>0</td></tr>
<tr><td>q 15</td><td>at Shackland q Alowe q Thomas Hargate</td><td>3</td><td>0</td><td>0</td></tr>
<tr><td>q 21</td><td>at Hanging Wonge q Henry Drake q Thomas Hargate at Charnellhowe</td><td>1</td><td>2</td><td>0</td></tr>
<tr><td>q 27</td><td>/Jo Law/ next West fenne q Henry Drake q Hargate</td><td>0</td><td>0</td><td>0</td></tr>
</table>

---

220. It is not clear what this larger total refers to.

pre 2	/q 6/ at Lambcote with a sponge q Thomas Hargate	1	1	0
q 8	at Over Jaberd an headland q Robert Chosell q Thomas Hargate	1	0	0
q 9	at Heachamgate q Linn q Thomas Hargate 2r – rent 1d	0	0	0
q 7	at Darrell wonge q Thomas Hargate	1	1	0
pre 3	/q 1/ at Docking Way q Thomas Hargate 4a 3½r rent 11¾d	0	0	0
	there q Robert Chosell q Thomas Hargate	2	0	0
q 2	/340/[221] at Heachamgate q Thomas Linne q Thomas Hargate 3r rent 2d	0	0	0
q 3	/343/ neare Heachamgate q Thomas Hargate	1	0	20
q 4	/345/ at Bishops Croft q Linn a Messuage decayed q Thomas Hargate	3	0	20
q 6	/388/ at Millstye q Thomas Hargate	0	3	20
q 8	/393/ at nether Heachamgate q Henry Drake q Thomas Hargate	0	3	0
q 9	/408/ at Windes gate q Thomas Linne q Thomas Hargate	0	3	20
q 12	at Goodacre q Thomas Hargate	0	2	0
	there more north q Thomas Hargate	1	3	0
q 13	neare Cheswick q Thomas Hargate	0	3	0
	there more west q Thomas Hargate	0	0	0
	/461/ at Cley pitt q Linn q Thomas Hargate 2r rent 1d	0	0	0
q 16	at Longe Cley land q Thomas Linn q Thomas Hargate	3	0	20
q 15	at Goodacre q Thomas Hargate	0	3	0
q 18	/493/ at Oxeland q Thomas Hargate called the Legge	0	0	25
	there q Thomas Hargate	0	3	20
q 20	/504/ at West Wonge q Thomas Hargate	1	1	0
q 22	at Ringsted Heaves q Thomas Hargate	0	0	0
pre 6	part of a close of 7a 2r wherof bond 5a 3r 10 p q Thomas Hargate	0	1	20
q 12	there more part of the same close	1	0	0
	there more part of the same close	0	2	0
	Sum	40	0	15

pre 3	/q 1/ <inclosed q Thomas Hargate 1a 3r>
q 1	<there next inclosed>
	/40a 15p/ the 629 piece q 6 n 218 in exchange qr

[p] 21 Willyam Guybons particular free rents to Sedgford Prior[222]

pre 2	a	r	[p]			d	
q 9	0	2	0	at Greengate q Thomas Hargate			
pre 3	4	3	½	/q 1/ neare Castle q Thomas Hargate		11	¾

---

221. Numbers (1–1759) for strips and closes start to appear in the LH margin; they have been moved to the central text to avoid confusion and to maintain the horizontal arrangement of the entry.

222. Alice developed a new system listing acreage details in the central text when columns record rents; note the separate column for halfpennies and farthings.

q 1	3	1	0	*q* Thomas Hargate wherof 7r inclosed. Rent for these a red rose		
q 2	0	3	0	*q* Thomas Hargate	2	0
q 13	0	2	0	/461/ at Cley pitts	1	0
pre 8	0	3	½	/q 28/ in Eaton a messuage *q* Colls, Costen hath ½r rent	1	0

[sub-total] /1s 4¾d/

pre 2	in Westgate Street with the cappitall messuage late Richard
q 1	Birdes conteyning 5r

6 0

Quere for the rent of 7r & 6r nn. 332, 333 /1s 10¾d/

		a	r	[p]
pre 1	Francis Guybons bond rents to Sedgford 1634	a	r	[p]
q 23	3a *q* Simon Ellgar neare greengate	3	0	0
pre 2	/q 1/ at Marlepitt a Messuage *q* Simon Ellgar	1	3	0
pre 3	/q 6/ neare Heacham gate *q* Simon Ellgar *Bird east*	1	3	0
pre 4	/q 2/ neare Broadgate *q* Simon Ellgar	0	3	20
	there more East *q* Simon Ellgar *7r the Lord east Attwood east*	0	3	20
q 4	neare Overseagate *q* Simon Ellgar *Banyard east Lawes west*	3	1	0
	there more east *q* Simon Ellgar *the Lord on both sides*	1	0	20
q 5	at Sweethouse *q* Simond Ellgar *he Lord east Gurling west*	1	1	0
q 6	/662/ neare Brancaster gate *q* Randall Ellgar }*Banyard east*	1	0	0
	/663/ there next *q* Randall Ellgar *q* Henry Clarke }the Lord west*	1	0	0

	7 Car Edmond Ellgar to Francis Guybon junior			
pre 4	/q 6, 662, 663/ the Lord west	2	0	0
[p 22]	20 Hen 8 Robert Ellgar to Ralph Lawes 2a at Smallstyes			

		a	r	[p]
	<Edward Arnolds bond rent to Sedgford 1634>	a	r	[p]
pre 3	/q 9/ <2r at Winesgate *q* Ellgar>[223]	0	2	0
	<there next called Meynes land an headland *q* Ellgar>	0	2	0
	<there *q* Francis Guybon *q* John Lawes>	0	2	0
q 17	<at Hundell an headland *q* Ellgar>	0	2	10
pre 4	/q 11/< at Longland Bottom *q* Simon Ellgar>	3	1	0

/5 1 10p/

[p] 23	John Lawes his bond rents to Sedgford			
pre 1	/q 5/ at greengate *q* Robert Rose *q* Ralph Lawes *q Folkes*	1	0	20
	there more south *q* Ralph Lawe *q Folkes*	2	0	0
	there more south *q* Ralph Lawes *q Folkes*	0	2	20
q 7	neare Heachamgate at Cote Crofte *q Robert Rust*	2	0	12
q 8	neare greengate *q* Ralph Lawes	0	2	0
q 10	neare Kimbaldin *q* Ralph Lawes	0	2	0

---

223. Entry mostly deleted.

		£	s	d
	there more south *q* Ralph Lawes	0	2	20
q 13	at Heydones *q* Ralph Lawes	2	0	0
q 14	neare Heacham Border *q* Robert Hargate *3 Car*	0	3	0
q 17	/96/ at Cote Croft *q* Thomas Hargate *4 Car Jo Cr*	5	0	0
	there called Pikes acre *q* the Pryor	1	0	0
	there *q* Francis Guybon *q* Simon Bloomfield	1	3	0
	there more west *q* Ralph Lawes *sometime in 2 pieces*	1	1	0
106[224]	there next *q* Willyam Banyard *Car 7*	1	3	2
	there next *q* Ralph Lawes	0	2	20
109	there bounded by itselfe *q* Thomas *4 Car* Hargate, *q* John Folkes part of 3s 7d	7	0	0
q 18	at Hanging Mere *q* Tho. Hargate *4 Car 2ac 2½r with 1r free*	2	1	0
q 19	at Heacham Border *q* Ralph Lawes	1	2	0
q 22	at Skottsyard furlong *q* Ralph Lawes	1	3	10
	there more east *q* Ralph Lawes	1	1	20
q 23	at Cote Croft with a messauge inclosed *q* Ralph Lawes	7	0	0
q 23	/154/ there *q* Francis Guybon *q* Lionell Bankes *called the Hermitage*	0	1	20
	there more south *q* Lionell Bankes *q* Francis Guybon	0	1	0
	there next with a messuage *q* Froskhole *q* Lionell Bankes*	4	2	0
	there next *q* Lionell Bankes	3	0	0
q 24	at Millstye *q* Ralph Lawes *q* Godfrey Rust	1	0	0
pre 2	at Caphill an Headland *q* Ralph Lawes	2	1	0
q 5	/210/ there more north *q* Thomas Hargate *4 Car*	3	0	0
	there next *q* Ralph Lawes	0	3	20
113	there *q* Thomas Hargate *q* John Alowe *q* Folkes part of 3s 7d *q* the Prior 4 Car*	0	3	20
114	there next *q* Thomas Hargate *q* John Folkes part of 3s 7d *q* the Prior 4 Car*	1	0	20
pre 1	/q 27/ neare Froskhole *q* Francis Guybon *q* Lionell Bankes	1	1	0
	there more south with the tenement froskhole *q* Francis Guybon *q* Lionell Bankes	1	1	0
	there more South *q* Francis Guybon *q* Lionell Bankes	1	1	0
pre 2	/q 10/ at Green gate *q* Ralph Lawes part of 4a	2	0	0
q 12	at Cheswick *q* Ralph Lawes	0	2	20
	there more west *q* Ralph Lawes	0	2	0
	there more west *q* Ralph Lawes	2	0	0
q 16	neare Hall Bottom *q* Ralph Lawes	0	1	20
q 17	at Darrell Wonge *q* Ralph Lawes	1	0	0
q 19	neare Hall Bottom *q* Ralph Lawes <an Headland with a start> *q* John Rust*	1	2	0

224. Numbers left in LH margin where no confusion with quarentia.

	there more north <an Headland> *q* Ralph Lawes *q* John Rust an			
	Headland	1	0	0
[*p 24*]	Sum [*sub-total*]	72	2	14
pre 3	neare Winesgate *q* Francis Guybon *q* Lionell Bankes *sold to			
q 9	Arnold*225	0	0	0
q 20	at West Wonge *q* Ralph Lawes	1	0	0
	there next more West *q* Ralph Lawes	1	0	0
	there more west *q* Ralph Lawes	0	2	0
q 24	near over Micklehowe gate *q* Ralph Lawes	1	0	0
	[*sub-total*]	/3	2	0/

Sum of bonde land is 76ac or 14p [*rent*] 25s 4¼d

pre 6	for bond rent of 1½r at Oldowne knoll part of 1a 2r *q* Randall	a	r	[*p*]
q 6	Ellgar and Thomas Bassam	0	1	20
q 6	/B Crisp/ there next part of the former 6r *q* Randall Ellgar 7 Car	0	0	0

/28 Hen 8/ Robert Ellgar to Ralph Lawes 5a in divers peices
q Thomas Orwell

9 Car   Francis Guybon to John Lawes on tenement & 12ac 2½r in
grosse <qr the fine> & 2a north upon Heachamgate:226

fur	[a	r	p]
104	17	3	0
154	23	0	1	1
155	23	0	1	0
156	23	4	2	0
157	23	3	0	0
167	27	1	1	0
168	27	1	1	0
169	27	1	1	0
415	9	0	2	0
[*Sum*]	14	0	1

/4 Car/ John Cremer to Jo Lawes 2ac 2½r in one piece neare Oldmill227
/114, 115 free 1½ / Brogg the Lord east, Jo Lawes west, south upon Sir
Hamon Le Strange

---

225. Fewer insertions on the even pages suggest that they might be later entries than the odd facing pages.

226. Alice adapted her new system of columns in the central text even when rents were not recorded in RH columns. Vertical columns were clearly used as an aid to adding up; the written total is 2r out. When this table was converted into continuous text, it demonstrated the difficulty of adding across horizontals.

227. Margins and columns have been removed for notes in the text and where no totals are involved.

/109 & 103/ 7ac in one piece more east of the last piece, John Lawes east
& west, north upon Richard Bird & to Pike acre

/96 &/ 5ac in one piece more east, Hen Minnes west, the way east, abutt
north at the last

/210 &/ 3ac more east, Jo Lawes north, Hen Minnes south, west upon the way

/213, 214 &/ 2ac q in 2 pieces more north of the last, Ri Bird north, Jo Lawes south

/4 Car/ Will Guybon to Robert Rose the cappitall messuage & 3r q Tho
Longstreth 2 Car

/7 Car/ William Banyward to John Lawes

[pre] /1, q 17, 106/ 1ac 3r 2p John Lawes east & west, north upon Tankard acre

7 Car Tho Longstreth of Hich[am] to John Lawes the halfe of ½ part of
a messuage called Julians with 57ac 10 perches Streetgate Way, west Ro
Banyard east, north upon Stowellstye

	John Lawes his free rent to Sedgford 1634	a	r	[p]
[p] 25				
pre 1	/BR/ at Hanging Mere q Ralph Lawes q Briggs *q Strasbrooke			
q 18	holden of Sedgford*	<8	o	o>
	there q Thomas Hargate q John Alowe	o	1	20
q 19	/BRIGS/ at Heacham Border with a pightle on the west ende of Ralph Lawes *6 Eliz*	1	o	o
	/BR inde 7r/ there more east q Ralph Lawes, q Robert Burnham *inde 7r Briggs 6 Eliz*	4	o	o
q 20	/BR/ at Hanging Wonge q Ralph Lawes *q Strasbrooke 1a holden of Sedgford*	o	o	o
q 21	/BR/ the last piece of the furlong bounded by itselfe q Ralph Lawes *q Alowe 6 Eliz*	2	2	o
q 27	neare West fenne q Willyam Guybon q Henry Drake	o	2	o
pre 2	/q 5/ neare Caphill q Thomas Hargate, q Alowe Jo Cremer	o	3	20
	Sum <18a 1r – 18¼d>	9	1	o
pre 1	/BR/ 2a free neare Greengate q Ralph Lawes particular rent 2d			
q 12	which is as the other free lands be rated q Burnham			
	the sum of John Lawes his free lands holden of the Pryor	11	1	10

9 Car Francis Guybon to John Lawes: 12ac 2r 20p with the
tennement Froskhole & to 2ac north upon Heachamgate

	John Lawes his free rents of lands holden of Sedgford Stranges			d	
pre 1					
q 18	8	o	o	at Hanging Mere q Strasbrooks q Brigges *6 Eliz*	4 ½
q 20	1	o	o	at Hanging Wonge q Strasbrooke q Briggs *6 Eliz*	o ½
q 23	4	o	o	inclosed in his homestead with a messuage decayed next the Hermitage	4 o
				Sum	9 o

[*p 26*]

		a	r	[*p*]
pre 1	Mr Waters his land bond of Sedgford			
q 11	neare Heachamgate an headland *q* Phillip Loads and Thomas Hill	1	1	0
pre 2	in Westgate <a messuage &> Crofft *q* Christopher Powly and			
q 1	Thomas Trevett abut north upon Heachamgate	1	1	0
q 1	in Westgate Street one <messuage with a> crofft *John Bird* *q* <Powly> *Mr Loads* and Laycock and Thomas Hill, Henry Minnes west, 2r free east, abut north upon Heachamgate, south upon Westgate	1	1	0
q 12	next Greengate *q* Phillip Loads and Laycock & Hill, <the Lord> east, Greengate Way west	0	2	0
q 15	neare Hall Bottom *q* Phillip Loades and Laycock and Hill, the Lord north	0	3	0
q 18	near Hall Botton *q* Phillip Loades and Laycock and Hill, Henry Minnes north	0	2	0
q 19	near Ringsted Way *q* Phillip Loads and Laycock and Hill, late Bird north	3	0	0

Sum bond 8ac 2r Rent 2s 10d[228]

q 1	2r with a messuage in Westgate *q* Mr Powly *John Bird* and Thomas Trevett abutt south upon Westgate north upon his bond. Rent 1d free

Christopher Powly clerke his land bond of Sedgford

		a	r	[*p*]
pre 2	in Westgate *q* John Folkes abut north upon Heachamgate south			
q 1	upon Richard Bankes	1	0	0
q 1	next and west *q* John Folkes and Rackey a messuage and crofft late Richard Bird east, abut south upon Westgate, north upon Heachamgate	1	3	0

Sum 2ac 3r – 11d Writt[229]

		a	r	[*p*]
	[*p 28*] <Christopher Pooly Clarke his bond rents to Sedgford 1634>[230]			
pre 1	at Our Ladyes Well called the Vickerage *q* Thomas Hargate			
q 27	W[*aters*]	1	0	20
	there more south called the Bond Close *q* John Alowe particular rent 4s W[*aters*]	2	0	0
pre 2	/q 1/ at Westage *q* Thomas Trevett *Mr Waters*	1	1	0

---

228. When 'sum' includes information on rent the format has been retained in its entirety.

229. Page 27 is blank.

230. On page 28 the two entries for Powly and Phillip Loades have been crossed and superseded by the entries on page 26, but they are of interest as they show the succession of clerks' holdings in Sedgeford.

	a	r	[p]
there more east a croft *q* John Folkes	I	o	o
there more east a croft *q* John Folkes	I	3	o
there a messuage with a croft *q* Thomas Trevett free 2r – Id *Mr Waters*			

Sum beside particular rent 5ac ½r – 20½d – 5s 9d

42 Eliz Mr Powly of Rackey 1ac and Messuage conteyning 2r & a
          crofft adjoining conteyning 7r>

		a	r	[p]
	<Phyllip Loades Clerke his bond rent to Sedgford 1634>			
pre I	*now Mr Waters*			
q II	/n 71/ neare Heachamgate an headland *q* Thomas Hill	I	I	o
pre 2	/q I/ in Westgate street a messuage with a croft *q* John Hendry	I	3	o
q 12	/n 269/ near Greengate *q* Thomas Hill	o	2	o
q 15	/n 284/ neare Hall Bottom *q* <Thomas Hill> *Jo Hendry*	o	3	o
q 18	/n 316/ near Hall Botton *q* John Hendry	o	2	o
q 19	/n 316/ near Ringsted Way *q* John Hendry	3	o	o
	Sum 7a 3r all bond			
pre 12	at Westgate *q* Thomas Trevett and Mr Powly			
q I	there with a messuage and crofft *q* Thomas Trevett 2r free Id >	I	I	o

		a	r	[p]
[p] 29	Robert Rose his bond rent to Sedgford 1634			
pre 5	/893/ at Berneswond *q* John Almans *Framingham east Will			
q 15	Banyard west 10 Jac*	I	I	o
q 18	there more west, at Mousehyde	I	I	o
	there next *q* Thomas Gogney part of Iac	o	2	20
q 19	at Mouse hide purchased of Roger Le Strange	o	I	20
	there next *q* Simon Smith	2	I	o
	there next *q* Brock	o	2	o
	there next Margery Clerkes	o	2	o
	there next Lingsty *q* Brock	o	2	o
	there more north *q* Thomas Longstreth	2	o	o
	/6ac Ir/²³¹			
q 20	at <Wrongland> *Greengate* *q* Willyam Crisp *q* Edmond Smith, *west upon Streetgate 10 Jac*	6	o	o
pre 6	/q 2/ at Streetgate *q* Edmond Smith}	I	3	o
	there more west *q* Thomas Orwell & Ed Smith }*10 Jac*	o	I	10
	there next *q* Willyam Crisp & Ed Smith }	2	o	o
q 3	at Oldownes *q* Edmond Smith *Fring way south Ra Hargate north east upon Gungore 10 Jac*	I	3	20
	there more north *q* Ralph Hargate *part 41a 2r 30p 7 Jac*	I	3	20

---

231. Total for the previous six entries (bracketted in the original text).

4 Car[232] there more north *q* Ralph Hargate *part 41a 7 Jac*	2	3	0
q 4 at Shortland *q* John Ellgar *q* Thomas Longstreth **q Will Guybon Wrongate**	3	2	0
q 5 /4 *Car*/ near Shortland a close *q* Edmond Smith **q Will Guybon**	2	0	0
q 6 at Oldbourne knoll *q* Edmond Smith	3	0	0
4 Car there more west 2 messuages**q Will Guybon** with 2 crofts /6a or di/ adjoining *q* Thomas Longstreth **part of 9a ½r**	7	1	0
there more west at Longlands *q* Richard Gogney *q* Orwell *q* Thomas Longstreth	7	2	0
there next *q* Thomas Longstreth	2	2	0
4 Car there more west next the path leading from Southgate to Eastgate **q Will Guybon**	4	1	0
there more west next Barkers mere	8	1	0
q 7 next Oldowneknoll *q* Thomas Orwell		3	20
there next 2r and 6r *q* Thomas Longstreth *this should be before the last 3½r*	2	0	0
there more *q* Collen *this Robert Collen to Ed Hargate 44 Eliz*	0	1	0
q 9 at the ende of the last furlong *q* Thomas Longstreth	0	3	10
there more south *q* Thomas Longstreth	0	2	20
/17/[233] there next *q* Thomas Longstreth	0	2	20
there more south *q* Thomas Longstreth	0	3	20
/18/ there more south *q* Thomas Orwell	1	0	0
q 10 /14/ at Stowell Stye *q* John Longstreth	3	1	0
/15/ there more west *q* John Ellgar **q Ralph Hargate part 41ac 7 Ja**	1	0	0
/16/ there more west *q* John Ellgar, *q* Ra Hargate part 41ac 7 Jac*	1	3	0
there more west *q* formerly in 3 pieces *q* John Longstreth	2	2	0
pre 7 /q 3/ at Fringhowe *q* Edmond Smith	1	1	0
there more north *q* Thomas Longstreth	1	2	0
there more north *q* Highmere *q* Willyam Roses	1	1	0
q 4 at gatewonge *q* Edmond Smith	2	0	0
there more *q* Godfrey Hargate *at Gate Wong under Hanging Mere part of 41ac 7 Jac*	3	3	0
4 Car there more west *q* Thomas Longstreths *Will Guybon*	1	0	0
Sum [*sub-total*]	90	1	20

---

232. Alice sometimes included a date in the LH margin, usually it superseded an earlier date in the central text; this format has been retained where it does not compete with other marginal entries.

233. These numbers in precincts 6, 7, do not relate to the map and may refer to an older survey.

[p 30]

pre 7	Robert Rose his bond rent [continued]	a	r	[p]
q 4	/4 Carl/ at gatewonge q Thomas Longstreth *q Will Guybon*	1	0	0
	/4 Carl/ there q Edmond Smith *q Will Guybon*	5	0	0
q 5	at greenhill a headland q Edmond Smith	1	1	0
	there more south q Thomas Lawes *an Headland*	2	0	0
q 6	at Bungeysty q Edmond Smith	1	2	30
	there more west q Willyam Rose	4	0	0
	there more west an headland q Ralph Hargate *part of 41a 7 Jac*	1	0	0
q 7	at Barblehowe q Edmond Smith	4	1	30
	there more south q Edmond Smith	0	1	20
	there next an headland q Willyam Rose	3	2	20
	there next called Checkerland q Thomas Brocks	0	1	0
q 8	at Hanging hill q Willyam Rose	1	0	0
q 11	/13/ at Cliprowe q Godfrey Hargate	3	0	0
	/12/ the more west an headland Cliprowe q Orwell q Willyam			
	Rose next Snetsham Bordure	5	0	0
q 12	/John 1128/ at Well Hill q Framingham *the Lord east*	0	0	20
	there next q Willyam Akers q Orwell	0	1	20
	there next q Willyam Rose	0	2	0
	there more west q Thomas Longstreth	1	0	0
4 Car	there next q Thomas Longstreth *q Will Guybn 4 Car*	1	0	0
4 Car	/10/ there more west q Thomas Longstreth *q Will Guybon			
	4 Car*	1	0	20
	there next q Thomas Longstreth	3	1	0
4 Car	/11/ there more west q Thomas Longstreth *q Will Guybon*	3	0	20
4 Car	/12/ there more west q Thomas Longstreth *q Will Guybon*	0	2	20
	/13/ there more west q Thomas Longstreth	1	0	0
	there more west q Godfrey Hargate	1	0	0
	there more west q <Willyam Rose> *Godfrey Hargate*	0	2	0
	there more west at Corpinhouse q Godfrey Hargate	0	1	0
	there next part of 6r q Willyam Rose	0	1	0
1163	there next <the other part of the 6r> q Thomas Longstreth	1	1	0
	there more west q Thomas Longstreth	1	1	0
q 13	at Westmere q Thomas Longstreth	1	1	0
q 14	at Westbarblehowe an headland q Thomas Longstreth	1	0	0
q 14	/John 1184/ there more south q Godfrey Hargate	2	0	0
q 14	/John 1185/ there q Frammingham	2	0	0
q 15	/John 1196/ at Wellhill *folpitt* q Frammingham *the Lord north*	1	0	20
q 16	at the south end of Wellhill q Willyam Rose q Godfrey Hargate	0	3	20
q 17	/15/ at Burdell q Godfrey Hargate	2	0	0
	there more north q Thomas Longstreth	1	0	20
	/16/ there next q Willyam Akers q Willyam Rose	2	1	0

		a	r	[p]
q 18	/Jo 1222/ there next q Willyam Akers at Eastbarblehowe	1	1	0
	/John Ro[se] 1223/ there next q Willyam Akers *q George Framingham at Longhow Ro Rose east*	1	1	0
q 19	/Jo 1226/ at \<Longhowe\> *East Barblehow* q Godfrey Hargates *Framingham Jo Ellgar south, Rose north*	0	1	30
	there next q Thomas Longstreth	0	1	30
q 20	at Mickle\<howe\> *wong* called Checkerland q Thomas Brocks	0	3	20
	/5/ there next q Willyam Rose	1	2	0
	/6/ there next more west q Willyam Rose	1	2	0
	Sum [sub-total]	71	0	30

		a	r	[p]
[p] 31	Robert Rose his bond rent [continued]			
pre 7	/4 Car, 19/ at west Barblehowe q Simon Ellgar part of 6a 3r			
q 21	*q Will Guybon*	2	2	0
q 22	/18/ at Titlehouse q Thomas Longstreth	0	2	20
q 23	at Overcawdell q Willyam Rose *11a 1r*	11	2	0
	there more east q Thomas Lawes	2	1	0
q 24	at nethercawdell q Edmond Smith	3	2	0
	/5/ there more west q John Akers q Thomas Hargate *7 Jac*	3	3	0
	/3/ there next at Lampitt Wonge	1	1	0
q 25	at Lampland an headland q Thomas Lawes	0	3	20
q 26	at Redhill q John Akers q Thomas Brocks *q Will Guybon*	3	0	0
4 Car	/9/ there next q Thomas Brock, q Will Guybon	1	0	0
	/10/ there more south an headland q Willyam Rose *Jo Ellgar north*	0	3	20
q 27	/2/ at Lampit Wonge q Willyam Rose	3	2	0
	there more west with a messuage q Simon Smith q Willyam Rose	1	0	0
q 28	/8/ at Winches Lane with a messuage next Chapmans Stye			
4 Car	q Thomas Brocks *q Will Guybon*	4	3	0
	there more west a messuage q Willyam Rose sometime in divers peices	3	1	0
q 30	/17/ at Woolfesdele q Willyam Akers	2	2	0
	there more south an headland q Thomas Hargate *7 Jac*	2	2	0
q 31	/14/ at Tokesbye q Thomas Longstreth	1	2	0
	there more north q Thomas Longstreth	1		20
q 12	neare west meare q Francis Guybon*} 9 Car these bought*	1	2	0
q 31	at Tokestye q Francis Guybon *} 9 Car Will Guybon 4 Car*	0	3	0
	Sum [sub-total]	55	1	20
	the whole sum of bond land is 216a 3r 30p at 4d – £3 12 3¾d			

		a	r	[p]
pre 5	/1635/ an headland at Olde Downe knoll q Martin Smith and			
q 14	Stone *Gurling q Crisp north*	2	0	0

q 15	/888/ at Leakeland q Gogney and Martin Smith Framlingham on both sides	2	2	0
q 21	/937/ next Fring Border q Willyam Acres, Will Guybon and Martin Smith *Rose north Fring field south west on Peders Way*	5	0	0
pre 6	/q 6/ at Olde Downe knoll q Longstreth and Martin Smith	0	2	0
q 7	/988/ in 3 pieces q Thomas Orwell and Martin Smith next Robert Attewood West	2	0	0
q 8	/989/ at Olde Downe knoll q Willyam Rose and Martin Smith *Ed Hargate south upon Ped[dars Way]*	1	1	0
q 8	next and north q Thomas Gogney and Martin Smith *Rob Banyard north south*	1	1	0
q 9	at Stowell Stye q Thomas Gogney and Martin Smith *Rob Collen north*	1	1	0
pre 7	at Whipplegate q Thomas Orwell and Martin Smith, Willyam			
q 3	Banyard north	1	3	0
	[Sum]	/17	2	0/

q 12	/1138/ John Rose for bond rent q Henry Mimes at Well Hill east upon Robert Rose 8 Car	0	1	0
9 Car	Robert Rose to Robert Rose his sonne and Ellen Riches all the lands X thus crossed with the number in the coppy sett upon them as they are disorderly taken up and some errors:			

[p 32] Rust Land				Chosells Land			
604	1	0	0				
725	1	3	0				
1001	0	1	0				
1012	1	3	0	548	0	2	0
1015	0	2	0	724	2	2	0
[Sum]	5ac 1r of Rusts			3ac of Chosells			

6 Ja	John Crisp is admitted to all following but a tent[ement] & a close called Wesenham			
567	1	0	1	q 2 precinct 4
	5	0	0	in 5 pieces q John Rust /5a 1r/
	3	1	0	in 3 pieces q John Chosell /but 3a/
	2	3	0	in 2 pieces q John Terror 20 Eliz
489	1	1	1	25 perches q 17 precinct 3[234]
554	1	0	0	q Thomas Mason & Brock q 1 precinct 4
564	2	1	0	there an headland q Gogney – this Bartle Crisp
815	1	3	0	q 3 precinct 5 q Thomas Brock & Wesenham now Ro Banyard 21 Eliz

---

234. Note 25 perches in column.

883	5	0	0	in one piece q Will Banyard it is but 4a 3r 10p 43 Eliz
364	1	3	0	in 2 pieces q 4 pre 3 q Randall Ellgar 44 Eliz
[Sum]	25	1	25p	

Mr Gurling hath as followeth besides lands not sett out:

567	1	0	1	
	5	1	0	of Jone Rusts
	3	0	0	in 2 pieces of John Chosells
489	1	2	0	
554	1	0	0	q Brocks
883	4	3	0	10p q Will Banyards
369	1	3	0	q Randall Ellgar
[Sum]	18	1	30	

4 Car Nicholas Dunn & Sarah daughter of John Crisp to Elizabeth
       Gurling all their land tenements in Sedgford videll 57a 2r 35p

		a	r	[p]
pre 5	Robert Rose his free rent to Sedgford 1634			
q 18	at Mousehide q Thomas Longstreth *917*	0	1	30
q 19	at Mousehide q Thomas Longstreth *924*	0	1	20
pre 6	7ac next Pedders Way q Ralph Hargate called Gunnymore			
q 1	particular rent 2s	7	0	0
	4 Car Robert Rose doth fealty for this 7r by the rent of 7d			
	[Sum]	/7	3	10/

		a	r	[p]
[p] 33	Mr Gurling Clerke for his bond rents to Sedgford			
pre 3	/365/ at Greengate bounded by it selfe q John Crisp *q Ra Ellgar			
q 4	to Jo Crisp 44 Eliz*	1	3	0
q 5	at Fricklesgate q John Crisp *North upon the Lord 378*	0	1	20
q 6	at Northgate q John Crisp*Will Banyard west north upon Bettsmere 385*	0	2	0
q 9	at <Willd>Widdersgate q Thomas Hargate *& Will Guybon forera next Brancast[er] 420*	1	1	0
q 10	a messuage with a croft *q Willyam Guybon* at Maynes Close <with a messuage> *q Robert Hargate 421*	0	2	0
	there more *next &* north q Robert Hargate *q Will Guybon 422*	1	1	0
	there next q Willyam Guybon *q Orwell & Hargate 423*	0	3	0
	there more north an headland q John Crisp *425*	0	3	0
	there <more> *next &* north q John Crisp *an headland next Streetgate Way east 426*	3	0	0
q 17	at Hundell q John Crisp *the Lord south 489*	1	2	0
q 18	at Exland q John Crisp *the Lord west 499*	1	1	20
q 19	neare Michill Hondgate q John Crisp *the Lord west 519*	3	2	0

q 20	at Over furlong *q* John Crisp *the Lord east Will Guybon west			
	526*	2	1	0
pre 4	at Brodgate *q* John Crisp *q* John Chosell the Lord on both sides			
q 1	548*	0	2	0
	there more north a messuage *q* John Crisp *552*	2	1	20
	there more north a messuage with a croft *q* John Crisp *next the			
	Comon Path north 553*	4	0	30
	there next with a croft *q* John Crisp *& Brock next the Comon			
	Path south 554*	1	0	0
q 2	/567/ neare Knattington greene *q* John Crisp *6 Jac the Lord west			
	Jo Ellgar east 567*	1	0	½
	there more east *q* John Crisp *q* Henry Clarke Ro Banyard east			
	570*	1	3	0
	there more east *q* John Crisp *the Lord on both sides 578*	0	3	20
q 3	neare Sedgford Common *q* John Crisp *the Lord west 597*	1	0	0
	/604/ there more west *q* John Crisp *q* John Rust Ric Banyard			
	east*	1	0	0
q 4	at Over Summergate *q* Willyam Guybon *the Lord east south			
	upon oversumerg 618*	1	1	20
q 5	at Sommerfeild Border *q* <Will Guybon> *Jo Crisp* <the Lord			
	east Hen Lawes west> * Francis Guybon east 632*	0	3	0
	there more west *q* John Crisp *633 *q* Finches*	1	0	0
	there next *q* John Crisp *634 Robert Banyard west 634*	1	1	0
5 Car	/641/ there more west *q* Simon Ellgar *Will Guybon Ro Bany			
	east Hen Lawes west 641*	2	0	14
5 Car	/643/ there more west *q* Simon Ellgar *q* Willyam Guybon at			
	Nettlebush *the Lord east Hen Lawes west*	0	3	30
	there more west *q* John Crisp* Ro Banyard west north upon the			
	Lord 644*	0	3	0
q 7	<there more> *at Gebdele bottom* north *q* Willyam Guybon *			
5 Car	Ro Banyard south & north 679*	3	0	0
5 Car	there more north *q* Willyam Guybon, *Henry Lawes south 685*	0	1	0
	there more north *q* Willyam Guybon *Robert Banyard north			
	686*	1	1	0
5 Car	there more north *q* Willyam Guybon *the Lord north 688*	2	1	0
5 Car	there more north *q* Willyam Guybon *the Lord north Ro			
	Banyard south 692*	0	3	20
q 9	neare Streetgate *q* Willyam Guybon *the Lord east north upon			
	the Lord 698*	3	0	0
q 10	at Highmere *q* John Crisp *the Lord west 706*	3	1	0
q 11	at Longeland *q* John Crisp *q* John Chosell, <the Lord> Richard			
	Banyard west 724*	2	2	0
Arnold	there next *q* John Crisp *q* Jone Rust late Simon Ellgar east 725*	1	3	0

		a	r	p
	there more east *q* Francis Guybon	3	0	0
5 Car	there next at Highmere *q* Francis Guybon *& Hargate Arnold next Hyghmere east 727*	3	0	0
[p 34]	[Sub-total]	60	1	4
pre 4		a	r	[p]
q 24	/5 Car/ at Jebdelehill *q* Willyam Guybon *the Lord east & west 765*	0	3	0
pre 5 q 1	at Summergate *q* <Robert Banyard> *Longstreth* *q* Willyam Guybon *the Lord west 787*	2	2	0
	there more west *q* John Crisp*the Lord east, Ro Banyard west 789*	1	0	0
	there more west *q* John Crisp *Anthony Dey late Acres east 792*	0	3	0
	there more west *q* Thomas Longstreth *q* Willyam Guybon *the Lord east 795*	0	2	10
	there next *q* Thomas Longstreth *q* Willyam Guybon *796*	6	0	30
	there more west *q* Willyam Guybon *q* Longstreth 797*	0	2	0
	there next *q* Thomas Longstreth *q* Willyam Guybon *798*	1	1	0
	there more west *q* Willyam Guybon *q* Longstreth 799*	1	2	0
	there next *q* Willyam Guybon *q* Longstreth Hen Lawes west 800*	0	2	0
q 5	/5 Car/ at Smallstyes *q* Willyam Guybon* the Lord east, Ro Attwood west 831*	2	3	20
q 11	/5 Car/ neare Podingland *q* Willyam Guybon * Ri Banyard east and west 843*	1	1	0
	there more west *q* John Crisp *abutt north upon an headland *q* Banyard 851*	1	1	0
q 13	at Bromyarde *q* John Crisp, *the Lord east Strange west 870*	2	0	0
	there more west *q* Willyam Guybon *the Lord on both sides 876*	2	3	0
q 14	at Stowellstye *q* John Crisp,*and Willyam Banyard and Ro Rose on both sides 883*	4	3	10
q 15	neare Streetgate *q* John Crisp,*Will Banyard on both sides 898*	2	0	0
6 pre q 8	next Stowell *q* John Crisp <and> *Jo Rust* <Willyam> *Rob Banyard south next Stowell Stye north 1001* /Rust/	0	1	0
q 10	neare Stowell Stie *q* John Crisp *& Jo Rust, Ro Rose east, south upon Stowell Stye 1012* /Rust/	1	3	0
	there more west *q* John Crisp *& Rust, Robert Attewood late Banyard 1015* /Rust/	0	2	0
	[Sub-total]	/35	0	0/

Sum <98a > 95a 1r 4p at 4d

pre 4 q 4	South upon Over Summergate *q* Richard Bird and Adler Billard an headland	1	1	0

/608, 609/ there next *q* Richard Byrd and Rob Pepper sometime in 2 pieces Robert Banyard east abut south upon oversumergate both ... 6 1 0

4 Car Nicholas Dunn to Willyam Gurling 57a 2r 35p

5 Car *qv* the roll for Will Guybon to Willyam Guybon

/601/ Mr Gurling for free rent of 1r in the 4 precinct and the 3 furlong neare Sedgford Common *q* John Crisp[235] ... 0 1 qr

3 pre

q 22 */540/* at Ringstead Heaves *q* Thomas Hargate and Willyam Guybon ... 1 1 1qr

[*p*] 35

		a	r	[*p*]
pre 1	Robert Attewood for bond rent to Sedgford 1634			
q 10	at Kembalding *q* Willyam Banyard *q* Edward Hargate **q* Chosell*	1	0	0
2 pre	*/q 6/* at Lampit *q* John Bird *q* Edward Hargate	1	1	0
	there *q* John Bird *q* Edward Hargate **q* Folke part of 3s 7d*		3	0
	there next more east *q* John Bird *q* Edward Hargate	1	2	0
q 9	neare greengate *q* John Bird *q* Edward Hargate	3	2	0
3 pre	neare Bishops Croft *q* Edward Hargate called Lowtes longe piece			
q 4	part of 5r **q* Clerke Ri Ban 1 rod*	1	0	0
	/347, 348/ there more east *q* Edward Hargate **part of 3a 3r Ri Bankes 3r *q* Clerk*	3	0	0
	/350/ there more east *q* Willyam Banyard *q* Edward Hargate **Chosell*	1	1	0
	/360/ there more east *q* Willyam Banyard *q* Edward Hargate, Chosell	2	3	0
q 7	*/400/* neare good acre *q* Willyam Banyard *q* Edward Hargate **Chosell*	3	0	0
	/405/ there most east called Good acre *q* Willyam Banyard *q* Edward Hargate **Chosell a headland*	1	0	0
q 9	*/414/* neare Winesgate *q* Willyam Banyard *q* Edward Hargate **q* Jo Crisp of Eaton & Ro Chosell*	2	2	0
q 13	neare Cheswick *q* Willyam Banyard *q* Edward Hargate **& Godfre Manning *	1	1	30
q 16	at Longe Cleyland *q* Willyam Banyard *q* Edward Hargate **Chosell*	1	2	0
pre 4	*/q 1/* at Broadgate *q* John Bird *q* Edward Hargate	2	1	0
	/557/ there next *q* John Bird *q* Edward Hargate	3	1	0
q 13	neare Jebdelebottome *q* John Bird *q* Edward Hargate	0	3	0
pre 5	*/q 2/* neare Pedders Way *q* John Bird *q* Edward Hargate	4	2	0
	/411/ there next *q* Willyam Banyard *q* Edward Hargate **Godfre Manning*	4	2	0

235. The reference 'qr' in the perches column probably means ¼ rod or 10 perches.

q 11	neare Smallstyes *q* Thomas Longstreth *q* Edward Hargate * 1 Ja 6r 30p*	2	0	0
	there next *q* Willyam Banyard *q* Edward Hargate	1	2	0
q 12	near Stowell Stye *q* John Bird *q* Edward Hargate	2	2	10
860	there more east *q* Thomas Longstreth *q* Edward Hargate *1 Jac*	3	0	0
861	there next *q* Willyam Banyard *q* Edward Hargate	4	2	10
	there more east *q* Thomas Longstreth *q* Edward Hargate *1 Jac*	1	0	10
	there more east *q* Thomas Longstreth *q* Edward Hargate *1 Jac*	2	1	0
	there next *q* John Bird *q* Edward Hargate		3	14
q 16	next Fring Border *q* Thomas Longstreth *q* Edward Hargate *16*	2	1	0
pre 6	near Oldowne knoll *q* Willyam Banyard *q* Edward Hargate			
q 7	*q Manning & Beale*	2	0	0
q 8	at Oldowne knoll *q* Willyam Banyard *q* Edward Hargate *q Beales*	2	0	20
	there more north *q* Robert Collen *q* Edward Hargate *44 Eliz*	3	1	20
q 10	neare Streetgate *q* Willyam Banyard *q* Edward Hargate *q Ni Smith*	1	0	0
	there *q* Willyam Banyard *q* Edward Hargate *Chosell*	0	2	0
	there more *q* Willyam Banyard *q* Edward Hargate <at Brock yard> *Chosell 42 Eliz *	5	0	0
	there more west *q* Thomas Drake *q* Edward Hargate *q Ellgar 44 Eliz*	1	1	0
	there an headland *q* Thomas Brock *q* Edward Hargate *& Will Banyard*	1	1	0
q 11	neare Chappell Croft *q* Thomas Brock *q* Edward Hargate *Will Banyard*	3	1	0
q 12	at Chappell Croft *q* Will Banyard *q* Edward Hargate *q Orwell*	1	2	0

there should be 34a of Will Banyard 42 Eliz beside marked 0

Sum 82ac 2r wanting a perch at 4d it is but 82

[*p 36*]

44 Eliz	Robert Collen to Edward Hargate 1r n 995 & 3a 1r n 997 this 1r Robert Rose hath qr [*query*] how *Rober[t]*
42 Eliz	Will Banyard to Ed Hargate 43a 1r 30p *videl* to 34 parcell of 40c 3r 30p parcel of 49a 3r 30p *q* Will et Jane Banyard 7 Eliz
347 & 348	4ac parcell of a messuage & 5a *q* Will Banyard & Ri Clerke 31 Eliz & to
1033 & 1037	4a 2r parcell of 8a 2r in divers pieces with a messuage *q* Will Banyard & Tho Brock 33 Eliz
42 Eliz	Will Banyard took up 40a 3r 30 p and 4a or 0p *q* Clarke & 4a 2r *q* Collen
42 Eliz	he sold to John Crisp 5ac and to Ro Hancell 1a. Remayne 34a 3r 30p for the death of Jone Banyard between 1 & 27 of Eliz

					[a	r	p]
1 Jac		Richard Bird to Edward Hargate 21ac 2r in grosse					
Bond	Robert Attewood hath of Willyam Banyards q Chosells				37	0	1
	he hath of Willyman Banyards and Richard Clerkes				4	0	0
	of Willyam Banyards and Thomas Brocks				4	2	0
	of Robert Collens 44 Eliz				3	1	1
	of Randall Ellgar q Drake *44 Eliz*				1	1	0
	of John Birds				21	0	19
	of Longstreths *taken up 10ac 40p 1 Jac*				10	2	10

Sum 82ac – want 1 perch

Robert Attewoods admittance in the next lease is to 76ac 2r 30p

	a	r	[p]			s	d
pre 3				Robert Attewoods free rents to Sedgfords			
q 7	1	1	0	/401/ neare Goodacre q Willyam Banyard *Chosell*			
				q Edward Hargate: particular		0	8	0
q 13	1	1	0	/448/ neare Cheswick q Willyam Banyard *Chosell*			
				at Cleyland		0	4	0
pre 6	0	3	½	neare Streetgate q Willyam Banyard *Chosell*			
q 10				q Edward Hargate *1017*		0	2	¾
	3	2	0	/1021,1026/ there more west q Willyam Banyard			
				Chosell q Robert Chosell *1022*		0	5	0
	0	3	½	10p /1029/ there q Willyam Banyard *Chosell*			
				q Edward Hargate *1025*		0	2	0
pre 5	0	3	0	neare Stowell Stye q Willyam Banyard *Chosell*			
q 12				q Edward Hargate *858*		0	1	0
pre 6	3	1	0	at Chappell Croft q Willyam Banyard *Messuage			
q 12				Chosell* q Edward Hargate *1046*		0	11	0
Sum	11ac 3r 10p					2	9	¾

				a	r	[p]
pre 4						
q 2	neare Broadgate q Willyam Banyard *Chosell* q Edward					
	Hargate			0	3	20
	/574, 583/ there more east q Willyam Banyard *Chosell*					
	q Edward Hargate *called Greenhow dele*			0	3	20
pre 5	/786/ neare Summergate q Willyam Banyard *Chosell rent*					
q 4	q Edward Hargate			0	2	0
pre 5	at Smallsties q Willyam Banyard q Edward Hargate *866, 830					
q 5	not Chosell*			0	3	20
pre 5	/867/ neare Stowellstie q Willyam Banyard *Chosell* q Edward					
q 12	Hargate *866*			0	3	20
pre 6	neare Streetgate q Willyam Banyard *Chosell* q Edward					
q 10	Hargate *1035*			1	0	30
q 12	at Chappell croft q Willyam Banyard *Chosell* q Edward					
	Hargate *1045*			1	0	20
	/3s 4d short 18d/ Sum 6ac 1r 10p at 1d – 6¼d					

1–2	Robert Chosell dyed sole seazed of one messuage & certayne free			
Mary	land to it belong by the rent of 4s 10d and that Jone the wife of			
	Will Banyard sole heyre of Robert Chosell payeth the release of			
1 Eliz	4s 10d Jone the wife of Will Banyard doth fealty for the same			

		a	r	[p]
[p] 37	Henry Lawes his heyres their bond rent to Sedgford			
pre 3	neare Bishops Croft q Thomas Hargate *with a messuage Acres			
q 4	east Bulliman west*	2	0	0
	there more east q Henry Clerke *Banyard east, Rob Atwood west*	4	0	0
	there more east q Henry Clerke, *an headland millway north, west upon Cranes croft*	1	3	0
q 6	neare Heachamgate q Bullwer q Thomas Brock *his owne east, Mr Gurling west*	1	2	0
q 7	neare Good acre q Fokes q Hargate *Ro Banyard west, Rob Atwood east*	2	1	0
q 9	at Winesgate q Nicholas Smith, *called Meaners lands W. Guybon east < his owne west>*	1	3	0
	there more west q John Ellgar *called Meaners lands Atwood west*	0	3	0
q 17	at Hundele the length of 2 furlongs *q John Brock H. Mims north*	0	2	0
q 18	at Exland q Thomas Brock *the Lord east and west*	0	3	20
q 19	a peice called Westwong q John Brock *neare Ringstedgate the Lord east, Mr Gurlin west*	2	0	0
pre 4	neare Broadgate q Thomas Brock *Mr Gurlin south, Attwood north*			
q 1		6	2	20
q 3	neare Sedgford Common q Thomas Brock * the Lord east, Mims west*	2	1	0
q 4	neare Over Summergate q John Brock q Thomas Hargate, at Nettlebush *W Guybon east, the Lord west*	1	0	20
q 5	neare Summer Border q John Brock *the Lord on both sides*	2	1	20
	there more west q Thomas Brock *Mr Gurlin east the Lord west*	1	1	
	there more west q Thomas Brock *Mr Gurlin on both pts*	0	3	0
	there more west q Thomas Brock *H. Mins east Rob Banyard west*	1	2	20
q 6	at Brancastergate q Thomas Brock *an headland Rob Banyard west*	0	2	20
q 7	at Jebdele bottome q Henry Clerke q Hargate *his owne north Ro Banyard south*	0	3	20
	there more North q Henry Clerke q Hargate *the Lord south Mr Gurlin north*	0	3	0
q 12	at Short Debdale an headland q Thomas Brock *Rob Banyard north*	0	2	0

q 13   neare Jebdele Bottome an headland *q* Thomas Brock *an

       headland the lord west*   1   1   0

       there more west *q* Thomas Brock *his owne west, the Lord east*   0   3 20

       there next *q* Thomas Brock *the Lord west*   3   0   0

q 24   at Jebdale Hill *q* Brock *q* Hargate *his owne on both sides*   1   3   0

       there more east *q* Henry Clerke *his owne on both sides*   0   3 20

pre 5   neare Broadgate sometime in the hand of the Lord *q* Brock,

q 1   the lord on both ptes*   1   0   0

q 2   neare Pedders Way *q* Thomas Lime *the Lord south Attwood

       north*   0   3   0

q 5   at Smallstyes *q* Thomas Brock *the Lord east Rob Banyard west* 1   0   0

q 13   at Bromyard 2ac 2r *q* Simon Smith and 2ac 2 rod *q* John Ellgar

       and 3ac 2r *q* Thomas Gogney now all in one piece *the Lord east,

       Rob Banyard west*   8   2   0

pre 6 at Chappell Croft *q* Nicholas Smith *q* Thomas Hargate *Jo Elgar

q 12   east the Lord west*   1   3   0

       there more west *q* John Brock purchased of Sr Roger Lestrange,

       Adams east   1   0   0

       there next more west *q* Thomas Brock *his mess[uage] west*   2   1   0

       there next more west with a messuage *q* Thomas Brock *Cremer

       east*   4   0   0

<N2   in Mickt furlong at Damastr Grove Lammin east Cremer west

q 29   *Lamins east, Cremer west*

                        < Summ 65 or 30p at 4d – 21s 8¾>

                14 Car [*Sum*] 64a 0½r at 4d [*rent*] – 21s 4¾d

pre 3 /*q 17*/ *q* Henry Minns   0   2   0

[*p 38*]

8 Jac Robert Chosell to Richard *Banyard* in mortgage:

592   3   0   0   abutt north upon Over Summergate

667   3   0   0   /*668, 669*/ in Jebdell bottom, south upon Brancastergate, this is

                   3a or di

       1   0   0   in Northgate Croffts

      Robert Chosell to Richard Banyard the 2 former 3ac and

10 Jac 1   2   0   inclosed and

388   1   0   0   at Sickles Crofft this is but 3r di Richard Banyard

7 Jac John Chosell taketh up and the same court selleth to Robert Chosell as

      followeth:

580   0   3   0   /*N61*/south upon Broadgate & an at the North End of the last,

591   3   0   0   these are <but> 6½r <no perches>

635   1   3   0   at Sweethouse – this Robert Banyard

722   2   2   0   at Longland – this Robert Banyard

716   2   3   0   there

611   1   2   0   /*612*/ at the north side of the East Hall this is <6> 5r 10p

		a	r	[p]
	Henry Lawes his free rents to Sedgford			
pre 3	/q 6/ neare Heachamgate q Thomas Linne	0	2	30
pre 4	/q 3/ neare Sedgford Common q Henry Drake	0	2	0
q 7	at Jebdele Bottome q Henry Drake	0	2	0
q 24	at Jebdele Hill q Henry Clerke	0	2	0
pre 5	/q 1/ neare Broadgate q Henry Drake	0	2	10
q 4	neare Shortlands q Thomas Hargate	0	2	0

Sum 3a 1r – 3¼d

pre 4 /q 24//1ac 1r at Jebdele Hill q Henry Drake particular rent 5d

5 Car	Robert Attewood & and Margarett:			
	43	1	30	q Will Banyard 42 Eliz
1 Jac	10	0	40	parcel of 74a 1r 30p q Gogney & Tho Longstreth
	21	2	0	q [?]
	1	1	0	at Stowell q Randall Elgar 44 Eliz 1 Jac
	0	1	0	parcell of 18a 7 furlong 6 pre and it is an headland
	0	0	0	which he had of [?] 44 Eliz
Sum	76	2	30	

917 /maz,²³⁶/ 8 Car John Crisp to Ro Banyard

486 1a 1r ½p Ro Banyard North q Simon Ellgar south east upon
Pedders Way part of 1a 2r di

10 Car John Crisp to Ro Banyard with a cottage

		a	r	[p]
[p] 39	Robert Banyards bond rent to Sedgford 1634			
pre 3	/q 4, 610/ neare Bishops Croft q John Chosell	2	0	20
	/611/ there more north q Thomas Orwell		1	20
q 6	/382/ neare Millstye q Edmond Smith q Willyam Banyard *Car 7, the Lord called Fickles Croft east*	1	2	0
	/386/ there more West q *Ed Smith* Willyam Banyard *Car 7, Ro Banyard 12a called Mayners west*	1	2	0
	there next q Robert Black beard *called Mayners land*	12	0	0
q 10	at Street Way q Robert Blackbeard	0	3	0
q 14	at Cheswick an Headland q Robert Blackbeard	0	3	0
q 17	/487/at Hundale q Robert Blackbeard <q J Crisp 7 Car 1a 2½r> *1a 2r 486*	1	2	0
q 17	/490/ there q Edmond Crisp q Willyam Banyard *Car 7 south upon Streetgate*	0	2	0
q 18	at Exland q Henry Clerke	1	0	0
pre 4	/q 1/ at Broadgate q John Rawlins q <Will Banyard >			
q 1	*Ro Hargate 558 2 Car*	2	2	20
	there more North q Adler Billard *Rob Hargate 559*	0	3	20

---

236. The Magazine.

	there more north part of 5ac at Preists land *q* John Rust *& Ro Hargate 560 2 Car*	3	0	0
	there part of the former 5ac *q* Willyam Banyards *561 7 Car*	2	0	0
	there *q* Willyam Banyard *562 7 Car*	0	3	0
q 2	neare Broadgate *q* Adler Billard *571*	1	0	0
	there more east *q* Godfrey Hargate *1 Car 572*	1	0	0
	there more east *q* Adler Billard *q* John Chosell taken up 8 Jac 580*	0	3	20
q 3	neare Over Summergate *q* Thomas Orwell *590*	1	1	20
	there more west *q* John Chosell *taken up 7 of Jac 591*	0	3	0
592	there next called Hanglemangle *q* Chosell his owne east north upon Over Summergate*	2	3	0
	there more west *q* Adler Billards *596*	1	3	0
q 4	at over Summergate *q* Thomas Orwell *610*	1	2	0
611	there more east *q* John Chosell *8 Jac 11 Jac*	0	3	20
612	there next *q* John Chosell *8 Jac 11 Jac*	0	1	30
q 5	/635/ at Summer Border *q* Adler Billard *q* John Chosell *11 Jac*	1	3	0
	there more west *q* Thomas Orwell *639*	1	2	0
	there more west sometime in the Lords hand *646*	1	0	0
	there next called Oldich *q* Thomas Orwell *647*	1	0	0
	there more west *q* Thomas Orwell *652*	2	2	0
653	there more west *q* John Chosell <7 Ja north of Easthall> *653*	1	2	20
	there more west and headland *q* Nicholas Browne *654*	1	1	0
q 6	at Brancaster gate an Headland *q* Adler Billard *655*	0	1	30
	there more east *q* Thomas Orwell *656*	2	1	20
<380>	there more east *q* Thomas Orwell *666*	0	3	20
667	there more east *q* John Chosell }	1	0	0
668	there next called Leech land *q* John Chosell }*8 Jac 11 Jac 3a*	1	2	0
669	there next an Headland *q* John Chosell }	0	2	20
q 7	at Jebdele Bottome part of 1a 2r *q* Adler Billards	1	0	0
	/677/ there more north *q* Adler Billard *q* John Chosell 11 Jac*	0	2	0
	there more north *q* Richard Smith	1	0	0
[p 40]	Sum [sub-total]	63	2	0
pre 4	/q 7/ at Jebdele Bottome more north *q* Adler Billards	1	0	0
	there more north *q* Adler Billards	0	3	0
	there more north *q* Thomas Orwell	1	0	0
q 9	at Streetgate an headland *q* Thomas Orwell	1	2	0
q 10	at Highmere sometime in the Lords hands *31 Hen 8*	5	2	0
	there next *q* Adler Billards	1	0	10
q 11	/716/ at Longland *q* John Chosell *7 Ja 11 Ja*	2	3	0
	there more east *q* John Chosell	0	2	20
722	there more east *q* John Chosell *7 Ja 11 Ja*	2	2	0
q 12	at Short Debdele *q* Brightmeres *31 Hen 8*	0	2	20

	there more north *q* Adler Billards	0	2	20
	there more north an headland *q* Adler Billards	0	2	20
q 13	at Jebdele Bottome *q* Thomas Orwell	2	0	20
	there more west *q* Thomas Orwell	2	1	0
	there next an headland *q* Banyards	2	0	20
q 24	at Jebdale Hill the first piece an headland *the crash* *q* Banyard *31 Hen*	0	2	10
	there next *q* Thomas Orwell	1	1	20
	there more north *q* John Chosell	0	2	0
pre 5	/q 1/ at Broadgate *q* John Chosell	0	2	0
	there more west *q* Adler Billards	1	0	0
q 2	neare Pedders Way *q* Purfer *q* Edmond Smith *q Orwell*	5	2	0
q 3	at Shortland *q* Robert Crisp the sonne of John Crisp, *Ri			
Car 5	Banyard south*	1	3	0
816	there more north *q* Henry Clerke }	0	3	0
817	there next *q* Henry Clerke }*q Will Banyard*	3	1	0
	there next an headland *q* Robert Finch *31 Hen 8*	0	1	20
q 5	at Smallstye *q* Thomas Orwell	0	2	0
	there more east *q* Adler Billards	1	3	0
q 11	neare Podingland *q* Thomas Orwell	2	0	0
	there more west *q* Adler Billards	3	1	0
q 13	/879/ neare Stowell Stye *q* Simon Smith at Bromyards *at Nepdich*	4	3	0
q 14	neare Stowell Stye *q* Adler Billard	0	3	0
	there next *q* Richard Smith *part of 3r 31 Hen 8*	0	2	½
pre 3	/Car 8/ at Hundele *q* Thomas Gogney *q* John Crisp* the sonne			
q 17	of Robert 1632 Hen Minns south*	1	2	0
pre 6	at Oldownekoll a messuage *q* Thomas Orwell *called Julians in			
q 6	Southgate*	6	1	0
q 8	neare Streetgate *q* Thomas Orwell	4	3	10
q 10	neare Stowell Stye *q* John Rust	1	2	0
1032	there more west *q* Thomas Longstreth	2	1	0
1036	there more west *q* John Bird an Headland	1	1	0
q 12	at Chappell Croft *q* Edmond Smith	4	2	30
pre 7	at Exmere with 2 pightles in the North ende *q* Thomas Longstreth	4	1	10
q 29	there next at the Reed Damm *q* Banyard	1	1	0
	Sum of bond 145a 2r 10p at 4d and 4a late Adams			
[p] 41				
1634	at Chappell Croft with a messuage with a croft *q* Nicholas Smith			
pre 6	*Henry Lawes west* late John Adams *Car 10 north upon the			
q 12	way to Dockin[g]*	4	0	0
	Sum	49	2	10

5 Jac   Robert Banyard *senior* to Robert his sonne & Jone Ellgar
           one messuage q Smith & 10ac q Longstreth as followeth:
second   7a 2r op parcell of 10ac in 4 peices q Thomas Longstreth 17 Eliz
first   this first and to all his messuages & lands q Richard Smith 21 Eliz
Except 7   3   10   perches of the grant of the Lord 31 Hen 8 and except
        1   1   0   sold to <Robert Collen> John Bird & except 6ac
       <1> 0   0   sold to <Robert Collen & except> inde
2²³⁷   2   2   0   in 2 peices sold to Godfrey Hargate &
1   2   2   0   sold <John Crisp> to Rob Collen
3   1   0   0   <query for Richard Smith 21 Eliz> to John Crisp
 [Sum] 13   1   0
        7   3   10   7 Car Will Banyard to Rob Banyard
382   1   2   0   the lord called Freckles Crofft <west> *east* south upon
                     Heachamgate
386   1   2   0   neare there Hen Lawes east Ro Banyard called Mayners land
                     west
490   0   2   0   the Lord north Mr Gurling south east upon Streetgate Way
562,   2   3   1   Ro Banyard south John Crisp north west upon Fring Way
568   this 2a 3r

pre 3   Robert Banyards free rents to Sedgford   a   r   [p]
q 4   neare Bishops Croft q Thomas Orwell   1   2   20
4 pre   at Brancaster gate q John Alowe q Robert Hargate   0   3   0
q 6   there next q Robert Hargate   0   2   20
q 7   at Jebdele Bottome q Willyam Banyard   0   3   ½
q 10   neare Highmere q Willyam Banyard   0   3   ½
                            Sum 3a 3½r – 3¾d
5 Jac   Robert Banyard *senior* to Robert Banyard his sonne all his lands except
         Belldams & he is adm[itted] to 15a or op parcell of 16a 1r with a tenement in
         Eastgate *of this 12a called Mayners is part* & to
870   4   3   0   in one peice in the East field at Nepdich, north upon
                     Stowellstye
816,   4   0   0   in 2 pieces q 3 pre q Will Banyard & to his father *Will
817   Banyard all q
1031   1   2   0   parcell of 3a 3r Tho Longstreth west, south upon Stowellstye &
                     to 2 Eliz
501   1   0   0   parcell of 2a 1r in the North field, Tho Hargate west, the Lord
                     5ac east q Will Banyard
1036   1   1   0   q 10 precinct 6 q John Bird & to 28 Eliz
1032   2   1   0   q 10 precinct 6 q Gogney & John Longstreth & to 38 Eliz
        5   2   10   in 2 peices q Richard Longstreth 23 March 34 Eliz

---

237. Numbers may refer to the number of pieces in the holding.

13 Jac Robert Banyard is admitted to the 7a 3r 10p the Lord 31 Hen 8
9 Jac   Robert Banyard senior to Will Banyard one tennement called Belldams with
969   a croft and 4a q Willyam Heres 34 Eliz who had it of executors of Margerett
        Longstreth
1 Car   Ralph Hargate to Robert Banyard
572   1 0 0   q 2 pre 4, the Lord east, Ro Banyard west
5 Car   John Crisp to Robert Banyard
815   1 3 0   /q 3 pre 5/ q Thom Brock Ri Banyard south, Ro Banyard north

[p 42]

	Richard Birds bond rent to Sedgford 1634	a	r	[p]
pre 1				
q 5	at Cote doore q Thomas Lestrange * n 26 in W*[238]	0	3	20
q 6	neare Heachamgate q Thomas Trevett sometime in 2 pieces *n 30 in W*	1	3	0
q 13	at Heydownes q Thomas Trevett *n 76 in Costen W*	0	3	20
q 17	at Cote Croft q Robert Cornell the 2 pieces following is the same:	0	0	0
	there called Wrongeland q Robert Cornell *n 108 Costen in W*	0	2	30
	there q Thomas Trevett next *n 108 Costen in W*	0	2	30
q 23	neare Hollway q Robert Burnham *n 149 }W*	1	3	0
	there more south q Robert Cornell *n 150 } Capell Close W*	2	1	10
	there more south q Robert Burnham *n 151 } Costen in W*	2	1	0
pre 2	/q 1/ at Westgate Street a messuage q Robert Burnham *n 185 in W*	2	0	20
	there more east q John Bird *n 186 in W*	0	2	30
q 5	neare greengate q Willyam Crisp *n 207 in Ben Crisp W*	1	2	0
	there more north at Peterpitt q Thomas Trevett, *n 215 Ro Banyard in W*	0	3	20
q 9	neare Heachamgate q Willyam Crisp *n 237Mar[tin] Carrew*[239]	1	3	0
	here more West q John Hendry *n 242 in W*	1	1	0
q 10	neare Cheswick q Willyam Crisp *n 250 MarCarrew*	2	2	20
q 15	neare Hallbottome an headland q Robert Hargate *n 282 in W*	1	1	0
	there more north q John Bird *n 283 in W*	1	1	0
q 18	neare Dorrellwonge q John Bird *n 313in W*	0	3	0
	there more south q Willyam Crisp *n 317 in W*	0	3	20
	there more south an headland *n 318 in W*	2	1	0
q 19	neare Ringstedgate *322 Mar Carrew*	1	3	20
	there more north q Robert Burnham *323 Mar Carrew*	1	0	0

238. 'W' on the RH side appears to be a later insertion than the numbers. It is not clear what 'W' refers to, possibly to 'Wallis' later on in Richard Bird's rental on page 43.
239. The identity of Martin Carrew is not clear either, he was possibly an earlier or later tenant.

		a	r	p
pre 3	/q 4/ neare Bishops Croft q Willyam Crisp *n 358 in W*	1	3	0
	there more east called Cranes Croft *q Willyam Crisp n 359 W*	1	3	0
q 6	neare Northgate q Willyam Crisp *392 WG[240] Mar Carrew*	2	1	0
	there more west q Willyam Crisp *free*	0	0	0
	there next q Willyam Crisp *next Francis Guybon 394 WG Mar Car*	1	2	0
q 7	near Goodacre q Willyam Crisp *396 Mar Car*	1	1	10
	there more east q John Bird *398 Mar Carrew*	0	2	0
	there more east q Willyam Crisp *402 Mar Carrew*	1	1	0
q 11	neare Brancaster *or Heacham Gate n 427 in W*	1		0
	there more South at West Croft q Willyam Crisp *n 432 in W*	1	1	0
q 12	at nether Heachamgate at Cleyland an headland q Willyam Crisp *n 440 in W*	0	2	0
q 13	neare Cheswick q Willyam Crisp *n 451 in W*	0	2	0
	there more West q Willyam Crisp *n 456 in W*	0	1	30
q 14	at Cheswick q Willyam Crisp *n 463 in W*	0	2	20
q 16	at Longe Cleyland q Willyam Crisp *n 475 in W*	0	2	20
pre 4	/q 4/ at Over Summergate an headland q Adler Billard *n 608 W*	1	1	0
	there next sometime in 2 pieces q Robert Pepir *n 609 W*	6	1	0

[p] 43	Richard Bird bond [rents] [continued]	a	r	[p]
pre 5	neare Broadgate with a Stert in the south end q Willyam Crisp			
q 1	*803 Mar Car*	0	3	0
	there next q Willyam Crisp *804 WG Mar Car*	1	2	0
	there more west q Willyam Crisp *806 Mar Carew*	0	3	0
q 11	neare Podingland q Thomas Crisp *n 852 in W*	0	2	0
q 13	at Bromyard q Willyam Crisp *873 Mar Carrew*	7	3	20
pre 6	/q 6/ neare the Reed Damme q John Bird *n 974 in W*	1	0	0
q 4	/in Heach[am] 942/ at Thorpgate in Heacham q John Bird next John Lawes *in W*	0	2	0
q 8	in Eaton q Constable at Beckmere *n 1490 Wallis*	0	1	20
q 15	in Eaton q Constable *n 1585 Wallis*	0	3	20
q 20	in Eaton q Constable *n 1631 Wallis*	0	2	0
q 26	in Eaton q Constable *n 1710 Wallis*	0	2	0
q 27	in Eaton q Constable called Heywards yarde *n 1722 Wallis*	0	1	20
q 28	in Eaton with a messuage q Constable *n 1736 Wallis*	1	3	0

Sum 70a 3r 10p 23s 6¼d

---

240. William Guybon.

	Richard Birds free rents to Sedgford	a	r	[p]
pre 2	at Westgate Street with a messuage q John Bird 5r 3 bind dayes			
q 1	in harvest 6d *W n 187*	o	o	o
pre 3	neare Northgate q Willyam Crisp *with a pitt in the south end			
q 6	called Burnham Pitt abut South upon nether Heachamgate W 393*	1	2	o
q 7	neare Goodacre q Thomas Line *n 397 Wallis*	1	3	20
pre 4	/q 5/ neare Summer Border q John Bird <628> *WG n 629 in*	1	3	o
pre 5	/q 4/ neare Shortland q Willyam Crisp *n 822 Wallis*	2	o	o
q 5	at Small Styes q Willyam Crisp *n 828 Wallis*	2	o	o
q 11	neare Podingland q Willyam Crisp *n 847 Wallis*	2	o	o

Sum 11¾d for 11a 0½r

and for 5r – 3 bind dayes 6d this Mr Wallis

13 Hen 8 Wrask a messuage & 7a

6 Hen 7 the Lord to John Chamberlayne one messuage & 18a late seized for a wast

16 Hen 7 Thomas Chamberlayne to John Chamberlayn one messuage, 18a 2r 15p et 8a 1r 20p

5 Hen 8 John Chamberlayn tooke up 19a 1r 10p with a messuage q John Morwick 21 Hen 7

32 Hen 8 John Chamberlayn 9a 3r di

38 Hen 8 James Anderson 9a 3r q Jo Foxe Executor to John Chamberlayn

4 Ed 6 Jac Anderson to Hargate 1a q Chamberlayn it is Inglolds acre

[p 44]	John Ellgar his bond rent to Sedgford 1634	a	r	[p]
pre 4	/568 Jo/ neare Broadgate q Willyam Rust *Gurling West*	1	2	o
q 2	/569/ there more east q John Rust *Gurling East q Ed Ellgar*	1	1	20
pre 5	/10 Jac/ neare Pedders Way part of 10a q Pursers q Edmond			
q 2	Smith	4	2	o
q 12	neare Stowell Stye q Henry Clarke *q Robert Collen*	1	3	o
pre 6				
q 12	/10 Ja/ neare Stowell Stye q Thomas Orwell q Edmond Smith	o	3	o
pre 7	/q 5/ neare Bungey Stye q John Ellgar with a stert in the east ende	2	2	20
q 8	at Hanginghill q John Ellgar	o	1	30
	there more west an headland q John Ellgar	3	1	o
q 10	at Clippgrowe q Godfrey Hargate	o	2	o
	there next q Edmond Ellgar	o	2	o
	there more south q Godfrey Hargate	2	o	o
q 11	/1119/ neare Clipprowe q Thomas Lawes	1	1	o
q 12	/1124/ at Wellhill q Thomas Lawes	1	3	o
	/1153/ there more west q John Ellgar <q Ro Collen>	o	2	o
	/1162/ there more west q John Ellgar <q Ro Collen>	1	1	o
q 13	at Westmere q Godfrey Hargate called Eastmere	o	2	10

	there next *q* Edmond Ellgar	0	2	10
	there more east *q* John Ellgar	2	0	0
q 14	at Westbarblehowe *q* John Ellgar	1	2	0
q 15	at Wellhill an headland *q* John Ellgar	0	2	0
q 17	/*1209*/ at Burdell an headland *q* Thomas Lawes	1	3	0
	there more north *q* John Ellgar	0	2	20
	/*1218*/ there next *q* Thomas Lawes <an headland>	1	1	0
q 19	at eastbarblehowe *q* John Ellgar	0	3	20
	there more north *q* John Ellgar	4	0	0
q 20	at Cattland *q* John Ellgar	1	0	0
	there more west *q* John Ellgar	1	2	0
q 22	at Tittlehouse an headland *q* John Ellgar	0	2	20
q 23	at Over Cawdle *q* John Ellgar	1	3	0
	there more east *q* John Ellgar	1	2	0
q 24	at Nether Cawdle *q* John Ellgar	3	2	10
	there more west *q* John Acres	1	1	0
	there next *q* John Ellgar	0	2	0
q 25	at Lampland an headland *q* John Ellgar	0	3	0
q 26	at Redhill *q* John Ellgar	0	2	20
q 27	at Wrennockdele *q* Thomas Longstreth called Wolvesdeale *q* in divers peices	8	0	0
	there more north with a messuage *q* John Acres neare Fibbesyard	0	2	0
q 28	neare Winches Lane inclosed called Mnescroft *q* John Akers	0	2	0
	there more west with a messuage *q* John Ellgar	1	0	0
	there more west next the messuage *q* John Ellgar	4	0	20
Jo[*hn*]	there more west a messuage called [?] *q* Thomas Longstreth neare Reyners Hill on the west *q* Thomas Beale *north upon the River*	17	0	13
[*p*] 45	Sum [*sub-total*]	81	2	33
pre 7	/*q 28 Jo*/[241] neare Winches Lane *q* Thomas Beale called Reyners Hill	10	0	10
Jo[*hn*]	there 3 pieces bounded by it selfe *q* Thomas Longstreth *& Beales* first piece 10p the second piece 4p the third piece 4 perches in all	0	0	18
q 3	at Toke Stye *q* John Ellgar Heardgonge	0	3	20
	there more north *q* John Ellgar	1	2	0
	there more north *q* John Ellgar	1	1	0
	there next *q* John Ellgar	1	0	0
	there more north *q* John Ellgar	1	1	0
	there more north *q* John Ellgar	0	2	20

---

241. John Ellgar junior, most likely.

q 24	/H12/[242] in Eaton q Edmond Constables			I	3	O
q 29	in Minks furlong q Edmond Constable			I	I	O

Sum qr [*query*] the 41 Eliz   19   2   28

Sum of John Ellgars bond lands 100a 1½r 1p at 4d, of this to
John Ellgar Junior 30a 18p 1638 *Car 14*

John Ellgar dyeth and John his sonne is admitted to 2 messuage 1 q Crisp 1
q Trevit

5 Ja	41	3	I	lying in 27 pieces & to
	2	3	O	/568, 569/ in 2 pieces q 2 precinct 4
	3	2	O	at Cliprow q Ralfe Lawes 34 Eliz it was 3ac di: 1166, 1147, 1118
	6	O	O	in 4 pieces in the South field q Thomas Lawes /1109, 1124, 1209, 1218, 5r, 7r, 7r, 5r/
	I	3	O	/858/ q 12 q Robert Collen beside 35ac & 18 perches q Tho Drake 43 Eliz

7 Ja	Tho Hargate to John Ellgar one messuage called Walls Coneyn			
	O	2	O	& to
	O	2	O	inclosed called Moonescroft &
	I	I	O	in nether Cawdell all q Edward Read 24 Eliz

43 Eliz Thomas Drake to John Ellgar one messuage called Longstreths q Beales
with 35a & 38p

<pre 8 /q 14, N2/ Godfre Hargate at Overcrowne Crosse q Ralph Hargate which he
had of the surender of Willyam Banyard 1635>

[*p 46*]

pre 1	Henry Minnes his bond rents to Sedgford 1634	a	r	[*p*]
q 5	neare Greengate q Simon Ellgar	5	O	O
q 7	neare Cote Stye q John Trevett	O	I	20
q 11	neare Heachamgate q John Costen	I	I	O
q 17	at Lampitt q John Trevett	I	O	O
100	there q Robert Ellgar *Si[*mon*] Ell*[243]	I	O	O
101	there q Robert Ellgar *Si Ell*	I	2	20
102	there q John Trevett	I	I	O
q 22	/145, 11 Car/ at Skotts yard furlong q Simon Ellgar	2	3	O
q 24	neare Mill Stye *the east* part of 7ac 3r q Bloomfield *whereof			
11 Car	1a free Si Ell*	6	3	O
pre 2	/q 1/ at Westgate q Trevett q John Costen	O	2	O
	there more east a messuage q John Trevett	I	O	O
q 5	/206/ neare greengate q Willyam Crisp *Si Ell*	I	O	O
11 Car	/208/ there more north somtime in the hands of the Lord *Si El*	3	O	O
	/209/ there more north q Willyam Crisp *Si Ell*	I	3	O

---

242. Heacham reference.
243. Clarifying succession in the Ellgar family.

		a	r	p
q 6	at Lampitt *q* Foakes *q* Thomas Brock	2	0	0
q 10	/246/ next greengate *q* Willyam Crisp *Si Ell*	0	2	20
q 11	at Cheswick *q* Thomas Linne *Si Ell*	8	3	20
11 Car	/251, 252/ there more north at Micklehowe *q* Richard Ogle *Si Ell* *q* Simon Bloomfield	2	1	0
	there more north *q* John Trevett	0	2	20
q 15	neare Hallbottome *q* John Costen	0	1	30
q 16	next the Lord *q* John Costen	0	2	0
q 17	neare Greengate *q* John Trevett	0	1	0
	there more west *q* John Costen	0	2	0
q 18	neare Hallbottome *q* John Trevett	0	1	10
pre 3	/q 6, 389/ neare Northgate *q* Willyam Crisp *q* *Si*Ellgar	4	0	0
q 6	/390/ there more west *q* Willyam Crisp *Si Ell*	1	0	0
q 7	/399/ neare Goodacre *q* Willyam Crisp *q* *Si* Ellgar	2	0	0
q 16	at Longe Cleyland *q* John Trevett with a gore at the south ende	1	0	0
q 17	/486 *Hen Lawes*/ at Hundele *q* Simon Ellgar *q* Francis Guybon	0	2	0
pre 4	{at Greenhowedel *q* Willyam Crisp *Hen Lawes east Banyard west*	1	2	0
q 3	{there more west *q* Thomas Orwell *Banyard east Lawes west*	2	3	0
Dey	{there more west *q* Thomas Orwell *Gurling east the Lord west*	1	2	0
q 4	/Dey/ near over Summergate *q* Willyam Crisp in exchange *Banyard*	1	0	0
q 5	/649/ neare Summer Border *q* Thomas Orwell	3	0	0
11 Car	/650/ there next sometime in the hand of the Lorde *Si Ellgar*	4	0	0
pre 7	/q 13, 1171/ at Westmere *q* Thomas Beale	1	0	0
q 21	/1249/ at West Barblehouse part of 6a 3r *q* Tho Longstreth *Si Ell*	4	1	0
q 29	/1310/ at Exmere *q* Simon Ellgar	0	2	20
q 32	/1345/ at Westlandele *q* Simon Ellgar	1	0	0

Sum bond 73ac 3r 10p at 4d
Henry Minnes 1a free *q* Robert Burnham *the west* part of 7a 3r
in the 1 precinct and the 24 furlong the other 6a 3r being bond –
1d. Sold 6ac 3r. Remain 67ac or 10p

[p] 47	Henry Minnes bond [rent] 1635	a	r	[p]
pre 4	/Dey/ <Henry Minnes a cottage with a curtledge *q* Edward			
q 4	Greene lateThomas Spallding near Bishops Crofft Bond> / *Wakefield*/	0	1	0
pre 4	/q 11/ <at Longeland *q* Lionell Bankes late Thomas Spallding>	0	3	0

	George Framingham his bond rents to Sedgford	a	r	[p]
pre 5	/q 12, 866/ neare Stowell *q* Willyam Rose	2	1	0
q 15	/887/ neare Streetgate *q* Willyam Akers *Will Banyard late Will Guybon east*	1	1	0

q 15	/889/ there more east q Willyam *Kath* Rose *Will Banyard late Will Guybon east*	1	1	0
q 15	/894/ there more east q Willyam Akers *at Redland*	10	1	0
q 15	/905/ there more east q Willyam Akers *an headland q Kath Rose*	0	3	20
q 16	/911/ neare Fringe field next Lingesty q \<Adler Billiard\> Thomas Longstreth *the Lord east*	0	2	30
q 17	/912/ neare Lingestt q Adler Billard	1	1	0
q 20	/935/ at Wronge Land q Willyam Akers	1	3	0
pre 6	/q 3, 947/ at Oldownes q Thomas Orwell Rose on both sides	1	0	0
q 3	/949/ there more north q Willyam Rose	0	3	20
q 3	/950/ there more north q \<William Rose q Godgrey Hargate\> *Thomas Orwell*	3	3	0
q 4	/952/ at Shortland q Willyam Rose q Godfrey Hargate /6 Carl/	1	3	0
q 4	/953/ there more north q Willyam Akers	0	1	30
q 5	/955/ next Fringate a Pightle q Willyam Akers	0	0	20
q 5	/956/ there more a messuage with a croft q Willyam Akers	2	0	0
q 5	/957/ there more north a messuage with a croft next Lingsty q Godfrey Hargare *south upon the way* /6 Carl/	4	0	0
pre 7	/q 4, 1079/ at Gatewonge q Thomas Orwell q Willyam Akers	3	0	0
q 4	/1080/ there next q Ralph Hargate /6 Carl/	2	0	10
q	/1081/ there next q Ralph Hargate /6 Carl/	2	3	0
[p 48]	[Sub-total]	/39	3	0/
q 4	/1082/ at Gatewonge q Willyam Rose *Robert Rose west*	0	2	10
	/1084/ there more west q Willyam Akers with a pightle q Thomas Orwell	3	0	0
	/1085/ there next q Willyam Akers *q Orwell*	1	2	0
q 8	/1101/ at Hanginghill q Willyam Rose *an headland* /6 Carl/	0	2	0
q 9	/1105/ at Hanging land an Headland q Willyam Akers	1	0	0
q 20	/1235/ at Kattland q Godfrey Hargate /6 Carl/	0	2	0
q 20	/1237/ there more west q Willyam Akers /6 Carl/	1	0	0
q 20	/1239/ there more west q Godfrey Hargate *the Lord on both sides*	1	0	0
q 20	/1241/ there more west q Godfrey Hargate /6 Carl/	2	0	5
q 23	/1260/ at Over Cawdell q Willyam Akers	1	2	0
q 24	/1264/ there more west q Willyam Akers at Nether Cawdell	1	3	0
q 24	/1268/ there more west q Willyam Akers	1	1	0
q 28	/1291/ next Winches Lane called Basterds yards q Willyam Crisp	1	0	0
	/1293/ there more west a messuage q Thomas Hargate	1	0	0
	Sum [sub-total]	17	2	15

the whole sum of bond land is 57a 1r 15p at 4d

pre 7	5r late Godfrey Ellgar *the north ende* of 3a \<0 1 16p\>			
q 28	q Thomas Lawes	1	1	0

q 28   /1300/ 1a 1r <16 perches> q Thomas Lawes the north ende of 3a
q Thomas Lawes and Beales with a messuage John Ellgar west,
Allain Collen east abutt north upon the river, south upon the way

7 Ja   /41a 2r 30p abut Ra Hargate/ 2 Ed 6

946	1	3	1	Rose
948	2	3	0	Rose
963	3	3	0	
966	7	2	0	/967, 968/ called Carseys & Hamons
1017	1	0	0	Rose
1020	1	3	0	Rose
1062	3	2	0	
1068	0	2	0	
1071	0	2	0	this is 3r di
1078	3	3	0	Rose
1080	0	2	0	10p Framingham
1096	1	0	0	Rose
1126	1	0	0	
1133	0	3	0	
1136	2	3	0	
1140	4	1	0	
1189	1	0	0	
	1	3	1	in 2 pieces /1199, 1200/
1191	0	2	0	
1289	1	2	0	

pre 7   /1086/ George Framingham with a pightle at Cattwonge q John   a   r   [p]
q 4   Pedder free   4   2   0
q 24   at Nether Cawdle q Willyam Akers free particular 1½d /2½r   0   2   0
                                                    Writt

7 Jac   /Ralph Hargate/ was admitted to beside 41a 2r 30p above as foll:

961	3	1	1	this is 3ac 1r
1152	6	0	1	/1211/ in the South field in 2 pieces q Orwell
	7	3	1	in the East field q Will Page *964, 965*
897	2	2	0	/899/ q Adler Billard
572	1	0	0	/Ro Banyard/ q Adler
879	1	0	0	at Bromyard q Wesenham
	0	1	0	with part of a messuage next Wesenham q Gitting 28 Eliz
1159	2	2	0	/1169/ in 2 pieces
1188	3	0	0	/1192/ in 2 pieces 9r q 14 & 3r q 14 this is 3r di

[Sum   27   2   20p   plus 41a 2r 30p =]   69   1   10

		a	r	[p]
[p] 49	Willyam Banyards bond rents to Sedgford			
pre 5	/q 13, 879/ at Bromyard q John Wesenham q Ralph Hargate *7 Ja*	1	0	0
q 15	/890/ neare Streetgate q Thomas Longstreth q Willyam Guybon *the Lord east* /5 Carl/	2	0	20
5 Car	/892/ there more east q Thomas Longstreth q Willyam Guybon* the Lord west* /5 Carl/	2	2	20
5 Car	/895/ there more east q Thomas Longstreth q Willyam Guybon *Framingham west* /5 Carl/	2	1	0
5 Car	/896/ there next east q Thomas Longstreth q Willyam Guybon	3	1	0
	/897/ there next more east q Ralph Hargate *& Adelar Billard*}	1	2	0
	/899/ there more east q Ralph Hargate *the Lord East q Adelar Billard} 7 Ja*	1	0	0
q 19	at Simons Pitt an headland q Thomas Longstreth *Will Guybon Linsty north* /5 Carl/	1	2	0
6 pre	/q 6/ at Oldowne knoll q Ralph Hargate *7 Jac 3a 1r 1p 961*	3	1	0
	there more west q <Ralph Hargate> *Will Rose & Acres 962*	1	0	0
963	there more west q Ralph Hargate *q Orwell <3a 1r > 7 Ja 963*	3	2	0
964	/11ac ½r/ there next q Ralph Hargate	5	0	0
965	there next q Ralph Hargate *q Will Page 7a 3r 1p 7 Jac*	2	2	20
	/Carseys in one piece & Hamons/			
	there more west q Ralph Hargate in Southgate *966*	2	3	0
	there next a messuage with a croft q Ralph Hargate *7 Jac 967*	2	2	0
	there next a messuage q Ralph Hargate with a croft *968*	2	1	0
	there more west q Thomas Longstreth *& Ro Banyard called Belldams* /9 Jac/	4	1	20
pre 7	at Street way q Ralph Hargate *7 Jac at the end of the Lords			
q 2	9ac east upon the way*	3	2	0
q 3	neare Fring Border q Ralph Hargate *Strange & north & south 7 Jac east upon the Lords 30a*	0	2	0
	there more north *the Lord south 7 Ja*		3	20
q 12	at Well Hill q Ralph Hargate *the Lord west south upon Snetsham to 7 Ja*	1	0	0
	there more <north> *west* q Ralph Hargate *Strange west 7 Ja*	0	3	0
	there q Ralph Hargate *Gogney east Strange west 7 Ja*	2	3	0
	there more west q Ralph Hargate *Strange east Orwell west 7 Ja*	4	1	0
	/1152/ there more west q Ralph Hargate <Gogney west> *q Orwell Strange North 7 Ja*	3		0
	/1159/ there more west part of 1a q Ralph Hargate	1	1	0
	there an headland q Ralph Hargate *7 Jac*	1	1	0
q 14	at West Barblehow q Thomas Longstreth q Ralph Hargate *7 Ja*	2	1	0
	there next q Ralph Hargate *Gogney south Strange north 7 Ja*	1	0	0
7 Ja	there more south q Ralph Hargate *Strang north Gogney south 7 Ja*	0	2	0
	there next q Thomas Longstreth *but 3r 7 Ja*	0	3	20

q 15   at Well Hill *q* Ralph Hargate } * upon 5a of the Lord   1   1   0
        there next *q* Ralph Hargate   } 7 Jac Strange on both sides
        East*   0   2 20

q 17   /1211/ at Burdale *q* Ralph Hargate *q* Orwell 7 Ja*   3   0 20

q 27   at Wrennocksdele a close called Tibbsyard *q* Ralph Hargate
        7 Ja   1   2   0
        the way on both sides abut upon the Comon Lane north west   0   0   0
                Sum all bond 72a 2r at 4d *this was cast short 1r di*   0   0   0

6 Car   Ralfe Hargate to \<Robert> Will Banyard 56a 1r 10p with 2 messuages called
       Hamons & Kerseys *qr* the roll 11 Car for joynture
1 Car   \<Ralph> Edmond Crisp to Willyam Banyard
7 Car   /to Ro Ban[yard]/ 1a 2r the Lord called Frickles Croft east Henry Lawes west
       1a 2r more west Henry Lawes east Ro Banyard 12a called Mayners west
2 Car   /Jo Crem [er]/ 2r John Crisp *q* Chosell South the Lord east upon Streetgate
       /to Will Bany[ard]/ 2a 3½r *q* 1 pre 4 John Crisp north *q* Yonges
[p 50] /43 Eliz/ Richard Banyard admitted to 9a stet \<parcell> of 49a 3r 30p *q* Will
       and Jone Banyard & to 12a 3r *q* Tho Banyard 17 Eliz and in the resitall of
       his fathers will it is expressed that he gave him beside 5a inclosed at Browes
       yarde & 3 halfe acres at Longeland & 3 halfe acres at Shortlands and 1 acre
       lying next East Hall which last it may be free. /in all 20a 3r fine 18s 1½d/

11 Jac and Ralph Hargate senior to Richard Banyard a messuage & 8[ac] *q* Kath
found Linne in grass

189	1	0	0	with a messuage		
201	2	0	0			
228	2	1	0			
235	0	3	0			
258	1	1	0			
312	0	3	0	[Sum] 8a *q* Katherin Linnes & to		
403	1	0	1			
224	2	2	0			
77	0	3	0			
110	1	1	0	/110/	a	r [p]
216	0	2	1	he hath in all of Hargate land	18	2 0
248	3	3	0	in Hall Bottom this is but 3a 2r		
249	1	0	0	there Richard Bird east Longstreth west		
227	1	3	0	in all of Hargates 20a 3r		

10 Jac John Chosell to Richard Banyard beside 3a n 592 & 3a in Jebdale 667, 668,
       669

654	1	2	0	inclosed &
388	1	0	0	at Fickles croft this is but 3r di
				all these Robert Banyard hath

|Bartholomew Crisp|

<table>
<tr><td></td><td></td><td>a</td><td>r</td><td>[p]</td></tr>
<tr><td>pre 4</td><td>/q 1/ <at Broadgate q John Crisp and Thomas Drake</td><td>1</td><td>0</td><td>0</td></tr>
<tr><td></td><td>there more north q John Crisp and Gogney an headland></td><td>2</td><td>1</td><td>0</td></tr>
</table>

11 Jac Robert Chosell to Richard Banyard one close in Northgate conteyne 3 acres
between Heachamgate way and Richard Banyard north abutt east upon
Streetgate Way west upon the Lord

9 Car John Lawes to Richard Banyard

236	1	1	0	/4r 30p/ an headland with a start east upon Henry Minnes
319	1	1	0	Ri Bird east the Lord west
474	1	1	0	Ri Bird west Ro Banyard east south upon Nether Heachamgate

pre 8 /q 28, free/ Francis Costen< for free rent of a bearne and halfe a rod part of
3r½ called Colles q Hargate>

[p] 51 Richard Banyards bond rents to Sedgford 1634

<table>
<tr><td></td><td></td><td>a</td><td>r</td><td>[p]</td></tr>
<tr><td>pre 1</td><td>/q 13/ at Heydones q Robert Hargate *John Lawes north, Will Guybon south*</td><td>0</td><td>3</td><td>0</td></tr>
<tr><td>q 17</td><td>at Cote Croft q John Alowe q Robert Hargate *next the way called Heachamgate north*/11 Ja/</td><td>1</td><td>1</td><td>0</td></tr>
<tr><td>q 21</td><td>next the land of John Lawes neare Bullards Hill q Thomas Linne</td><td>1</td><td>0</td><td>0</td></tr>
<tr><td>2 pre</td><td>at Hollway a messuage *in Westgate* with a croft q Thomas</td><td></td><td></td><td></td></tr>
<tr><td>q 1</td><td>Linn q Robert Hargate *Hall Green east Gibs Green west* q Thomas Linn q Robert Hargate *11 Ja*</td><td>1</td><td>0</td><td>0</td></tr>
<tr><td>q 3</td><td>next Hollway at Over Jaybert q Thomas Linn q Robert Hargate* next Holway west* /11 Ja/</td><td>2</td><td>0</td><td>0</td></tr>
<tr><td>q 6</td><td>at Lampitt an headland q Robert Hargate *Randall Ellgar east* /11 Ja/</td><td>0</td><td>2</td><td>20</td></tr>
<tr><td></td><td>there q Thomas Hargate *Will Guybon free east his owne free west* /11 Ja/</td><td>2</td><td>2</td><td>0</td></tr>
<tr><td>q 7</td><td>at Mill Hill q Robert Hargate with the Mill Hill in the west ende /11 Ja/</td><td>1</td><td>3</td><td>0</td></tr>
<tr><td></td><td>there more south q Thomas Linn q Robert Hargate *abutt west upon Hunston way* /11 Ja/</td><td>2</td><td>1</td><td>0</td></tr>
<tr><td>q 9</td><td>at Greengate q Nicholas Smith q Robert Hargate</td><td>0</td><td>3</td><td>0</td></tr>
<tr><td>q 10</td><td>next Greengate q Nicholas Smith q Robert Hargate</td><td>2</td><td>2</td><td>20</td></tr>
<tr><td></td><td>there next q John Rust q Robert Hargate</td><td>1</td><td>0</td><td>0</td></tr>
<tr><td>q 11</td><td>at Cheswick q Thomas Linn q Robert Hargate</td><td>1</td><td>1</td><td>0</td></tr>
<tr><td>q 18</td><td>neare Hallbottome q Thomas Linn q Robert Hargate</td><td>0</td><td>3</td><td>0</td></tr>
<tr><td>pre 3</td><td>/q 5/ neare Mill Stye q John Chosell</td><td>0</td><td>3</td><td>20</td></tr>
<tr><td></td><td>there more north q Adler Billard *q John Chosell*</td><td>0</td><td>1</td><td>30</td></tr>
<tr><td></td><td>there next a decayed messuage q Adler Billard *q John Chosell*</td><td>0</td><td>2</td><td>0</td></tr>
<tr><td></td><td>there q Adler Billard q John Chosell</td><td>0</td><td>1</td><td>½</td></tr>
</table>

	there more north *q* Adler Billard *q* John Chosell */3a Jac 11/*[244]	0	2	0
376	there with a pightle in the east ende *q* Adler Billard *q* <Willyam Banyard> *John Chosell*	0	3	0
377	there more north a Messuage decayed *q* Thomas Orwell *q* Willyam Banyard	1	3	0
q 6	*/380/* at Northgate *q* Adler Billard *q* John Chosell *10 Ja*	0	3	20
q 7	at Goodacre *q* Gogney *q* Robert Hargate *q Crisp west Poly east*	1	0	10
pre 4	*/q 3/* at Over Summergate *q* *Robert* Chosell *q* Willyam Banyard	0	3	0
	there next *q* Adler Billard *q* Willyam Banyard	0	1	0
q 7	at Jebdele Bottome *q* Adler Billard *q* Willyam Banyard part of 6r in 2 peices	0	2	0
q 8	*/this is free/* part of 7a of the Lords at Pedders Way which Richard Banyard claymeth	0	3	0
q 10	at Highmere *q* Robert Chosell	1	2	0
q 11	at Longeland *q* Robert Chosell <43 Eliz>	1	2	0
q 13	next Jebdele Bottome *q* Adler Billard *q* Willyam Banyard *2r free*	0	0	0
pre 5	*/q 3/* at Shortland an Headland *q* Nicholas Smith *q* Willyam Banyard		2	0
q 11	at Small Stye *q* Nicholas Smith *q* Willyam Banyard	1	3	0
	there *q* Willyam Banyard *q Beales*	1	2	0
q 12	neare Stowell Stye *q* Nicholas Smith *q* Willyam Banyard	2	3	0
pre 6	*/q 10/* at Stowell Stye *q* Nicholas Smith *q* Willyam Banyard	3	0	0
q 10	there more east *q* Nicholas Smith *q* Willyam Banyard	1	3	0
pre 2	[9 Car] neare Heachamgate *q* John Lawes in 2 pieces *Bird east the Lord west*	1	0	30
q 19	neare Hall Bottom *q* John Lawes an headland with a start *Bird			
9 Car	North*	1	1	0
pre 3	[9 Car] at Longe Cleylands *q* John Lawes *q* Towne Land *Ri			
q 16	Banyard east south upon nether Heachamgate*	1	1	0

Sum 46a 3½r 10p at 4d

43 Eliz 46a or 10 p – 15s 4¼d

[p 52]

pre 3	Richard Banyards land free of Sedgford			
q 5	*/369/* neare Mill Stye *q* Willyam Banyard and Adler Billard *Jo Chosell*	0	1	30
q 5	*/374/* there next & north with a messuage *q* Willyam Banyard and Adler Billard *Jo Chosell*	0	2	0
q 5	*/375/* there next in the same croft *q* Adler Billard his bond land *Jo Chosell north*	1	1	0

244. Total for 5 previous entries.

q 6	/379/ at Northgate an headland q Willyam Banyard & Adler Billard *Jo Chosell*	0	1	30
q 6	/391/ there more west q Robert Chosell and Robert Hancell, Henry Minnes east *q Ro Chose[ell]*	1	2	0
pre 4	/q 4, 623/ at Over Summergate q Willyam Banyard	0	1	0
q 8	/696/ neare Peders Way by the Lords 18a	0	3	0
q 6	/664/ neare Brankaster Way q Willyam Banyard & Adler Billard	0	3	0
q 13	/738/ next Jebdale Botton q Willyam Banyard and Adler Billard	0	2	0
pre 5	/q 11, 844/ at Small Styes q Robert Chosell	0	2	0
pre 6	/q 7, 993/ neare Stowell Stye q Willyam Banyard Robert Rose east	0	2	0
	/2s 2d, 4½/ Sum 6a 2r – 6½d and particular rent is 8½d			

Richard Banyards free rents to Sedgford

	a	r	[p]		s	d
pre 1						
q 1	n 1	3	0	0	at Stump Crosse inclosed q Robert Hargate	0 5 ½
pre 2	223	1	0	0	/q 6/ at Lampitt q Robert Hargate q John Creamer	0 2 0
pre 4 q 2	581	0	3	½	at Broadgate q Adler Billard and Willyam Banyard *Ro Chosell*	0 1 ½
q 3	593	0	2	10	at Over Summergate q Ro Chosell q Willyam Banyard	0 1 0
pre 5 q 4	820	0	1	30	neare Shortland q Robert <Hancell> *Chosell* 0	½
q 11	840	1	3	0	at Small Styes q Willyam Banyard *Ro Chosell* 0	3 ¾
	842	1	1	½	there more west q Willyam Banyard *Ro Chosell*	0 2 ¾
q 12	863	1	0	0	near Stowell Stye q Willyam Banyard *Adelar*	0 2 ¾
q 11	845	0	1	30	q Willyam Banyard *Ro Chosell*	
	10	1	0	Sum	free particular rent	1 8 ½

pre 3	[*Richard Banyards land free of Sedgford*][245]	a	r [p]
q 5	<neare Mill Stye q Adler Billard and Willyam Banyard>	0	1 30
	<there more north q Adler Billard and Willyam Banyard>	0	2 0
	<there next q Adler Billard and Willyam Banyard>	0	1 20
q 6	<at Northgate an headland q Adler Billard an headland q Willyam Banyard>	0	1 30
	<there q Robert Hancell>	1	2 0
pre 4	/q 4/ <at Over Summergate q Willyam Banyard>	0	1 0
q 8	<part of the Lords 18ac>	0	3 0
q 6	<neare Brankastergate q Willyam Banyard & Adler Billard>	0	3 0

---

245. Entry crossed out and updated above, with numbers and more detail added.

q 13   <next Jebdale Botton *q* Adler Billard and Willyam Banyard>   0   2   0

pre 5   /*q 11*/ <at Small Styes *q* Robert Chosell>   0   2   0

pre 6   /*q 7*/ <neare Stowell Stye *q* Willyam Banyard>   0   2   0

Sum free 5a 3r[246] at 1d is 5¾d

[*p*] 53 <Robert Creamer> Randall Ellgar is admitted to:

3 Ja   2   1   0   at Mousehode, and to the Lord in the tenure of Longstreth
                           north & south

     1   0   1   *q* Will Crisp *south upon Brankestergate* pre 4 & to one mess
                           & 20a *videll* in 4 pieces

     4   0   0   with the messuage: the 1 [*piece*]

     3   0   0   the 2 piece

     4   0   0   the 3 piece

     9   0   0   the 4 piece & to

     1   0   0   1a parcell of 1a di & to

     1   0   0   parcell of 1a di & to

     0   2   0   *q* Allaine Clarke

[*Sum*] 25a 3r di   fine 25s

/*Edmond*/ Randall Ellgars heyres for bond rent to Sedgford   a   r   [*p*]

pre 1 /*q 17*/ at Cote Croft *q* Richard Ogle   5   0   0

       there *q* Thomas Deerham *3 Jac*   4   0   0

2 pre /*203*/ next Hollway *in Westgate* a messuage with a croft

q 4   *q Ogle* *q* Simon Bloomfield *3 Ja 4ac*   3   1   0

q 6   at Lampitt *q* Simon Bloomfields   3   3   0

q 7   at Mill Hill an Headland *q* Richard Ogle *2 Ja 3ac*   3   1   0

Sum bond 19a 1r at 4d 6s for free 1¼d

q 4   /*202*/ for free rent next Hollway *q* Simon Bloomfield 1¼d for   1   1   0

Willyam Minnes his bond rent to Sedgford 1634   a   r   [*p*]

pre 2 < at Eastgate *q* Richard Deerham *q* Thomas Hargate *Jo Roll*>   0   2   0

q 2   <there more east a messuage with a croft *q* John Collen *Jo

       Roll*>   1   3   0

       <2r next *q* Simon Ellgar particular rent 10d *Jo Roll*>   0   2   0

pre 4 /*q 4*/ <at Olditch *q* John Yonges *q* Willyam Green *Dey*>   1   2   0

pre 5 /*q 1*/ <at Broadgate *q* John Yonges *q* Willyam Green *Dey*>   0   2   0

Sum 4a or 16p – 16¼d and 2r bond particular 10d

pre 2 Willyam Minnes *John Roll* 2½r <free> *q* John Collen

q 2   particular rent of <Mayden fee> 1d

---

246. Note the incorrect total and the need to renew the entry.

		a	r	[p]
[p 54]	/1634/<John Crisp the sonne of Robert his bond rent to Sedgford>			
pre 4	/q 1/ <at Broadgate q Thomas Drake *Bartle Crisp 1638*>	1	0	0
	<there more North an headland q Gogney>	2	1	0
pre 6	<t Oldknowne knoll a messuage with a croft q John Wesenham>	1	2	20
q 6	<there q Francis Costen & Randall Ellgar>	1	0	0

	Robert Lawes his bond rent to Sedgford 1634	a	r	[p]
pre 1	/q 5/ neare Greengate q Ralph Lawes	0	3	20
	there more south q Ralph Lawes	0	2	20
	there more south q Ralph Lawes	0	1	20
	there more south q Ralph Lawes	1	3	0
pre 2	/q 2/ at the Reed Damme a messuage with a croft q Ralph Lawes	1	0	16
q 10	neare Hall Bottome part of 4a q Ralph Lawes	2	0	0

/5 Car 6a 3r di/

		a	r	[p]
pre 3	/Anthony/ Robert Dey his bond rent to Sedgford 1634			
q 4	/358/ at Eastgate q Thomas Akers free	1	0	0
q 4	/359/ there more east q Thomas Akers free	1	3	0
q 18	at Exland q Thomas Akers free	1	1	0
5 pre	/q 1/ neare Broadgate q Thomas Akers free	0	3	0
q 12	neare Stowell Stye q Thomas Akers free	1	0	0
7 pre	/q 10/ at Clipprowe q Thomas Lawes	4	0	0
5 pre	/q 17/ neare Linge Sty q Thomas Longstreth *q Will Guybon*	1	1	0
4 pre	/q 4/ at Oldich q Willyam Minnes & John Yonges *14 Car*	1	2	0
5 pre	/q 1/ at Broadgate q Willyam Minnes and John Yonges *14 Car*	2	0	
4 pre	/q 11/ at Longland next, Fringe way on the west /1639/ of Minnes	3	0	
		6	3	0

Sum bond 7a 3r, free 3a 1r

		a	r	[p]
[p] 55	Allen Robert Collen his bond rent to Sedgford 1634			
pre 5	/885/ next Streetgate Way sometime in 3 pieces q Allen Collen			
q 15	*the Lord east*	6	1	0
q 16	/Dey 14 Car/ next Fring Border an headland q Adler Billard	1	0	0
q 17	/Dey 14 Car/ neare Linge Stye an headland q Adler Billard *next Fring Border south*	1	1	0
pre 6	/q 2/ neare Streetgate an headland q Margery Clarke	1	3	0
q 6	at Oldowne Knoll q Margery Clarke	2	3	0
q 7	neare Stowell Stye q Margery Clarke	1	1	0
q 9	at Stowell Stye q Henry Clarke *Rose on both sides*	0	3	20
	there more south q Henry Clarke *Rose on both sides*	2	1	30
pre 7	/q 20/ at Cattland q Thomas Orwell	3	0	0
q 24	at Nether Cawdell q Margery Clarke	2	0	0
	there more west q Thomas Beale	1	1	0

	there next *q* Thomas Beale	3	0	0
	there more west *q* Thomas Beale	1	0	0
	there next *q* Thomas Beale	6	2	0
q 27	at Wrennock Deale *q* Margery Clarke	1	1	0
	there more west *q* Thomas Beale	4	1	20
q 28	neare Winches Lane a messuage with a croft *q* Margery Clarke *in Southgate Rose east*	1	2	0
	there next a messuage with a croft *q* Margery Clarke *north upon the river*	1	2	0

[Sum] /44 1r 10p/

q 29	at Exmere *q* Margery Clarke	1	1	0
pre 7	<neare Winches Lane> a messuage *q* Thomas Lawes <part of			
q 28	4a 2r 1 10 perches whereof 5 Godfre Ellgar> *abut north upon the river, the way goeth on south on the way	1	2	16
	there next & west at the south end of 3ac Ellgar west abut north upon the way	1	3	0

Summ 44a 1r 10p all bond at 4d
3a 1r 16p sold to Dey 2a 1r di

pre 2	John Roll his lande bond of Sedgford	a	r	[p]
q 2	/198/ a messuage in Eastgate inclosed *the way east & north* *q* Willyam Minnes and <Richard Dearham> *John Collen*	1	3	0
q 2	/195/ there *q* Willyam Minnes *Hargate* Willyam Crisp and Richard Dearham	0	2	0
q 2	/199/ one pightle bounded by it selfe *q* Willyam Minnes and Simon Ellgar, the Reed Damm south, Bearsty north, abut west upon the Lord rent 10d for	0	3	0
q 2	/free/ 2r di inclosed in the croft *q* *Hargate* Willyam Minnes and John Collen his bond land west abut north upon the way, south upon Bearstye, rent 1d for	0	2	20
pre 7	</Allen/ Collen for bond rent near Winches Land *q* Thomas			
q 28	Lawes part of 4a 2r 10p whereof Godfrey Ellgar hath 5r> <1r 36p the north ende <east side> of 1a 36p with a tenement *q* Thomas Lawes>	3	1	36

pre 7	/1638/ <George Framingham>			
q 28	<Godfrey Ellgar for bond rent part of 4a 2r 10p *q* Thomas Lawes>	1	1	0

[p 56]	Robert Hancell his bond rents to Sedgford 1634	a	r	[p]
pre 3	neare Bishops Croft *q* Willyam Banyards *voyd* a messuage			
q 4	with a croft *q Finches* /42 Eliz/	1	0	½
	there more east *q* Robert Banyard *in Eastgate with a ten[emen]t*	1	1	0

		a	r	[p]
pre 5	neare Purfers Croft *q* Robert Collen *with a spong in the north*			
q 4	/fine 5s & 2s 9d/ 4 Jac taken up and the first pcicc takcn but 1ac	2	0	0
pre 6	/Sold 1634/ John Adams for bond rent at Chappell Croft a			
q 12	messuage with a croft *q* Nicholas Smith *q* Thomas Crisp to Ro			
	Banyard	4	0	0

/Edmond Arnolld/

		a	r	[p]
pre 3	Richard Bankes senior his bond rents to Sedgford 1634			
q 21	at Overfurlong *q* Henry Drake	1	1	0
pre 4	/q 11/ at Longland *q* Adler Billard	0	2	½
q 13	at Jebdele Bottome *in Eastgate* *q* Adler Billard *q* John Chosell	1	0	0
	there *in Eastgate* next *q* Robert Woodthorp *q* John Yonges	1	0	0
pre 6	/q 10/ at Stowell Stye *q* Thomas Gogney	0	3	20
	there next *q* John Ellgar	0	2	0
q 12	/854/ at Chappell Croft *q* John Rust *q* Robert Banyard	2	1	0
pre 3	/349/ neare Bishops Croft *the south end* <parcell> of 5r called			
q 4	Lowtes piece *the way south* *q* Clarke	0	1	0
q 4	/350/ there next a messauge *the south end* <part >of 3a 2r *q*			
	John Rust *the way south*	0	2	0
q 4	/351/ <there next with a messuage *q* Spallden *Attwood east the			
	way south*>	0	1	0
q 9	at Winesgate *q* Ellgar	0	2	0
q 9	there next *q* Ellgar an Healand called Meynes Land	0	2	0
q 9	there *q* Francis Guybon and John Lawes	0	2	0
q 17	at Hundell an headland *q* Ellgar	0	2	10
pre 4	/q 11/ at Longeland Bottom *q* Simon Ellgar	3	1	0
	Writt [Sum] /13a 2r 1/			

		a	r	[p]
pre 3	/349 Wakefield 1637/ Thomas Spalding for bond rent of a cottage			
q 4	with a curtleage *q* Edward Greene *& Rust* neare Bishops Croft			
	the way south *12 Car*	0	1	0
pre 4	/H Minnes/ at Longeland *q* Lionell Bankes			
q 11	Sold to Henry Minnes 1635 to Dey 1639	0	3	0

		a	r	[p]
[p] 57	John Lingey his bond rents to Sedgford 1634			
pre 3	/q 1/ at Westgate at cottage called Castle *q* Thomas Collen	0	1	0
q 9	at Winesgate *q* Thomas Collen	0	2	0
q 16	at Longe Cleyland *q* Thomas Collen	0	3	0
pre 4	/q 9/ neare Streetgate *q* John Collen	1	0	0
	there next *q* Thomas Collen	2	0	0
q 10	at Highmere *q* Thomas Collen	2	0	0
pre 5	/q 5/ at Small Styes *q* John Lawes *but 2a 6 Car qr 18 Jac*	2	2	0

		o	2	o
q 12	/855/ neare Stowell Stye q Thomas Collen	o	2	o
	there next q Thomas Collen	o	3	20
pre 6	at Streetgate q Thomas Collen	o	3	20
q 10	there next q Thomas Collen	o	2	30
	Writt	/11	3	30/
pre 6	Willyam Adams for bond rent of 7½r at Oldowne Knoll of 9a			
q 6	½r q Robert Rose	1	3	20
pre 8	in the Minkt furlong Creamer and Awdly 1637 *the Lord on			
q 29	both sides*	1	o	o
pre 6	Thomas Outlawe for bond rent of ½ rod at Oldowne knoll part			
q 6	of 6r q Randall Ellgar Thomas Bassam having 1r ½ of the same			
	piece this is 30 per*	o	o	30
	/977/ 4 Jac <Thomas> Rich Outlaw to Anne Armes 15p q Tho			
	Drake 42, 45 Eliz			
pre 6	Thomas Bassam *John Lawes* for bond rent of 1½r at Oldowne			
q 6	knoll part of 1a 2r q Randall Ellgar *4 Eliz Drake to Fewter			
	1r 10p*	o	1	10

Edmond Person, Thomas Wallden, Woollston

pre 5	/881/ Willyam Byrd for bond rent of a piece of neare Stowell			
q 14	Style wheron the mill doth stand q Robert Banyrd part of 3r *q			
	Richard Smith*	o	o	20

[p 58]

pre 6	/1638 Will Guybon/ <Richard Gould for bond rent at Oldowne	o	1	o
q 6	knoll q Thomas Brock>			
pre 3	/354/ Willyam Billement for bond rent of a cottage in Eastgate	1	o	o
q 4	q John Yonge *Ro Banyard late Chosell west the messuage of			
4 Car	Tho Hargate q Dungle & Hen Lawes east* 3r abutt south upon			
	the way *to Docking* Robert Banyard west			
pre 2	Richard Bankes junior for bond rent of a cottage in Westgate	o	2	o
q 1	streete q Thomas Hargate			
	Writt			
pre 8	/N2/ Godfrey Hargate for bond rent in Eaton [247] q Creamer and			
q 14	Godfrey Hargate *at Overcrowne Crosse, Cremer south*			
	/1576/ John Ellgar north east upon Hounsbush 11 Car	o	1	30

---

247. N2 reference is to land in Heacham paying rents to Sedgefords Manor, Sedgeford.

pre 2   <Willyam <<Greene>> Crisp for bond rent of a messuage with a   1   1   16
q 1   croft at Hall Greene *q* David Greene>
      <7 Car Will Crisp to John a messuage & 5r. So 16 perches short>

      <Edmond Arnold for bond rent of>
pre 2   John Crisp the sonne of Willyam holdeth 5r 16p with a messuage
q 1   and a shoppe on Hall Greene by rent 5¾d   1   1   16

pre 6   <Francis Costen for bond rent of 1a *q* Randall Ellgars sold to
q 6   Bartholomew Crisp 1635 and to John Crisp 1638 14 Car>   1   0   0

      <Robert Larke for bond rent of>

		a	r	[*p*]
[*p*] 59	Mrs Dorothe Redmans bond rent to Sedgford 1634			
N18[248] at Thorpe Street *q* Chafer *17 Eliz* *q* John Rolph *17 Eliz et 24				
q 42	to Rolfe *q* Plumm 24 Hen 7 15 Hen 8*	2	0	0
N29	at Findelowes Calke Pitt with a Calkepitt in it *q* Pryore of			
q 55	Norwich *q* John Rolph *q* Folkes 9 Eliz both, 17 Eliz to Eustace			
	Rolfe*	1	2	0
	Sum 3a 2r in Heacham field taken up <8 Eliz 17r> Eliz 37			
	<39 Eliz fine 10s> 42 Eliz fine	3	2	0

		s	d	
	Edmond Jenners bond rent to Sedgford 1634			
q 65	1ac neare Collens Close *q* Willyam Raven *q* Strange n 65 n 10*	1	0	0
q 66	3ac in West Meddow furlong *q* Willyam Raven *n 9*	2	6	0
	1ac there more east *q* Willyam Raven *n 11*	0	9	0
	1ac there more east *q* Willyam Raven *n 14*	0	9	0
	2ac there more east *q* Willyam Raven *n 17*	2	0	0

            Sum 8a 1r – particular rent 7d
      taken up 17 Eliz fine 8s: 39 Eliz fine 10s: 42 Eliz fine 7s granted
      38 Hen 8 fine 6s 5½d
pre 8   /Willyam Adams 1637/ Thomas Awdly for bond rent of 1ac in the
q 29   Minckt furlonge in Sedgford *q* Edmond Creamer

					Edmond Creamers rent to Sedgford bond	s	d	
[pre 1]	1	3	0		/136/ late Hargates called Skotts yarde sold to Sir			
q 22					Ni[*cholas*] Lestrange 1634	0	7	0
		1	1	0	late Hargates next the River sold to Sir Nicholas			
					Lestrange 1634	0	5	0
q 25		0	3	½	late Hargates and abuts upon Otterhole sold to Sir			
					Hamon Lestrange 1634	0	3	½

---

248. In Heacham, hence the different numbering system.

pre 6	2	1	0	/q 12/ late Ralph Hargates sold to Henry Creamer			
				1634	0	9	0
pre 8	1	0	10	/q 14/ in 2 pieces late Hargates sold to Henry			
				Creamer 1634	0	4	¼
q 2	1	1	0	in Eaton betwixt Henry Lawes and Richard Byrd			
				to Henry Creamer	0	5	0
q 29	0	2	0	in Eaton q Thomas Hargate Robert Creamer hath it	0	2	0

Sum 2s 11¾d

Edmond Creamer payd 3s 5d so 5¼d to[o] much

John Fisher's Survey of Sedgeford, 1631

Sedg[e]ford Breck & Infield Lands 1631[249]
by Mr Fisher

Sedgeford Breck Booke 1631

Look what lands soever any man hath in the first breck, he is to have exchange for it in the fift[h] breck, & what soever he hath in the fift[h] breck, he is to have exchange for it in the first breck

For lands in the second breck, look for exchange in the sixt[h] breck, & for lands in the sixt[h] breck, look for exchange in the second

For lands in the third breck, look for exchange in the seaventh, & for lands in the seaventh, look for exchange in the third

For lands in the fo[u]rth breck, look for exchange in the eight, & for lands in the eight, look for exchange in the fo[u]rth

Southfeild [*7 precinct*][250]   **The First Breck**

2 fur[251] the first breck contayneth one peece   a   r [p]   whereof H. Myns hath
1065   of land of the Lords wch by Mr   in exchange 1r, Jo. Ellgar
    Shepheards booke is 30 acres, but for   1ac, Ro. Rose 8a 2r
    divers yeres last past it hath bene   W. Banyard 11a 2r[252]
    letten for 24 acres & was by measure   24   1   0   & letten for barly 3ac

---

249. LEST/IC58.

250. The text by John Fisher is laid out diagrammatically across the page in neat, tiny writing; there are no formal margins or columns. For clarity, the entries for the precinct, furlong and numbers have been consolidated into a LH margin. As in the 1634 rental, the numbers post-date those for the precinct and furlongs hence the gaps in the sequences.

251. Abbreviations have been retained where they are standard ie 'wch', 'wth' 'wthin' and for the names of tenants in the narrow columns. Otherwise, contractions are extended.

252. Abbreviations for acre have been standardized to 'ac' when standing alone; otherwise 'a' 'r' 'p'.

3 fur	the 6 first peeces of the third furlong				
1066	where the Lord hath	12	0	0	letten wth the great fearm
1067	Sir Hamon le Strange[253]	1	2	0	letten wth the great fearm
	William Banyard	0	2	0	
1069	Sir Hamon le Strange	0	2	0	letten wth the great fearm
1070	the Lord	3	0	0	letten wth the great fearm
	William Banyard	0	3	20	
9 fur	the fifth peece of the 9 furlong wch				
1108	is the Lords & conteyneth	5	0	0	letten wth the great fearm
1109	the fifth peece wch is Sir Hamon le Strange was	2	3	0	letten wth the great fearm
1110	<three acres part of the next peece> of Lords 5 acres	5	0	0	whereof Ro. Rose hath in exchange 1ac & the shepheard for covenants 2ac
17 fur					
1219	the Lords part of 3 acres	0	2	0	
1220	Sir Hamon le Strange	1	0	0	
18 fur	all the 18 furlong where Sir Hamon le				
1221	Strange hath	2	2	0	letten wth the great fearm
1222	Robert Rose in 2 peeces	2	2	0	
1204	the Lords part of 5 acres	0	2	0	
19 fur	all the 19 furlong where Sir Hamon le				
1224	Strange hath	0	3	20	
	John Elgar	0	3	20	
	Robert Rose	0	1	30	
	the same Robert	0	1	30	
	John Elgar	4	0	0	
1229	the Lord	1	3	20	} Jo. Elgar hath in
1230	Sir Hamon le Strange	1	3	20	} exchange
	The whole some [sum][254] of the Lords land & Sir Hamon le Stranges	64	0	20	

The sum of:

John Elgar	4	3	20							
Robt Rose	3	1	20							
Wm Banyard	1	1	20	9	2	20	*vidz* to:			
							11	2	0	W. Banyard
The sum of the exchange that here to be allowed to the tenants wthin this breck is							10	1	20	Ro. Rose
							5	3	0	Jo. Elgar
			27	3	20		0	1	0	H. Myns
To the shepheard for his covenants			2	0	0					

---

253. Fisher's use of lower case as in 'le' Strange has been retained for this survey.
254. Some replaced by 'sum' from this point.

The exchange lands & shepheards covenants
being deducted there will remayne clerely of
the Lords land in the first breck   30 1 0 whereof
     letten wth the great fearme 27 1 0
    So remain to be letten for barly 3 0 0

<table>
<tr><td>This breck will be in the
yeare ending at Michaelmas
1631   last crop   1639
1636   somerlay
1637   first crop
1638   second crop</td><td>Memo[255] that in the yeare ending at Michaelmas 1631 onely Allan Collin hath in this breck 3ac: for Fr. Guybon 1ac & Osborne 3r 20p, for wch they are to pay fearm barly. But when this breck come to be broken up againe, there will be but 3ac onely to be letten for barly, wch difference ariseth by reason that Ro. Rose in the yeare ending at Michaelmas 1631 hath 2a 3r 20p in exchange on the north side for his land on this side, wch hereafter he shall have in this breck</td></tr>
</table>

Memo that Tho Longstreth is to have 1ac di of the
last crop in the Southfield every yeare, as Mason had
with his lease

Southfeild [7 precinct]   ## The Second Breck

			a	r [p]	
15 fur					
1202	Sir Hamon Le Strange part of 6a 3r		6	2	0
1203	the last peece of the 15 furlong wch				W. Banyard hath 4ac in
	is the Lords was	14	0	0	exchange
					Robt Rose 4a 3r 20p
1204	the Lord part of 5ac	0	2	0	Jo. Elgar 5a or 20p
14 fur	the first two peeces of the 14 furlong	1	0	0	
1183	*vidz* Ro. Rose				
1184	and the same Robert	2	0	0	
21 fur	all the 21 furlong where the Lord				W. Banyard 7ac & Ro.
1246	hath	9	0	0	Rose 2ac in exchange
1247	Sir Hamon le Strange	6	0	0	Ro. Rose 3a 1r in exchange & 2a 3r letten wth the great fearme
1248	the Lord	1	1	0	Ro. Rose hath in exchange
1249	Henry Myns	4	1	0	
1250	Robert Rose	2	2	0	
1251	Sir Hamon le Strange	2	0	0	Ro. Rose hath 1a 3r in

---

255. For standard abbreviation of memoranda.

exchange & for covenants
the shephcard hath 1r
[*and below*]

| 1252 | the Lord | 1 | 3 | 0 | the shepeard hath for covenants |

1243	the Lord	5	0	0	
1244	John Elgar	1	2	0	
1245	the last peece of the 20 furlong wch is the Lords was	18	0	0	Ro. Rose hath 3a 3r in exchange, W. Banyard 1a 2r 20p, letten wth the great fearm 12a 3r 20p

22 fur	all the 22 furlong in wch the Lord				Fr. Guibon *Ro. Rose*
1253	hath	1	1	0	hath 1a 2r
1254	Sir Hamon le Strange	1	1	0	H. Myns hath 1ac in exchange

| 1255 | Robert Rose | 0 | 2 | 20 | |
| 1256 | Sir Hamon le Strange | 1 | 1 | 0 | Jo. Elgar hath it in exchange |

| 1257 | John Elgar | 0 | 2 | 20 | |

13 fur there is one peece of the Lords inclosed conteyning 3ac adjoining to the
1182 South Close wch is bounded by it self after the end of the 13 furlong, wch
3 ac (before it was inclosed) did lye wthin the compasse of this second
breck, & now is again added to this second breck

The whole sum of the Lords land: a   r [*p*]
Sir Hamon le Strange   67   3   0
Little South Close   3   0   0

The sum of:
Robert Rose   6   0   20
Henry Myns   4   1   0
John Elgar   2   0   20   12   2   0

vidz to
16   3   20   Robert Rose
12   1   0   W. Banyard
6   1   20   John Elgar
1   2   0   F. Guybon
1   0   0   Hen Myns

The sum of the exchange lands that
are to be allowed to the tenants wthin
this breck is   38   0   20

The exchange lands & shepheards covenants
being deducted there will remayne clearly of
the Lord land wthin the second breck besides
the sd 3ac inclosure wch is all letten wth the
great fearme   15   2   20

1631   second crop   1639
1632   last crop   1640
1637   somerlay
1638   first crop

Southfield [7 *precinct*]   The Third Breck

		a	r	[*p*]	
31 fur 1337	the Lord called Eastlarksdile	16	o	o	F. Guibon 2r, Jo. Elgar 3ac in exchange
30 fur 1312	20 acs part of 32ac of the Lords wch is first peece of the 30th furlong	20	o	o	The shepheard 2ac for covenants Great fearme 12ac & letten for barly 2ac 2r
1314	next that Sir Hamon le Strange hath	2	3	30	Ro. Rose 2ac 2r 20p, F. Guibon 1r in exchange & letten to Guibon for barly 10p
1313	Robert Rose	2	2	o	
1315	Sir Hamon le Strange	4	2	o	John Laws 2ac, H. Myns 1ac in exchange & letten for barly 1a 2r
1316	Robert Rose	2	2	o	
1317, 1318	<1339, 1340> The peeces bounded by themselves before the end of the 30th furlong wherof the one contayneth 18ac of the Lords & is furgrownd				
1318	the other is the Lords called Claypit peece cont 24ac whereof 2r lye in the Claypit: so rem[ain]	23	2	o	Jo. Elgar 3a 2r in exchange Great fearm 20ac

	a	r					
The whole sum of the Lords land, beside the 18ac of furre ground & 2r in the Claypitt of Robert Rose	66	3	30				
	5	o	o			*vidz* to:	
				6	2	o	Jo. Elgar
				2	2	o	Ro. Rose
The sum of the exchange lands that are to be allowed to the tenants wthin this breck				2	o	o	Jo. Lawes
				o	3	o	Fr. Guibon
	12	3	20	1	o	o	H. Myns
The shepheard for his covenants	2	o	o				

1631	first crop	1639	The exchange lands & shepheards covenants being deducted there will remayne clearly of the Lords land in the third breck	a	r	p
1632	second crop	1640		36	o	10
1633	last crop	1641				
1638	somerlay					
			whereof letten to the great fearme	32	o	o
			So remain to be letten for barly	4	o	10

Southfeild [7 precinct]   The Fourth Breck

30 fur	twelve acres, the residue of the aforesaid	12ac	
1312	32ac, wch is the first peece of the 30 furlong	12ac	whereof to the shepheard for covenants 2ac
31 fur	the last peece saving two of the 31 furlong		
1338	wch is the Lords & contayneth	48ac	Great fearm
29 fur	the last peece of the 29 furlong wch is the		
1311	Lords called Dumplin & contain	5ac	Great fearm
	The whole some of the Lords land	65ac	whereof
	letten wth the great fearme	53ac	
	to the shepheards for his covenants	2ac	
	So remain to be letten for barly	10ac	So here are 63ac, besides the shepheards covenants

				Grasscroft by Mr Shepheards book contain 16ac,
1631	somerlay	1639		but is not above 11ac by measure, whereof 3ac are
1632	first crop	1640		inclosed & accompted wth Church medow amongst
1634	second crop	1641		the infield lands, & the residue lyeth always for the
1634	last crop	1642		sheepe & yeldeth noe other profitt

Southfeild [7 precinct]   The Fift[h] Breck

		a	r	[p]	The shepheard hath it for
9 fur	<two acres of the Lords part of 5ac				
1110	being the last peece in the 9th furlong> *laid into the first breck*	2	0	0	covenants
1111	one peece bownded by itself after the end of the 9 furlong wch is Sr Hamon le Strangs & conteyneth	11	0	0	Great fearm
1112	another peece next that bownded by itself wch is the Lords & conteyneth	7	0	0	Great fearm
17 fur	all the 17 furlong where John Elgar				
1209	hath	1	3	0	
1210	Robert Rose	2	0	0	
1211	William Banyard	3	2	20	
1213	Robert Rose	1	0	20	
1214	Sir Hamon le Strange	0	2	0	Great fearm
1215	Sedgfords	1	0	0	Great fearm
1216	the Lord	2	0	0	Great fearm
1217	John Elgar	0	2	0	
1218	the same John	1	1	0	
1219	the Lord part of 3ac *2r of this added to the first*	2	2	0	Great fearm

1220	*this is 1ac added to the first breck*	4	0	0
1204	one peece bownded by itself after the end of the 15 furlong wch is the Lords *part of 5acs* *2r of this added to the first & 2r of this added to the second*			
16 fur	all the 16 furlong where Sr Hamon	2	0	0	Ro. Rose in exchange
1205	le Strange hath			
1206	Robert Rose	0	3	20
1207	Sir Hamon le Strange	1	3	0	Ro. Rose in exchange 1a 1r 20p whereof letten to barly 1r 20p
1208	the Lord	1	1	0	Jo Elgar 1ac in exch & the rest being by measure 1r let to him
15 fur	all the 15 furlong saving the last peece,	0	1	20
1194	where John Elgar hath			
1195	Sir Hamon le Strange	2	1	0	Jo. Elgar in exchange
1196	Robert Rose	1	0	20
1197	the Lord	0	2	0
1198	Sir Hamon le Strange	0	1	0
1199	Sir Hamon le Strange	1	0	20	W. Banyard in exchange
1200–1	William Banyard somtymes 2 peeces	1	3	20
1202	Sir Hamon le Strange *part of 6a 3r* /6a 2r of this added to the 2nd breck/	0	1	0	<whereof> Willm Banyard 1r exchange
12 fur	all the beginning of the 12 furlong the			
1122	Lord hath	0	3	0
1123	Sir Hamon le Strange	1	0	0
	John Elgar	1	3	0
1125	the Lord	1	3	0	Jo. Elgar in exchange
	W. Banyard	1	0	0
1127	the Lord	1	1	0
	Robert Rose	0	0	20
1129	Sir Hamon le Strange	0	1	20
1130	Robert Rose	0	1	20
1131	the same Robert	0	2	0
1132	Sir Hamon le Strange	0	2	0
1133	William Banyard	0	3	0
1134–5	Robt Rose in 7 peeces	2	0	0
1136	W. Banyard	2	3	0
1137	Sir Hamon le Strange	1	0	0
1138	Henry Myns	0	1	0

1139	Sir Hamon le Strange			1	0	0		
1140	William Banyard part of 4ac 1r			2	0	0		
	The whole sum of the Lords land			45	0	0		
	Willm Banyard 11 2 0							
	Robt Rose 10 1 20							
	John Elgars 5 3 0							
	Henry Myns 0 1 0		27	3	20		*vidz* to:	
						4 3 0	Jo. Elgar
						3 1 20	Ro. Rose
	The sum of the exchange lands to be							
	allowed to the tenants in this breck		9	2	0	1 1 20	W. Banyard
	To the shepheard for his covenants		2	0	0		

1632	somerlay	1640	The exchange lands & shepheards		a	r [p]
1633	first crop	1641	covenants being deducted there will			
1634	second crop	1642	remayne clerely of the lords land in			
1635	last crop		the fift breck	44	1	0

whereof		
Letten wth the great fearm	24	2	0
So remain to be letten for barly	19	3	0

Southfeild [*7 precinct*]   **The Sixt[h] Breck**

		a	r [p]		
12 fur	the residue of the 12 furlong beginning				
1140	wth the remainder of Will Banyards				
	4a 1r, *vidz*	2	1	0	
1141–2	Robert Rose in 2 peeces	4	1	20	
1143	the Lord	7	0	0	
1144	Sir Hamon le Strange	0	2	0	
1145	Robert Rose	3	0	20	
1146	Sir Hamon le Strange	0	1	20	Ro. Rose in exchange
1147	Robert Rose	0	2	20	
1148	the Lord	1	0	0	Ro. Rose in exchange
1149	Robert Rose	1	0	0	
1150	Sir Hamon le Strange	1	0	0	H. Myns in exchange
1151	Robert Rose	1	0	0	
1152	W. Banyard	3	0	0	
1153	John Elgar	0	2	0	
1154	Robert Rose	0	2	0	
1155	Sir Hamon le Strange	1	0	0	Ro. Rose in exchange
1156	the Lord	2	0	0	Ro. Rose in exchange
1157–8	Robert Rose somtymes 2 peeces	0	2	0	
1159	W. Banyard	1	1	0	
1160	the Lord	1	2	0	H. Myns in exchange

1161	Sir Hamon le Strange	1	1	0	H. Myns 2r 20p, Jo. Elgar 2r 20p in exchange
1162	John Elgar	1	1	0	
1163	Robert Rose	1	1	0	
1164	Sir Hamon le Strange	1	0	0	the shepheard [2ac]
1165	The Lord	1	0	0	for covenants
1166	Francis Guibon *Ro Rose*	1	0	2	
1167	the Lord	1	3	0	Ro. Rose in exchange
1168	Robert Rose	1	1	0	
1169	W. Banyard	1	1	0	
13 fur 1170	all the 13 furlong where the Lord hath	9	0	0	Great fearm
1171	Henry Myns	1	0	0	
1172	the Lord	3	0	0	Great fearm
1173	Sir Hamon le Strange	2	0	0	
1174–5	John Elgar somtymes 2 peeces	1	0	20	*Jo. Elgar 1a 2r in exchange for this peece n. 1244 layd into the second breck*
1176	the Lord	7	0	0	Great fearm
1177	Sir Hamon le Strange	2	0	0	H. Myns 1a or 20p exchange & letten for barly 3r 20p
1178	Robert Rose	1	1	0	
1179	the Lord	1	3	0	
1180	John Elgar	2	0	0	
1181	Sir Hamon le Strange 11acs called the South Close	11	0	0	<this is accompted amongst the Infield lands>
14 fur	for Sharnborne Close				
1185	all the 14 furl saving the 2 first peeces, *vidz* Ro. Rose	2	0	0	
1186	Sir Hamon le Strange	1	2	0	Base
1187	John Elgar	1	2	0	
1188	W. Banyard somtymes 2 peeces	3	1	0	
1190	Sir Hamon le Strange	0	2	0	
1191	W. Banyard somtymes 2 peeces	1	1	20	
1193	Sir Hamon le Strange	1	1	0	

The whole sum of the Lords land & the 11acs (the South Close) *letten with the fouldcourse always to lye for the sheepe*47 1 20

        Robert Rose   16   3 20

        W. Banyard   12   1 20

John Elgars   6   1 20
F. Guibon   1   2   0
Henry Myns   1   0   0   38 0 20

vidz to:

6   0 20 Ro. Rose

The sum of the exchange lands to be   4   1   0 Henry Myns
allowed to the tenants in the breck   11 0   0   0   2 20 Jo. Elgar
The shepheard for his covenants   2   0   0

1633	somerlay	1641	The exchange lands & shepheards covenants being
1634	first crop	1642	deducted there will remayne clerely of the lords
1635	second crop		land in the sixth breck 45 1 20
1636	last crop		whereof letten wth the great fearm 32 0 0
			So remain to be letten for barly 13 1 20

Southfeild [7 precinct]   ## The Seaventh Breck

		a	r	[p]
31 fur	all the 31 furlong (saving the 3 last			
1319	peeces) *vidz* the Lord	2	2	0
1320	More the Lord	1	0	0
1321	John Lawes	0	2	0
	John Elgar	0	3	20
	Robert Rose	1	2	0
	John Lawes	1	0	0
1325	Francis Guibon *Ro Rose*	0	3	0
	John Elgar	1	2	0
	John Lawes	0	2	0
1328	Sir Hamon le Strange	2	2	0 Ro. Rose exchange
	Robert Rose	1	0	20
	John Elgar somtymes iii peeces	3	2	0
1333	Sir Hamon le Strange	8	1	0 Great fearme
	John Elgar	0	2	20
1335	Sir Hamon le Strange	2	2	0 Ro. Rose exchange
1336	Sir Hamon le Strange	2	1	0
1337	/no furrs/ *now 3 Breck*			Great fearme
32 fur	all the 32 furlong (saving the 3			
1345	first peeces) Hen. Mins	1	0	0
1346	Sir Hamon le Strange somtymes			
	7 peeces	5	0	0 Great fearme
1346	Sir Hamon le Strange	2	2	0
1347	the Lord	1	0	0
1348	Sir Hamon le Strange	1	0	0
1349	the Lord	1	3	0

1350	Sir Hamon le Strange	1	3	0	
1351	the Lord	4	0	0	
1352	Sir Hamon le Strange	1	1	10 }	
1353	the Lord	2	2	0 }	
1354	the Lord	1	0	0 }	
1355	Sir Hamon le Strange	2	0	20 }	Sharnborne Close
1356	two peeces bownded by themselves after the end of the 32 furlong where Sr Hamon le Strange hath	1	0	0	Great fearme
1357	two acres part of 5ac of the Lords	2	0	0	
1358	the residue of the same 5ac of the Lords	3	0	0	
33 fur	in the 33 furlong Sir Hamon le Strange				
1359	somtymes 3 peeces	3	1	0	
1360	the Lord	5	0	0	
1361	Sir Hamon le Strange	5	2	0	whereof the shepheard hath 1r
1362	the Lord	1	3	0	shepheard covenants

The whole sum of the Lords lands <besides 1ac ½ of furrground>		64	1	30	<78a 3r 30p>

			John Elgars	6	2	0		
1634	somerlay	1642	Robt Rose	2	2	20		
1635	first crop		John Lawes	2	0	0		
1636	second crop		F. Guibon	0	3	0		
1637	last crop		Henry Myns	1	0	0	12	3 20

Exchange lands to be wthin this breck allowed to Robert Rose	5	0	0
to the shepheard for his covenants	2	0	0
wch being deducted there will remayne clerely of the lords land in the 7 breck	71	3	30
whereof letten wth the great fearme	37	2	30
So remain to be letten for barly	34		0

Southfeild [7 precinct]

1342	the 3 first peeces of the 32 furl vidz			
1343–4	Sir Hamon le Strange somtymes in 2 peeces			
1363	the residue of the 33 fur vidz Sir Ham le Strange	7	1	0

The Eighth[b] Breck

24ac whereof great fearme 17ac 2ac wch the shepheard hath for covenants

1364	Sir Hamon le Strange	1	1	0	great fearme
1365–6	the said Sir Hamon somtymes 2 peeces	4	3	20	great fearme
1367	the said Sir Hamon	3	2	0	great fearme
1368	the said Sir Hamon	1	0	0	great fearme
1369	the said Sir Hamon	1	0	0	great fearme
1370	the said Sir Hamon	1	3	0	great fearme
1371	all the 34 furlong *vidz* Sir Hamon	2	1	10	great fearme
1372	somtymes 2 peeces				
1373	the said Sir Hamon	1	1	0	great fearme
1374	the said Sir Hamon	2	2	0	great fearme
1375	the said Sir Hamon	1	0	0	great fearme
1376	the Lord	12	0	0	great fearme
	The whole sum wthin this breck wch is all the Lords	65	2	30	whereof
1635	somerlay for the shepheards covenants	2	0	0	
1636	first crop so remain:	63	2	30	
1637	second crop letten wth the great fearme	49	1	30	
1638	last crop & letten for barly	14	1	0	

The whole sum of the all the Lords lands
in the South pasture, beside the South
Close contain 11ac 510a 2r 30p

North Pasture [*1 & 2 precincts*]

The First Breck

2 fur	all the second furlong of the first	a	r [*p*]		whereof the shepheard
n 2	precinct wch is the Lords & contayneth	16	0	0	hath 2ac Mr Loades 2r in exchange
3 fur	all the third furlong wch is the Lords				Mr Guibon 5r
n 3	& contain	20	0	0	W. Guibon 3ac
14 fur	part of the 14 furlong of the second				
276	precinct where the Lord hath	5	0	0	
	W. Guibon	1	0	0	
278	the Lord	1	1	0	
279	the Lord	1	1	25	
280	Sedgfords, part of the next peece di now 5ac	0	2	0	Sold to W. Guibon 1634
13 fur	the first peece of the 13 furlong wch	4	0	0	Ric Bird 3r in exchange
270–1	are the Lords contain				Ric Banyard 3r
273	the other 3 peeces wch are the Lord				H. Myns 1a 20p & furr
274–5	cont 4ac & are furr grounds				ground 2r allowed 1641
	The sum of the Lords land,				*1641
	besides the 4ac of furre ground	48	1	5	47a 3r 5p*
	and Will Guibon	1	0	0	

1634 somerlay   1642
1635 first crop   *vidz* to:
1636 second crop   1   1   0 W. Guibon
1637 last crop   1   0 20 H. Myns
                                                0   3   0 Ric Banyard
The sum of the exchange land to be   0   3   0 Ric Bird
allowed to the tenants wthin this breck 4   1 20   0   2   0 Mr Loades
to the shepheard for his covenants   2   0   0
The exchange lands & shepheards covenants   *1641
being deducted clearly of the Lords land in the   41a 1r 25p*
first breck to be letten for fearme barley   41   1 25
whereof abate 3ac new exchange & 2r   *1641
sold to W. Guibon & so rent for barly   38   1 25   37a 3r 25p*

North pasture [2 *precinct*]   ## The Second Breck

14 fur Sedgfords the residue of the 5ac di   a   r [*p*]
280   in the 14 furlong   5   0   0 sold to W. Guibon 1634
281   the Lord, next that   7   0   0 Edw. Hargate 1ac, Mr
                                                            Wallis 3r di in exchange;
                                                            Mr Guibon exchange 3r
                                                            new

12 fur all the 12 furlong where Jo. Lawes hath 0   2 20
263   the Lord   8   0   0 Shepheards covenants 2ac
                                                            Jo. Lawes exchange 2r 32p

        John Lawes   0   2   0
265   Sedgfords   7   0   0 Jo. Lawes in exchange
266   the Lord by Mr Shepheards booke 5ac,   Jo Lawes 1a 1r, Ro. Lawes
        but it contayneth not above   4   0   0 2a 3r in exchange
        John Lawes   2   0   0
268   the Lord   1   2 20 W. Guibon exchange
269   Philip Loades clerke   0   2   0
286   the last peece of the 15 furlong *vidz*
        the Lord   3   0 10 W. Guibon exchange new
15 fur Henry Myns   0   1 30
288   the Lord   0   1 30 H. Myns exchange
16 fur all the 16 furlong where Hen. Myns
        hath   0   2   0
290   the Lord   0   2   0 H. Myns exchange
291   the Lord   7   0   0 whereof Ric Bird exch
                                                            2a 2r 20p *whereof
                                                            W. Guibon exchange 4a
                                                            1r 20p new*

		a	r	p	
292	Sedgfords	9	0	0	Sold to W. Guibon 1634 whereof W. Guibon 9ac exch
293	the Lord	0	1	30	W. Guibon exch 1r 30p new
294	John Lawes by Mr Shepheards booke 1r 30p but by measure it is bigge enough for	1	0	0	
295	the Lord	2	1	0	
258	the last 4 peeces of the 11 furlong *vidz* Richard Banyard	1	1	0	
259	The Lord	3	0	0	W. Guibon exchange new
11 fur	Henry Myns	0	2	20	
261	The Lord	0	2	20	W. Guibon exchange new

Sum of the Lords land 58				2	30	
John Lawes	4	0	20			
Hen. Myns	1	2	10			
Rich. Banyard	1	1	0			
Mr Loades	0	2	0	7	1	30

vidz to:

1635	somerlay	10	1	20	W. Guibon
1636	first crop	8	3	32	Jo. Lawes
1637	second crop	2	3	0	Ro. Lawes
1638	last crop	2	2	20	Ric Bird
		1	0	0	Ed. Hargate
	The sum of the exchange lands to be	0	3	20	Mr Wallis
	allowed to the tenants wthin this breck 27 1 2	0	3	30	H. Myns

to the shepheard for his covenants wch
being deducted there remain to be 2 0 0
letten for barly 29 1 18
whereof sold to W. Guibon 14ac & new exch 3a 1r.
So remain for barly 12a or 18p

North Pasture [*3 precinct*] **The Third Breck**

		a	r	[p]	
493	all the 18 furlong of the 3 precinct where W. Guibon hath	0	0	35	
494	the Lord	0	1	0	W. Guibon exchange
18 fur	the heire of Henry Lawes	0	3	20	
496	the Lord	1	1	0	
	Robert Dey	1	1	0	
	W. Guibon	1	1	20	

499	Mr Gurling clerke	I	I	20	
500	the Lord	5	o	o	
	Robert Banyard	I	o	o	
	W. Guibon	o	3	o	
503	the Lord	o	3	o	W. Guibon exchange
	W. Guibon	o	3	20	
505–7	the Lord somtymes 3 peeces	2	3	o	W. Guibon exchange
	Willm. Guibon	o	3	o	
509	the Lord by booke 3ac but by accompt & measure	3	I	o	Whereof Mr Loades 5r, W. Guibon 3r in exchange
510	Sedgfords	4	o	o	
511	the Lord	I	2	o	whereof H. Myns 5r exchange
19 fur	all the 19 furlong, the Lord somtymes	8	2	o	
512–3	4 peeces				
514–5	William Guibon	o	3	o	
517–8	the Lord somtymes 2 peeces	4	o	o	
519	Mr Gurling	3	2	o	
	Henry Lawes	2	o	o	
521	the Lord	2	o	o	
20 fur	all the 20 furlong, John Lawes somtymes 2 peeces	2	o	o	
	Willm Guibon	I	I	o	
525	the Lord	3	o	o	
	Mr Gurling	2	I	o	
527	Sedgfords, two furlong long	3	o	o	sold to W. Guibon 1634
	John Lawes	o	2	o	
529	the Lord somtymes 2 peeces	8	I	o	
530					
531	all the 21 furlong, the Lord somtymes	4	2	o	whereof the shepheard 2ac
532	2 peeces				
21 fur	Richard Bankes	I	I	o	
534	the Lord, besides 1ac of furrs	7	o	o	
535–6	the Lord somtymes 2 peeces	4	o	o	
537	all the 22 furlong: the Lord	5	o	o	Jo Lawes 2a 3r exchange
22 fur	John Lawes by Mr Shepheards booke 3ac but by his copies	3	2	o	
539	the Lord	3	o	o	
	William Gurling clerke	I	I	o	
541	all the 23 furlong, the Lord	3	o	o	
23 fur	William Guibon	I	2	o	

543	the Lord	7	0	0
544	all the 24 furlong: the Lord	0	3	0
24 fur	John Lawes	1	0	0
546	the Lord	1	0	0

Sum of the Lords land, besides 1ac of
furre ground   82   3   0

W. Guibon	7	1	35
Mr Gurling	8	1	20
John Lawes	7	0	0
Henry Lawes	2	3	20
Robt Dey	1	1	0
Richard Bankes	1	1	0
Robert Banyard	1	0	0 29 0 35

1631   last crop   1639
1636   somerlay   *vidz* to:
1637   first crop   4   2   0   W. Guibon
1638   second crop   2   0   0   Jo. Lawes
                                            1   1   0   Mr Loades
The sum of the exchange lands to be   1   1   0   H. Myns
allowed to the tenants wthin this breck 9   3   0   0   3   0   Edw. Lawes
to the shepheard for his covenants   2   0   0
The exchange lands & shepheards covenants
being deducted there remain clerely of the Lords
and in the third breck to be letten for barly   71ac   wherof
abate 3ac sold to W. Guibon. So remain for barly   68ac

Memo: that for the year ending at Michaelmas 1631 onely, Ro. Rose hath 3ac in this breck, whereof he ought to have 2a 3r 20p in lieu of so much of his land, which lyeth in the South pasture, for wch he hath noe exchange there & for the other 20 perches he must pay fearme
So the clere some of the Lord land in this breck for the year
ending at Michaelmas 1632 onely will be   60a or 20p

North pasture [3 precinct]   **The Fourth Breck**

                                              *Wm Guibons exchange
                                              to lye all together*

		a	r [p]	
11 fur	the third peece of the 11 furlong & so forth, Sedgfords	14 0 0		Sold to W. Guibon 1634. Martin Cob 4a 2r,
254	the Lord	1	1 0	W. Guibon 3a 20p exchange
255	the Lord	4	0 0	shepherds covenants 2ac H. Myns 2ac exchange

256	Sedgfords	9	0	0	whereof 2a 1r on the
257					south side sold to
					W. Guibon & Wm.
					Guibon 1r 20p for barly
					new

17 fur

296	part of the 17 furlong, the Lord	3	0	0	
297	the Lord	0	3	0	
	Henry Myns	0	1	0	
	John Lawes	1	0	0	
300	the Lord	1	0	0	
322	all the 19 furlong saving the first	1	3	20	
	peeces Richard Bird				
	the same Richard Bird	1	0	0	
324	the Lord by Mr Shepheards booke 4 ac,				
	but it is so little that it may goe for	3	0	0	H. Myns exchange
	William Guibon	1	1	0	
	John Lawes	1	2	0	
327	the Lord somtymes 2 peeces	2	0	20	whereof Jo Lawes &
328					Robt Lawes in exchange
					1a 1r 20p
329	John Lawes	1	0	0	

	Sum of the Lords land				38	0	20
	John Lawes	3	2	0			
	Rich. Bird	2	3	20			
	W. Guibon	1	1	0			
	Hen. Myns	0	1	0	7	3	20

1631	Second crop 1639				*vidz* to:
1632	Last crop 1640		5	0	0 Hen. Myns
1637	Somerlay		4	2	0 Mr Cobs
1638	first crop		3	0	20 W. Guibon
	Sum of the exchange lands to be allowed		0	3	20 Ro. Lawes
	to the tenants wthin this breck	14	0	0	0 2 0 Jo. Lawes
	to the shepheard for his covenants	2	0	0	

The exchange lands & shepheards covenants being
deducted there will remain clerely of the lords land
in the 4th breck to be letten for barly   22   0   20   wherof
sold to W. Guibon 16a 1r. So remain for barly   5   3   20

North pasture [2 *precinct*] The Fift[h] Breck

		a	r	[*p*]	
					W. Guibon 2r exch new
285	in the 15 furlong of the second precinct, the Lord	20	0	0	W. Guibon 1ac exchange Shepheards covenants 2ac
301–3	the residue of the 17 furlong, the Lord sometime 3 peeces	1	2	0	
17 fur	W. Guibon	1	1	0	
	Henry Myns	0	2	0	
306	the Lord	0	1	30	
	Sedgfords	3	0	0	Sold to W. Guibon 1634
308	all the 18 furlong, saving the 2 last peeces. The Lord	0	3	0	
309–11	the Lord, somtymes 3 peeces	8	0	0	
18 fur	Richard Banyard	0	3	0	
	Richard Byrd	0	3	0	
314	the Lord by Mr Shepheards booke but Hen. Mines doth sold it as his owne	0	1	10	
	Henry Myns	0	1	10	
	Philip Loades clerke	0	2	0	
	Sum of the Lords land	33	2	30	

W. Guibon	1	1	0		1631	first crop	1639
Hen. Myns	1	0	20		1632	second crop	1639
Rich. Banyard	0	3	0		1633	last crop	1640
Rich. Bird	0	3	0		1638	somerlay	
Mr Loades	0	2	0	4	1	20	

Exchange lands to be allowed in this
       breck to W. Guibon 1 0 0
  to the shepheard for his covenants 2 0 0
wch being deducted there will remayne clerely of
the Lords land in the 5 breck to be letten for barly 30a 2r 30p whereof
sold to W.Guibon 3a & new exchange 2r. So remain 27a or 30p

North pasture [1 *precinct*] The Sixt[h] Breck

		a	r	[*p*]	
5 fur	all the 5 furlong, saving the 5 first				
10	peece where the Lord hath	2	2	0	whereof the shepheard 2ac
11	Sedgfords	3	0	0	wherof Jo. Lawes exch 2ac
	Robert Lawes	0	2	20	
13	the Lord	0	2	20	Jo. Lawes in exchange
	John Lawes	1	0	20	
15	Sedgfords	1	0	20	Jo. Lawes in exchange
	Robert Lawes	0	1	20	

17	the Lord	0	1	20	Jo. Lawes in exchange
	Robert Lawes	1	3	0	
19	the Lord	5	0	0	W. Guibon in exchange new
20	Sedgfords	2	0	0	Sold to W. Guibon 1634
	John Lawes	2	0	0	
	William Guibon	3	0	0	
	the same William	2	0	20	
	the same William	1	1	20	
25	Sedgfords *|whereof 5r sold to W. Guibon 1634 on south side|*	2	2	0	whereof Ric Banyard 5r exchange
	Richard Bird	0	3	20	
	John Lawes	0	2	20	
6 fur	all the 6 furlong, William Guibon	0	3	20	
	Mr Wallis	0	3	20	
	Richard Bird	1	3	0	
7 fur	all the 7 furlong, William Guibon	0	2	0	
	John Lawes	2	0	12	
33	the Lord	1	1	0	H. Myns in exchange
	Henry Myns	0	1	20	
35	the Lord	0	2	20	Mr Loades 2r, H. Myn 20p in exchange
	William Guibon	0	1	20	
37–8	the Lord, somtymes 2 peeces	2	1	20	
	Henry Myns	0	1	20	
40–1	the Lord, somtymes 2 peeces	6	0	30	whereof H. Myns 30p exch
42	Sedgfords	7	0	0	
	John Lawes	2	0	0	
44–5	the Lord, somtymes 2 peeces	4	3	0	
59	all the 10 furlong, saving the 6 first peeces. The Lord	2	0	0	
10 fur	Willm Guibon	0	2	20	
	Edward Hargate	1	0	0	
	John Lawes	0	2	0	
63–6	the Lord somtymes 4 peeces	15	3	0	whereof 5a 2r 20p for W. Guibon exchange new
	John Lawes	0	2	20	
68	the Lord	0	2	20	W. Guibon exchange new
	William Guibon	1	2	0	
70–1	the Lord, somtymes 2 peeces	2	3	0	W. Guibon exchange new
	Sum of the Lords land	60	1	30	
	William Guibon	10	1	20	

John Lawes	8	3	32
Robert Lawes	2	3	0
Richard Bird	2	2	0
Edward Hargate	1	0	0
Mr Wallis	0	3	20
Henry Myn	0	3	0

27 1 12

1631	Somerlay	1639
1632	First crop	1640
1633	Second crop	1641
1634	Last crop	1642

vidz to:

4	0	20	Jo. Lawes
1	2	10	H. Myns
1	1	0	Rich. Banyard
0	3	0	Mr Loades

Sum of the exchange lands to be
allowed to the tenants wthin this breck 7 1 30
to the shepheard for his covenants 2 0 0
wch being deducted there will remain clerely of the Lords
land in the sixt breck to be letten for fearme barly   51ac whereof
sold to W. Guibon 3a 1r & new exch. So remain for barly   33a 3r

North pasture [*1 precinct*]   **The Seaventh Breck**

		a	r	[p]	
11 fur	all the 11 furlong *vidz* Mr Loades	1	1	0	
	Henry Myns	1	1	0	
74	Sedgfords	5	0	0	Jo. Lawes in exchange
13 fur	all the 13 furlong saving the 2 last				
78	peeces Jo. Lawes	2	0	0	
79, 80	the Lord somtymes 2 peeces	1	1	0	Jo. Lawes in exchange
81	W. Guibon	0	2	0	
14 fur	all the 14 furlong Edward Lawes	0	3	0	
83	Sedgfords by Mr Shepheards booke 7ac				
	but by measure it is not above	6	0	0	W. Guibon in exchange
	W. Guibon	1	0	0	
85	Sedgfords	6	0	0	R. Bankes 5r, Ro. Dey 5r, Jo. Lawes 3r, Ro. Banyard 1ac, Mr Girling 1r, W. Guibon 1a 1r 35p in exchange & W. Guibon 5p for barly
86	a peece of the Lords contain	2	2	0	W. Guibon exchange new
87, 88	all the 15 furlong. The Lord somtymes				
	2 peeces	4	0	0	Mr Girling exchange
89	Sedgfords	4	0	0	Mr Girling exchange
15 fur	the Lord	3	0	0	H. Lawes 2a 3r 20p, Mr Girling 20p in exchange
90					

	W. Guibon		3	0	0	
92	*lafter the 15 furl* A peece of the Lords					whereof W. Guibon exch
	contain		5	0	0	2r new
95	*lafter the 16 furl* A peece of the Lords					whereof the shepheard
	cont		I	0	0	2ac

Sum of the Lords land	38	0	0			
W. Guibon	4	2	0			
John Lawes	2	0	0			
Mr Loades	I	I	0			
Henry Myns	I	I	0			
Edw. Lawes	0	3	0	9	3	0

vidz to:

7	I	35	W. Guibon
8	I	20	Mr Girling
7	0	0	Jo. Lawes
2	3	20	H. Lawes
I	I	0	Ro Dey
I	I	0	Rich Banks

1632	somerlay	1640
1633	first crop	1641
1634	second crop	1642
1635	last crop	

29	0	35

To the shepheard for his covenants   2   0   0
wch being deducted there will remayne clerely of the Lords land in the
7 breck to be letten for fearme barly 6a 3r 5p whereof to W. Guibon for
new exchange 3ac.
So remain for barly 3a 3r 5p

So Crispe (who was predecessor to Mr Girling) had aunciently in the third breck but
7a 20p for wch he had (of old) the 2 four acre peeces & the 20p above menconed in
exchange. Mr Girling hath lately bought 5r in the third breck for wch he hath noe
exchange. He is quite insted out of the 6ac pece above menconed (where he should
have had 1r) and therefore he must have his 5r out of the Lords 5ac (n. 92) & so then
will remain in this breck to be letten for barly 2a 2r 5p

North pasture [1 precinct]				The Eight Breck

16 fur	the 16 furlong of the first precinct	a	r [p]	W. Guibon exchange
93	wch is the Lords and somtymes was			new.
94	2 peeces contayning together	9	3	20
10 fur	the 6 first peeces of the 10 furlong			
	where Mr Martin Cobb hath	3	0	0
	W. Guibon	I	I	0
55	the Lord	I	I	0	W. Guibon exchange
56–7	the Lord	3	2	0	W. Guibon exchange
58	Sedgfords in Mr Shepheards booke 3ac,			
	but in respect of the greatness of Ric.			
	Birds peece in may goe for	2	3	20	Ric. Bird exchange

8 fur	all the 8 furlong where W. Guibon hath	1	1	0	
	John Lawes	0	2	0	
48	the Lord	0	2	20	whereof Jo Lawes 2r exch
49	Sedgfords	3	0	0	Jo. Lawes exchange
50	the Lord	1	1	0	
9 fur	The 9th furlong where W. Guibon hath	0	2	20	
	Martin Cobbe	1	2	0	
5	all the beginning of the 5 furlong, the Lord	4	2	0	
6	the Lord	1	1	0	whereof W. Guibon 2a 3r 20p exchange new & the other 20p for barly
7	the Lord	1	3	0	
	Robert Lawes	0	3	20	
	Henry Myns	5	0	0	
4 fur	The 4th furlong wch is the Lords, contain	24	0	0	whereof H. Myns 1r exchange shepheard 2ac

Sum of the Lords land	53	3	20

Hen. Myns	5	0	0
Mr Cobbe	4	2	0
W. Guibon	3	0	20
Robt. Lawes	0	3	20
John Lawes	0	2	0

14 0 0   *vidz* to:

3	2	0	Jo. Lawes
2	3	20	Ric Bird
1	1	0	W. Guibon
0	1	0	H. Myns

Sum of the exchange lands to be allowed to the tenants wthin this breck   7 3 20

to the shepheard for his covenants   2 0 0

wch being deducted, there will remayne clerely of the Lords land in the 8 breck to be letten for fearme barly 44ac wherof to W. Guibon for new exchange 16a 1r.

So remain for barly 27a 3r

1633	somerlay	1641	
1634	first crop	1642	
1635	second crop		
1636	last crop		

The whole some of the Lords land in the North pasture is 418a 3r 15p

*The number of the furlongs here have relacons to the book
or platt of Sedgford made in the yeare of our Lord 1631*

Eastfield [4 precinct]   The First Breck

14fur   the 14 furlong of the 4 precinct, wch is
746²⁵⁶   all the Lords & contayneth by measure
         24a 1r 3p & is accompted by comon
         reputacon   20ac
15 fur   the 15 furlong wch is all the Lords, &   whereof F. Guibon 1a
747   contayne by measure 29a 3r 34p & is   or 20p, Edw. Hargate 3r
         accompted   30ac   20p in exchange; the
                                                                    shepheard 2ac, Great
                                                                    Farm 26ac

            Sum of all the Lords land in the first 50ac
         breck whereof allowed to F. Guibon*1ac
            or 20p* & Edward Hargate *3r 20p*
                              in exchange   2ac
            to the shepheard for his covenants   2ac
         so remain clerely of the Lords land there 46ac
            whereof letten wth the great fearm   26ac
            so remain to be letten for barly   20ac

1632   somerlay   1640   1641 Robert Attwood hath used his owne 3r 20p late
1633   first crop   1641   Edward Hargate for divers years past as infield &
1634   second crop   1642   noe exchange hath been allowed to him in this breck.
1635   last crop   So remain clerely of the Lords land in this breck 46a
                               3r 20p

Eastfield [4 precinct]   The Second Breck

16 fur   the 16 furlong wch is all the Lord   a   r [p]   shepheard 1ac,
748   contayning by measure 19a 1r 14p & is   20   0   0   Great fearme 19ac
         comonly accompted   shepheard 1ac,
17 fur   the 17 furlongwch is all the Lords contayn by   Great fearm 25ac
749   measure 35a 3r 15p & is comonly accompted 30 0   0
7 fur   the 5 last peeces of 7 furlong vidz Robt   1   0   0
691   Banyard Mr Girling   0   3 20
         1641 it is intended that these 2 peeces shall be used as infield
693–5   the Lord in 3 peeces contayn by the booke
         12a 3r 20p and are comonly accompted   12   0   0

256. The numbers for the brecks in East Field differ slightly from the maps indicating
ongoing modification to the organisation of these brecks. The Brecks in East Field are thus
divided, 1641. The acreages in the Breck Book show the approximations as well as the figures
by measure.

1641 it is intended that this shall be laid into the infield and so there will remayne clerely of the Lords land in this breck 50 acres

		a	r	p	
	Sum of all the Lords land in the second breck	62	0	0	
	Robt Baynard	1	0	0	
	Mr Gurling	0	3	20	1 3 20

1633 somerlay 1641
1634 first crop 1642
1635 second crop
1636 last crop

	a	r	p
to the shepheard for his covenants	2	0	0
so remain clerely of the Lords land there	60	0	0
whereof letten wth the great fearme	44	0	0
so remain to be letten for barly	16	0	0

Eastfield [4 precinct]   The Third Breck

		a	r	[p]	
18 fur	the 18 furlong wch is all the Lords				Ro. Banyard ½ ac
750	contayning by measure 22a 3r 29p & is comonly accompted	20	0	0	exchange, shepheard 2ac covenants
19 fur	the 19 furlong wch is all the Lords				
751	contayning by measure 35a 3r 24p & is comonly accompted	30	0	0	Great fearme

Stormhill Close contayning by measure 6ac 20p & by estimacons 5acr, adjoynurth to this breck, but it lyeth always for the sheepe, & yeldeth noe other profit.

		a	r	[p]	
7 fur	One peece of the Lords in the 7 furlong				whereof Great
690	contayning	20	0	0	fearme 12ac

1641 It is intended that 20ac (n. 690) shall be laid into the infield & so there will remayne clerely of the Lords land in this breck 47a 2r

	a	r	p	
Sum of all the Lords land in this breck (besides Stormhill Close)	70	0	0	whereof
allowed to Robt Banyard for exchange	0	2	0	
to the shepheard for his covenants	2	0	0	
so remain clerely of the Lords land there	67	2	0	*1641 47a 2r*
whereof letten wth the great fearme	42	0	0	
so remain to be letten for barly	25	2	0	*whereof furs 2r*

Eastfield [4 precinct]   The Fourth Breck

		a	r	[p]	
20 fur	the 20 furlong wch is all the Lords				The shepheard 1ac
752	contayning by measure 27a 3r 3p & is comonly accompted	20	0	0	Great fearme 19ac

		a	r	p	
22 fur 754	the 22 furlong (wch by Mr Shepheards book is called the 25 furlong) & is all the Lords contayning by measure 19a 2r 37p is comonly accompted	18	0	0	The shepheard 1ac Great fearme 17ac
5 fur 628	one peece of the Lords abutting upon Brancaster way towards the North, wch seemeth to be pt of the first peeces of the 5 furlong, & is accompted	3	0	0	
	Richard Bird hath the next peece	1	3	0	
630	the Lord next that	0	2	0	
	Francis Guibon next that	1	1	0	
	Sum of the Lords land there	41	2	0	

1635	somerlay	Richard Bird	1	3	0		
1636	first crop	F. Guibon	1	1	0	3	0 0
1637	second						
1638	last crop						

		a	r	p	
	allowed to the shepheard for his covenants	2	0	0	
	so remain of the Lords land there	39	2	0	whereof
	letten wth the Great fearme	36	0	0	
	so remain to be letten for barly	3	2	0	

Eastfield [4 precinct]   The Fift[h] Breck

		a	r	[p]	
4 fur 627	the last peece of the 4 furlong wch is the Lords contain	9	0	0	Great fearm
626	Francis Guibon next before that	1	0	20	
625–4	the Lord before that, in two peeces	5	2	0	
3 fur 586–7	the second and third peece of the third furlong, wch are the Lords & contayne	5	0	0	Great fearm
585	part of the first peece of the third furlong, which in the Lords contain 25ac, whereof 10ac furground. Remain	15	0	0	Shepheard 2ac Great fearme 12ac
2 fur 584	part of the last peece of the second furlong, wch is the Lords contain 15ac, whereof 10ac furground. So remain	5	0	0	Great fearme.
	1641 It is intended that this 5ac shall lye continually for the sheep				
583	The peece next before that wch is Edw. Hargates	0	3	20	
582	A peece of the Lords next before that, cont[ain] 3	3	1	0	Great fearme
	1641 These acres now used as infield				
	Sum of the Lords land there	42	3	0	*1641 34a 2r*

1635	somerlay	1639	of Francis Guibons	1	0	20		*1a or 20p*
1636	first crop		Edward Hargate	0	3	20		
1637	second crop		[sum]	2	0	0		
1638	last crop							

allowed to the shepheard for his covenants	2	0	0
so remain of the Lords land there	40	3	0
whereof letten wth the great fearme	34	1	0
So remain to be letten for barly	6	2	0

2ac
whereof
1641 32a 2r

Eastfield [4 precinct]   The Sixt[h] Breck

24 fur the 24 furlong wch is all the Lords   a   r [p]
        contayning by measure 52a 1r 16p, &   40   0   0
        it is accompted

1641 There will be noe cause to allow any exchange to Mr Girling & Ro. Banyard in this breck, by reason that they shall use their own land in the second breck as infield

        whereof allowed to Mr Girling for exchange   0   3   20
                    to Robt Banyard for exchange   1   0   0

1631	second crop	1639	to the shepheard for his covenants	2	0	0	
1632	last crop	1640	so remain of the Lords land there	36	0	20	whereof 38ac
1637	somerlay		letten wth the great fearme	29	0	20	
1638	first crop		so remain to be letten for barly	7	0	0	

Eastfield [4 precinct]   The Seaventh Breck

23 fur The 23 furlong wch is all the Lords   a   r [p]
755   contayning by measure 57a 3r 5p, & it is
        accompted   30   0   0
        1641 pt of this 30ac is taken from the 7th breck and added to the 8th. so rest 20ac
        whereof allowed to Robt Banyard for exchange   0   2   0

1631	second crop	1639	to the shepheard for his covenants	2	0	0	
1632	last crop	1640	So remain of the Lords land there	27	2	0	whereof17a2r
1633	somerlay	1641	Letten wth the great fearme	14	0	0	
1638	first crop		So remain to be letten for barly	13	2	0	

Eastfield [4 precinct]   The Eight[h] Breck

1641 10ac taken out of the 7th breck and added to the 8th breck wch make 30ac

						a	r	[p]
5 fur	It contayneth part of the first peece of the 5 furlong							
628	wch is all the Lords (the residue thereof *vidz* 3ac							
	being in the 4th breck) wch peece contayneth by							
	measure 30a 2r 16p is comonly accompted				20	0	0	whereof
			allowed to Francis Guibon for exchange		1	1	0	
1631	somerlay	1639	to Richard Bird for exchange		1	3	0	
1632	first crop	1640	to the shepheard for his covenants		2	0	0	
1631	second crop	1641	so remain of the Lords land there		15	0	0	*25ac*
1632	last crop	1642	wch is all letten wth the great fearme					

774   The three last furlongs of the fourth precinct contayning together by Mr
775   Shepheards book 2ac (but by measure 26a 14p, doe always lye for the sheepe
776   & yeld noe other profits

Ro. Banyard hath half an acre lying in the sheepes pasture on the south
side of the way leading from Sedgford to Docking for wch he is to have
exchange continually either in the third or seaventh breck

All the pasture lands on the south side of Docking way, wth the 11 acre
close by Docking field for many yeares last past have bene laid continually
for sheep, & hath yelded noe other profit: they doe contayne all together
267a 1r 28p whereof:
The Lord hath 263a 3r 28p

Mr Girling 2ac, Hen. Lawes 1ac for wch they have exchange in the infield
Ro. Banyard 2r for wch he hath exchange either in the 3 or 7 breck, as
abovesaid

	[a	r	p]
The whole sum of all the Lords land in the East brecks wth 20ac of furground	381	1	0
more on the north side of Docking way of the Lords	26	0	14
on the south side of Docking way of the Lords	263	3	28
Sum total in the East pasture	671	1	2
Sum on the north side	418	3	15
Sum on the south side (beside South Close)	510	2	30
Sum total of all the Lords land in all the fouldcourses, besides South Close	1600	2	7

New brecks in the Eastfield of Sedgford
on the south side of the way from Sedgford to Docking

		acres
1.	The first breck broken up at Candlemas 1631, contayneth	33
2.	The second breck adjoyning to Docking border, & to the 11 acre close, to be broken up at Candlemas 1632, contayneth	40
3.	The third breck, on the east side of the Whin Close, to be broken up at Candlemas 1633, contayneth	40 or 35
4.	The fourth breck, more north on the east side of the infeild, to be broken up at Candlemas 1634, besides Lawes his acre, & Ro. Banyard half acre, contayneth	55
5.	The fifth breck, being new pit peece, wch contayneth 18 acres & the 11 acre close, to be broken up at Candlemas 1635	29
6.	The sixth breck, lying in the midst between the Whin Close & the 11 acre close, to be broken up at Candlemas 1636, contayneth	40

Rents to be paid for these brecks
At Michaelmas 1633 for the first breck   33 acres
At Mich 1634 for the first & second   73 acres
At Mich 1635 for the second & third   80 or 75 acres
At Mich 1636 for the third & fourth   95 or 90 acres
At Mich 1637 for the fourth & fifth   84 acres
At Mich 1638 for the fifth & sixth   69 acres
At Mich 1639 for the sixth onely   40 acres

Memo: that the second breck extendeth 17r & half westward from the south east corner of the first breck & southward to the way leading from Suggate to Docking. The third breck extendeth eastward 10r short of the south west corner of the first breck & from thence southward by a great thorne (where a crosse is made) to acrosse in the side of a pit hole, & from that crosses to the south east corner of the Whin Close. But if it shalbe thought fitter to preserve the covert in that place, then the bank may goe from the said great thorne to the south east corner of the Whin Close & so that breck will contayne but 35 acres. The sixth breck extendeth southward to the way leading from Suggate to Docking.

The Brecks in the Eastfield are thus divided 1641

1. /757/ The first breck lieth at Blackhyrne, between Ringstead field on the   acres
north & the second breck here next menconed on the south & abbutteth
upon Ringstead field in part & upon the 6th breck in pt towards the east &
upon Ringstead field towards the west & contain by statute measure 53ac
3r but by comon etimacon *at 5r to an acre* it lyeth for *whereof laid to
Ringstead Flock 3ac*   43

2. /758/ The second breck lieth there more south, between the first breck
on the north & the third breck on the south, & ab[ut] upon the sixth breck
towards the east, & upon Ringstead field in part, & upon the 7th furlong at
Jebdale bottom in part towards the west, & contain by measure 50ac & by
comon estimation   40

3. /759/ The third breck lieth there more south, between the second breck
on the north & the 4th breck on the south, & abut upon Stormhill close in
part & upon the 7th breck in part towards the east & upon Jebdale bottom
towards the west *& it hath a sneck on the south side* and contain by
measure 50ac & by comon estimation   40

4. /760/ The 4th breck lieth there more south, between the third breck on
the north & Jebdale hill in part & Brancaster gate in part on the south, &
abut upon the 8th breck towards the east, & upon Jebdale bottom in part,
& upon a pece of 3ac of the lords wch Wm Girling clerk hath in exchange
towards the west *and it hath a sneck on the north side* & contain by
measure 50ac & by comon estimation   40

5. /585, 586, 587, 624, 626, 628, 629/ The fifth breck is entred in the drag book
in the beginning of the third furlong In the end of the 4th furlong & in
the beginning of the fift[h], whereof in the third furlong by measure 18a 2r
15p, but accompting 5r to an acre (as in all the former brecks) it contain 14a
3r 20p; and in the 4th & 5th furlong there are 8 severall peces (whereof Fr.
Guibon hath 2 peces cont 2a 1r 20p *n 626 & 631* & Wm Guibon late Ric
Bird hath 7r * n. 629* wch 8 pcs contain together by estimation 25a or 20p.
So that in this breck also partly by estimation, & partly at 5r to an acre,
there are likewise *whereof the Lords 35a 3r 20p & the tenants 4a or 20p*   40

6. /761/ The sixth breck lieth farre more north, between Ringstead field in
part & a small parcell of the first breck in part on the north, & Stormhill
Close in part & the 7th breck in part on the south, & ab. upon the first &
second brecks towards the west, & upon Somer border towards the east, &
contain by measure 50ac by estimation   40

7. /762/ The 7th breck lieth there more south between the sixth breck in part, & Stormhill close in part on the north & the 8th breck on the south *in part & a pece in the 4th breck in part*; & abut upon Stormhill Close in part & upon the third breck in part *& upon part of the 4th breck in part* towards the west, & upon Somer border towards the East, & contain by measure 50ac & by comon estimation   40

8. /763/ The 8th breck lieth there more south betweene the 7th breck on the north & a pece of furground of the lords in the beginning of the third furlong of this 4th precinct on the south & abut upon the 4th breck in part & upon the 5th breck in part towards the west, & upon Somer border towards the east & contain likewise by measure 50ac & by estimation   40

Stormhill Close

The Lords land in the Eastfield Brecks 1641

Eastfield Brecks

#	a r [p]		a	r	[p]	a	r	[p]		a	r	[p]
1	43a 757	to F. Guibon in exchange	2	1	20	remain:			for barly	10	0	0
	whereof	to Wm Guibon late Birds	1	3	0	36	3	20	great farm	26	3	20
		to the shepheard	2	0	0							
2	40a 758	to the shephead	2	0	0	38	0	0	for barly	10	0	0
									great farm	28	0	0
3	40a 759	to Ro. Banyard	0	2	0				for barly	10	0	0
		to the shepheard	2	0	0	37	2	0	great farm	27	2	0
									whereof furs 2r			
4	40a 760	to the shepheard	2	0	0	38	0	0	for barly	10	0	0
									great farm	28	0	0
5	35a 3r 20p	to the shepheard	2	0	0	33	3	20	for barly	10	0	0
									great farm	23	3	20
6	40a 761	to the shepheard	2	0	0	38	0	0	for barly	10	0	0
									great farm	28	0	0
7	40a 762	to Ro. Banyard	0	2	0	37	2	0	for barly	10	0	0
		to the shepheard	2	0	0				great farm	27	2	0
8	40c 758	to the shepheard	2	0	0	38	0	0	for barly	10	0	0
									great farm	28	0	0

In Febr 1641 there was 3ac (at 5 roods to an acre) taken out of the north west corner of the first breck & layd to Ringstead *South* fouldcourse & other exchange in the infield was allowed to Francis Guibon, Willm Guibon & Robert Banyard, so that now there wilbe incl[uded] 40ac in every breck of wch the shepheard is to have 2ac; letten for barly 10ac & letten wth the great fearm in every breck constantly 28ac. The 3ac above mentioned is added to the first breck of Ringstead South fouldcourse & wilbe somerlay in 1644

Sedgford Infield Lands 1631

An abstract of all the Infield Land in Sedgford, wch belong to Sir Hamon le Strange knight, either by virtue of his lease from the Deane and Chapter of Norw[i]ch, or otherwise, wth the names of the severall fearmors of those lands for the yeare ending Michaelmas 1631

fur	/1 precinct/	a	r	p	
18	the Lord of Hecham in Hecham accompt	5	2	0	Philip Loades, clerk
	the Lord of Hecham in Hecham accompt	1	1	0	Philip Loades, clerk
19	Sedgfords, a pightell contain	1	0	0	Fr. Guibon,[257] Great fearme
	the Lord of Hecham	1	0	0	Mr Loades in
	the Lord of Hecham	4	0	0	Hecham accompt
20	the Lord of Hecham	5	0	0	[ditto][258]
	the Lord of Hecham	1	1	0	[ditto]
22	/n. 140/[259] Sedgfords	7	0	0	Fr. Guibon, Great fearme
	/143/ Sedgfords	1	2	0	Philip Loades, clerk
	/145/ Sedgfords	3	0	0	Mr Loades
24	/160/ Sedgfords	14	0	0	Fr. Guibon, Great fearme
26	/165/ Sedgfords	5	0	0	[ditto]
27	/171/ the Lord 10ac West Fen, whereof	9	0	0	[ditto]
	/171/ & the residue thereof	1	0	0	Tho. Longstreth added to his leased lands
	/172/ the Lord called Waterhallyard	1	0	0	Fr. Guibon, Great fearme
	/175/ Sedgfords, called Sedgfordyard	4	2	0	[ditto]
	/2 precinct/				
1	/191/ the scite of the mannor of Westhall contayning 7ac	7	0	0	Fr. Guibon, Great fearme
2	/194/ Sir Hamon L'Estrange[260] called Nethergeyberds	7	0	0	Fr. Guibon, Great fearme
	/1341/ [precinct 7] the Lord, called Reed dam medow	1	0	0	Fr. Guibon, Great fearme left out by Mr Shepheard
3	/200/ the Lord called Uppergeyberds	18	0	0	Fr. Guibon Great fearme
4	/204/ the Lord	5	0	0	Fr. Guibon for barley

257. Abbreviations for tenants retained as in the document.

258. In this survey there is much bracketing of entries which is difficult to replicate on the printed page, so the word 'ditto' has been used instead to avoid any ambiquity.

259. As with the Breck Book, there are no formal margins or columns for the Infield Lands, although they are firmly indicated. A narrow LH margin has been created for the furlongs, while the precincts and new numbers for the strips and closes form part of the central text. A central column identifies the acreage.

260. L'Estrange showing an apostrophe, but more often Le Strange or Lestrange; Le Strange is used in this section of the survey, see above, p. 61.

9	/238/ Sedgfords	1	1	0	W. Guibon
10	/243/ Sir Hamon L'Estrange Halbottom Close	9	0	0	Fr. Guibon, Great fearme
	/247/ Sedgfords	3	0	0	W. Guibon
	/3 precinct/				
6	/381/ the Lord called Ficklecroft /after the/	7	0	0	Fr. Guibon, Great fearme
9	/419/ the Lord called Windes peece	12	0	0	[ditto]
11	/428/ the Lord called Blackland	5	0	0	[ditto]
13	/460/ Sedgfords	0	3	0	[ditto]
	/462/ the Lord	0	3	20	W. Guibon
16	/473/ the Lord 3ac whereof	1	2	0	[ditto]
	/473/ & the residue thereof	1	2	0	Rich Banyard
	/476/ the Lord	3	0	0	Fr[ancis] Guibon for barley
	/483/ the Lord	5	0	0	Wid[ow] Acres
17	/488/ the Lord	1	2	10	W. Guibon
	/491/ the Lord	1	2	10	Rich Banyard
[p]	/Sum 148a 2r/[261] beside the scite of the manor				
	/4 precinct/				
1	/547/ the Lord	5	0	0	Jo. Adams
	/549, 550, 551/ the Lord in 3 peeces inclosed	5	0	0	Fr. Guibon, Easthall fearme
2	/565/ the Lord called Knattington greene	5	0	0	Fr. Guibon, Great fearme
	/566/ the Lord	10	0	0	[ditto]
	/573/ the Lord called Inglands	0	2	20	Fr. Guibon, Easthall fearme
	/577/ the Lord	0	3	20	[ditto]
	/579/ the Lord by Bulls whins	1	3	0	[ditto]
3	/598, 599, 600/ the Lord 2ac, 1ac, 5r	4	1	0	John Adams
	/606/ the Lord whereof part is inclosed	18	0	0	Fr. Guibon, Great fearme
	/607/ the scite of the mannor of Easthall 6ac whereof the house & yards	2	0	0	Fr. Guibon, Easthall fearme
	& the residue thereof	4	0	0	Fr. Guibon, Great fearme
4	/613, 614, 616/ the Lord 12ac, 1ac, 1½ac	14	2	0	Fr. Guibon, Easthall fearme
	/619/ the Lord	1	2	20	Jo. Adams
	/620/ the Lord called Mareland	7	0	0	Fr. Guibon, Great fearme
5	/636/ the Lord called Wrongland	0	2	20	Rich Banyard
	/638/ the Lord	0	2	20	Wid Acres

261. A total is given at the end of each page; the beginning of the next page is shown in the margin.

	/642/ the Lord 5ac whereof	2	2	o	Jo. Adams
	& the residue	2	2	o	Martin Smith
	/648/ the Lord	3	0	o	Mr Loades
6	/659, 660, 661/ the Lord 1½ac, 2½r, 1½ac	3	2	20	Mr Loades
	/665/ the Lord	4	3	o	Mr Loades
7	/671/ the Lord	o	2	o	Jo. Adams
	/676/ the Lord	o	2	o	[ditto]
	/681/ the Lord 1ac whereof	o	2	o	Rich Banyard
	& the residue thereof	o	2	o	W. Guibon
	/683, 689/ the Lord 1ac, 2ac	3	0	o	W. Guibon
8	/697/ the Lord 18 ac whereof	5	0	o	Rich Banyard
		10	0	o	Martin Smith
		3	0	o	Wid Acres
9	/699/ the Lord 4ac whereof	2	0	o	Wid Acres
		2	0	o	Martin Smith
	/700/ the Lord 4½ac whereof	2	0	o	Mr Loades
		2	2	o	Rich Banyard
10	/704/ the Lord 5ac whereof	2	0	o	Mr Loades
		3	0	o	Rich Banyard
	/707/ the Lord	o	3	o	Jo. Adams
	/709/ the Lord	o	3	o	Wid Acres
11	/714/ the Lord	1	1	o	[ditto]
	/715/ the Lord	1	0	o	W. Guibon
	/717/ the Lord	1	1	o	[ditto]
	/720, 721/ the Lord 2½r, 1½ac	2	0	20	Wid Acres
13	/733/ the Lord hath this in exchange	o	3	20	The heire of H Lawes hath

/in exchange for 1ac of his at Pothow 5 pr[ecinct], 1 fur[long], third peece n 781/

[p] [Sum] /141a 2r/

13	/736/ the Lord 3ac whereof	2	0	o	Rich Banyard
	& the residue thereof	1	0	o	W. Guibon
	/737/ the Lord	3	0	o	W. Guibon
	/741/ the Lord in 2 peeces 7r whereof	o	3	20	Rich Banyard
		o	3	20	Wid Acres
	/758/ the Lord	1	0	o	Jo Adams
21	/new, 24 old,[262] 764/ The Lord	o	2	o	Rich Banyard
	/5 precinct/				
1	/788/ the Lord	1	3	o	Mr Girling hath this in

exchange for 2 acres of his, in the 5 precinct, the 13 furlong & the second peece n 870

	/794/ the Lord	1	2	o	W. Guibon

---

262. Number of old furlongs in new brecks Eastfield.

	/802/ the Lord, called Flinthill	20	0	0	Fr. Guibon, Great fearme
	/805/ the Lord	3	1	0	W. Guibon
	/807/ the Lord	2	2	0	[ditto]
2	/813/ the Lord	0	3	0	Tho Viccars
4	/823/ the Lord by the Whin Close	14	0	0	Fr. Guibon, Great fearme
5	/826/ the Lord	2	0	0	W. Guibon
11	/838/ the Lord, called the Whin Close	34	0	0	Fr. Guibon, Great fearme
12	/868/				
13	/875/ the Lord	2	3	0	Fr. Guibon for barley
	/877/ the Lord	6	0	0	[ditto]
	/880/ the Lord	16	0	0	Martin Smith
15	/886/ the Lord	1	0	0	Mr Girling hath had this

peece, & the 4th peece next following in exchange for 1½ac in the 13 furlong of the 5 precinct lately bought of Thomas Longstreth. But it appeared by the Court Rolls 21 Eliz 24 that Mr John Lestrange did buy that land of old Thomas Longstreth half a yeare after the book made by Mr Shepheard. And Thomas Longstreth doth acknowledge that he paid fearme continually to Mr Stubbs for this said acre, & the forth peece following: & therefore Mr Girling ought to also pay fearme for the same.

	/891/ the Lord	1	0	20	W. Guibon
	/900/ the Lord	5	0	20	Martin Smith
16	/907, 908/ the Lord 1½ac, 3½r	2	1	20	Martin Smith
	/910/ the Lord	0	2	20	Mr Girling, as before appeareth
17	/913/ Sir Hamon Le Strange	9	0	0	Martin Smith
18	/916/ Sir Hamon Le Strange	1	1	0	[ditto]
20	/934/ the Lord	3	0	0	[ditto]
	/precinct 6/				
9	/1010/ the Lord	0	1	0	[ditto]
10	/1024/ the Lord	3	0	0	Martin Smith
11	/1037/ the Lord above Chapplecroft	14	0	0	Fr. Guibon, Easthall fearm
12	/1043/ the Lord called Chapplecroft	7	0	0	Fr. Guibon, Great fearme
	/7 precinct/				
1	/1061/ the Lord	9	0	0	W. Guibon
2	/1063/ the Lord	0	2	0	[ditto]
	/1064/ Sir Hamon Le Strange	2	3	0	[ditto]
3	/1075/ Sir Hamon Le Strange	1	0	0	[ditto]
9	/1106/ the Lord	2	2	0	[ditto]
	/1107/ Sir Hamon Le Strange	2	2	0	Martin Smith
10	/1114/ the Lord	0	3	0	[ditto]
	/1115/ Sir Hamon Le Strange	1	0	0	[ditto]

[*p*] [*Sum*] /181a 2r/

13 /1181/ The great South Close contayining 11ac & the little South Close
    containing 3ac are not cast up amongst the brecks because they may be plowed
    up at any time. And it is intended that Mr Guibon shall pay for the great
    South Close at all tymes when Sharnborn Close is not in tilth. But when
    Sharnborn Close is in tilth Mr Guibon shall pay for that & then the South
    close shall be for the sheepe   11 0 0 Fr. Guibon, Great fearme
20 /1236, 1238/ the Lord 1½ac, ½ ac   2 0 0 Martin Smith
    /1240/ the Lord   1 0 0 [*ditto*]
    /1243/ the Lord   5 0 0 W. Guibon
31 /1339/ Grasscroft is set downe in the booke for 16acs. It contayneth by measure
    but 11acs whereof 3acs are inclosed & is afterward set down wth Church
    Medow, & the residue lyeth for the sheeps pasture, & yieldeth no other profit
    /1340/ Sir Hamon Le Strange reserveth his part of the Reed dam wch
    contayneth 8ac in his own hands
    /8 precinct/
    The whole content of Beales his croft by Mr Shepheards booke is 18a 2r 20p.
    By measure it is but 15a 1r 20p whereof sold to Fr. Costin 2ac 1r & letten to him
    1ac & the residue being 12a 20p in letten to Fr. Guibon & is set down in the
    two somes following:
1   In Beales Croft 15a 1r 20 p whereof   12 0 20 Fr. Guibon, Great fearme
                                                            1 0 0 Fr. Costen
    /1377/ Sir Hamon Le Strange   2 1 0 sold to F. Costin
    /1378/ [*ditto*]   0 1 30 in Beales Croft
    /1379/ [*ditto*]   6 0 0 [*ditto*]
    /1380/ [*ditto*] *lib de Hecham*   0 1 20 [*ditto*]
    /1382/ Sir Hamon Le Strange   1 0 0 Mr Loades
    /1383/ Sir Hamon Le Strange   2 0 0 Fr. Guibon, Great fearme
    /1384/ Sir Hamon Le Strange 5a 1r whereof 2   1 0 Fr. Guibon, Great fearme
                                                            3 0 0 Mr Loades
    /1385/ Sir Hamon Le Strange   1 0 0 4ac Fr. Costin for 16s
    /1386/ [*ditto*]   1 1 0 [*ditto*]
    /1388/ [*ditto*]   1 3 0 [*ditto*]
    /1392/ the Lord *Sr H L Str*   0 2 0 Bartholomew Crisp
    /1404/ Sir Hamon Le Strange   0 3 0 [*ditto*]
2   /1415/ Sir Hamon Le Strange   1 1 0 Fr. Costin
3   /1420/ Sir Hamon Le Strange   0 2 20 Tho. Longstreth
    /1421/ [*ditto*]   0 2 20 Tho. Longstreth lease
    /1422/ [*ditto*]   0 2 20 Tho. Longstreth
    /1423/ [*ditto*]   2 2 20 Tho. Longstreth
    /1426/ [*ditto*]   2 2 20 Tho. Longstreth lease
4   /1427/ Sir Hamon Le Strange   1 1 0 Fr. Costin

/1429/ [ditto]	1	1	0	[ditto]
/1433/ [ditto]	0	2	0	[ditto]
/1434/ [ditto]	2	0	0	[ditto]
/1437/ [ditto]	0	1	20	[ditto]
/1439/ [ditto]	0	1	20	[ditto]
/1440/ [ditto]	1	1	20	[ditto]
/1441/ Sir Hamon Le Strange	1	0	0	Tho. Longstreth lease
/1443/ Sir Hamon Le Strange	0	3	0	[ditto]
/1445/ [ditto]	4	3	0	Fr. Costin
/1448/ Sir Hamon Le Strange	0	3	20	in Beales croft

5 /1449/ Sir Hamon Le Strange 1½r. Half of this is in Beales Croft & the other
half in the field & the heire of Hen Lawes hath 1½r lying on the south side
thereof, whereof our half is in Beales his croft also and the other half in the
field. Sir Hamons fearmor useth all that is in the close & the heyre of Henry
Lawes useth all that is in the field.

[p] [Sum] /67 1 20/

/1451/ Sir Hamon Le Strange	0	3	20	Fr. Costin
/1455/ [ditto]	0	3	20	[ditto]
/1457/ [ditto]	0	2	20	[ditto]
/1459/ [ditto]	1	1	0	[ditto]
6 /1464/ Sir Hamon Le Strange	0	1	20	Fr. Costin
/1466/ [ditto]	0	1	30	[ditto]
/1468/ [ditto]	2	2	0	Mr Loades
7 /1470/ Sir Hamon Le Strange	0	1	20	[ditto]
/1471/ [ditto]	0	1	30	[ditto]
/1472/ [ditto]	1	1	0	Fr. Costin
/1475/ [ditto]	0	3	0	[ditto]
/1476/ [ditto]	0	2	0	[ditto]
8 /1478/ Sir Hamon Le Strange	0	3	0	Tho. Longstreth
/1487/ [ditto]	0	2	0	[ditto]
/1488/ [ditto]	0	1	0	[ditto]
/1491/ [ditto]	0	3	20	[ditto]
/1492/ [ditto]	0	3	20	[ditto]
/1495/ [ditto]	0	1	0	Tho. Cremer *now sold*
/1497/ [ditto]	0	3	20	[ditto]
9 /1501/ Sir Hamon Le Strange	1	0	0	Tho. Longstreth by lease
/1502/ [ditto]	0	2	0	[ditto]
/1503/ [ditto]	0	2	0	Tho. Longstreth by lease Hitchins accompt
/1504/ [ditto]	1	0	0	Tho. Longstreth by lease
/1509/ [ditto]	0	2	0	[ditto]
/1510/ [ditto] Ashyard	3	0	0	Th. Longstreth for 13s 1d

/1511/ [ditto] late Hargates		I	o	o	Th. Longstreth for 4s
/1513/ Sir Hamon Le Strange in Beales Croft	o	3	30		
/1514/ [ditto]		o	I	20	
/1515/ [ditto]		o	3	o	
/1516/ [ditto]		3	I	o	1ac part hereof letten to Fr. Costin
/1517/ [ditto] * lib of Ingoldsth[orpe]		o	2	o	1r part of this 2r} sold to
/1518/ [ditto] not of Hech[am]*		o	2	o	1r part of this 2r} Fr.
/1519/ [ditto]		I	o	o	all this acre } Costin
/1520/ [ditto]		2	o	o	

*Agreed with Fr. Costin that hee shall have about 2ac 3r *viz* 5r q 1 [*quarentia*] & 6r q 9 paying yearly *per annnum* freely to Hecham 5d

10	/1521/ Sir Hamon Le Strange	o	2	o	Tho Longstreth
	/1524/ [ditto]	o	3	20	by lease
	/1525/ [ditto]	o	3	20	Tho Longstreth
	/1526/ [ditto]	o	3	20	Tho Longstreth by lease
	/1527/ [ditto]	o	2	o	Mr Loades
	/1532/ [ditto]	4	o	o	Fr. Costin
	/1533/ [ditto]	o	2	20	Tho Longstreth
	/1536/ [ditto]	I	I	o	[ditto]
	/1539/ [ditto]	I	I	o	[ditto]
	/1540/ [ditto]	I	o	o	[ditto]
11	/1544/ Sir Hamon Le Strange	o	I	o	Fr. Costin
	/1546/ [ditto]	I	I	o	[ditto]
	/1547/ [ditto]	o	2	o	[ditto]
	/1549/ [ditto]	o	2	20	[ditto]
	/1551/ [ditto]	o	I	20	[ditto]
	/1556/ [ditto]	o	I	20	[ditto]
	/1560/ [ditto]	o	3	o	[ditto]
	/1561/ [ditto]	o	2	20	[ditto]
	/1563/ [ditto]	I	o	o	[ditto]
12	/1569/ Sir Hamon Le Strange	o	2	20	Tho Longstreth
13	/1573/ Sir Hamon Le Strange	3	o	o	Tho Longstreth by lease
[p]	[Sum] /43ac/				

15	/1582/ Sir Hamon Le Strange	o	2	o	Jo Crispe
	/1590/ [ditto]	I	I	o	Tho Longstreth by lease
16	/1596/ Sir Hamon Le Strange, sold	o	3	o	Mr Loades
	/1601/ [ditto]	o	2	o	Tho Longstreth
17	/1606/ Sir Hamon Le Strange	I	I	o	Salter
	/1608/ Sir Hamon Le Strange /after the 17 furl/	o	2	o	Fr. Costin

18	/1610/ Sir Hamon Le Strange	0	3	0	[ditto]
	/1611/ [ditto]	0	1	0	Tho Longstreth
	/1612/ [ditto]	0	3	20	[ditto]
	/1615/ [ditto]	3	0	0	Fr. Costin
19	/1618/ Sir Hamon Le Strange	0	2	20	[ditto]
	/1619/ [ditto]	0	1	30	Tho Longstreth
	/1620/ [ditto]	1	0	0	*all sold*
	/1621/ [ditto]	0	1	30	[ditto]
20	/1632/ Sir Hamon Le Strange	0	1	30	Rich Bird
22	/1669/ Sir Hamon Le Strange	0	2	30	Tho Longstreth by lease
24	/1673/ Sir Hamon Le Strange	3	0	0	W. Burnham in
	/1675/ [ditto]	1	1	0	Hecham accompt
27	/1715/ Sir Hamon Le Strange	1	1	0	Tho Longstreth
	/1718/ [ditto]	1	0	0	*wth the house*
	/1719/ [ditto]	0	2	0	Tho Longstreth
	/1720/ [ditto]	1	0	0	by lease
	/1721/ [ditto]	1	2	0	[ditto]

/After the 27 furlong/

/1729/ Sir Hamon Le Strange called Sedgfords	4	0	0	Fr. Guibon, Great fearme
/1730/ [ditto] 5r	1	1	0	[ditto]
/1731/ [ditto] called Sedgfords dam	2	0	0	[ditto]
/1732/ [ditto] our Aldercarre	0	2	0	[ditto]

28	/1744, 1745/ Sir Hamon Le Strange called Dingles pightell	1	2	0	Fr. Guibon, Great fearme
	/1754/ Sir Hamon Le Strange called Ingolds	1	0	0	[ditto]
	/1755/ Sir Hamon Le Strange	1	3	0	[ditto]
	/1758/ The Lord called Church Medow	6	3	0	[ditto]
	/1759/ The Lord part of Gresscroft inclosed	3	0	0	[ditto]
	/1763/ Sir Hamon Le Strange	1	0	0	Fr. Costin
	/1765/ [ditto] /Menght Furlong /	1	1	0	[ditto]
	/1767/ [ditto]	0	3	0	[ditto]
	/1772/ [ditto]	1	2	0	Tho Longstreth
	/1779/ [ditto]	0	2	0	Tho Longstreth

/Snetisham Field/

/1784/ Sir Hamon Le Strange more west abbutt upon Robert Rose north	0	3	0	Tho Longstreth by lease
/1786/ Sir Hamon Le Strange more west abutting upon John Ellgar in part & upon the land given by Thomas Mason to the towne of Sedgford in part towards the north	0	3	0	Tho Longstreth by lease

[Sum] /49 3 30/

Sum total of all the Infield Land expressed in this book with the great South Close containing 11acs wch lyeth in the sheepes pasture, besides the scite of the mannor of Westhall wch contayneth 7ac & the Reed dam containing 8ac amounteth to 631a 2r 30p

[p] Infield Land letten for money 1631

	a	r	p		£	s	d
Francis Guibon hath wth the great fearme which at 5s an acre amounteth to	267	I	20		66	16	10½
He hath Easthall fearme	038	3	0		06	19	6
Thomas Longstreth hath of lease lands besides 2r for wch he payeth 2s in Hecham accompt, & besides 1½ac wch he hath yearely in the Southfield with the last crop	021	0	20		04	18	0
More he hath in the Ashyard wch contayneth	003	0	0	for	00	13	1
He hath more next that, late Hargates	001	0	0	for	00	4	0
Francis Costin hath in the 1 furlong of the 8 precinct	004	0	0	for	00	16	0
Tho Cremer hath in the 8 furlong of the 8 precinct	001	0	20	for	00	6	8
Sum of acres [*sub-total*]	336	I	20				
Sum of money					80	14	1½

Infield land letten for Barly 1631

	a	r	p
To Francis Guibon	16	3	0
W. Guibon	44	I	10
Mr Loades	27	2	20
Richard Banyard	18	0	10
Widow Acres	14	I	20
John Adams	15	3	20
Martin Smith	68	2	0
Thomas Longstreth	20	I	0
Francis Costin	38	3	20
Thomas Viccars	00	3	0
John Crispe	00	2	0
Richard Bird	00	I	30
Bartholomew Crispe	01	I	0
Salter	01	I	0
Mr Girling ought to pay for	01	2	20
Sum [*sub-total*]	270	I	30
wthin Hecham accompt	22	I	0
The tenants have in exchange	02	2	20
Sum total	631	2	30
More letten to Hitcham men at Cattgore in Hecham which is usually put into Sedgford accompt	12	0	0

Extracts from the Sedgeford Firmall and Breck Book, 1647–1650

Seg[d]ford Firmall & Breck Book 1647/8/9 & 1650
Sedgford Southfeild Brecks at large & the East Brecks
and the North Brecks in short & large²⁶³

*Page²⁶⁴

---

263. From LEST/IB90.

264. The table of contents is written in a different hand and appears to be inserted at a later date with the insertions in the directions for using brecks.

1. The directions for the using of all Sedgford Brecks as they be new sett out

The Northfeild Brecks letten for 2 bushell of barly the acre

[a   r   p][265]

1	Breck summerly	1642	and in 1650	and in 1658	and in 1666
		*1674	and in 1682	and in 1690	and in 1698*
2	Breck summerly	1643	and in 1651	and in 1659	and in 1667
		*1675	and in 1683	and in 1691	and in 1699*
3	Breck summerly	1644	and in 1652	and in 1660	and in 1668
		*1676	and in 1684	and in 1692	and in 1700*
4	Breck summerly	1645	and in 1653	and in 1661	and in 1669
		*1677	and in 1685	and in 1693	and in 1701*
5	Breck summerly	1646	and in 1654	and in 1662	and in 1670
		*1678	and in 1686	and in 1694	and in 1702*
6	Breck summerly	1647	and in 1655	and in 1663	and in 1671
		*1679	and in 1687	and in 1695	and in 1703*
7	Breck summerly	1648	and in 1656	and in 1664	and in 1672
		*1680	and in 1688	and in 1696	and in 1704*
8	Breck summerly	1649	and in 1657	and in 1665	and in 1673
		*1681	and in 1689	and in 1697	and in 1705*

The Southfeild Brecks letten some for 5s the acre and some for barly[266]

		[a	r	p]				
1	Breck summerly	*34	3	0*	1644	in 1652	in 1660	in 1668
	inde for barly	10	0	0	*1676	in 1684	in 1692	in 1700*
2	Breck summerly	*30	0	0*	1645	in 1653	in 1661	in 1669
	inde for barly	10	0	0	*1677	in 1685	in 1693	in 1701*
3	Breck summerly	*52	0	0*	1646	in 1654	in 1662	in 1670
	inde for barly	10	0	0	*1678	in 1686	in 1694	in 1702*
4	Breck summerly	*58	0	0*	1647	in 1655	in 1663	in 1671
	inde for barly	15	0	0	*1679	in 1687	in 1695	in 1703*
5	Breck summerly	*23	1	14*	1648	in 1656	in 1664	in 1672
	inde for barly	10	0	0	*1680	in 1688	in 1696	in 1704*
6	Breck summerly	*32	3	1*	1649	in 1657	in 1665	in 1673
	inde for barly	10	0	0	*1681	in 1689	in 1697	in 1705*
7	Breck summerly	*57	1	30*	1650	in 1658	in 1666	in 1674
	inde for barly	15	0	0	*1682	in 1690	in 1698	in 1706*
8	Breck summerly	*63	2	30*	1651	in 1659	in 1667	in 1675
	inde for barly	20	0	0	*1683	in 1691	in 1699	in 1707*

---

265. The LH column showing the acreages of the brecks has been worn away, leaving just the perches column as a clue to its existence; to avoid confusion it has not been included here.

266. See fn. 264 above; the acreages shown in the document are a later insertion.

The Eastfeild Brecks letten some for 5s 6d and some for 2 bushll barly the acre[267]

		a	r	p				
1	Breck summerly				1640	in 1648	in 1656	in 1664
	inde for barly	10	0	0	*1672	in 1680	in 1688	in 1696*
2	Breck summerly				1641	in 1649	in 1657	in 1665
	inde for barly	10	0	0	*1673	in 1681	in 1689	in 1697*
3	Breck summerly				1642	in 1650	in 1658	in 1666
	inde for barly	10	0	0	*1674	in 1682	in 1690	in 1698*
4	Breck summerly				1643	in 1651	in 1659	in 1667
	inde for barly	10	0	0	*1675	in 1683	in 1691	in 1699*
5	Breck summerly				1644	in 1652	in 1660	in 1668
	inde for barly	10	0	0	*1676	in 1684	in 1692	in 1700*
6	Breck summerly				1645	in 1653	in 1661	in 1669
	inde for barly	10	0	0	*1677	in 1685	in 1693	in 1701*
7	Breck summerly				1646	in 1654	in 1662	in 1670
	inde for barly	10	0	0	*1678	in 1686	in 1694	in 1702*
8	Breck summerly				1647	in 1655	in 1663	in 1671
	inde for barly	10	0	0	*1679	in 1687	in 1695	in 1703*

2. A note how the Brecks in the North Pasture will fall in tilth

			a	r	p	
<1647>	6	Breck summerly	25	0	14 }	
<1655>	5	Breck first crop	37	0	10 }	
<1663>	4	Breck second crop	28	2	27 }	118a 1r 38p at 2 bushel
<1671>	3	Breck last crop	27	2	27 }	Barly 59 comb 1 bushel
<1679>						
<1687>						
1695						

			a	r	p	
<1648>	7	Breck summerly	27	0	20 }	
<1656>	6	Breck first crop	25	0	14 }	
<1664>	5	Breck second crop	37	0	10 }	117a 3r 31p at 2 bushel
<1672>	4	Breck last crop	28	2	27 }	Barly 58 comb 3 bushel 3 peck
<1680>						
<1688>						
1696						

			a	r	p	
<1649>	8	Breck summerly	26	0	34 }	
<1657>	7	Breck first crop	27	0	20 }	115a 1r 38p at 2 bushel
<1665>	6	Breck second crop	25	0	14 }	Barly 57comb 3 bushel
<1673>	5	Breck last crop	37	0	10 }	
<1681>						
<1689>						
1697						

---

267. See fn. 264 above.

\<1650\>	1	Breck summerly	28	1	14 }	
\<1658\>	8	Breck first crop	26	0	34 }	106a 3r 2p at 2 bushel
\<1666\>	7	Breck second crop	27	0	20 }	Barly 53 comb 1 bushel 2 peck
\<1674\>	6	Breck last crop	25	0	14 }	
\<1682\>						
\<1690\>						
1698						

\<1651\>	2	Breck summerly	28	0	28 }	
\<1659\>	1	Breck first crop	28	1	14 }	109a 3r 16p at 2 bushel
\<1667\>	8	Breck second crop	26	0	34 }	Barly 54 comb 2 bushel 2 peck
\<1675\>	7	Breck last crop	27	0	20 }	
\<1683\>						
\<1691\>						
1699						

\<1652\>	3	Breck summerly	27	2	27 }	
\<1660\>	2	Breck first crop	28	0	28 }	110a 1r 23p at 2 bushel
\<1668\>	1	Breck second crop	28	1	14 }	Barly 55 comb 0 bushel 3 peck
\<1676\>	8	Breck last crop	26	0	34 }	
\<1684\>						
\<1692\>						
1700						

\<1653\>	4	Breck summerly	28	2	27 }	
\<1661\>	3	Breck first crop	27	2	27 }	112a 3r 16p at 2 bushel
\<1669\>	2	Breck second crop	28	0	28 }	Barly 56 comb 1 bushel
\<1677\>	1	Breck last crop	28	1	14 }	
\<1685\>						
\<1693\>						
1701						

\<1654\>	5	Breck summerly	37	0	10 }	
\<1662\>	4	Breck first crop	28	2	27 }	121a 2r 16p at 2 bushel
\<1670\>	3	Breck second crop	27	2	27 }	Barly 60 comb 3 bushel
\<1678\>	2	Breck last crop	28	0	28 }	
\<1686\>						
1694						
1702						

1655	6	Breck summerly	25	0	14 }	
*enterd	5	Breck first crop	37	0	10 }	118a 1r 38p at 2 bushel
above*	4	Breck second crop	28	2	27 }	Barly 59 comb 1 bushel
	3	Breck last crop	27	2	27 }	

The will of Sir Hamon Le Strange

The will of Sir Hamon Le Strange, kt proved 7th July 1654[268]

/Sir Ham[on]L'estrange militis/ In the name and feare of God I Hamon L'estrange of Hunstanton in the county of Norf[olk] Knight of sound and perfect memory (for which I praise God) this second day of July in the yeare after the incarnation of our blessed Saviour one thousand six hundred and fifty two, renouncing all former wills by me heretofore made doe now make and ordaine my last will and testament as followeth. First, I render unto thee o[h] heavenly all possible praise for thine election of mee before the beginning of the world in thine onely sonne unto eternall salvation. To vouch[s]afe me thine appointed meanes to be borne a man, begotten and bred of believing and religious parents; to be watered with the dew of thy Grace and sealed with baptisme into the name of thine only sonne and myne alone Saviour; to have been nursed with the pure milke of the doctrine of his incarnation, passion, resurrection and ascention and instructed in the precious knowledge and participation of that heavenly food of souls the Manna of the Sacrament of his supper; all which fully, firmely and stedfastly to believe and live thereafter is life everlasting. So I believe Lord helpe myne unbeliefe.

I thanke thee for the grete mesure of dayes where with though hast filled my glasse of time and abundantly for that comfortable union and blessed harmony which I have for many yeares enioyed with that life of my life my deare wife whose jointure is already provided for by assurance. And further moved by long experience of her ever deare esteeme of my life and pson, and her most pious and painfull care in the education of my children, those olive branches where with God hath pleased to bless our table, and to propagate my name and family, and her ever incessant industry in straynes of knowledge above her sex to the just faithfull and laudable advantage and advancement of my estate I doe further enlarge myself as followeth. I give unto her a silver Magdalene cupp with a cover, and another small cupp of silver with a cover, and six silver spoons with gilt knaps, and one silver ladle with a broken end, and

---

268. PROB 11/238/248. There is a copy of the will in the Norfolk Record Office, 'transcribed' which contains several errors, *see* LEST/AE8.

one silver pottager, most of which her owne before marriage but that I thinke fitt to express them to prevent question.

Item I give unto her the green russell[269] bed in the parlour chamber with all the proper and usual bedding thereunto belonging, and all the chaires and stooles of the same stuff thereunto belonging.

Item I give unto her the green broadcloth cupboard cloth embroydered about the skirts with orange tawny silke twist upon purple velvett.

Item I give unto her the blewe bed furnished where on I use to lodge in the chamber over the kitchin. And all those beds in the darinx[270] chamber over myne owne lodging chamber and all those beds in the inner chamber south of the darinx chamber.

Item I give unto her the green velvet canopy and bedding with the chaires and stooles of snakes velvett[271] mixed black and greene thereunto belonging. And in all the beds I menconed I intend also the bedsteads, matts, cords and bedstaves belonging to the same.

Item I give unto her the halfe part of all myne houshold linnen.

Item I give unto her six cushions of needlework which were her mothers and six other Turkye work cushions.

Item I give unto her halfe my brass and halfe my pewter and six trunkes or chests indifferently to be taken by her and my small coach and harness thereto.

Item I do ratify and confirme unto my sonne and heir Sir Nichs L'estrange, Baronet, all former conveyances made by me unto him or to any other person or persons in trust for him or to his use. And further I give unto his wife, my daughter Ann L'estrange my wa[t]ch.

Item I give unto their second sonne Nicholas L'estrange my great English bible with gilt leaves and fower old angells.

Item I give unto his brother John my base violl and case and books of violl lessons and two old Angells and my biggest birding peece usually standing in the parlour.

Item I give unto his brothers W[illia]m, Edward and Charles five pounds a peece; to Roger and Thomas my godsons tenne pounds a peece.

Item I give unto my second sonne Hamon L'estrange his heires and assignes all my right, title and interest of in or to the part or parts allotted or to be allotted unto me

---

269. Russell was the Netherlandish name for Lille where the cloth, a smooth satin of wool, originated, *see* Yaxley, *Glossary*, p. 174.

270. Corruption of dornix, fabric of wool, linen silk or mixture, used for hangings, coverlets, table carpets etc, *see* Yaxley, *Glossary*, pp. 63, 68.

271. Velvet which has a pretty mottle, like snakeskin. My thanks to Jean Agnew.

upon myne adventure in the East and West Fenne of Boston, Lincolnshire or either of them.

Item I give unto his wife tenne pounds, his eldest sonne Hamon (my godsonne) tenne pounds, to his sonne Nicholas five pounds, to his son W[illia]m five pounds, to his daughter Dorothie my god daughter tenne pounds, to his daughter Elizabeth five pounds.

Item I give unto my sonne in law Sir W[illia]m Spring, Baronet, my crusado or porteyn of gold.[272] To my daughter Spring my black enameled diamond ring. To her sonne W[illia]m (my godson) my eare ring set with diamonds and two old angells. To her sonne Thomas Spring five pounds and to her daughter Dorothie five pounds.

Item I give unto John Fisher of Honing, gent., five pounds and to Mary his wife five pounds and to there sonne John (my godson) tenn pounds.

I doe constitute and ordayne my said sonne Sir Nich[olas] L'estrange executor of this my last will and testament for the payment of my debts and legacies and for the receiving, sueinge for and recovery of all moneyes and debts anyway due and payable unto me. And for a further legacy of my love I give unto the said Dame Alice my wife £100. And I will that all my gifts and legacies (by me bequeathed by this my last will and testament now declared as aforesaid and which shall be menconed in a schedule to this my last will annexed) and shall be paide and delivered within halfe a yeare next after my decease and that soe long tyme also myne house shall be kept and maynteyned by myne executor with sufficient dyett for the benefit of my servants so to continue and provide for themselves elsewhere before or at the end of the expiracon of the said halfe yeare. I will and desire that the poore people of Sedgeford and Heacham may be looked upon with a mercifull eye and considered with a charitable hand out of the severall and respective impropriations there. And the Vicar also of He[a]cham taken yearely under the like care.

Nowe having taken leave of the world and the blessed porcons which God have vouch[s]afed of my wife, family and estate, I leave them this legacy of counsell to all my children and family to be affable, meeke, courteous, peaceable, easy to be entreated in all honest and lawfull things and that they practice the blessed rule and lesson taught us by our Saviour, Learne of me for I am humble and meeke, My body (that tabernacle of clay wherin my soule hath a long time sojourned upon earth I render to earth) againe to be buried by the care and direction of myne executor within the chancell of Hunstanton there to sleepe until it be awakened by the blast of the last trumpett when all human flesh shall rise and this my soule and spirit (which now thus acts and indites) shall be revested[?] with its owne body and with those (and none other) eyes I shall behold my blessed redeemer in whose presence is the fullness of joyes and at his right hand pleasure for evermore. (I desire to have

272. Crusado: a Portuguese coin bearing the figure of the cross, *see Shorter Oxford English Dictionary*.

a plain black marble stone and in a plate of gilded brasse thus graven, *In terris peregrinus eram nunc Incola coeli,* In heaven at home a blessed change who while I was on earth was Strange.[273] Every word, letter and particle of this my last will and testament with the owne hand of me the testator Hamon L'estrange. I will that at least halfe of the yearely profit of the land (which escheated unto me by the felony of Robert Overman in the murther of his wife for which he suffered death) be yearely forever bestowed in some charitable way to the reliefe of the poor people and the first whole yeares profitts to be expended in the making of a fencewall for the almshowses in Brancaster.

Hamon L'estrange, February 27th 1652. This codicil or addicon I thinke fitt to subioyne and annex to my last will and testament and to ratifie and confirme the same:

1. I give to Thomas Ferrow mine old shagge bayes gowne and my blacke figured satin suite and my darkest colour cloth suite.

2. To Francis Dusgate my grey cloke lined and open at the armes with flatt buttons ash colour and tawny and five pounds in ready money.

3. To Henry Coppin eight pounds in money.

4. To my Cooke forty shillings in money.

5. To my Groome twenty shillings in money.

6. To my Bayliffe twenty shillings in money

7. To my two husbandmen twenty shillings a peece in money. To William Bateman twenty shillings in money.

9. To Margaret Guybon five pounds in money.

10. To Elizabeth Guybon five pounds in money.

11. To the Dairy maide twenty shillings in money.

12. To Elizabeth Hunt twenty shillings in money.

13. To Jean Frost twenty shillings in money.

To and amonge the poore people of Sedgeford, Heacham, Hunstanton, Ringstead and Holme, the summe of twenty pounds to be distributed amonge them in such proportions as my executor shall thinke meete. All mine old jerkins and coats and remnants of wearing things, except my velvet jacket and furr of fitches[274] and squirrell furre sleaves I will that they be distributed as may be most fitly and with best direction of my executors amonge my servants. I advise my executor Sir

---

273. No second bracket, but there is a large gap at this point.
274. Fitch was a polecat, www.oed.com.

Nicholas L'estrange that he will consider of his owne and my library, and where he finds double books that he will bestowe one or two bookes upon every of the ministers who have any relacon to me by Rectory or Vicarage.

Hamon L'estrange sealed and subscribed in the presence of me: Fra[ncis] Dusgate

This will with this codicil annexed was proved at Westminster before the judges for probate of will and granting administracons, the seaveth day of July in the yeare of our God, one thousand, five hundred fiftee and foure, by the oath of Sir Nicholas L'estrange, Baronet sole executor named in the said will to whome administracon of all and single[275] the goods, chattless and debts of the said deceased was comitted, he being first sworne by vertue of a comission to that effect, well & truly to administer the same.

---

275. 'Singular' as in Alice's will, see below, p. 362.

The will of Dame Alice Le Strange

The will of Dame Alice Le Strange of Sedgeford proved 28 Feb 1656/7[276]

/Dame Alice Lestrange/ In the name of God Amen the sixteenth day of October in the yeare of our Lords one thowsand six hundred fifty and six. I, Dame Alice Lestrange of Sedgford in the Countie of Norf[olk] relict of Sr Hammon Lestrange Kn[igh]t of Hunstanton in the said Countie deceased being sound in minde and in perfect memorie God be praised revokeing all former wills, doe make and ordaine this my last will and testament in manner and forme followein. That is to say, first I yield up my soule into the handes of Almightie God firmely beleiveing to be saved by and through the merrite and passion of my blessed Saviour and Redeemer Jesus Christ. Next I bequeath my body to the earth in sure and certain hope of a resurreccon to eternall life, the same to be decently interred in the chancell of the church of Hunstanton aforesaid neere to the body of the said Sir Hamon Lestrang[e] my late deare husband. And as for my wordly goodes which the Lord hath given me I will and bequeathe them as followeth.

First I give and bequeath unto Sir Nicholas Lestrange Bar[one]t, my breweing copper mash fatt, gile fatt, weete fatt cooler and underbecke with the dales[277] belonging to the brewhouse, the plankes and shelves in the larder and boulting house, the table and pressing board in the smothering roome, the shelves and plankes in the dayry, my washing copper and milke copper in the washing house, the shelves in the storehouse, the plankes and shelves in the pastry and scullery with the iron oven lid, the plankes and shelves in the kitching, the tables and shelves in the pantry, the beerestooles in the seller and buttery, the table and cupboard in the parlour, the tables and cupboard in the dineing roome and my serge bedd lyned with pentado,[278] the bedstead bedding and all that belongeth to it with the chaver stooles and carpett suteable to the bed.

---

276. PROB 11/262/.
277. Wooden trough, *see* Yaxley, *Glossary*, p. 62.
278. For the purchase of some of these items *see* Whittle & Griffiths, pp. 119–31.

Item I give and bequeath unto Dame Anne Lestrange my daughter in law my lesser bard chest with all the linnen therein,[279] my sealeskin box with all the pillowbeers therein, the bedstead with curtaines, vallance tester bed and bedding as it standeth in the celler chamber, the greene canopy with the bedstead and bedding as it standeth in the buttery chamber, the bedstead with the tester and curtaines of greene russetts with all the bedding as it standeth in the hall chamber, the bed of blew serge in my owne chamber with the bedding as it standeth, six stoles of crosse stitch, one dozen of silver fashond pewter, ten pewter dishes of seaven severall sorte, a long swan dish, a longe pasty plate and three other pyeplates all marked A. eS,[280] one dozen of silver spoones and my biggest silver ladle, and my coach with the new harnesse. Also I give and bequeath unto the said Dame Anne Lestrang[e] my greate bard chest with all the linnen therein except one paire of three breadth sheetes of fine holland, one suite of diaper and one sute of damske wrapped in a cloth in the same chest which I will and bequeath unto Dame Elizabeth Spring my daughter.

Item I give to Dorothy Spring my grandchilde my aggate jewell.

Item I give unto Sir William Spring Bar[one]t and Thomas Spring his brother my grandchildren forty shillinge a peice.

Item I give and bequeathe unto Roger Lestrang[e] my sonne forty pounde.

Item I give and bequeathe unto Judith Lestrang[e] my daughter in law my greene silverd grogram petticoat, my silver inkehorne, my silver mawim cup with a cover,[281] my second silver ladle and my blacke cabinet, all the linen in the wainscot box according to the inventary.

Item I give unto John Lestrang[e] my grandchilde five poundes and unto Thomas Lestrang[e] my grandchilde and godsonne five poundes.

Item I give unto William Lestrang[e], Edward Lestrang[e], Roger Lestrang[e] and Charles Lestrang[e] my grandchildren forty shillinges a peice.

Item I give unto Dorothy Lestrange daughter of my sonne Hamon Lestrange esq[uire] my border of gold. Item I give unto Hamon Lestrang[e] brother of the said Dorothy my wedding rich [ring] and forty shillinges.

Item I give unto Nicholas Lestrang[e] my godsonne another of the brothers of the said Dorothy five pounds and to William and Elizabeth Lestrang[e] brother and sister of the said Dorothy forty shillinges a peice.

Item I give unto my nephew Charles Spelman my little diamond ring.

---

279. Barred chests used for travelling were often reinforced and protected with iron bars and bands, see Yaxley, *Glossary*, p. 41.

280. *ie.* A[lice L]e S[trange].

281. This item is probably the Magdelene cup given to Alice by Sir Hamon in his will, see above, p. 353.

Item I give unto my neece Katherine Anderson my greene tabby petticoate, two fine holland shiftes, two fine holland aprons and my least hoop ring.

Item I give unto my neece Anne Willson wife of Townesend Willson clerke my hoope ring with the motto (rejoyce for my gaine).

Item I give to my cousin Margaret Fisher, wife of John Fisher of Honing, my rideing coate, my cedar cabinet, two fine holland shiftes and two fine holland aprons. [282]

Item I give to Amy wife of Edward Phillip Loades of Ringstead clerke one booke intitled Mr Greenhams workes.[283]

Item I give unto William Waters clerke vicar of Sedgford aforesaid Doctor Gawdens booke and twenty shillinges in monie.[284]

Item I give unto the poore of Sedgford aforesaid forty shillinges. Item I give unto Francis Guybon my servant forty shillinges.

Item I give unto Elizabeth Guybon his daughter my servant six and twenty pounds in monie and the bedstead blankete and darnix covering on the bed whereon the dayry maide lyeth (the bed and boulster being already the said Elizabeth Guybons). Also I give unto the said Elizabeth my ordinary weareing apparel and the residue of my weareing linen not herein before bequeathed.

Item I give unto Sarah Laster my dayry maide, to Beatris Paule my cooke maide, to Margaret Rix and John Overman my servants to every of them tenne shillinges a peice.

Item I give unto Katherine Anderson my neece over and besides the legacie therein before bequeathed unto her one laced hankercheife all of which said legacies of monie herein above bequeathed I doe hereby declare and appoint to be paid by my executor hereafter named within six moneths after my decease. And further if any goodes, sume or sumes of monie be hereby given and bequeathed to any person or persons under the age of one and twenty years then my will and minde is that my executor hereafter named shall pay the same into the hands of the father or mother of the said person or persons whichsoever of them be then living.

Lastly I doe hereby constitute and ordaine my beloved sonne Hamon Lestrang[e] of Pakenham in the Countie of Suff[olk] esq[uire] sole executore of this my last will and testament, to whom I give and bequeath all the residue of my goodes and chattels

---

282. See fn. 49, p. 77 concerning the different identities of John Fisher and different names of his wife.

283. R. Greenham, *The Works of the Reverend and Faithful Servant of Jesus Christ, M. Richard Greenham, Minister and Preacher of the Word of God,* collected into one volume, (various editions, 1559–1612).

284. John Gawden, 1605–1662, bishop and author of religious texts, associate of John Collinges and a staunch royalist, see www.worldcat.org, as Gauden.

whatsoever, for the paying of my debtes and legacyes and performeing this my last will and testament and bringing my body decently to the earth.

In witness whereof I have hereunto subscribed my name and seald it with my seale the day and yeare above written, Alice Le Strang[e], the said testatrix did seale and declare this to be her last will and testament in the presence of us John Fisher, Francis Guybon sen[ior], William Doodes.

This will was proved at London before the judges of probate of will and granting administracons lawfully authorized the twenty eight day of February in the yeare of our Lord one thowsand six hundred fifty six English stile by the oath of Hamon Lestrange her sonne and executor named in the said will to whome administracon was committed of all and singuler the goodes and chattels and debte of the said deceased he being first sworne by vertue if a comission truely to administer etc.

Index

Places in Norfolk unless otherwise stated

Errata to pages 59–60 – *Notes to the Reader*

The original order of the Sheep Accounts in LEST/P10

'Accounts of Flocks & Foldcourses by the Lady Alice L' Estrange' ~~[pp. 46–103]~~ [*pp. 121–85*]

Sheep accounts 1625–43 ~~[pp. 46–74]~~ [*pp. 121–52*]

Plundering of the flocks by parliamentary forces 1643 ~~[p. 74]~~ [*p. 152*]

Cullett sheep, tithe wool & lamb accounts, grandchildren's sheep ~~[pp. 74–95]~~ [*pp. 152–76*]

'A reckoning of the sheep of Nicholas Le Strange, my grandchilde' ~~[pp. 95–7]~~ [*pp. 176–9*]

'A reckoning of the profit of my grandchilde Nicholas Le Stranges sheepe' ~~[p. 98]~~ [*p. 179*]

'A note of what sheep were layd upon Barrett Ringsted ground' ~~[p. 98]~~ [*p. 180*]

'A note for laying of sheepe at Ringstead' ~~[p. 100]~~ [*p. 182*]

'A reckoning for sheepe beginning from Midsomer 1653' ~~[pp. 100–2]~~ [*pp. 182–4*]

'A reckoning of the Kitching Sheepe 1654' ~~[pp. 102–3]~~ [*pp. 184–5*]

'Accounts of the charges and profitts of a shippe in divers voyages' ~~[pp. 110–12]~~ [*pp. 195–8*]

Children's accounts, 1618–1627 ~~[pp. 15–35]~~ [*pp. 87–108*]

A note of the tenants' sheep on the South Flock of Ringstead in 1643, and a note of flocks, foldcourses and shepherds' covenants ~~[pp. 108–10]~~ [*pp. 191–3*]

Alice Le Strange's own sheep account, 1617–1625 ~~[pp. 35–46]~~ [*pp. 109–21*]

Wool accounts 1642–1654 ~~[pp. 103–8]~~ [*pp. 185–91*]